Greening Aid?

Greening Aid?

Understanding the Environmental Impact of Development Assistance

Robert L. Hicks, Bradley C. Parks,
J. Timmons Roberts, and Michael J. Tierney

OXFORD
UNIVERSITY PRESS

OXFORD

UNIVERSITY PRESS

Great Clarendon Street, Oxford OX2 6DP

Oxford University Press is a department of the University of Oxford.
It furthers the University's objective of excellence in research, scholarship,
and education by publishing worldwide in

Oxford New York

Auckland Cape Town Dar es Salaam Hong Kong Karachi
Kuala Lumpur Madrid Melbourne Mexico City Nairobi
New Delhi Shanghai Taipei Toronto

With offices in

Argentina Austria Brazil Chile Czech Republic France Greece
Guatemala Hungary Italy Japan Poland Portugal Singapore
South Korea Switzerland Thailand Turkey Ukraine Vietnam

Oxford is a registered trade mark of Oxford University Press
in the UK and in certain other countries

Published in the United States
by Oxford University Press Inc., New York

British Library Cataloguing in Publication Data

Data available

Library of Congress Cataloging in Publication Data

Data available

Typeset by SPI Publisher Services, Pondicherry, India
Printed in Great Britain
on acid-free paper by
Clays Ltd, St Ives plc

ISBN 978-0-19-921394-8

1 3 5 7 9 10 8 6 4 2

Preface and Acknowledgements

From the first earth summit in Stockholm in 1972 to the 2005 G-8 meeting in Gleneagles and the 2006 climate change negotiations in Nairobi, the issue of how foreign aid can damage or protect the global environment has been the source of protest, legislative debate, and reform efforts at development agencies around the world. Repeated complaints by environmentalists and by scientists raise pointed questions: has foreign assistance actually been 'greened' as many donors claim? Are aid agencies still funding 'mega-projects' with severe negative environmental consequences like roads, dams and lumber mills in rainforests? Are donors increasingly financing environmental protection and clean-up as they have promised? Is environmental foreign assistance flowing to the places of greatest environmental need? What explains patterns of environmental aid allocation—is it received by countries with the greatest environmental problems? Is it being used to offset the impact of other types of aid, or addressing geopolitical, rather than environmental concerns? Which countries give and get environmental aid, and why?

Despite a smattering of NGO reports and numerous scholarly case studies, we still lack a complete and coherent account of whether aid has changed in response to new information, increased criticism, other factors, or at all. The lack of knowledge about environmental aid has been exacerbated by three related factors. First, previous scholars have not yet collected and analyzed all the available data on bilateral and multilateral environmental aid. Extant studies are based on incomplete information; therefore, their inferences may be incorrect. Instead, different groups of scholars have often looked at either multilateral or bilateral aid, rather than analyzing both types simultaneously. Second, when both types of aid are analyzed within a single study, scholars typically have relied on small samples or country studies that obscure the broader patterns that emerge when analyzing the full population of donors and a longer time series. Third, because donor organizations have their own criteria for identifying and counting what is and what is not environmental aid (and these criteria often change over time within a given organization), it has been very difficult to make comparisons across donors or over time. In the past, there has been no systematic way to track changes in the amount or allocation patterns of environmentally damaging aid, which funds primarily infrastructure, agro-business, energy, and extractive (e.g. mining and drilling) industry projects that may fall into a number of sector categories. While prior studies provide tantalizing and important hints about the allocation and environmental impact of aid, they present an incomplete picture of development assistance worldwide.

In this book, we rectify these shortcomings by gathering, categorizing, and analyzing development projects from over fifty official donors (sovereign governments, multilateral grant-making agencies, and multilateral development banks) to more than 170 recipient countries for the twenty years where the data are most complete and reliable (1980–99). We employ the Project-Level Aid (PLAID) database to describe trends in aid allocation. The PLAID database now comprises over 428,000 individual projects and we continue to expand the database. We employ a systematic and replicable coding system that classifies every aid project in terms of its likely impact on the natural environment. No comparable dataset has ever been constructed, either by academic researchers or a donor organization. We analyze this dataset using straightforward rankings and analysis of trends, eighteen comparative case studies of nations and sectors, and econometric models in order to better understand where environmental aid (and traditional aid) is going and why. Thus, this study breaks important ground by providing not only descriptive data about long-term trends in environmental aid, but the first systematic statistical analysis of all bilateral and multilateral environmental aid to date.

The focus of this book is primarily on issues of aid allocation. However, we strongly believe that purpose-specific measures of aid allocation are a vital component to understanding aid effectiveness. The PLAID database will provide a valuable resource to those interested in evaluating the effectiveness of specific types of aid (e.g. health, infrastructure, education, democracy-promotion, as well as environmental). The empirical study of whether, how, and to what extent the receipt of foreign aid influences development outcomes is fraught with challenges. An emerging consensus among development researchers suggests that future research should ideally evaluate the impact that specific types of aid have on specific development outcomes. However, because analysts lack complete and systematic categorizations of aid flows by sector, we have witnessed a surge of econometric work on the relationship between total aid flows and outcomes like economic growth and poverty alleviation.[1] Such research designs cannot gauge the effect that specific types of aid have on their stated objectives.[2] Aid that targets biodiversity

---

[1] Boone (1996); Burnside and Dollar (2000a, 2000b); Hansen and Tarp (2001); Easterly et al. (2004a, 2004b); Collier and Dollar (2002); Easterly (2003); Roodman (2003). All these studies assume that aid is largely fungible. Conversely, Tierney (2003) argues that the fungibility of aid varies dramatically with the type of aid given.

[2] For recent efforts to solve this problem see Fitzgerald and Sloan (2006); Bermeo (2006); and Clemens et al. (2004).

protection or sewage treatment surely affects economic growth, infant mortality, and, indeed, biodiversity, differently than road construction, electricity grids, and oil derricks do. However, scholars have thus far had no way of subjecting such hypotheses to empirical tests with comprehensive and accurate data. It is our hope that the PLAID database and the methodology employed in this book will bring analysts a step closer to understanding the effects of development assistance, from start to finish.

We have worked across disciplinary lines to produce a book that will appeal to a broad audience. This collaborative research has broadened our individual viewpoints and in this book we have approached the problem of understanding aid without the usual disciplinary blinders. At times, we have had predictable debates about topics such as the terminology that should be used throughout, the level and type of empirical analysis, and the target readership of the book. Our final goal is a compromise that seeks to translate the academic content of this book to a broad readership. Therefore this book is designed to be useful to environmental and development practitioners, policy-makers, students, and researchers in economics, political science, environmental studies, geography, and sociology. We seek to inform debate on international environmental policy, but also believe the case of foreign assistance for the environment provides an opportunity to test hypotheses derived from work in international relations and economics, as well as illustrate the utility of new data for cross-national research on development assistance. Far from the last word on the matter, we are well aware of the exploratory nature of this study and how individual cases might diverge from the overall patterns this analysis reveals. The models and theories in this book are intended to raise important issues, synthesize numerous academic theories, and provide some of the first empirical evidence on a range of questions surrounding development assistance and the environment.

The compilation and analysis of the PLAID database that forms the backbone of this book has put us in the debt of many people, most of all our amazing students who were instrumental in developing this resource. A team of fantastic students worked at William and Mary over four years, and we are deeply grateful to all of them: Charles Adair, Ken Baldassari, Julie Brockman, Erica Chiusano, Jeff Crowley, Keith Devereaux, Elizabeth Dewey-Vogt, Jessie Di Gregory, Morgan Figa, Rachel Fitzgerald, Josh Geiger, Alexander Goodspeed, Mike Goudey, Tina Ho, Ryan Hodum, Lauren Howard, Emily Hughes, Miranda Hutten, Charlotte Jackson, Marc Johnson, Scott Johnson, Ian Keene-Babcock, Amelia Kissick, Sarah LaVigne, James Long, Doug McNamara, Summer Marion, Caitlin Moorman, Rosalind O'Brien, Scott Parks, Brad Potter, Ryan Powers, John Rogers, Katie Ross-Kinzie, Laura Sauls, Klaus Schultz, Corey Shull, David Sievers, Megan Smith, Kaity Smoot, Nino Stamatovic, Emily Thompson, Lauren Triner, Erin Ward, Jack Warner, Joanna Watkins, Josh Wayland, Mary Kate Weaver, Mike Weissberger, Melissa White,

Brendan Williams, Heather Winn, and Dana Wojno. We would also like to recognize both the help and enduring patience of our information technology support, especially David Reed and Will Armstrong. Chris O'Keefe, Josh Loud, Kaeli McCall, Rich Nielsen, and the rest of the team at Brigham Young University provided crucial assistance in boosting the quality and quantity of data on several multilateral funding agencies. We also owe a tremendous debt of gratitude to Sue Peterson, Carl Strikwerda, Gene Roche, and others in the William and Mary administration who have given us the continued feedback, support, and assistance needed to get the PLAID project off the ground. Sarah Caro and Jennifer Wilkinson at Oxford University Press have been a pleasure to work with and extremely understanding of our rolling deadlines. Dan Neilson gave us tremendously detailed comments and raised a host of questions that improved the manuscript immensely. We owe our greatest single debt to Jess Sloan who read the entire book more times than any human should have to endure. Jess corrected errors, reconceived the organization of the book, and managed the egos and the prose of four authors from different disciplines. She is a gem.

This book benefited greatly from feedback that we received at professional conferences and invited talks where individual chapters were presented or where our coding procedures and data protocols were subjected to probing questions from both scholars and practitioners. Specifically, we thank Arnab Basu, Julia Benn, Sarah Bermeo, Tim Büthe, George Carner, Marty Finnemore, Jeff Frieden, Valerie Gaveau, Clark Gibson, Joanne Gowa, Jean-Louis Grolleau, Tami Gutner, Peter Haas, Barak Hoffman, Robert Keohane, David Lake, Maria Carmen Lemos, Tammy Lewis, Eric Lief, Matt McCubbins, Phillip Mann, Helen Milner, Dick Morgenstern, Eric Neumayer, Dan Nielson, Phil Roeder, Steve Rothman, Justin Tingley, Erik Voeten, James Vreeland, and Kate Weaver.

Finally, we would like to thank our families for their love and support through the endless meetings and late nights this project demanded of us. A special thanks to Jen Tierney for the delicious barbecues that accompanied many of these 'working' meetings.

Of course, all the hard work in the world would have done little without the generous funding and support we have received over the years. Key funding for the PLAID project has come from National Science Foundation grant #SES-0454384, which supported much of three years of data compilation. Additional private funding from Benjamin Berinstien provided critical support for meetings, field research, and research assistance. Student summer funding was provided through the Andrew W. Mellon Foundation support of the Environmental Science and Policy program at William and Mary; further funding was granted through William and Mary's Roy R. Charles Center. Additional funding for student research and meetings was provided by Brigham Young University. The book was completed while Roberts was funded in part by a fellowship as James Martin 21st Century Professor at Oxford University's

Environmental Change Institute and a Faculty Research Assignment from the College of William and Mary. We want to thank the Economics, Government, Public Policy, and Sociology departments at William and Mary for space and resources over these several years, in which the PLAID team expanded and spread across several offices and computer labs. In Sociology, we thank especially Dee Royster and Dianne Gilbert, and at Oxford University, we thank Diana Liverman, Jane Applegarth, and Sue King.

Our goal is to provide a useful resource for understanding and improving the role of foreign assistance in protecting the global environment and improving the lives of people living in both developed and developing countries. The recent report from the Intergovernmental Panel on Climate Change suggests that the stakes for current and future generations are even higher than when we launched this project many years ago. We hope that what follows is both interesting, informative, and makes a small contribution to our understanding of a very large problem facing this generation and future generations.

Of course, we are entirely responsible for any errors that remain in this manuscript, and the views expressed in this book are those of the authors and do not necessarily represent those of their employers.

Williamsburg, Washington, DC, and Oxford
July 2007

Contents

List of Figures

List of Tables

List of Acronyms

ADBISF	Asian Development Institute Special Fund
AFDB	African Development Bank
AFDF	African Development Fund
ASDB (ADB)	Asian Development Bank
ASDF (ADF)	Asian Development Fund
CDB	Caribbean Development Bank
DBD	'Dirty' Broadly Defined (with likely negative environmental impacts)
DSD	'Dirty' Strictly Defined
EBD	Environmental Broadly Defined
EBRD	European Bank for Reconstruction and Development
EIB	European Investment Bank
ESD	Environmental Strictly Defined
EU	European Union
G-7	Group of Seven: Canada, France, Germany, Italy, Japan, the USA, and the UK
G-8	Group of Eight: The G-7 plus Russia
GEF	Global Environment Facility
IADB (IDB)	Inter-American Development Bank
IBRD	International Bank for Reconstruction and Development (World Bank)
IDA	International Development Association (World Bank)
IDB FSO	Inter-American Development Bank Fund for Special Operations
IIC	International Investment Corporation (part of IADB)
IO	International Organization
ISDB	Islamic Development Bank
LDCs	least developed countries
MDB	Multilateral Development Bank
MGA	Multilateral Grant Agency

MIGA   Multilateral Investment Guarantee Agency

N   Neutral aid (neither environmental nor 'dirty')

NDF   Nordic Development Fund

NGO   non-governmental organization

NIB   Nordic Investment Bank

PLAID   Project-Level Aid database

1

From Rio to Gleneagles: Has Aid Been Greened?

A Brief History of Environmental Aid

In the summer of 1992, the Brazilian army patrolled the freshly scrubbed streets of Rio de Janeiro to safeguard 30,000 visitors arriving from 172 countries. Kings, Premiers, Presidents, and Prime Ministers had all flown in for one of the largest gatherings of state leaders in history: the United Nations Conference for Environment and Development, known as the Earth Summit. Inside the official conference site, dignitaries discussed the world's ecological challenges, debated the links between environment and development, and fought pitched diplomatic battles over proposed solutions to those issues. Outside, at Flamengo Park, thousands of NGO activists held parallel events; building networks, issuing statements to the press, and adding to the pressure already felt by the conference participants.

In the months preceding the Earth Summit tension between developed and developing countries ran high. Environmentalists and voters in Western countries pressured their elected officials to 'do something' about issues like deforestation in the Amazon, ozone depletion, and global climate change. But with some of the richest stores of biodiversity, natural resources, and carbon located in poor countries, the potential for environmental damage was greatest in places outside the sovereign control of Western governments. A central dilemma facing negotiators was to determine how less developed countries could be encouraged to act on issues that were often far below security, development, health care, and education on their domestic agendas. An even deeper conflict existed: fencing off forests and controlling carbon emissions would almost certainly slow developing countries' economic growth, especially in the shorter term.

The 'Grand Bargain' at Rio was that wealthy countries agreed to underwrite the participation of less developed countries in any global environmental accord to come out of the meetings. Most developing countries, however,

1

feared this new concern for environmental protection would 'crowd out' foreign aid for basic human needs and economic development. Drawn up jointly by developed and developing countries, a document called Agenda 21 was designed to break this impasse. Agenda 21 was a 700-page plan for 'sustainable development' that sought to bring poor countries into environmental agreements while simultaneously supporting their economic development. Chapter 33 of Agenda 21 states that 'The implementation of the huge sustainable development programs . . . [would] require the provision to developing countries of substantial *new and additional* financial resources.' The estimated cost of implementing Agenda 21 was $561.5 billion a year, with the global North bankrolling $141.9 billion (or 20 per cent of the total cost) with low or no-interest concessional lending and developing countries footing the rest of the bill.[1] Of the assistance to developing countries, about $15 billion a year was supposed to be devoted to global environmental issues, with the rest targeting more localized sustainable development programs within developing countries.[2]

The Rio debate reflected the tensions that surfaced during the years of preparatory conferences leading up to the event. A year earlier, developing country governments issued the strongly worded Beijing Ministerial Declaration on Environment and Development. The document identified poverty as the main driver of environmental degradation and argued for 'a special Green Fund [to] be established to provide adequate and additional financial assistance' to developing countries.[3] In the Kuala Lumpur Declaration on Environment and Development signed 29 April 1992, developing countries argued that 'funding should be provided in addition to, and separate from, Official Development Assistance (ODA) target commitments by developed countries. A specific and separate fund for the implementation of Agenda 21 should be established.' Additionally, the Beijing Declaration called for the Fund to 'cover the costs of the transfer of environmentally sound technologies

---

[1] United Nations Conference on Environment and Development (1992: section 4, chapter 33). A few recent studies provide the data and economic analyses that explain these figures. Water-related diseases are estimated to cost the global economy US$125 billion per year, while alleviating such diseases would cost from US$7–50 billion per year (Gleick 1998; also see *UNEP Global Environmental Outlook*). With respect to global climate change, Grubb estimates that the global South will require financial transfers of $100 billion a year (Grubb 1990: 287). Hayes and Smith (1993: 166) put the figure at $30 billion a year. Victor (1999) claims a funding mechanism for climate change that actually slowed the rate of warming would be somewhere in the range of tens or hundreds of billions of dollars. See also Luterbacher and Sprinz (2001); Schelling (2002); Barrett (2003b).

[2] Robinson (1992) puts the number at over $125 billion in concessional financing, from which the $15 billion was to address global issues.

[3] Sjoberg (1999). This Fund would specifically target those problems that were not covered by specific international agreements, such as 'water pollution, coastal pollution affecting mangrove forests, shortages and degradation of fresh water resources, deforestation, soil loss, land degradation and desertification.'

and the costs for building up national capabilities for environmental protection and for scientific and technological research.'[4] The assistance would range from support for national park creation to improvement of power plant efficiency to sustainable forestry efforts in the tropics.

In Rio, developing country governments proposed that funding to the Global Environmental Facility (GEF) be tripled and a special 'Earth Increment' be added to the World Bank's development assistance funds in order to 'provide virtually free environmental aid to the very poorest nations.'[5] Under all of these proposals, developing countries stressed that 'new and additional' funds would need to exist, so that environmental protection funds would not be diverted from existing development aid budgets.

Yet shortly after the agreements were signed at Rio, the 'Grand Bargain' between the global North and South began to unravel. The 'Earth Increment,' which was supposed to be a 15 per cent boost in International Development Association (IDA) funding to the World Bank, failed to materialize.[6] The proposed tripling of GEF funds proved to be a political non-starter, especially for the United States. Because of the strong pushback from donor governments, the Green Fund, which would support local Agenda 21 projects, also became a casualty of the negotiating process. When developing countries—as a second-best solution—attempted to integrate issues of local and national environmental concern into the GEF's mandate, which was originally designed to fund *global* environmental protection, fierce Northern resistance quashed their efforts.[7]

Thirteen years later, in the summer of 2005, the leaders of the G-8 countries—the United States, Germany, France, Britain, Italy, Japan, Russia, and Canada—met at the Gleneagles golf resort in Scotland. British Prime Minister Tony Blair, who was serving as G-8 president in 2005, set two priorities for the G-8 meeting: a substantial increase in aid, especially for Africa, in order to 'make poverty history,' and more progress on addressing global climate change. Despite the focus on poverty, environmental aid was again showcased at Gleneagles to demonstrate Western governments' commitment to global environmental issues. The G-8 made promises to help poor countries more

---

[4] Sjoberg (1999: 27). See 'Beijing Ministerial Declaration on Environment and Development' (A/46/293). It was adopted by 41 developing countries in Beijing on 19 June 1991.

[5] Lewis (1992: A6). This idea was publicly supported by then-World Bank President Lewis Preston.

[6] Donor governments also delivered only a fraction of the bilateral environmental funding promised at Rio. Fairman and Ross (1996).

[7] Another early indication of the West's reluctance to commit to more environmental aid came during negotiations on desertification, when donor governments argued for a 'Global Mechanism' that would mobilize and coordinate existing funds, rather than provide additional funds (Najam 2004).

readily access clean energy technologies in the Gleneagles Plan of Action.[8] To a roaring crowd outside the Gleneagles meeting, rock superstar Sting echoed Blair, urging world leaders to address global climate change and to boost aid for Africa. Sting vowed that the world would pay attention, and would not accept leaders who broke promises on foreign aid. 'Every step you take, every vow you break, we'll be watching you...' he sang. Once again, it seemed environmental aid would soon be on the rise.

Yet after only three years, it appears that Gleneagles may be Rio all over again. Besides being almost an exact repetition of promises made in 1992, the Gleneagles declarations were very similar to those made at the first Earth Summit held in Stockholm, Sweden, three decades before. The 1972 Stockholm Declaration included a Resolution on Institutional and Financial Arrangements, which called for an 'Environmental Fund' that would assist developing countries in their efforts towards sustainability.[9] While the same measures have been called for repeatedly over the past thirty-five years, it is not clear how much real progress has been made in transferring resources to developing countries in order to mitigate, prevent, or remediate damage to the environment.

Despite numerous and substantial promises, little research exists on how much environmental money is new, and whether the promises of previous environmental summits have been met. Since the mid-1980s, MDBs like the World Bank have been harshly criticized for funding road-building, mining, and dams which displace large numbers of people. How much do contemporary aid flows reflect these traditional funding patterns? If aid designed to address environmental issues has increased, which countries are receiving the most? Why? Which donor governments give the most? Which multilateral donors are the 'greenest?' What explains these trends? In order to begin to answer these questions and others, we need a more complete picture of aid and the environment, as well as rigorous analysis of what might explain these patterns. This book takes an important step toward painting that picture and conducting that analysis.

---

[8] It read: 'We acknowledge the valuable role of the Global Environment Facility in facilitating co-operation with developing countries on cleaner, more efficient energy systems, including renewable energy, and look forward to a successful replenishment this year, along with the successful conclusion of all outstanding reform commitments from the third replenishment.' G-8 leaders also pledged to 'explore opportunities within existing and new lending portfolios to increase the volume of investments made on renewable energy and energy efficiency technologies consistent with the MDBs' core mission of poverty reduction...' (G-8 Gleneagles 2005).

[9] Haas et al. (1992). The 'Resolution on Institutional and Financial Arrangements' from the 1972 Stockholm conference recommended that this Fund finance programs such as regional and global monitoring, assessment and data-collecting systems, environmental quality management and research, and public education.

Why Study the Environmental Impacts of Aid Allocation?

Each year, billions of dollars flow from Western governments to private organizations and governments in developing countries for the stated purpose of addressing environmental problems. Why do donors provide environmental aid to developing countries? Are donors concerned with the environmental 'rate-of-return' they receive on their aid investment? Are they buying political cover at home, or interested in achieving geo-strategic and commercial aims? What are the likely implications of aid allocation patterns for the alleviation of local, regional, and global environmental problems?

The stakes in this debate are enormous. Approximately 1.6 million people die prematurely every year from indoor air pollution, and 1.7 million people die prematurely every year due to unsafe water, sanitation, and hygiene.[10] Lead exposure, urban air pollution, and pesticide poisoning claim more than a million additional lives annually. At the same time, millions of hectares of forests are lost each year to clear-cutting, burning, and desertification, while biodiversity is in rapid decline both on land and in the oceans. After fifteen years of painstaking global climate negotiations, most scientists consider the Earth's climate to be edging perilously close to a tipping point.[11]

The study of environmental aid is important not only for these substantive reasons, but also because it provides new empirical terrain in which to test hypotheses developed in the fields of international relations, comparative politics, and development economics. In many respects, environmental aid represents a 'least likely' case for a successful international financial transfer.[12] According to mainstream theories of international cooperation, successful interstate financial transfers are more likely to occur when donor governments and recipient governments are willing and able to honor their policy commitments.[13] For recipients, this often entails making policy adjustments to create an enabling environment so that foreign assistance can have its intended effect. For donors, this means reducing funds when recipients renege on policy reforms that are necessary for the success of the financial transfer.[14] Yet

[10] UNDP (2006).　　[11] IPCC (2007); Roberts and Parks (2007a); Shellenhuber (2006).
[12] Eckstein (1975) explains that a case is least likely when it is used to test a theory under conditions that would be least likely to prove the theory correct.
[13] Keohane and Nye (1993); Haggard and Moravcsik (1993); Tierney (2003).
[14] There are a number of reasons why donors might be unwilling or unable to cut off funding. If a donor country possesses intense preferences for a collective good like global environmental protection, it may be unable to credibly threaten environmental aid withdrawal from countries of global or regional environmental significance. For example, in Indonesia, 'donor governments were so pressed to find projects to appease strong "save the rainforests" movements within their own countries that they were unable to coordinate their efforts to bargain collectively with the Indonesian government for macro-policy changes. Already deluged with aid projects for rainforest protection, the Indonesian government could afford to reject loans with conditionality aimed at reforming commercial logging policies'

environmental aid transfers rarely occur under such circumstances. Typically, recipients are more interested in addressing their own local environmental issues than in the regional and global problems donors want them to address,[15] and may well lack the institutional capacity to put external funds to good use. Consequently, donors are often put in the awkward position of needing to fund an international public good when recipients have insufficient institutional capacity for successful implementation. In these cases, donors might undermine the effectiveness of an environmental aid transfer if they are unable or unwilling to provide predictable funding to well-governed countries or withhold funding from non-credible partner countries.[16] As such, the study of environmental aid may hold valuable lessons for students of both development and international cooperation.

In one of the path-breaking works on this topic, *Institutions for Environmental Aid*, Robert Keohane concludes that 'constraints on [donor-recipient partnerships] are strong.'[17] Recent World Bank data on project success rates lend strong support to this conclusion. Across nine sectors, environmental projects were the least successful projects in the World Bank's FY01–FY03 portfolio. Only 25 per cent of Bank-financed environment projects during this period received a 'satisfactory' project outcome rating, compared with 100 per cent of education projects, 86 per cent of health projects, and 87 per cent of infrastructure projects.[18] Given such challenges, why would donor governments continue to allocate increasing amounts to environmental programs?

One possible explanation is that environmental aid can be effective under certain conditions. Concessional finance has, after all, proven essential to securing the participation of Southern governments in several international

---

(Connolly 1996: 339). Easterly offers a different explanation for the same phenomenon: 'Most donor institutions are set up with a separate country department for each country or group of countries. The budget of this department is determined by the amount of resources it disburses to recipients. A department that does not disburse the loan budget will likely receive a smaller budget the following year. Larger budgets are associated with more prestige and more career advancement, so the people in the country departments feel the incentive to disburse even when the loan conditions are not met' (Easterly 2001: 116). Van de Walle (2000: 4) also points out that donor agency 'staff may well lack the discipline not to lend to marginally deserving or temporarily virtuous countries if professional advancement continues to be related to the size of one's portfolio of projects.'

[15] Connolly (1996: 330) rightly argues that 'the provision of financial transfers for environmental problems typically amounts to an attempt to persuade recipient countries to do something that donor countries consider a priority rather than to provide the resources that would enable recipients to take the environmental actions of highest priority to them'. The central problem, according to Heltberg and Nielsen (2000: 276), is that poor nations sit on 'another segment of their welfare function where they have higher marginal utility of wealth and lower marginal utility of environment as compared to donors.'

[16] This is of course far from an exhaustive list of all the factors that reduce the effectiveness of environmental aid. See the chapters that follow.

[17] Keohane (1996).   [18] World Bank (2005c).

environmental agreements.[19] For example, the Montreal Protocol Fund played a central role in creating virtually universal participation by paying poorer countries to replace ozone-damaging chemicals with newer ones.[20] This ensured they couldn't lose by signing. The resulting cooperation has facilitated significant reductions in the global production and consumption of ozone-depleting substances compared to a counterfactual world with no financial transfer.[21] The ozone treaty has been held up as a potential model for other subsequent environmental agreements.

It is also possible, however, that environmental aid is no different from other types of foreign assistance: increasing and decreasing for reasons completely unrelated to environmental protection. Donor rhetoric about altruism and public good provision may simply be window dressing for aid with geopolitical and commercial motives, or used to buy political support at home. Barbara Connolly and her colleagues argue that 'donors do not always provide aid in order to solve *environmental* problems. Often, aid programs are about solving *political* problems. So why do donors bother? It is possible that donor governments, or some elements within them, sometimes care more about the *appearance* of doing something to solve international environmental problems than about finding genuine solutions to the problems.'[22] We explore these various explanations of donor motivation in the chapters that follow.

Studying aid allocation provides crucial information about how tax dollars are actually spent, as well as insight into donor and recipient preferences. In addition, aid allocation can tell us a great deal about aid effectiveness, even when effectiveness is not tested directly. If donors are selective in the agents they employ to allocate aid—by investing in a credible domestic aid agency or delegating development assistance to a respected multilateral organization or an NGO—and the recipients they choose to fund, we should expect these same donors to be concerned about the implementation of aid projects to ensure that their money is not wasted or misused. Is environmental aid given primarily to countries with governments capable of delivering public goods and implementing sound policies? Does it differ from non-environmental aid in this respect? If so, such an allocation pattern would speak directly to

[19] Roberts and Parks (2007a); DeSombre (2000a); Sell (1996); Barrett (2003a); Ferroni and Mody (2002); Kaul et al. (1999, 2003); Barrett (2003b); Adam and Gunning (2002); Stiglitz (1999); Albin (2003); Kanbur et al. (1999a); Anand (2004); Arce and Sandler (2002); Peterson and Wesley (2000).

[20] Barrett (1999a: 216).

[21] DeSombre (2001). Side payments to developing countries have proven equally important in a number of other international efforts to protect the environment (Weiss and Jacobson 1998).

[22] Connolly (1996: 333). The pessimistic view of Todd Sandler and James Murdoch closely resembles the argument made by Connolly: '[T]he Montreal Protocol may be more symbolic than a true instance of a cooperative equilibrium' (1997b: 332).

the likely effectiveness of these two different types of aid.[23] Throughout the rest of the book, we will explore whether environmental aid has the same characteristics as development aid in general, or whether it is allocated to more capable recipients, and is thus potentially more effective at achieving its stated purposes.[24]

Gaps in Understanding Aid Allocation and the Environment

Since the Rio Earth Summit in 1992, scholars and policy analysts have produced a number of books and articles on the topic of environmental aid to developing countries. The lack of comprehensive data on aid projects from both bilateral and multilateral donors, however, leaves these analyses incomplete. In order to address sectors, donors, recipients, regions, and other attributes of interest, researchers need detailed information on each aid project across the complete range of donors and recipient countries. Until now, those data did not exist. The lack of good data is made worse by the habit among some scholars of making generalizations based on only a few cases.[25] Mitchell and Bernauer remind us that 'conclusions drawn from qualitative case studies are often difficult to generalize, and such research can only test

[23] In a broad assessment of environmental aid effectiveness, Connolly writes that 'donor interests dominated the agenda-setting phase, [but] recipient interests become much more critical determinants of effectiveness in the implementation phase. In fact, recipient political commitment is probably the key constraint on the implementation of pro-environment policy reforms (1996: 334).'

[24] Neumayer (2003a, 2003b); Kenny (2006); Burnside and Dollar (2000a, 2004); Radelet et al. (2004). Burnside and Dollar's much-celebrated (2000a) study concludes that aid would be effective if *it were allocated to* countries with sound institutions and good policies. The entire basis of the Millennium Challenge Account and (much earlier) the IDA is that aid will have a real, measurable impact on its goals if it is channeled to the right places. Collier and Dollar (2002: 1477, emphasis added) 'estimate that . . . aid as currently allocated sustainably lifts 10 million people per year out of poverty. The same volume of assistance, *allocated efficiently*, would lift an estimated 19 million people out of poverty. Thus, the productivity of aid could be nearly doubled if it were allocated more efficiently.'

[25] Examples from the environmental aid literature include Chatterjee and Finger (1994); Connolly (1996); Lofstedt and Sjostedt (1996); Young (2002); Congleton (2003); and Lewis (2003). The work of Chatterjee and Finger (1994) is illustrative. As part of a larger litany of criticisms, they suggest, 'The purpose of most loans and of many grants is to generate profit for the donor country and its industries. Much of the profit generated from aid stems not simply from the lucrative construction contracts for building roads, dams, and factories, but also from the commodities and labor exploited as a result of this new infrastructure.' This generalization is quite plausible (and we provide some additional support for this claim later in the book), but it is not an inference that follows from analysis of an unbiased sample of a large number of aid projects. As King et al. (1994) explain, case studies are useful for tracing causal processes, generating hypotheses, and establishing the scope conditions of more general theories. However, no matter how compelling the case studies, they cannot alone bear the weight of the broad theoretical generalizations found in the works cited above. On issues of external validity and causal inference see King et al. (1994); Dessler (1999); Sprinz and Wolinsky-Nahmias (2004); Brady and Collier (2004).

the causal relationships between a relatively few [independent variables] and one [dependent variable] at a time.'[26] Through case studies and small-*n* qualitative research, scholars have learned a great deal about a few well-studied sectors, agencies, and donor governments, as well as comparative foreign policy in general. In doing so, they have begun to untangle complex causal processes. Yet, we still lack a complete and coherent account of the causes and consequences of environmental assistance to developing countries as a whole. If we cannot first describe the overall pattern of aid allocation, we cannot understand how it affects the natural and human environment on a global scale.

Although numerous, efforts to fill this empirical gap have been neither systematic nor comprehensive. In 1998, a team of researchers at the World Resources Institute's International Financial Flows and the Environment project reported that most data are aggregated by donors into their own arbitrary categories, 'thereby failing to provide much guidance for strategic planning related to particular environmental issues or areas of geographic interest.' Similarly, the Intergovernmental Panel on Climate Change found in 2001 that 'data are simply not collected and analyzed in a manner that informs policy makers interested in the issue.' The European Commission reported that 'along with other donors, [we face] a number of difficulties in calculating the precise amount of environmental expenditure. There is no generally accepted definition of an "environmental project" or of the environmental component of an integrated development/environment project.' They concluded that their 'statistical system does not enable an environmental analysis of aid flows.'[27] Connolly, Gutner, and Bedarff (1996) echo this concern: '[A]vailable data are highly distorted by the lack of any common definition of what is or is not "environmental assistance".'[28]

Fairman and Ross (1996) reflect the general sentiment of most environmental aid scholars when they skeptically state that, 'Although funders have increasingly embraced the rhetoric of sustainable development, it is not clear how much their words represent a real change in beliefs and values.'[29] We would add that, more important than beliefs and values, rhetoric doesn't always correlate with changes in actual lending and grant-giving behavior. Even if beliefs and values regarding the environment change, environmental

---

[26] Mitchell and Bernauer (1998: 14).   [27] European Commission (2006: 133).

[28] Connolly et al. (1996: 286). Peter Haas in 2004 argued that quantitative data collection efforts have not improved much since the publication of the Keohane and Levy book. 'As a social scientist, how do you systematically study an issue—environmental politics—for which we have no good data? The data that we do have just stinks.' Quoted from panel discussion at the American Political Science Association meeting, Chicago, September 2004. In email communication, Barbara Connolly expressed skepticism about measurement efforts in this area, arguing that donors are 'internally inconsistent in what they classify as "environmental" aid, and comparisons across donors are even more precarious' (Barbara Connolly, email communication with authors, 2003).

[29] Fairman and Ross (1996: 39).

protection and remediation in the developing world still costs an enormous amount of money. Especially in democratic countries, funding increases have a long series of checks, balances, budgets, committees, agencies, and other political and institutional hurdles to pass. Thus, while our empirical analysis in this book includes a series of case studies for illustrative purposes, our inferences rely primarily on changes in actual environmental aid allocation over time and across donors and recipients. We believe such systematic quantitative analyses provide a necessary complement to the existing literature on aid and the environment.

Despite the fact that there is now a body of scholarship on environmental aid, the existing literature has offered few generalizable findings. Research designs that allow for a comparison of the relative weights of alternative explanations are pursued infrequently, and testable propositions are rarely exposed to empirical disconfirmation.[30] For example, it remains unclear whether and to what extent environmental aid donors are concerned with crafting efficient aid contracts, making symbolic gestures to constituents, getting money 'out the door,' or pursuing geo-strategic and commercial interests. Some scholars argue that environmental aid donors have good intentions and are primarily motivated by the environmental rate-of-return on their aid investment.[31] Others reason that the environmental policy preferences of voting citizens in Western countries are the primary determinant of support for environmental aid budgets.[32] Another group of authors contend that environmental aid is given for reasons that have little to do with actual environmental improvement. Connolly et al. (1996) suggest that 'non-environmental incentives, such as export promotion or appeasing domestic political constituencies by creating the appearance of significant action, figure prominently in donors' decisions to provide [environmental] aid.'[33] While there are good reasons to think that both of these factors are important, it is difficult to judge which of them matters more, whether they are among the most important, and if so, under what conditions. Answering these questions requires both

---

[30] In the mid-1990s, Breitmeier suggested why such research has been lacking: 'For understandable reasons, case selection in most studies [on international regimes] has been driven by practical considerations instead of methodological requirements. Moreover, the choice of both dependent and independent variables for systematic attention in these small-n case studies has failed, in general, to produce a cumulative and consistent set of information on an agreed-upon set of important variables. Each study, in practice, has tended to select idiosyncratic variables, or operationalize common ones in radically different ways. As a result of these limitations, the study of international regimes stands out as somewhat peculiar in its absence of systematic, large-n studies making use of quantitative methods, methods which have advanced the state of the art in almost all other areas of political science' Breitmeier et al. (1996: 1). Also see Moravcsik (2003).

[31] Lofstedt (1995); Hassler (2002); Sell (1996); Parks and Tierney (2004); Darst (2001, 2003).

[32] Keohane and Levy (1996), Connolly (1996: 332–3), Sjoberg (1999), Streck (2001), and Nielson and Tierney (2003).

[33] Connolly (1996: 339).

a systematic, global analysis as well as the closer look provided by case studies.

The existing literature is similarly divided on which recipients receive more environmental aid and why. Some scholars argue that donors favor recipient countries that are willing and able to implement sound environmental policies; others contend that donors are most interested in helping countries with low levels of environmental concern and capacity. Connolly (1996: 328), for example, argues that in order to enhance national concern for environmental protection and strengthen weak environmental institutions environmental aid is often used to specifically target those countries with poor environmental policies. Yet the picture is mixed. Michael Ross (1996: 180) claims that '[p]artly due to its reputation for corruption, the [Philippine] Forest Management Bureau . . . received little [environmental] assistance.' Elsewhere, Connolly (1996: 291) suggests that 'Poland, the Czech Republic, Slovakia, and Hungary have received far more [environmental] assistance than other countries . . . in part because they were the first to initiate broad reforms and have stronger institutional capacity compared with their neighbors.'[34] There is surprisingly little consensus on who receives the greatest share of environmental aid: those furthest behind or those making the greatest strides forward.

Donor countries face a variety of specific choices when considering the allocation of aid. Donors make some of these decisions sequentially and others simultaneously. Similarly, while some decisions are institutionalized in multi-year contracts, others are re-negotiated on an annual basis or even more frequently. More specifically, donors must decide what type of aid to give (grants or low-interest loans for project or budget support, etc.), how much to give, which agent should deliver the aid and manage the projects (national donor agencies or multilateral organizations like the World Bank or the UN), which countries should receive the aid, and within recipient countries which public or private institutions should receive the aid.

To date, no theoretical framework has been employed to analyze the feedback loops and linkages between these various stages in the environmental aid transfer process. Yet the literature suggests that the effectiveness of environmental aid is endogenous to allocation decisions—meaning decisions by states and international organizations on the amount and type of environmental aid to give are influenced by the expected environmental 'rate-of-return' on their investments.[35] Some have suggested that environmental aid will be less effective when industry and/or

[34] DeSombre and Kauffman (1996: 120–1) also suggest that donors are highly selective in the types of projects that they approve for implementation. In fact, the authors write that 'it is this function of the Fund that is the most surprising and worthwhile' (1996: 120).

[35] Dollar and Levin (2004); Neumayer (2003c); Adam and Gunning (2002); Martens (2001); Milner (2006); Ross (1996: 180); Gibson (1999); Nielson and Tierney (2003); Parks and Tierney (2004).

environmental lobbying groups 'capture' policy at the agenda-setting stage of the decision-making process. Others argue that bilateral environmental aid is less effective than multilateral aid because delegation to an independent agent enables donors to achieve scale and scope economies; gather, interpret, and disseminate costly information to overcome coordination and collaboration dilemmas; and facilitate collective decision-making. Some also see multilateral donors as better able to resolve disputes, make credible commitments, and 'lock-in' unpopular reforms.[36] Others claim that the formal decision rules of multilateral development banks enable them to provide more effective aid than multilateral grant-making agencies.[37] Another body of literature identifies the criteria by which aid is allocated among recipient countries as a key determinant of environmental aid effectiveness.[38] Whether the type of donor and the formal decision rules within such multilateral donors affect environmental aid allocation is explored in Chapter 8.

Understanding Environmental Aid: The Principal–agent Framework

What motivates increases and cutbacks in the environmental aid budgets of donor countries? Why do some environmental aid donors channel funds through multilateral agencies, while others use their own bilateral agencies? Why do some recipient countries get more environmental aid than others? Why are some types of environmental aid more effective than others?

Although most scholars deal with each of these questions using distinct analytic frameworks, these decisions by donors do not necessarily operate independently of each other. Therefore, we argue that it is important to have a single explanatory framework that can accommodate the wide range of considerations facing the key actors involved at each stage of the aid allocation

---

[36] For example, Milner (2006) argues that 'states...appear to give foreign aid to gain influence over recipients (a private benefit) but find themselves, collectively, giving too much aid to some and not enough to others—thereby hindering the overall goal of development. Although states still want to preserve some private benefits by allocating aid themselves, they have delegated some aid functions to IOs to help overcome this lack of coordination.' In other words, states may look 'down' the decision tree at their menu of options and choose to delegate in the interest of cost efficiency or political expediency. Though agents often hide information, conceal actions they have taken, or use their delegated authority to undermine their political masters, principals reserve the right to re-contract, nullify violated contracts, employ oversight mechanisms, institutionalize administrative checks and balances, and so on. See Martens et al. (2002); Congleton (2003); Nielson and Tierney (2003); Boulding (2004); Hawkins et al. (2006); Milner (2006).

[37] Peterson and Wesley (2000); Kaul et al. (1999, 2003); Anand (2004).

[38] Ross (1996). 'Credible' governments—those governments with the demonstrated willingness and ability to honor their policy commitments—are hypothesized to offer donors a higher rate-of-return on their environmental aid investment than non-credible recipients.

Figure 1.1. Nested principal–agent relationships in aid allocation bargaining process

process. We employ a variant of the strategic choice approach—principal–agent theory—that focuses attention on the causes and consequences of different choices made by donors in the aid allocation process. This book models the environmental aid allocation process as a series of nested games between strategic actors.[39]

The game is based on bargaining. Vertical bargaining takes place between constituents and their elected representatives within donor countries and between elected leaders and aid agency bureaucrats. Horizontal bargaining occurs between different domestic interest groups within donor countries, as well as between donors and recipients in the international arena. Finally, bargaining occurs between recipient countries and donor institutions, as recipients may not accept what donors may prefer, and vice versa. Ultimately, environmental aid allocation is a function of all these bargaining games. The outcome within any one game is a function of that particular game, plus those preceding or following it.

One way to think about the process of foreign aid allocation is as a series of principal–agent relationships.[40] While potentially very complex, this delegation chain contains some key relationships for understanding environmental aid allocation and is represented in Figure 1.1 above. Voters in donor countries delegate authority to elected officials to make public policy, including allocation decisions about foreign assistance. Political leaders often find it beneficial to further delegate authority to specialists who are better equipped to make informed choices about aid allocation and then implement those decisions. Typically, this means tasking an existing government bureaucracy within the executive branch with this job, or creating a new organization to

[39] See Bergman et al. (2000); Martens et al. (2002); Gibson et al. (2005); Nielson and Tierney (2003); Milner (2006).

[40] Following Hawkins et al. (2006), we define delegation as 'a conditional grant of authority from a *principal* to an *agent* that empowers the latter to act on behalf of the former. This grant of authority is limited in time or scope and must be revocable by the principal.'

carry out this function. Elected officials could alternatively choose to delegate allocation decisions to a multilateral agent such as the World Bank, UNDP, or the GEF.[41] Finally, aid agencies—either domestic or multilateral, depending on the preceding step—decide which potential recipient countries will receive how much and what type of aid. This requires aid agencies to negotiate cooperative aid contracts with potential recipients, since the development agency requires, at a minimum, the consent of the recipient government to operate within the territory of that state. As UK Secretary of State for International Development Hillary Benn said in response to a question about whether his government would withhold £50m from the World Bank: 'I've got a choice on where I want to put my aid money. I could put it in our bilateral agency or in multilateral institutions. Donors will make a choice on where it will make the most difference.'[42]

A Roadmap for the Rest of the Book

This book is divided into nine chapters. In Chapter 2, we document the broadest trends in environmentally damaging, environmentally neutral, and environmentally beneficial aid over the last two decades. We find that in a relatively short period of time, donors have substantially cut funding for development projects that damage the environment, while modestly increasing assistance for environmental protection/remediation, and steeply ramping up 'do-no-harm' projects that fall somewhere in between. Additionally, we examine four types of environmental aid in greater depth, allowing us to explore the causal mechanisms that purportedly drive aid allocation. We begin with two issues of global concern: biodiversity loss and climate change. First, we review the growing literature on biodiversity hotspots and explore the extent to which funding labeled as biodiversity aid actually flows to regions where species loss is most critical. Next, we examine the broadest trends in funds to address climate change, an issue that has been the subject of a decade of debate around three funds created to support the Kyoto Protocol. As aid for climate adaptation and mitigation activities could soon eclipse all other environmental aid, we return to this issue in the book's conclusion.

The last two case studies take a closer look at aid for local environmental issues, which recipient governments often deem the most critical. Land use

---

[41] After these basic decisions about delegation have been made, there are often numerous additional delegations from both bilateral and multilateral bureaucracies to other government bureaucrats, research scholars, private contractors, or non-governmental organizations that implement projects on the ground. We do not analyze such agency relationships in this book but other scholars have used a similar principal–agent framework to do so. See Cooley and Ron (2002).

[42] Hillary Benn. Speech at the University of Oxford, Global Economic Governance Series, October 2006.

and desertification have arguably created the greatest numbers of environmentally related deaths over the past two decades. Yet we find this type of aid is relatively neglected and funding does not appear to be flowing to the places where it is most needed. Finally, since great proportions of deaths and illnesses in the developing world are also related to unsafe drinking water and contaminated waterways, we explore the patterns in aid for water and sanitation projects. In all four of these environmental issue areas we employ quantitative and qualitative data to illustrate a broad picture and gain insights into some important details of the environmental aid sector. Comparing the needs assessments made at Rio in 1992 for each environmental sub-sector with actual funding received in the 1990s shows that there is a huge gap between the 'prescription' of scientists and the actual 'dosage' of environmental aid delivered. Funding for water nearly reached the prescribed dose, but funds for desertification, climate change, and biodiversity were just 2, 4, and 7 per cent of what experts said was needed, respectively. Shifting priorities in environmental aid at the end of our study period showed climate change and biodiversity aid increasing, but water and land aid dropping. These case studies lay some groundwork and highlight the need to understand what is driving the allocation of environmental aid.

In Chapters 3 and 4, we analyze an important bargain in the aid allocation process by empirically evaluating how donors allocate environmental (and other) aid among recipient countries. The sharply conflicting ideas on what drives aid referred to above have dramatically different observable implications and consequences for future support of Western environmental aid budgets. In Chapter 3 we present the major trends in which countries receive the most environmental aid by ranking recipients in the 1980s and 1990s and then looking at the top ten recipients and their top donors. By taking a closer look at five different recipients, China, India, Brazil, Egypt and Kenya, we attempt to understand the rise and decline of environmental aid in each country's national context. China and India were at the top of the list of recipients as developing nations with huge populations and quickly rising economies, and shared the same major donors of environmental aid. Brazil and Kenya are both of biological importance to donors with their rainforests and 'charismatic' fauna. Egypt lacks both of these, but receives great amounts of environmental aid because it is a geopolitical keystone in its region, especially to the United States. The chapter raises the core question of whose needs get met—donors' or recipients'?

Chapter 4 is the core of this book: this is where we build and test statistical models to evaluate which recipient countries get environmental aid and why. We model inter-recipient environmental aid allocation as a two-step process. In the first so-called gate-keeping stage, a donor country or multilateral agency decides whether or not to give a recipient country aid. Once a recipient country has passed the gate-keeping stage, the donor government then gives a portion of its overall aid budget to the recipient country in what is called the allocation stage. Limited dependent variable models allow us to measure the impact of donor and recipient characteristics on environmental (and non-environmental) aid allocation in ways that account for the peculiarities of aid data.

Our results from Chapter 4 suggest that the extant literature on aid allocation and effectiveness has over-generalized its conclusions. While many types of aid are allocated in a dysfunctional manner, there is little evidence that environmental aid allocation fully conforms to this pattern. Some hypotheses based on an 'eco-functionalist' distribution of aid (that environmental aid goes where it is needed most) are supported. However, they do not explain the overall pattern of environmental aid allocation: national income, population size, and colonial history are also good predictors of who receives environmental aid. Contrary to the expectation that political loyalty (as measured by voting with the donor country in the United Nations General Assembly) would bring more aid to certain recipient countries, the opposite was true. Overall the picture was more heartening than many analysts would suggest: bilateral donors overall were more responsive than multilateral donors to a recipient country's global and regional environmental significance, policies and institutions, and poverty level. Bilateral aid for global environmental issues also appears to be more responsive to factors signaling the project's likely success. We conclude that environmental aid flows are generally not well understood because the scholarly literature has lacked sufficient data on aid flows or systematic empirical tests of competing hypotheses, and we suggest important areas for future research in this area.

In Chapters 5 and 6 we examine which donor governments spend the most on foreign assistance for the environment and why? Total environmental aid from bilateral donors skyrocketed in real terms during the 1980s and 1990s, from $5.8 billion in the first five years of the 1980s to $27.4 billion in the latter half of the 1990s. Meanwhile, funding for aid projects with overall negative environmental impacts declined significantly over the 1990s, from about 45 per cent of grants and loans to just over 20 per cent. The net effect of these two trends is considerable; at the beginning of the 1980s, bilateral donors on average gave eleven times as much money for dirty projects as for environmentally beneficial ones. By the early 1990s, this ratio was below 4 : 1, and by the end of the decade it was 2 : 1. By the late 1990s, no major bilateral donors were out of line with this standard, and some were even funding more environmental projects than dirty projects. Descriptive statistics reveal that some governments spend under 5 per cent of their total aid budget on environmental programs, while others give three times that amount. Chapter 5 ranks the donors on their 'greenness,' and then looks at five major bilateral donors in more depth: two leaders (Denmark and Germany), two laggards (the UK and the US), and Japan, which, in a single decade, went from laggard to global leader in total environmental aid. The Second World War and the Cold War factor strongly in the disparate histories of these donors, but this analysis shows an important convergence in their behavior towards the environment, shaped of course also by their internal politics and institutional issues.

In Chapter 6, we describe the political market for environmental aid in wealthy countries, and draw on principal–agent theory to explain cross-national patterns in environmental aid donation. We empirically evaluate whether citizens of developed countries authorize and financially empower their elected officials to resolve specific regional and international environmental problems, or whether they find their primary motivation in a broader set of values. We also test for the impact of interest group influence by environmentalist, dirty industry, and green technology lobbies. Additionally, we examine political institutions that may promote or hinder the passage of environmental policy in general, and environmental foreign aid policy in particular. Hypotheses tying aid allocation to high GDP per capita and 'post-materialist values' are supported, but they are better able to explain the fall in 'dirty' aid than the rise in environmental aid. Environmental lobbies appear to be reducing the share of aid allocated for 'dirty' projects and increasing 'green' project amounts for global public goods like biodiversity and climate change, but they may also be reducing funding shares for water projects. The most perplexing finding is that strong national environmental policies are negatively related to environmental aid expenditures. These issues arise again in the final three chapters of the book.

In Chapters 7 and 8 we examine the arrangement between donor governments and their own bilateral aid agencies, and choices related to the delegation of development assistance to multilateral institutions. We investigate why some countries choose to delegate more to multilaterals and whether this tendency varies across environmental and other types of aid. Chapter 7 documents the relative 'greening' of the major multilateral aid agencies. While multilateral organizations have tended to give somewhat more environmental aid than bilateral agencies, their overall 'greening' occurred later, and appears significantly less complete than the bilateral aid agencies. That is, most still provide four times as much funding for infrastructure likely to harm the environment as for specifically pro-environmental projects. We rank the 'greenest' multilaterals, and then go on to examine the greening process within the World Bank, the Asian Development Bank, and the OPEC Fund for International Development. Fifteen multilateral agencies gave over $75 billion in environmental aid over the two decades, but the group of donors providing environmental aid is extremely concentrated: five multilateral agencies gave 90 per cent of all funds. This suggests why a few agencies get so much attention from environmental and human rights campaigners and the media. The World Bank occupies the rest of this chapter, since this single agency is responsible for a third of all environmental aid and has led others in approaching the issue. The cases provide a striking contrast, describing the creation of the first major international agency for addressing the global environmental needs of developing countries, the Global Environmental Facility, and the OPEC Fund for International Development, whose funding choices reveal a different set of priorities.

Chapter 8 seeks to explain why donor governments delegate the allocation and implementation of billions of dollars worth of environmental aid to multilateral agencies. Again, we draw on principal–agent theory and argue that states often out-source the allocation and delivery of environmental aid to resolve free riding issues and other collective action problems. In particular, we test the hypothesis that states delegate environmental allocation and implementation responsibilities to international organizations in order to enhance the credibility of their own policy commitments. We also subject a series of alternative hypotheses to empirical scrutiny. We suggest that donor governments with small or ineffective bilateral aid agencies may be more likely to delegate authority to a multilateral agency. Countries with less bargaining power in the international arena, such as those with small populations or small economies, may also prefer multilateralism, as it leverages their influence over recipient countries. Additionally, multilateral agencies may offer economies of scale and scope and cost advantages when implementing environmental projects relative to bilateral aid agencies.

Chapter 8 also explores the factors that drive donor governments to support certain types of multilateral agencies, based on the agency's environmental expertise, track record, and formal decision-making rules. As expected, smaller countries use multilaterals for specialized issues like the environment, and larger donors use multilaterals more for 'dirty' projects, perhaps as a way to avoid criticism from local environmentalists. The findings on a series of expectations about more selective bilateral donors delegating based on recipient performance were mixed, and contrary to our expectations, high overhead costs in bilateral agencies were not associated with higher levels of supranational delegation. Overall the picture was quite complex and extremely rich in implications for future research and policy.

In Chapter 9 we conclude by revisiting our core questions, and consider the policy implications of the previous chapters' findings. We discuss the future of environmental aid, focusing on the surge in funding for developing countries to adapt to climate change. At the time of this writing, the Kyoto Protocol's special funds for climate change adaptation and mitigation activities are just beginning to function, and the core questions of this book remain very relevant to that debate. A final point concerns the effect of reducing dirty aid and increasing environmental aid on the social development of the poorest states. There are many 'lost' countries that receive little aid of either type, and often these are the most needy and vulnerable countries. Ideally aid helps address environment and development issues, and by doing so is more effective. Yet the reality is that sometimes aid will successfully address only one mission. Finally, the idea of measuring where environmental aid is needed most is a contested one; even under ideal circumstances it is difficult to evaluate the performance of the donor community. While we readily acknowledge the methodological difficulties of such analysis, in this concluding chapter, we underscore the importance of continuing to systematically measure how aid is being allocated. Our final task in the book is to lay out a dozen 'principles' that we believe should guide the allocation of environmental aid. We hope this research spawns critiques and methodological improvements; it is by no means the last word. With billions of dollars and enduring environmental problems at stake, we believe the issues addressed here will require substantial research in the future.

2

Billions for the Earth? Patterns of Environmental Assistance

Has aid been greened since the promises made at the 1992 Rio Earth Summit? In order to accurately describe what has happened over time and across donors, and in order to evaluate the political claims and scholarly theories about aid and the environment, a comprehensive project-level database covering the universe of development finance is needed. As briefly described in the Preface to this book, we have developed such a database, cataloguing and categorizing over 428,000 individual aid projects from all major donors over three decades from 1970 to 2000. The ongoing goal of the Project-Level Aid (PLAID) database project is to collect and standardize data on every individual development assistance project committed by official donors since 1970.

This chapter provides a concrete description of the trends in aid and its likely environmental impact. We briefly describe how the dataset was built and how projects were categorized by likely environmental impact. We then describe how aid has changed since 1980, contrasting aid that tends to have positive environmental impacts with the far greater number of projects which tend to have negative impacts. More detail about the dataset can be found in the notes to this chapter, the Appendices, and the extensive documentation available on the PLAID website. Our analysis, which focuses on aid commitments, shows a significant greening of foreign assistance. It also suggests that while donors experienced significant environmental reform throughout the 1980s and 1990s, the behavior of multilateral donors remained relatively unchanged through the mid- and late 1990s. The second half of the chapter begins the effort of disaggregating 'environmental aid.' We first track project funding for international and local environmental issues over time. We then examine two types of environmental projects in each of these categories. First, we analyze land degradation and water projects. The experience of these two sectors differs dramatically: water projects attract over two-thirds of all environmental aid, while desertification and land degradation consistently receives very little despite repeated appeals from scientists and international agencies. The second set of environmental aid sub-sectors contrasts the rapid rise of funding to protect biodiversity in the late 1990s with much more expensive projects to reduce greenhouse gas emissions—both issues of global concern but which potentially constrain national and local development plans.

The analysis in the second half of the chapter required that we search the some 39,000 projects that have been individually coded as 'environmental' and sort these by issue area. We performed this query using three techniques: (1) keyword searching of project descriptions, (2) analysis of OECD DAC dataset sector codes, and (3) follow-up research using the documents of donors and recipients.[1] These sectoral datasets were analyzed for trends in the number of projects and total funding amounts over two decades, the largest donors and recipients, and for the type of projects most common in these sub-sectors. We subsequently surveyed primary documents and secondary literature to identify and analyze the largest and most common types of projects within each sector.

These funding patterns raise some of the main research questions of this book. Do donor and recipient interests coalesce around certain types of environmental aid projects? If so, is this where we can expect the most environmental funding to flow? When donors' and recipient interests do not align, do recipient countries accept external assistance grudgingly? How do these factors impact the effectiveness of different types of environmental assistance? Finally, we evaluate whether the 'objective' requirements of environmental protection are being met. For this task, we compare actual funding with the Agenda 21 estimates of need published at Rio in 1992. The disparities between projected need and actual funding are large (and revealing) between the different sectors of environmental aid. However, before turning to the most basic descriptive statistics, we describe how we built our dataset and the methodological decisions we took to categorize projects.

Building the PLAID Dataset; Categorizing Aid Projects by their Likely Environmental Impacts

The PLAID database provides the most extensive coverage to date of projects financed by donor governments and international organizations (IOs). The

---

[1] We employed these three methods in order to ensure that we could identify the entire population of cases within each sector. We found that any list of potential keywords captured a large percentage, but not all projects in that sector. For example, not every project where 'water' appears in the title or project description is actually a water project. Conversely, some water projects will not include 'water' in the title or the description. In order to create these four sectoral datasets we went through the project documents, annual reports, and the secondary literature. Each relevant project was then sorted into one of the four sectoral datasets.

data are compiled from a range of official sources, including the OECD CRS database and annual reports and project documents from both bilateral and multilateral aid agencies. Additional variables have been created specifically for the PLAID database in an effort to standardize traditionally problematic fields in existing datasets (such as country names and dollar amounts). Our primary purpose is to provide scholars with a comprehensive tool to test hypotheses and understand trends in (overall and purpose-specific) development assistance both across countries and over time. However, such knowledge can also help inform policy-makers within donor governments, ensuring that these substantial sums of money can be directed through aid agencies and toward recipients where they can do the most good.

The majority of the PLAID data were obtained from the Organization for Economic Cooperation and Development's (OECD) Creditor Reporting System (CRS). The CRS data are the original source for 76.7 per cent of the project records in PLAID, covering the years 1973–2001.[2] The vast majority of the data taken from the CRS are bilateral aid projects, although small portions of the multilateral aid data are also from OECD sources. The CRS data rely on information from surveys that donor governments and multilateral organizations submit through the CRS about their aid projects each year. This reliance on donor reporting causes the OECD database to be incomplete, in particular for the early years of the CRS system.[3] The remaining 100,054 records included in the PLAID database were gathered directly from donor organizations. A significant portion of foreign aid comes from multilateral organizations that are not covered or covered incompletely in the CRS data. To fill these gaps, we collected project-level data from many multilateral organizations directly (including some that have periodically reported using the CRS system) for increased accuracy.[4] This increased coverage is important because while bilateral funders provided 77 per cent of total donor projects

---

[2] OECD (2002b).

[3] For a list of the specific gaps in coverage see Appendix A. These data were provided by OECD staff in July of 2003.

[4] The following is a complete list of independently collected multilateral donors as of January 2005: African Development Bank (AFDB), Asian Development Bank (ASDB), Carbon Offset (World Bank Group), Caribbean Development Bank (CDB), Council of Europe Development Bank (COEB), European Bank for Reconstruction and Development (EBRD), European Investment Bank (EIB), European Union (EU), Global Environmental Facility (GEF), Inter-American Development Bank (IADB), Inter-American Investment Corporation—IADB Group (IIC), International Bank for Reconstruction and Development—World Bank Group (IBRD), International Development Association—World Bank Group (IDA), International Finance Corporation—World Bank Group (IFC), Islamic Development Bank (ISDB), Montreal Protocol Fund (MPF), Multilateral Investment Fund—IADB Group (MIF), Multilateral Investment Guarantee Agency—World Bank Group (MIGA), Nordic Development Fund (NDF), Nordic Investment Bank (NIB), North American Development Bank (NADB), OPEC Fund for International Development Rainforest Trust (World Bank Group), United Nations Children's Fund (UNICEF), United Nations Development Programme (UNDP), United Nations Population Fund (UNFPA).

between 1970 and 2000, they provided less than half of the total money flowing from official sources.

The PLAID database covers the vast majority (perhaps over 90 per cent) of official commitments to development assistance projects 1970–2000.[5] For the purposes of this book, we define development assistance as loans or grants from governments, official government aid agencies, and inter-governmental organizations (IGOs) with the promotion of the economic development and welfare of developing countries as its main objective. With the exception of certain debt reorganization commitments, at least 25 per cent of a loan must consist of a grant in order to be considered official development assistance (ODA). However, PLAID also includes loans at near-market rates if these loans are designed for the broad purpose of fostering development. Our data include commitments that offer finance to developing countries in the form of grants, mixed loans and grants, loans at discretionary rates from multilateral agencies, loan guarantees at market rates, technical assistance, and sector program aid transfers.[6]

In the PLAID database, we have categorized all development projects as likely to be positive in their environmental impact, environmentally neutral, or likely to have negative environmental impacts, which we describe in shorthand as 'dirty.' Each project was assigned one of five values, from the most environmentally beneficial to the least: Environmental Strictly Defined (ESD), Environmental Broadly Defined (EBD), Neutral (N), Dirty Broadly Defined

---

[5] PLAID contains observations of money flows from donor entities to recipient countries for specific purposes. In the majority of cases, this means that a row of our data corresponds to a donor giving a recipient money in a particular year for a specific project, or one row of data per project. Under two conditions it is possible that a single project may appear multiple times in our data: when multiple donors give to the same project, or when a single donor commits new money to the same project in more than one year. If the original project was scheduled to be disbursed in yearly increments or periodic tranches over multiple years, this is captured on a single project line. However, on some occasions donors commit additional funds to existing projects. As these represent new funding commitments and separate funding decisions, they are listed as distinct projects. This means the following: assuming that each row in PLAID is a unique project will lead to an overestimate of the number of development projects. In some instances, PLAID allows users to track projects having multiple donors. For the large majority of our data it is impossible to know for sure whether each row is indeed a unique project. This drawback is characteristic of all large multi-donor databases currently in existence. Assuming redundant projects are coded into sectors consistently, summing commitment dollar amounts across donor, recipient, and year will lead to a good measure of a donor's commitments to particular recipients for a given year.

[6] The PLAID database does not include data from non-governmental organizations (NGOs) or contributions from private investors, banks, or foundations. The development assistance information in PLAID also does not currently include military aid from either bilateral or multilateral donors. The following is a list of the types of financing which PLAID does not currently include: Military equipment and services; military stock of debt; aid flows from non-governmental organizations; private long-term capital; grants by private voluntary agencies; member's contributions to multilateral agencies; loans made out of funds held in the recipient country; foreign direct investment (FDI), un-guaranteed bank lending, portfolio investment. Some or all of these data may be included in future iterations of the PLAID database.

(DBD), and Dirty Strictly Defined (DSD).[7] We provide a brief description of each value here. A full listing of specific criteria is available in Appendix A.

Environmental Strictly Defined (ESD) projects are those that one might expect to have an immediate positive impact on the environment. Such projects usually have clear, measurable goals and criteria for success with immediate environmental impacts. We consider these projects to be the most beneficial to the environment. ESD projects include projects targeting energy conservation, biodiversity protection, soil conservation, watershed protection, reforestation, access to clean water, and air pollution mitigation.

Environmental Broadly Defined (EBD) projects include those projects that have less definable, longer-range positive environmental effects than ESD projects or are preventive in nature. Such projects do not have an immediate or direct positive impact on the environment, but tend to be good for the environment over a longer time period. Examples of EBD projects include energy efficiency, industrial reforestation, family planning, desalinization, genetic diversity, sustainable development, and Agenda 21 projects.

In addition, all environmental projects (ESD and EBD) in the PLAID database are divided into two categories: **Green** and **Brown**. Green projects are designed to address global and regional environmental problems, such as biodiversity loss and trans-boundary air pollution. Brown projects, on the other hand, address local problems such as land erosion, sewer systems, and water pollution. This designation is described in greater detail below.

Neutral (N) projects include those projects that one might expect to have no immediate environmental impact or projects with positive and negative effects that can be expected to roughly balance out. These projects generally come in one of four forms.[8] First, many of them are economic in nature— promoting free trade, providing balance of payments support, helping small and medium enterprises, or promoting exports. Second, many environmentally neutral projects assist the health and education sectors. Third, a large number of neutral projects finance telecommunications and telecommunications infrastructure. Finally, many neutral projects provide emergency aid for disasters such as floods, earthquakes, and droughts. Such projects have negligible or uncertain environmental impacts and are therefore considered neither beneficial nor harmful.

---

[7] Some projects could not be coded due to missing or unintelligible descriptions. In such cases, we left the variable Env_Impact value blank. Depending on the research question, one may or may not want to include these 'blank' projects in the denominator when calculating percentages or conducting analyses. For discussion see Nielson and Tierney (2005).

[8] Before classifying any particular type of project we did research in the secondary literature, consulted ecologists and environmental economists, and debated whether they generally had a neutral environmental impact. For instance, many telecommunications projects include the installation of telephone poles. However, the environmental impact from these projects is so small, inconsistent, and often indirect that they do not belong in the same class as truly 'dirty' projects.

Dirty Broadly Defined (DBD) projects are those projects that will likely have a moderate or long-term negative impact on the environment. Overwhelmingly, these projects finance the agricultural sector. We recognize that different crops can have very different environmental impacts. However, information on the specific type of agriculture being financed was unavailable for the majority of the projects. Since most agricultural projects have a moderate negative effect on the environment we code all agricultural projects as DBD. DBD projects also include projects related to biotechnology, electricity generation and distribution, engineering, forestry, hydroelectric power, and mass transportation projects. While the term 'dirty' comes with negative connotations, we use it merely as shorthand, not because we believe that all such projects are 'bad.' We simply have not found a better shorthand term for 'likely to create negative environmental impacts overall.'

Finally, **Dirty Strictly Defined (DSD)** projects are those that one might expect to severely and immediately harm the environment. These projects may strip the environment of irreplaceable natural resources, as in the case of extractive industries (i.e. mining or logging old growth forest), or severely pollute/degrade the environment, with immediate measurable implications; examples include road and air transport, as well as heavy industry (such as fertilizer, tire, and brick-making factories).

There were three broad guidelines taken into consideration when coding for the environmental sector.[9] First, our coding rules disregard the positive intentions and/or humanitarian dimensions of projects. A project's potentially positive overall impact on a recipient's population is analytically distinct from a project's environmental impact. For instance, agricultural projects

---

[9] Every coded row in the PLAID database was coded individually for our environmental variables by at least two members of the research team. Researchers were trained on a set of practice projects using our coding criteria, available in Appendix A, and were only able to begin coding after they reached an 85% accuracy threshold. Subsequent tests for PLAID 1.1 put coder accuracy at above 95% for every single coder. Each project was then coded at least twice by separate researchers to establish inter-coder reliability. Projects that did not receive matching codes were referred to a senior researcher for a final decision before being added to the master database. However, many projects in the database contain only very brief and generic descriptions, and a few contain no description at all. Projects with short descriptions or which included only project titles were coded based on this limited information, while projects with no descriptive information received no code for our environmental variables. This decision makes our estimate of environmental aid very conservative, since a project description must specifically indicate that a project is environmental for us to code it as such—information which is not often included in short or incomplete project descriptions. If one calculates the total number or the percentage of environmental projects (or project dollars) with the total number of development projects in the denominator, then one undercounts the number of projects and the dollars spent on environmental foreign aid. However, since projects with no descriptions tend to fall early in the time series when there were fewer environmental projects being committed, we expect that excluding blanks from the denominator will overestimate the proportion of environmental projects and project dollars.

are coded as DBD. While agriculture projects frequently benefit citizens within the recipient country by raising incomes or providing sustenance, on average they negatively impact the country's natural environment through habitat conversion, increased erosion from tilling, synthetic fertilizer and pesticide use, etc. Thus, they are classified as dirty. Not all good development projects are good for the natural environment. The reverse is also true. Hence, for this variable we focused on likely environmental impact, rather than other positive or negative development impacts on the recipient country.

The second guideline addresses the issue of multi-sector projects. Many development projects address multiple purposes and cover multiple sectors (e.g. a project with one component helping the environment and another harming it). For these projects it isn't usually possible to aportion funds to each sector. Therefore in multi-sector projects, the code of the project is the value falling between the values we would normally assign to each sector. For instance, a rural education project that included the construction of schools and the financing of teacher education (which we categorized as neutral) and contained a bridge-building component (which we called DSD) designed to enable the transportation of school children from outlying areas would be coded as DBD, since this category falls between DSD and Neutral on our ordinal scale. However, multi-sector projects with adjacent codes, such as projects with split DBD and DSD components, were given the dirtier code, in this case DSD, in the interest of reporting a conservative estimate of environmental aid. Projects with both 'dirty' and environmental purposes often balanced out to 'neutral.'

Our final guideline concerns the intentions of the donor government or multilateral organization financing the project. Intentions were ignored in our coding rules. Instead, values were assigned based on the expected environmental impact of the project as described.[10] Although information on donor intent is available in some instances and would undoubtedly be of use in ambiguous cases, the lack of information on donor intentions for the vast majority of projects forced us to exclude this information while coding for the environmental impact of a project. Instead, we attempt to capture the likely impact of the project if implemented as described in the project documents.

---

[10] Since we accept that knowledge cannot directly impact the environment, we conceivably could consider any project funding research as neutral. However, we assume that most research informing a particular sector probably supports that sector. Further, typically research aimed at improving the environment is described as such in project descriptions. Therefore, all research was coded with the sector it informed. The same was done for investment, education, construction, and administration projects, which when specified as belonging to a particular project type were coded with the sector they contributed to (e.g. mining education was considered mining, DSD).

Trends in Environmental Aid: 1980–1999

Assembling the PLAID dataset revealed that data quality and completeness are significantly worse before 1980 and after 2000. We would encourage readers, for this reason, to be cautious of claims based on very recent aid data, since they may be incomplete.[11] As such, our analysis in this book focuses on the 1980s and 1990s, allowing us to analyze a significant time period and assess the impacts of the Rio de Janeiro Earth Summit, reform at the World Bank, and other important events. Figure 2.1 documents the broadest trends in environmental aid over our study period. While far more environmental projects are undertaken by bilateral aid agencies, environmental aid from multilateral development banks (MDBs) and other multilateral agencies substantially outstrips bilateral contributions in absolute dollar amounts. Both bilateral and multilateral commitments for projects with positive environmental impacts have been increasing since the 1980s, although bilateral commitments peaked in 1996, and multilateral commitments peaked a couple of years earlier and fell more sharply at the end of the decade.

Figure 2.2 shows the aggregate trends in dirty, neutral, and environmental aid from 1980 to 1999. Dirty aid shows a modest decline over the period, having risen in the late 1980s from around $30 billion a year to over $40 billion before falling back in the late 1990s below $30 billion. The rise in environmental aid appears much more modest when placed in this larger context, remaining only a small fraction of total aid despite the large increase in percentage terms over time. The most striking trend is the steep rise in environmentally neutral assistance: neutral aid doubles from $20 billion a year in the early 1980s to about $40 billion by the early 1990s, and then jumps to over $60 billion by the late 1990s.

These broad trends obscure some dramatic changes in the overall picture of environmental aid allocation. Creating a ratio of dirty aid to environmental aid (Figure 2.3) supports the argument that there has been a major shift in aid's likely environmental impact. As the 1980s began, dirty projects received *ten times* the funding of explicitly pro-environment projects on average. By the end of the 1990s, the ratio was only about *three to one*. As illustrated below in case studies of national agencies like USAID and DFID, bilateral funders greened their aid portfolios earlier and more thoroughly than multilateral funders (Chapters 5 and 6 address bilateral funding changes, 7 and 8 report on changes in the multilaterals). The World Bank, Asian, Islamic, and African Development Banks have also greened substantially over these pivotal decades by this composite measure, but continue to give about four times as much for dirty projects as environmental projects. Yet interestingly, they

---

[11] We are currently creating PLAID 1.2, which updates the time series, includes even more donors, and fills in gaps in PLAID 1.1 where new data have become available.

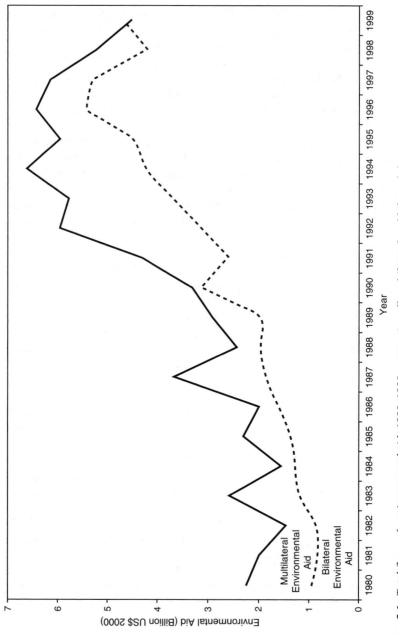

Figure 2.1. Total flows of environmental aid, 1980–1999, comparing all multilateral and bilateral donors

Note: Data shown utilizes only categorized aid data; see Appendix for details.

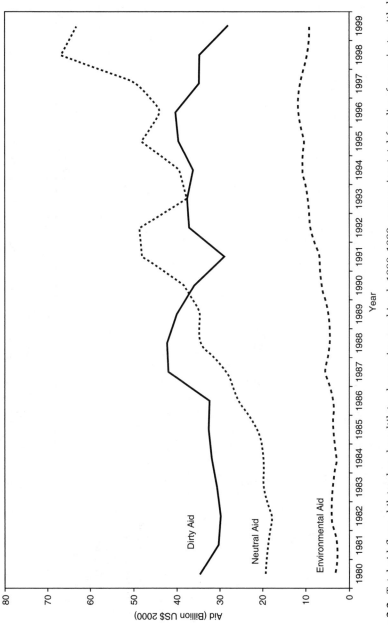

Figure 2.2. Total aid flows, bilateral and multilateral agencies combined, 1980–1999, comparing total funding for projects with likely positive environmental impacts, likely negative impacts ('dirty'), and those neutral or uncertain in impacts

Note: Data shown utilizes only categorized aid data; see Appendix for details.

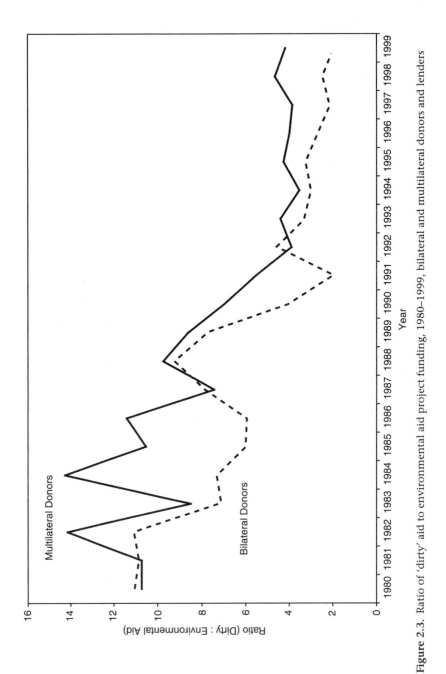

Figure 2.3. Ratio of 'dirty' aid to environmental aid project funding, 1980–1999, bilateral and multilateral donors and lenders

effectively stopped greening their portfolios in 1992, the year of the Rio Earth Summit.[12] While aid has been partly greened, the change has come gradually and sporadically, and with major differences in the efforts of different donors.

Types of Environmental Aid: Green and Brown

Does environmental aid from the industrialized world primarily target international or local environmental issues? As described briefly above, all environmentally friendly projects—those which received an ESD or EBD designation—were also coded into one of two environmental aid type categories designed to indicate the scope of the project: Green and Brown. A **Green** code designates projects that address global or regional environmental problems, and encompasses projects that positively affect environmental outcomes outside the recipient country. They either enhance or preserve global environmental resources and include projects that address climate change, CFC emissions, and biodiversity, or address regional issues such as transboundary air and water pollution. **Brown** codes indicate projects that focus primarily on local environmental issues and which improve environmental outcomes or reduce environmental degradation in a specific country or locality. These most often include drinking water treatment, soil erosion, and sewerage projects. By a significant margin, the most common types of brown projects deal with sanitation issues.

Figures 2.4 and 2.5 show the net total of green and brown aid projects in the PLAID database. Brown aid dwarfs green aid in aggregate terms—both for bilateral and multilateral donors, and both for the 1980s and the 1990s. While rates of giving among donors for both brown and green projects were relatively flat in the 1980s, a sharp increase in both types of aid occurred in the first half of the 1990s. Largely because of water projects after the Rio Earth Summit, brown aid rose from about 5 per cent of all aid to about 9 per cent in the mid-1990s, returning to earlier levels in the last two years of the decade. At the same time, green aid went from just 1 per cent of all aid during the whole 1980s to around 3 per cent in the 1990s. Over time, green aid is becoming a larger proportion of environmental aid, expanding from a fifth at the beginning of the 1980s to about a third in the last years of the 1990s. Together, green and brown projects constituted about 12 per cent of all foreign assistance for about six years: 1993 to 1997. In all other years, environmental aid was less than a tenth of all foreign assistance.

---

[12] This assumes that stand-alone projects are a good measure of the degree of greening at the multilaterals. If, as some MDBs claim, they are 'mainstreaming' environmental aid into all of their lending, then our measure displayed here may underestimate the degree of 'greening' in MDB portfolios.

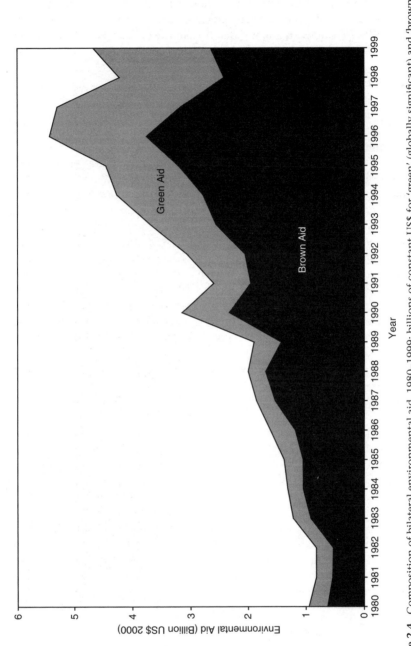

Figure 2.4. Composition of bilateral environmental aid, 1980–1999: billions of constant US$ for 'green' (globally significant) and 'brown' (local issues) projects

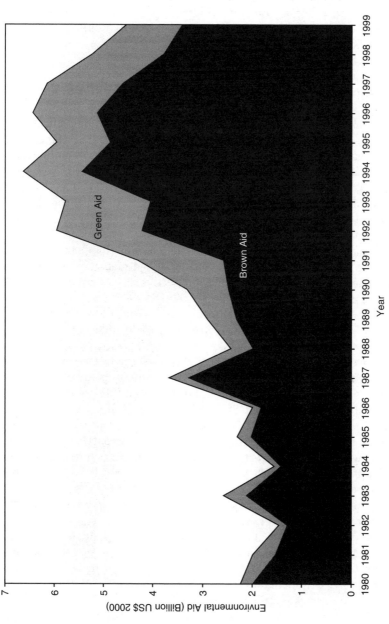

Figure 2.5. Composition of multilateral environmental aid, 1980–1999: billions of constant US$ for 'green' (globally significant) and 'brown' (local issues) projects

Interestingly, bilateral agencies have always been more dedicated to green issues than multilaterals, and this difference increased in the 1990s. In Chapters 5 and 7, we explore what is driving these changes through case studies of Germany, the United States, and Japan, and of multilateral agencies like the World Bank.

Contrasting Fates: Green and Brown Environmental Aid Sectors

Donor and recipient governments use aid to address very different ecological and political problems. Annual reports and websites of donor agencies frequently feature locals standing by rainforest parks and reforestation projects, but do these images represent the reality of environmental aid? We suspect that donors often want to fund projects that are less than perfectly aligned with the preferences of host country governments. But what is the concrete outcome of this tension? Whose priorities are funded and where does the money actually go?

To conduct this part of the analysis, we examined environmental aid projects in four sectors: water, biodiversity, land degradation, and climate change. These projects include two different sectors categorized as green environmental issues (biodiversity and climate change) and brown environmental issues (land degradation and water). We attempt in this section to understand who the big funders and recipients are in each sector, the types of projects that received funding, and what changes occurred with respect to funding levels.

Assistance for biodiversity protection and climate change, we argue, should be more attractive to voters in wealthy donor countries because of its properties as a global and regional public good. However, this type of assistance generally offers few direct and 'targetable' benefits to politicians or their constituents in recipient countries. Water and sanitation projects, on the other hand, tend to be favored by developing country governments because of their localized health benefits and the fact that large infrastructure projects can provide opportunities to steer profitable contracts to loyal companies (that can reciprocate with campaign contributions) and employ large numbers of relatively unskilled and poor workers. Water and sanitation projects can also lead to lucrative contracts for Western construction, equipment, and consulting firms, creating a political constituency for such support within donor countries. As such, we expect there to be significant funding for water and sanitation projects. Funding to control land degradation represents a more ambiguous case. On one hand, politicians in developing countries may use such aid to dole out political patronage, especially to rural regions that have proven their loyalty to the national leadership. In Brazil, for example, rural laborers and farmers are reported to have historically traded their political support for small material pay-offs from politicians often linked to wealthy landowners, who receive government subsidies. On the other hand, projects designed to control local land degradation in developing countries offer few direct benefits to voters in wealthy countries, and may garner less support from voters and interest groups in Western donor countries.

The following two figures show these four environmental sub-sectors and how they have changed between 1980 and 1999 (Figures 2.6 and 2.7). As expected, funding for water and sanitation outstrips funding for the other environmental sub-sectors. Biodiversity and climate change projects are more numerous than projects that target land degradation. In the remainder of this chapter, we explore these four sectors in detail to illustrate the divergent preferences and strategies of the different actors in the aid allocation process. We first compare the two local environmental brown issues, water and land degradation, and then move on to the green issues. In each section, we briefly compare how the need for aid in these sectors was expressed in the Agenda 21 document at Rio in 1992. We then move on to compare how much aid they have actually received, for what types of projects, in what countries, and from which donors. Each of these sections concludes with preliminary theory-building on why some issues receive funding or not, placing them into the framework of donor and recipient interests that we began to develop in the first chapter. These case studies provide a glimpse into the world of environmental aid, complementing the qualitative and quantitative evidence to come, and the econometric models in subsequent chapters.

Brown Funded and Brown Forgotten: Water and Land Degradation Projects

In order to describe the most significant trends in environmental aid, the data suggest that we start with water projects. There are many reasons for international assistance to focus on water and sewage provision to developing countries, but key questions arise about where the money flows and why. The basic facts are startling: every year, 1.7 million people die unnecessarily from unsafe water and sanitation, and the vast majority of these deaths are children.[13] Untreated sewage, illegal dumping of trash, soil contamination

[13] Limited access to these basic public services undermines economic growth and poverty reduction by increasing illness and death, reducing labor productivity, shrinking the size of the working-age population, delaying the demographic transition, and increasing the cost of health care for low-income families (United Nations Development Program (2006); Markandya (2005); Cole and Neumayer (2006); Fay et al. (2005); Esrey et al. (1991); Cutler and Miller (2005); and Gundry et al. (2004)). Low levels of access to water and sanitation also influence levels of educational attainment, gender equality, and environmental sustainability. In areas with inadequate water supplies, children—particularly girls—are often denied an education because they must spend a significant amount of time fetching water for their household. Many others are deterred by the lack of separate and decent sanitation facilities in schools. UNDP estimates that 443 million school days are lost every year due to water-related

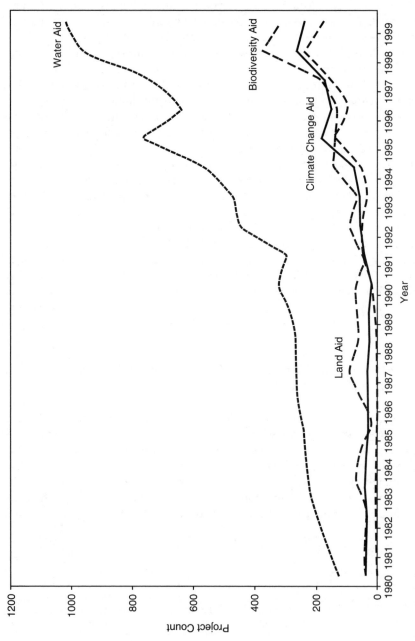

Figure 2.6. Count of aid projects by type of environmental aid, 1980–1999

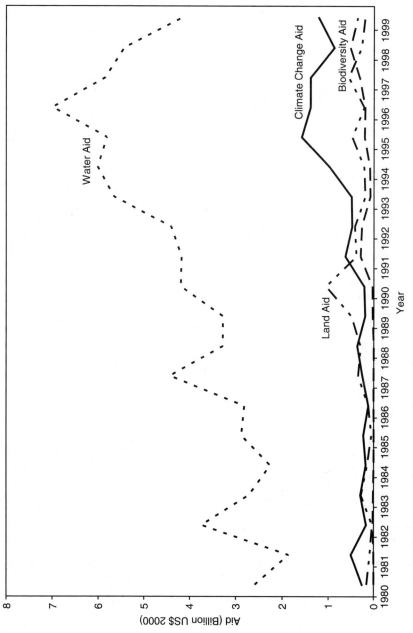

Figure 2.7. Amount of aid from all donors to environmental aid of four types, 1980–1999

from industrial facilities, and unchecked urban growth stress freshwater resources.[14] Many of these issues can be addressed at a reasonably low cost, through information and hygiene campaigns, spigots, chlorination, filtration, and solar disinfection technologies.[15] Cutler and Miller estimate that the benefit-to-cost ratio of investing in clean water technologies may be as high as 23 : 1.[16]

Land degradation is also reaching dangerous levels throughout the developing world: almost three-quarters of Africa's farmland suffers from severe nutrient depletion.[17] Central America and the north-east of Brazil are severely degraded; China has an annual soil erosion rate of five billion tonnes a year, and losses due to desertification are affecting more than a quarter of the country.[18] At the time of the Rio Earth Summit in 1992, it was estimated that desertification affected nearly 70 per cent of all fragile dry lands, approximately one-sixth of the world's population, and one-quarter of the world's total land area.[19] Land degradation has led to sharp declines in agricultural productivity, more frequent flooding and drought, malnutrition and food insecurity, mass migration and armed conflict, as well as ecosystem breakdowns.[20] Yet there are cost-effective interventions for improving soil

illnesses. Women also forgo significant opportunities for income generation, education, and leisure due to water collection responsibilities Cosgrove and Rijsberman (1998); UNDP (2006).

[14] In 2006, 1.4 billion people resided in river basins where water consumption has outstripped recharge rates UNDP (2006).

[15] Curtis and Caimcross (2003); Varley et al. (1998); Caimcross (2003); Han and Hlaing (1989); Huttly et al. (1997); Wilson et al. (1991); Hoque et al. (1995); Shahid et al. (1996); Checkley et al. (2004); Clasen et al. (2004); Reiff et al. (1996); Center for Global Development (2006); Esrey (1996); and Jalan and Ravallion (2003). Donors and host country governments can also improve water service delivery by introducing greater competition into the water sector, stepping up efforts to meter water supply connections, improving the integrity of regulatory systems, and adjusting water subsidy policies to reduce the upfront cost of getting connected to a water network. See World Bank (2003); World Bank (2004b). In Argentina, private competition led to a significant decline in child mortality from infectious and parasitic diseases, and had a disproportionately beneficial impact on the poorest regions because those without a connection to the water network gained the most from network expansions. See Galiani et al. (2005).

[16] Cutler and Miller (2005).   [17] Dugger (2006).

[18] Datong n.d.; People's Daily (2001).

[19] Desertification is defined there as 'land degradation in arid, semi-arid, and dry sub-humid areas resulting from various factors, including climatic variations and human activities.' FAO (1993).

[20] Sanchez et al. (2005); Levy et al. (2005); André and Platteu (1998); Niemeijer and Mazzucato (2002); Urdal (2006); Meier and Bond (2006). Sub-Saharan Africa loses 3% of its agricultural GDP every year to land degradation. It also costs the Indian economy $2.4 billion, or 1% of GDP every year UNEP GEO (2003). In China, where environmental degradation accounts for losses of 3–15% of GDP a year, land degradation has been identified as the single most costly environmental problem Varley (2005). Research also suggests that land degradation is particularly threatening to poor people and vulnerable groups. The rural poor depend heavily on the land for water, food, fiber, and firewood, but often lack the knowledge, tenure security,

health and combating land degradation including erosion control, sediment recapture, fertilizers, green manure, fertilizer trees, crop residues, and water conservation.[21]

At the Rio Earth Summit in 1992, the international community estimated that approximately $6.1 billion a year of water and sanitation assistance would be needed to satisfy global needs.[22] More recently, UNDP has argued that '[a]chieving the Millennium Development Goal target of halving the proportion of people without access to water and sanitation would cost about $10 billion annually for low-cost, sustainable technology,' and '[u]niversal access would raise this figure to $20–$30 billion, depending on technology.'[23] To address the problem of land degradation, Agenda 21 estimated that about $18.2 billion would be needed every year from the international community on grant or concessionary

and financial resources needed to make long-term investments in its productivity Vedeld et al. (2004).

[21] Sanchez et al. (2005: 107). Agro-forestry fertilizer trees can increase maize yields, reduce the spread of weeds, recycle soil nutrients, and increase the water-holding capacity of the soil. In addition, farmers can sell surplus wood to generate extra income, as well as reduce the burden on surrounding natural forest areas Sanchez et al. (2005: 204–5). Donors have achieved some significant successes in this sector. The Red Soils Project used China's many small eroded or barren areas to integrate livestock crops, land conservation, and water conservation practices into a sustainable framework. The Loess Plateau Project, in a similar fashion, has reduced soil erosion and improved local watershed management. According to the World Bank's Operations Evaluation Department, the Loess Plateau Project in China 'has been one of the most successful erosion control programs in the world, using indigenous ecological engineering to allow efficient use of watershed resources and reverse soil deterioration.' Another example of a successful donor-funded intervention is the Uttar Pradesh Sodic Lands Reclamation Project, which used gypsum to increase productivity of sodic soils, improve drainage, and introduce improved seed varieties and fertilizers to increase cropping intensity from 37% to 230%. It also used satellite Remote Sensing Application technology to determine the best places to farm, resulting in more efficient agriculture and rising incomes. The project is called an 'unqualified success' by one IEG report, because it 'has struck at the heart of the environmental dilemma in India: how to alleviate poverty without further damaging the environment' Ringskog and Chow (2002: 11–12).

[22] The Agenda 21 agreement mentions it twice: in chapter 18, 'Protecting the Quality and Supply of Freshwater Resources,' and chapter 21, 'Environmentally Sound Management of Solid Wastes and Sewage-Related Issues.' Chapter 18 stresses the importance of adequate water supplies for economic development and calls for 'holistic management of freshwater as a finite and vulnerable resource.' Its overall objective, to satisfy the freshwater needs of all countries for their sustainable development, was estimated to cost just $115 million annually. Chapter 21 outlines four waste-management program areas, two of which relate to water and sanitation: 'Environmentally Sound Waste Disposal and Treatment,' concerned with fecal matter treatment and disposal, and 'Extended Waste Service Coverage,' concerned with sanitation in poor urban areas. These programs were anticipated to cost the international community $6 billion annually, with additional costs being borne by the developing countries themselves.

[23] United Nations Development Program (2006).

terms.[24] Counterpart funds were expected to exceed international commitments.

The previous paragraphs indicate that land degradation and water quality are very serious environmental problems, but where are the actual funds flowing? Foreign aid agencies financed 7,660 water and sanitation projects, amounting to $78 billion, between 1980 and 2000, or about $3.9 billion a year.[25] All other environmental causes received just $51 billion over the same period. Overall, bilateral donors spent $31.7 billion to finance 6,682 water projects from 1980 to 1999,[26] while multilateral donors funded 980 much larger projects totaling $46.2 billion.[27] This figure is well below the

[24] Chapters 12 through 14 of Agenda 21 discuss the various aspects of land degradation. Agenda 21 outlines six program areas and justifies the annual cost to remedy each problem. First, 'strengthening the knowledge base and developing information and monitoring systems for regions prone to desertification and drought' was predicted to cost $175 million per year. Second, '[c]ombating land degradation through, *inter alia*, intensified soil conservation, afforestation and reforestation activities' was tagged at $3 billion per year. Third, '[d]eveloping and strengthening integrated development programmes for the eradication of poverty and promotion of alternative livelihood systems in areas prone to desertification' was tied to global goals of combating poverty and promoting sustainable agriculture. These were estimated by the Secretarial at $15 billion a year and $450 million a year in foreign aid needed, respectively. Fourth, '[d]eveloping comprehensive anti-desertification programmes and integrating them into national development plans and national environmental planning' was priced at $90 million annually. Fifth, '[d]eveloping comprehensive drought preparedness and drought-relief schemes, including self-help arrangements, for drought-prone areas and designing programmes to cope with environmental refugees' was expected to cost $1.2 billion. Finally, 'encouraging and promoting popular participation and environmental education, focusing on desertification control and management of the effects of drought' was listed at $500 million. The estimated cost of enacting the Agenda's program to combat desertification and drought as outlined in chapter 12 is approximately $5 billion a year. In addition, chapter 13 carries a price tag of about $1.95 billion for Sustainable Mountain Development. Although its program overlaps somewhat with that of chapter 21, the program for Sustainable Agriculture and Rural Development under chapter 14 would cost an additional $5.075 billion per year. Adding chapter 11, Combating Deforestation, with a price tag of approximately $6.2 billion, brings Agenda 21 projections to a total cost of about $18.2 billion per year for land degradation. United Nations Conference on Environment and Development (1992).

[25] The annual number of water projects rose overall from 123 in 1980 to 935 in 1990. After a slow but steady increase throughout the 1980s, the annual number of projects skyrocketed in 1992 to over 400, and continued to increase rapidly throughout the 1990s. Annual funding increased overall from $2.4 billion in 1980 to $4.2 billion in 1999, but unlike the number of projects, the increases were not consistent from year to year.

[26] Patterns of aid from bilateral donors were somewhat different from the patterns seen in multilateral donors. The number of projects funded annually by bilateral donors increased steadily from ninety-one in 1980 to 881 in 1999, with an especially large spike after the Rio Summit. The annual level of bilateral aid increased 200% over the period, climbing from $600 million in 1980 to $1.8 billion in 1999. Annual bilateral aid peaked in 1996 at just over $3 billion.

[27] The number of water projects funded by multilateral agencies increased much more modestly, but they were larger on average in terms of money spent. Over the two decades, multilateral projects increased from thirty-two in 1980 to fifty-four in 1999, and annual aid increased from $1.8 billion in 1980 to $2.3 billion in 1999. In the 1980s, multilateral donors' giving patterns showed far more variability than bilaterals', but in the 1990s, both displayed

$6.1 billion level of annual funding called for in Agenda 21 or the UNDP's $10–30 billion. However, in the years following the publication of Agenda 21 (1993–9), the average annual amount of water aid rose to $5.6 billion—only $500 million short of the original estimated amount needed.[28]

By contrast, funds to combat the destruction of soil resources are only trickling in from the aid community. There were only 1,537 land degradation assistance projects between 1980 and 1999, with an allocated total of approximately $4.6 billion over the entire period. This is a small fraction of the *annual* funding needs identified in Agenda 21: about 2 per cent of the annual Rio goals. Of all environmental aid given in the twenty-year period covered here, aid to address land degradation represents only 3.23 per cent.[29] Despite continued warnings about land degradation, it appears to be a very low priority for donor countries.

A closer look at who is funding what in these two program areas is instructive. The World Bank is by far the largest water donor, having lent approximately $25 billion over the twenty-year period. Japan gave $11.7 billion to fund 504 projects over the two decades, one of which cost almost $1 billion and was the largest project in either decade by a wide margin. By comparison, Germany and the United States—the next two largest bilateral donors—gave $5.2 billion and $3.5 billion, respectively. The top multilateral donors for both decades were the IBRD, IADB, and IDA, with $18.9 billion, $10.2 billion, and $5.5 billion, respectively.

The average cost of a bilateral water project was $4.7 million, while the average cost of a multilateral water project was ten times that—$47.1 million. Bilateral and multilateral agencies also finance different kinds of water projects, with multilaterals (especially the development banks, see Chapters 7 and 8) funding large infrastructure projects (many with loans) and bilateral agencies funding smaller local projects (many with grants). The late 1990s saw a surge in the number of water projects at the same time as a decrease in total water aid, suggesting that in recent years, these types of smaller, grant-funded projects have become more prevalent. Bilateral and multilateral donors also support different countries. The top three recipients of bilateral water aid were

much the same pattern, with a rise in the mid-1990s followed by a decline in the late 1990s back to pre-Rio levels.

[28] Funding spiked in the mid-1990s following Rio when the $6 billion goal was met for five consecutive years, but after the high of $6.5 billion in 1996, water aid levels dropped precipitously back down to pre-Rio levels, despite the continued increase in the number of projects.

[29] Signs of progress in closing this funding gap are few. The United Nations Conference on Desertification (UNCOD) adopted an action plan in 1977 to combat desertification in the 1980s. However, the PLAID data show that in the 1980s only about $1.1 billion (about $100 million a year) was appropriated to land degradation as a whole, amounting to only 2.85% of total environmental aid. In 1991, UNEP concluded that 'the problem of land degradation in arid, semi-arid and dry sub-humid areas had intensified, although there were "local examples of successes."'

Egypt, India, and China, while the top three recipients of multilateral water aid were Brazil, Mexico, and China. Overall, Brazil was the top recipient of water aid, with $6 billion over twenty years, virtually all of which came from multilateral donors. China barely reached the top ten for water aid recipients in the 1980s, but shot to the top of the list in the 1990s, and unlike Brazil, a significant portion of this aid came from bilateral donors.[30]

Land degradation aid hovered near or below $100 million a year until 1987, when two large projects boosted the traditional annual totals. That year, the IADB Fund for Special Operations provided $75 million for a reforestation project in Ecuador and the ADB gave $49 million for a reforestation project in Côte d'Ivoire. In 1990, a $350 million afforestation project funded by the World Bank's IDA—over four times larger than any previous project—was given to China. The years following the Rio Earth Summit in 1992 suggest that the issue of land degradation was overshadowed by other concerns. Land degradation aid fell in 1993 to around $260 million and followed a roller-coaster ride of highs and lows over the next six years, with aid dipping to $178 million in 1996 and peaking in 1997 at $575 million. Looking back at twenty years of project-level data, the shifting size and types of land degradation aid projects reveal much about donors' intended goals. While there are a handful of large land degradation projects, notably to China and India in the early 1990s, most aid given to countries comes in quite small packages averaging $2.4 million in the 1980s and $4.1 million in the 1990s. For example, a 1996 project from Canada to Haiti for $3.9 million sought to promote 'soil degradation control.' A project from Denmark to Zimbabwe for $2.3 million was designed to increase 'productivity in community land in five districts in eastern Zimbabwe through sustainable use of forests and trees.' These projects suggest narrowly targeted interventions with limited funds.

Although land degradation assistance makes up only a small portion of environmental aid, there are a handful of donors who have made the issue a priority. The largest bilateral donors in the 1980s were the United States, Sweden, and the Netherlands. In the 1990s, Japan, Germany, and the United Kingdom were the leading donors. Japan is a particularly interesting case, as it donated only 2.4 per cent of total land degradation aid in the 1980s, but was the largest land degradation aid donor by the end of the 1990s, with 27.2 per cent total land degradation funding. As we document in Chapter 5, China's dust storms seriously affect Japanese air quality, and these storms are the direct result of land degradation.

The pattern of multilateral aid for land degradation is one of very inconsistent attention,[31] and while multilaterals make up 41 per cent of total land

---

[30] Mexico saw a similarly large increase from the 1980s to the 1990s, from $810 million to $3.6 billion, funded almost entirely by multilateral donors.

[31] The ASDB gave in 1986, 1988, and 1989 while the IDA only gave in 1980, 1983, 1987, and 1989. The AFDB donated in 1980, 1985, and 1987, while the IADB only gave in 1981. In

degradation aid, they usually did so in large, one-time projects, unlike bilateral donors who gave in smaller projects over a number of years.[32] Over the 1980s and 1990s, the greatest recipients of land degradation aid were China (15.5 per cent of all land degradation aid), India (11.6 per cent), and the Philippines (9.2 per cent).[33]

Shifting Brown Aid Priorities

The observed pattern of water aid allocation raises an important question: If donors have effectively filled the 'financing gap' for most of the 1990s, and resource mobilization is a key constraint to success, why have we not witnessed more significant improvements in the provision of water and sanitation services worldwide?[34] Research suggests that donors have achieved limited success in the water and sanitation sector largely because of poor pricing policies, corruption, political targeting of public expenditure, insufficient buy-in from local communities, weak citizen–state accountability mechanisms, and low levels of capacity within recipient countries.[35] According to the World Bank's own measures of project success, 'the [water and sanitation] sector continues to rank last or next to last relative to other sectors.'[36]

the 1990s, the ASDB donated in 1992, 1996, 1999, at which time the IDA only gave in 1990, 1991, and 1999, and the AFDF only put money toward land preservation causes in 1992 and 1994. There is no quantitative pattern to the aid being given by these organizations in these years. In fact, no more than twenty projects were given by any of these donors in order for them to appear in the top three donors in their respective decades. The only multilateral organization that gives with any regularity to make an appearance in the top donors list is the GEF, which donated twenty projects in seven of the ten years between 1990 and 1999.

[32] While bilateral aid has accounted for nearly 60% of total land degradation aid 1980–99, multilateral donors have also made substantial contributions. The largest multilateral donors in the 1980s include the ASDB (21.04% of multilateral land degradation aid), the IDA (10.25%), and the AFDB (6.87%), while in the 1990s the largest donors include the ASDB (17.68%), the IDA (11.69%), and the GEF (3.09%).

[33] In the 1980s, Pakistan (21.6%), Ecuador (6.9%), and China (6.0%) attracted the largest percentage of land degradation aid, while China (18.70%), India (14.73%), and the Philippines (7.07%) weighed in for top percentages in the 1990s. In the case of China, the largest projection was a major $350-million afforestation loan from the World Bank's IDA. In the case of India, three Japanese projects were financed through the Overseas Economic Cooperation Fund (OECF), one in 1991 for $140 million for land use management work and two others in 1997 for afforestation projects totaling around $140 million and $120 million, respectively. The Philippines received $130 million in aid for land reclamation in Cebu through a series of large donations from the OECF. Pakistan shot up the recipients list thanks to a reclamation project in 1989 for $145 million from the ASDB. The IADB Fund for Special Operations gave Ecuador a $76-million reforestation project in 1987, pushing the country to the top three recipients during the 1980s.

[34] United Nations Development program (2006).

[35] Davis (2003); Whittington (2003); United Nations Millennium Project, Task Force on Water and Sanitation (2005); World Bank (2003); Isham et al. (1995); Isham and Kähkönen (2002, 2003).

[36] World Bank (2003: 11).

Unlike broad-based public services like public education and health care, water and sanitation infrastructure is a more 'targetable' good.[37] That is, water and sewerage projects are highly visible, location-specific, and of immediate benefit to specific communities.[38] They also provide opportunities to target jobs and steer large contracts to loyal companies that offer campaign contributions.[39] Brazil's Social Action in Sanitation Program, funded by the IADB in the 1990s, is typical in this regard: '[The project] was conceived and structured to generate double benefits... At the same time that it enabled temporary solutions for critical unemployment problems, it increased the coverage of sanitation services.'[40] In 1997, the IBRD financed a massive project in Wanjiazhai, China, in the northern Shanxi province that is home to three of China's fastest growing industrial areas. The project included not only the physical structures needed to transfer and purify water from the Yellow River, but also institutional reform in the agencies that manage water and resources to halt industrial pollution and overuse of the local water supply. The project's total cost was $1.5 billion, $400 million of which was financed by the IBRD loan. In addition to its primary purpose of alleviating water shortages, it was also intended to be a source of jobs, much like the Brazilian project.

These project characteristics have important implications for the effectiveness of donor assistance, because targeting of expenditures along political lines can significantly reduce the overall productivity of such spending.[41] Another key constraint is that many households in developing countries have un-metered private connections to water networks, and are charged a flat rate, regardless of how much water they consume. This provides no incentive for water conservation and leads to wasteful consumption of clean water. Inefficient and inequitable water subsidy schemes have also undermined the efforts of many donor agencies and host country governments.[42]

---

[37] Keefer and Khemani (2005); Robinson (2005); Ferejohn (1974); Bates (1981).

[38] When deciding which provinces, clans, or villages will receive the benefit of the aid, politicians often choose to reward loyalty to the governing party. According to Keefer and Khemani (2005: 13, emphasis added), '[c]ompetitive elections were a regular feature of the political landscape of Pakistan during the 1990s, but credible promises by political parties or political leaders to voters were supported largely by clientelist relationships and related to targeted transfers rather than broad public services. There is little evidence of political competition on the basis of broad policy promises, nor of distinctions among the major parties by their stances on broad policy issues. In this kind of environment, the provision of broad-based public goods would be expected to be low and the provision of targeted goods to be emphasized. Indeed, compared with countries with similar incomes per capita and demographic characteristics (age and proportion rural), primary school enrollment in Pakistan in 2000 was twenty percentage points less than would be expected. *Access to potable water, however, was twenty-five percentage points higher than expected. Investments in potable water, particularly in rural areas where they consist largely of well-drilling, are particularly easy to target and their benefits are immediately accessible and observable.*' Also see World Bank (2002b); Keefer et al. (2006); Moser (2005); Khemani (2004).

[39] Wade (1991).   [40] United Nations (1997).

[41] Robinson and Torvik (2005); Keefer and Knack (2007).

[42] Gómez-Lobo and Contreras (2003).

Donors themselves may also be responsible for failed water and sanitation projects if they are unwilling or unable to withhold, suspend, or terminate assistance. Pressure to continue disbursements and complete projects can come from very different quarters. Bilateral and multilateral agencies may face political pressure from their domestic principals to reward geo-strategic allies and trading partners, regardless of their commitment to sound development policies. Contractors interested in ensuring the steady flow of aid may lobby donors for continued disbursements.[43] Donors may want to avoid the public embarrassment of being responsible for a 'white elephant' project that could undermine their domestic support. There are also internal incentive structures within donor agencies that promote rapid and continued disbursements.[44]

Why then does water and sanitation aid remain so popular among donors compared to land degradation? One possibility is that the 'poverty aversion' of donors leaves them in a "Samaritan's Dilemma". That is, for donors who are truly altruistic and motivated by reducing poverty and expanding access to environmental services, it may be difficult to credibly threaten aid withdrawal when recipients fail to meet agreed-upon performance targets, backtrack on previous commitments, or adopt unhelpful policies that undermine a project's viability. Water and sanitation assistance may also be popular because, for practical and political reasons, there is a high level of demand for these sorts of projects among developing countries.[45] The urban poor are more able to organize and put pressure on politicians than rural poor and they represent very easily mobilized blocks of voters. Since land degradation projects tend to get implemented in rural areas, it is possible that there is less political demand for such projects. Large sewerage projects in cities do not suffer from similar

[43] Kanbur (2000).

[44] Easterly (2001: 116). Many donors are also guilty of adopting 'top-down' approaches to project design that fail to elicit buy-in from local communities and account for local knowledge and culture. In the area of rural water supply, Pritchett and Woolcock (2004: 198) identify three 'systemic failures.' 'First, decisions about the location and design of the project were made on a "technocratic" and "expert" basis almost exclusively; there was little effort to incorporate local knowledge. This led to insufficient knowledge about local conditions being taken into account, leading to avoidable technological mistakes. This was systemic in that improvement was not simply a matter of identifying better expert decisions; failure was inherent in the design of projects that did not allow for or encourage beneficiary engagement. Second, the assumption that there was a need produced a complete lack of attention to what people actually wanted from improved water supplies—i.e., to the demand for improved water services. This meant that the systems often did not meet the demands of the users, and hence there was little local commitment to the projects by the beneficiaries. This low commitment led to low and improper maintenance, and chronic underfunding and underprovision of recurrent inputs. Third, providers could abuse their discretion. The difficulty of observing in detail the quality of the services rendered from either the beneficiaries themselves (who were kept in the dark about costs) or from managers above (who did not know about beneficiary satisfaction) meant that projects often had considerable "slack." These monies were often siphoned off in various ways to bureaucrats and politicians. There were few pressures for cost-efficiency and actual delivery of services.'

[45] Keefer and Khemani (2005); Moser (2005); Nielson and Tierney (2001).

problems. It is also important to note that water and sanitation aid, unlike some other types of environmental assistance, may provide lucrative contracts for Western firms, creating a political constituency in donor countries for continued assistance.

The strong support that water and sanitation aid enjoys stands in sharp contrast to the response that land degradation has elicited from the international community. Experts argue that low levels of land degradation funding are linked to the broader North-South divide on desertification. Since the Rio Earth Summit, industrialized countries have refused to accept developing countries' claim that desertification is a global issue, so rather than agreeing to new and additional funding for land degradation, developed countries agreed to create a Global Mechanism (GM) that would help coordinate existing land degradation aid flows from bilateral and multilateral agencies.[46] According to Najam (2004: 150), 'the desertification case represents an important role reversal. Unlike most other global environmental negotiations where the North is the one pushing for a treaty and the South is resisting on the grounds that there are other more pressing global concerns that should be addressed first, this was a case where it was the South calling for a treaty and the North resisting for exactly the same reasons.' Our findings suggest that in these cases funding will be allocated at a far lower level than needed.

Green, Global, and on the Rise: Biodiversity and Climate Aid

Isolated and modest efforts to create national parks and preserves in the developing world existed prior to the 1980s, but the term 'biodiversity' was invented by biologists in 1985 to implant the protection of species in their ecosystems in the minds of policy-makers and the general public.[47] In 1992, Agenda 21 stated that while the campaign for biodiversity protection was growing, it was falling short of levels that would ensure a sustainable global commons: 'Despite mounting efforts over the past twenty years, the loss of the world's biological diversity, mainly from habitat destruction, over-harvesting, pollution, and the inappropriate introduction of foreign plants and animals has continued...Urgent and decisive action is needed to conserve and maintain genes, species, and ecosystems.'[48] Our findings suggest that soon thereafter the political project for biodiversity preservation bore more fruit. A decade after the term was coined, the tiny number of projects in the 1980s with terms in their titles such as 'Protection,' 'Parks,' and 'Reserves' were replaced by hundreds in the 1990s with the new buzzword, 'biodiversity

---

[46] Najam (2004); Porter et al. (2000: 134).

[47] Biologist E. O. Wilson is credited with first publishing a book with the word 'biodiversity,' a term he credits W. G. Rosen with inventing. The term was invented and disseminated specifically to create more political will to protect species.

[48] Chapter 15, UN Conference on Environment and Development (1992).

preservation.' The issue was successfully reframed as a global public good and bigger sources of foreign assistance began to materialize.

A series of abnormally hot years and scientific observations in the late 1980s also suggested that human activity was driving changes in the global climate.[49] As described in the first chapter, this issue is close to a paradigmatic case of global public good under-provision, where all people on earth contribute to the problem and all suffer the consequences of collective inaction. In the twenty years that climate change has been seriously debated, deep tensions have emerged between developed and developing countries. Scientists have warned of rising sea levels threatening low-lying countries and small islands, spreading deserts that will jeopardize the survival of millions farming marginally arid lands without irrigation, and devastating heat waves, hurricanes, floods, and droughts that could potentially set some developing countries back decades in their effort to build strong economies.[50]

Developing countries are both particularly susceptible victims of climate change and great potential contributors to controlling greenhouse gas emissions.[51] Lacking flood protection and secure food and water systems, poor countries are the most vulnerable to climate disasters. They need assistance to build expensive floodwalls and emergency response systems to protect their populations from such disasters. At the same time, the booming economies of China and India are rapidly increasing their energy consumption, and will soon become the world's largest sources of carbon emissions. Mitigation comprises all human activities aimed at reducing the emissions or enhancing the sinks of greenhouse gases such as carbon dioxide, methane, and nitrous oxide. Some aid projects seek to prevent new carbon emissions, while others focus on improving the efficiency of existing energy sources. Donor countries have an incentive to seek carbon reduction opportunities in developing countries where doing so is cheaper than in industrialized countries. By contrast, aid for adaptation to climate change tends to have local rather than global benefits. Adaptation projects generally help developing countries prepare for and cope with the detrimental effects of climate change, including coastal erosion, desertification, and severe weather.

The prescriptions to solve these two environmental crises could not be more different. Compared to other programs, the estimated cost in Agenda 21 of global biodiversity conservation seems low: roughly $1.75 billion annually from the international community. Aid for biodiversity protection usually involves creating and maintaining protected areas, such as national parks and wildlife preserves, drafting legislation, and developing national plans for conserving species diversity. By contrast, building high-technology

---

[49] IPCC (2001, 2007); Houghton (1999).
[50] IPCC (2001, 2007); Roberts and Parks (2007a).
[51] See for example Roberts and Parks (2007a).

power stations and improving the efficiency of industry and transportation infrastructure was expected to cost more than ten times as much. Measures to reduce carbon emissions (and other emissions) by encouraging efficiency and environmentally friendly alternatives to conventional development were estimated in Agenda 21 to require $20 billion annually (in 1993 dollars) in foreign assistance.

Our analysis of the 1,267 biodiversity projects during the 1980s and 1990s revealed that only $2.35 billion in aid was allocated for biodiversity over the whole period between 1980 and 1999, or about one-fifteenth of the Agenda 21 annual estimate of need ($120 million a year on average).[52] However, only $47 million was given between 1980 and 1989 (2 per cent). The remaining 98 per cent was transferred between 1990 and 1999. Annual project counts and total funding rates increased from just one project and $339,224 in 1980 to 292 projects with funding of $311,650,735 in 1999. In the 1990s, bilateral donors spent $825 million on 874 biodiversity projects, while multilaterals donated almost $1.5 billion for 374 projects.[53] The largest bilateral donor of biodiversity aid over the period was the United States, which donated $200 million, or 9 per cent of all biodiversity aid (with a sharp upward trend in the late 1990s, reaching $67 million in 1999 alone). Unsurprisingly, Brazil and Kenya received the most biodiversity aid over the period—most likely because they possess high-profile ecosystems in the Amazon and game-rich savannas. Other countries topping the list of hotspots per country and ranking relatively high in aid dollars received included Mexico, Indonesia, India, Costa Rica, Mozambique, and South Africa. These target areas for the biodiversity protection also support some of the largest branches of the eco-tourism industry. These descriptive patterns are consistent with a recent GEF evaluation which shows a strong bias towards 'mega-diverse' countries.[54]

Funding for climate aid projects was on a totally different scale, jumping from $2.33 billion total in the 1980s to $8.4 billion in the 1990s.[55] Even before

---

[52] In order to isolate biodiversity projects in the database, terms were chosen to use in keyword searches of the datasets. These included: Biodiversity, Bio-diversity, Biodiversidad, Biodiversité, Protection, Conservation, Reserves, Nature Reserves, Parks, Nature Parks, Shorebirds, Fauna, Flora, and Wildlife. As described above, after keyword searches proved incomplete, we went line by line through each of the 70,000 environmental projects to uncover the 1,267 biodiversity projects.

[53] The largest donor of biodiversity aid is by far the GEF. Providing 33% of total biodiversity aid and 43% of total multilateral biodiversity aid, the GEF is the largest influence on biodiversity aid trends. The reason for the GEF's high level of involvement in biodiversity stems from its responsibility to the Convention on Biological Diversity and resulting charters. 'Biodiversity conservation constitutes one of the GEF's greatest priorities... As the financial mechanism for the Convention on Biological Diversity (CBD), the GEF helps countries fulfill their obligations under the CBD.' Donations by other multilateral sources are insignificant in comparison to the GEF and top bilateral donors. UNDP (2007).

[54] Global Environment Facility (2005).

[55] Almost all types of climate aid show a large jump from one decade to the next. Only one type of project breaks the trend, geothermal power. Donors gave $1.04 billion in the

the threat of climate change weighed on the minds of policy-makers, donors funded energy efficiency, renewable power generation, forest fire control, and other similar types of projects that are now classified as climate aid. A total of $676 million was given for energy efficiency in the 1980s. In comparison, donors gave $4.54 billion for energy efficiency during the 1990s. Donors also increased their funding for renewable energy from $1.57 billion in the 1980s to $2.95 billion in the 1990s. By dollar value, the largest multilateral donors of climate aid during the 1990s were the Asian Development Bank ($2.3 billion), the International Bank for Reconstruction and Development ($1.4 billion), and the Global Environment Facility ($1.1 billion). The three largest bilateral donors for the decade were Japan ($1.08 billion), the United States ($897 million), and Germany ($342 million). The GEF's $1.1 billion in climate aid was spread across 248 climate change projects through 1999. One hundred and nine projects were 'enabling activities' that funded recipient efforts to comply with their UNFCCC commitments by developing carbon inventories and making plans for addressing climate change, totaling only $44 million. In contrast to these relatively small projects, energy sector loans can be massive, with values in the hundreds of millions of dollars.[56]

Recipient governments play an important role in determining which climate projects are carried out. A striking example is one of the largest climate aid projects in the PLAID database, a 1994 IBRD loan for $251 million towards

1980s and only $1.16 billion in the 1990s—a relatively moderate 11.5% increase. As well as attempting to mitigate climate change, donors began in the very late 1990s to fund projects for adaptation to its consequences. For the 1990s, the PLAID database only shows five projects whose descriptions indicate a primary focus on adaptation. One such project funded by the GEF was Caribbean-wide: a $7.4 million project for monitoring sea levels, assessing vulnerabilities, and planning for future policy implications of climate change. Global Environment Facility (2002). Other projects have descriptions that mention making plans for adaptation but not a primary focus on it. Some aid geared towards adaptation may very well not be intentionally designed to address climate change impacts. Projects in response to natural disasters, coastal erosion, and desertification may effectively be adaptation aid without being classified as such. A USAID document speaks to the classification problem: 'USAID works to incorporate climate change adaptation planning into mainstream development assistance activities. While strengthening the capacity of developing countries and countries with economies in transition to prepare for and adapt to the impacts of climate variability and change, the Agency focuses on existing projects in the water, coastal zone management, and agriculture sectors.' This is increasingly the case with all aid agencies—'mainstreaming adaptation' is the new buzzword in the development community. USAID (2005).

[56] However, often only a small component of such projects is directly relevant to lowering carbon emissions or improving energy efficiency. For instance, the IBRD approved the largest climate change project of the decade. In 1991, the IBRD made a commitment of $388 million for heat supply restructuring in Poland. PLAID database information on the project does not specify greenhouse gas control as an objective of the project, but a study on the Polish energy sector by the World Bank does discuss the program. The study points to district heating systems, centralized systems that provide heating for large residential and commercial areas, the focus of the IBRD project, as one of the largest sources for carbon dioxide emissions. The study also says that greenhouse gas reduction is an overall objective of the World Bank's energy program in Poland. United Nations (1994).

the Leyte Luzon geothermal power plant in the Philippines. The plant alone would have been more expensive to operate than a coal-fired plant, so the recipient country had to be convinced that it was a·worthwhile investment. A $30 million supplementary grant from the Global Environment Trust Fund (GET) financed one-third of the added expense of the facility. According to the World Bank's project documents, the GET grant played an important role in convincing the Philippines government to undertake the geothermal plant. The Bank estimated that the grant eliminated one metric ton of carbon emissions for every $1.60 of GET funding.[57] This case illustrates the contentious issue of 'additionality': that aid should be used to persuade recipients to invest in projects not likely to be undertaken in the absence of the subsidy. It also explains why the Philippines was the third largest recipient of climate change aid in the 1990s following India and China, which received, respectively, $1.59 and $1.40 billion in climate change aid.

While one can imagine a variety of potential projects that would bring benefits either to recipients (local needs) or donors (global concerns), many of the projects being funded by donors (in the area of climate change and biodiversity preservation) tend to address both global effects sought by donors and local effects that benefit recipients. Forest fire prevention projects, for example, create a global benefit by preserving carbon sinks and preventing carbon emission from smoke, but also provide recipients with a means to protect the safety of their citizens and economic resources such as timber. They can also be justified as protecting biodiversity. Energy efficiency projects make more usable energy available to recipient countries while reducing greenhouse gas emissions, and renewable energy projects are especially useful in rural areas where stringing power lines from centralized power stations may not be economically feasible. Setting up nature preserves is usually far more difficult than most outsiders realize, since local peoples in or near the protected areas are often cut off from key resources they need for food, fodder, fuel, fiber, shelter, and trade. Even in areas with thriving eco-tourism opportunities, locals seldom gain many benefits from Western-style parks.[58] The equivalent

---

[57] United Nations Environment Programme (2002). This geothermal plant accounted for a substantial portion of the $852 million the Philippines received in climate aid during the 1990s. During the 1980s, the Philippines actually received more climate-type aid than any other country, $532 million. Brazil and Pakistan followed with $532 million and $361 million respectively. China and India trailed far behind in the 1980s, coming in seventh and sixteenth on the list of climate aid recipients.

[58] E.g. Brechin et al. (2003); Neumann (2002); Roberts and Thanos (2003); Brandon et al. (1998). At Komodo National Park in Indonesia, locals living within and nearby the park indicated in a 1996 survey that they felt eco-tourism brought little to no economic benefit to local economies as the tourism companies were foreign or non-locally owned. Elsewhere in Indonesia, studies conducted in 1994 and 1995 at the Bunakin National Marine Park, Bogani Nani Wartabone National Park, and Tangkoko Duasudara Nature Reserve found that 'the ideal symbiotic relationship between people enjoying sustainable resource use and protected areas receiving support by resident environmental activists is not being realized.' Locals resented

for climate change might be the planting of large agricultural or pasturage areas with trees for carbon sequestration, or other more industrial projects that offer few jobs to locals. These are classic cases of global public goods being net liabilities for local peoples. Although there has been a recent push in the development community towards 'participatory' development, several recent studies show few social development benefits associated with the carbon trading mechanisms under Kyoto.[59] The Holy Grail of environmental assistance is identifying the 'win-win' projects that help locals directly and protect global public goods. Unfortunately, a significant number of critical projects serve only one need or the other.

The Direction of Environmental Aid

In terms of meeting the Agenda 21 recommendations, climate funding represents only 4 per cent of the prescribed allocation, and biodiversity attracted only 7 per cent of the prescribed allocation. Even worse is land degradation funding, which appears to have received just 2 per cent of the suggested amount (Table 2.1). If we want to understand why these environmental crises have not been solved, Table 2.1 suggests one part of the explanation: the necessary resources have not been provided.[60] At the same time, donors have generously bankrolled water and sanitation projects, and only modest improvements occurred during the period in which the funding was provided.[61] This suggests that while funding may be a constraint, it is likely not *the* most important constraint to improved environmental outcomes. Donors have also placed a significant (and increasing) amount of financial support behind the creation and maintenance of 'protected parks.' Yet, new research suggests that legally protected land may in fact be less effective at reducing biodiversity loss than areas that are not legally protected.[62] This reinforces the point that funding is only one of the many ingredients needed to protect the environment.

what they perceived as economic and political exclusion from the park management. In addition to poor relationships with locals, Ross and Wall (1999) concluded that 'natural ecosystems are not being protected' in these areas.

[59] e.g. Ellis et al. (2007); Boyd et al. (2007); Cole and Roberts n.d.; Young et al. (2001).

[60] See Bruner et al. (2004); Struhsaker et al. (2005).   [61] UNDP (2006).

[62] Using data on 163 forests in 13 countries, Hayes (2006) poses a serious empirical challenge to the assumption that legally protected areas are the optimal way to manage forests. She finds that the ability of the *users* of the forest to make the rules is positively correlated with vegetation density. An independent review of GEF-funded biodiversity projects also found that 'more than half of the completed protected area projects... reported few or no biodiversity impacts, and other projects reported possibly negative impacts. For example, in the Kerinci Sablat Integrated Conservation and Development project in Indonesia, the greatest loss of forest cover during the project occurred in the two districts that received the largest proportion of Village Conservation Grants' (GEF 2005: 22).

Table 2.1. 1990s environmental aid by sector: comparison of agenda 21 prescriptions for needed aid with actual dose delivered, four sectors.

	Dose prescribed $b/yr	Dose received $b/yr	Percentage of dose received
Water	6.1	5.6	92%
Land	18.2	0.35	2%
Climate change	20	0.84	4%
Biodiversity	1.75	0.125	7%
Total	46.05	6.915	15%

These four case studies also reveal some interesting trends in funding for environmental projects and the tensions between objective environmental needs, donor interests, and recipient interests. Water aid dwarfs all other environmental sub-sectors, and remains dominant through the twenty years analyzed in this study. Climate change aid and biodiversity projects rise sharply in numbers and amounts in the later 1990s, but funding to assist poor countries in addressing the crisis of desertification and other types of land degradation does not. Water projects remain popular among recipients—perhaps due to the high visibility of the projects for politicians and their ability to funnel this aid to domestic construction firms that support their political campaigns. The increased funding for sewage treatment in 1993 was at least in part attributable to the shock experienced by delegates at the Rio de Janeiro Earth Summit visiting its bay and spectacular beaches regularly contaminated with untreated sewage.

These brief sectoral studies provide some initial insights into the world of aid allocation, but we will provide significantly more detail in the chapters to come. Some analysis of these sectors suggests that biodiversity aid tends to flow to countries with high numbers of biodiversity hotspots as defined by groups like Conservation International and World Wildlife Fund. These groups actively lobby donor countries for increased funding to these projects. However, large allocations to the water and sanitation sector appear to conform more closely to geopolitical or commercial interests. Again, land degradation is a major problem, but it garners little aid except from some small European donors who, unlike larger bilateral donors, appear less likely to use aid as a geopolitical tool. Biodiversity and protected parks are attracting more funding over time, but it appears sporadic and mostly since the term biodiversity gained notoriety in the mid-1990s.

Climate aid, on the other hand, became prominent late in our study period, in the early 1990s. In spite of its late start, this type of environmental foreign assistance may soon overshadow all other environmental sub-sectors, with massive funding coming from Clean Development Mechanism (CDM) projects under the Kyoto Protocol. The CDM allows wealthy countries who cannot meet their promised carbon emissions reductions under Kyoto to buy carbon from developing countries by paying for projects like reforestation, power plant energy efficiency, and capturing methane from landfills. The CDM also will place a levy on these purchases, which will go into a fund for the least developed countries, to assist them with 'adaptation' projects that will help them deal with the consequences of climate instability. Since this is such a potentially important and complex issue, we return to it in more detail in the book's final chapter.

Environmental aid is quite diverse in terms of who benefits from the projects, who is funding them, and at what level they are funded. We have seen a substantial rise in funding from both bilateral and multilateral donors in the 1990s, but we have more work to do in order to understand which donors are giving this aid, and to whom. We turn to this question next: which countries are receiving the greatest amounts of environmental aid and are these allocation patterns consistent with the greatest environmental needs and opportunities for change? The sectoral studies in this chapter suggest that more aid may be needed to address some environmental issues effectively— the current flow of environmental aid makes only a small contribution towards protecting biodiversity, increasing energy efficiency, and slowing land erosion. The needs are great, and the funds are limited.

3

Who Receives Environmental Aid? Patterns of Allocation and Case Studies of Five Major Recipients

Donor governments see the periodic funding replenishments of multilateral aid agencies as their best opportunity to reform them, and the third replenishment of the Global Environment Facility (GEF) in the summer of 2002 was no exception. This time, the disagreement was over which countries were to be favored in receiving environmental aid. In the United States, the Bush administration pushed for greater selectivity to steer GEF funds away from 'corrupt and inefficient governments.' As part of a wider effort to impose strict performance requirements on multilateral aid agencies, the US Treasury offered the GEF $70 million in additional support—over and above their standard $107.5 million replenishment contribution—if the GEF could put in place a 'transparent performance-based allocation system.' US negotiators argued that the GEF should reward political, economic, and environmental reformers with larger environmental aid allocations, and punish institutional 'basket-cases' and countries slow to implement environmental reforms by withholding funds. John Taylor, Under Secretary of the Treasury for International Affairs, said, 'President Bush wants to ensure that the Global Environmental Facility has the funding it needs to meet its program priorities and the policies in place to use those funds effectively . . . and the policy reforms and performance targets that have been agreed by donors, are vitally important steps forward in meeting these critical objectives.'[1]

This 'performance-based' allocation plan sparked a heated debate between donor and recipient governments over the future of environmental aid allocation, and provoked conflict between the leader of the GEF, Mohammed El Ashry, and the largest contributor to the GEF, the United States.[2] The very idea

[1] US Department of the Treasury, Office of Public Affairs (2002).
[2] According to a top GEF official, 'The U.S. government basically blackmailed the GEF and the other donor countries by saying, "you do it our way, or else we are pulling our money out."' Whether one describes the US policy as blackmail or as a member government of the

of a performance-based allocation scheme prompted a furious response from the developing countries of the G-77 and China. The loudest criticism was that this kind of aid would become a political football and the funds would not reach the places where they were needed most. The G-77 stressed that the secret of the GEF's success was its availability to all developing countries, and any infringement upon that basic principle would benefit neither recipient countries nor the organization as a whole. Any limits on recipient countries' ability to access GEF funds, they argued, would 'fundamentally [change] the nature and the objectives of the GEF [and would] not be accepted by the developing countries.'[3]

Some Western governments also expressed serious reservations about a single-minded focus on countries' environmental policies and institutions as cues to the credibility of the recipient government's commitment on environmental issues. Germany's representative to the GEF stated that his country would not agree to an allocation system based strictly on country performance. In his words, 'To implement a GEF funded project according to *national* indicators would undermine the unique global character of the GEF. To forsake a project just because the host country is a bad economic or political performer could affect the whole [of] mankind in a negative manner.'[4] A coalition of NGOs staked out a similar position: '[The] GEF, based on its mandate, should be primarily focused on global environmental priorities, rather than country performance for its resource allocation.'[5]

Three Western governments—Canada, France, and the United Kingdom—sided with the United States in favor of an *ex ante* performance-based allocation system, but Belgium, Germany, Denmark, and Switzerland argued that such changes would violate the core principle of 'equal opportunity to access GEF resources.' Others supported a different sort of targeting, arguing that GEF funding would be most effective in countries that have the greatest potential to deliver global environmental benefits. As the Netherlands representative put it: 'The GEF, based on its mandate, should be primarily focused on global environmental priorities, rather than country performance for its resource allocation.'[6]

This public debate at the GEF offers a rare glimpse into the debates over environmental aid allocation. It shatters the myth of G-7 homogeneity, showing instead the variation in donor government beliefs about how their environmental aid funds should be spent. It also illustrates key differences

---

GEF using its authority and resources to realize its policy goals is certainly debatable, but the US did end up getting much of what it wanted to the dismay of GEF staff, most recipients, and some donors. Personal interview (2005).

[3] al-Nasser (2004).   [4] Steinke (2004).   [5] Global Environment Facility (2004c).
[6] Van Voorst tot Voorst (2004).

between many recipients and donors over rules that will shape subsequent aid allocations. In the case of the GEF's third replenishment, the United States and its allies got much of what they wanted, and the GEF eventually agreed to implement a performance-based allocation system. This reform could mark a sea change in the way that donors allocate their resources, a hypothesis we evaluate later in this book.

In this chapter, we explore the global allocation of environmentally beneficial, environmentally neutral, and environmentally damaging foreign assistance. The PLAID database allows us to compile the first systematic ranking of recipient countries by amount of environmental aid received during the 1980s and 1990s. We then briefly examine five major recipient countries in greater detail: China, India, Brazil, Egypt, and Kenya. We quickly explore each country's local, regional, and global environmental significance; domestic environmental policies and institutions; role, posture, and reputation in international environmental politics; and environmental funding sources and priorities. We also reflect on the relationship between foreign aid and environmental protection. These case studies provoke broader questions about why some countries receive more environmental aid than others, a question we attempt to answer in the next chapter.

Who Gets the Most? Allocation Patterns of Environmental Aid

If you asked someone with passing familiarity of environmental issues about which countries likely receive the most funding from international donors to address environmental problems, you would probably hear the names of Brazil, Kenya, Costa Rica, Ecuador, India, and China. The first four countries might make the list because of their world famous ecological resources and national parks; the latter two because of their huge populations and urban environmental problems. An environmentalist concerned about rising water levels due to climate change might also mention Bangladesh and small island states in the Pacific, or countries in Sub-Saharan Africa because of their severe vulnerability to drought and desertification. How well do these speculations match up with the facts?

Figures 3.1a and 3.1b show the total amount of environmental aid received by the top ten recipients of the 1980s and 1990s. These totals are also disaggregated into aid that was given to address global (green) and local (brown) environmental issues. Appendix B lists the total environmental aid received by all 200 nations and groups of countries in the 1980s and 1990s. There are several unsurprising countries on the leader list, such as Brazil, India, China,

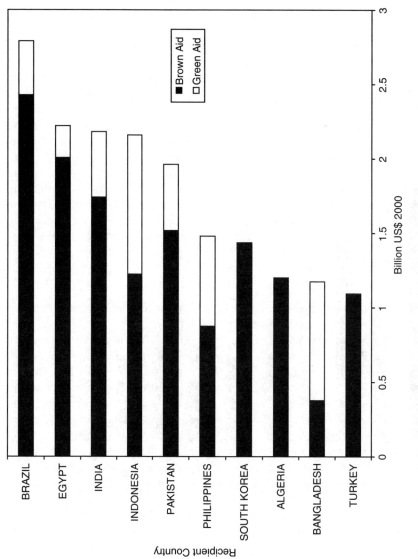

Figure 3.1a. Top ten recipients of environmental aid, by type, 1980–1989

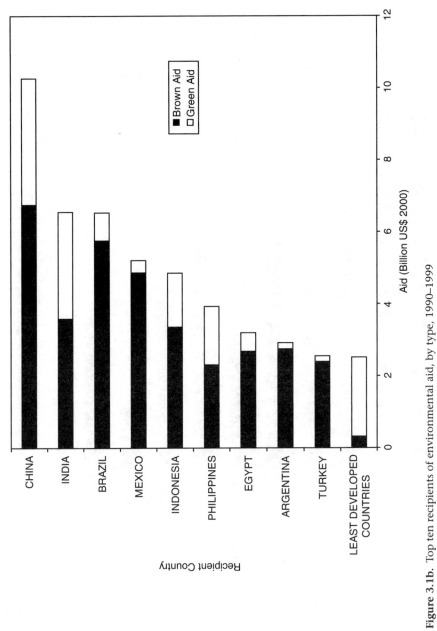

Figure 3.1b. Top ten recipients of environmental aid, by type, 1990–1999

Note: Utilizes only categorized aid data; See Appendix A for details. See note 8 on page 59 on LDCs.

Indonesia, Mexico, and Bangladesh.[7] However, there are some surprising entries that received over $1 billion in environmental aid in the1980s: Egypt, Pakistan, South Korea, Turkey, and Algeria. Without well-known environmental crises or globally critical biological resources, environmental aid to these countries would appear to be driven by their geopolitical importance to large donor states—perhaps in the context of the Cold War or in their efforts to influence security policy in the Middle East. China, which was not among the top ten recipients of environmental aid in the 1980s, skyrockets to first place with over $10 billion in environmental assistance in the 1990s. Major changes from the 1980s to the 1990s include some significant dry spells: Pakistan, for example, dropped from fifth to fourteenth in environmental aid; Kenya dropped from eleventh to twenty-fifth; and Algeria fell from eighth to forty-second. Among the next tier of recipients in the 1980s, El Salvador drops to sixty-seventh, Dominican Republic drops sharply to eighty-ninth, Ethiopia to sixty-first, and Haiti to seventy-first. Moving up significantly into the top twenty-five are Mexico, Vietnam, Peru, Russia, Bolivia, and Ghana.

In the 1980s, about a fifth of environmental aid received was earmarked for green environmental issues like biodiversity and climate change (see Chapter 2), but there was substantial variation, with Turkey, South Korea, and Algeria receiving only brown aid, and Bangladesh, Kenya, and Indonesia getting considerable assistance for green issues. In the 1990s, while brown aid continues to be the largest category, both China and India receive substantially more green aid. In a marked change from the 1980s, all of the top ten environmental aid recipients of the 1990s attracted at least some funding for green issues.

Table 3.1b lists the top ten recipients of environmental aid over the 1990s and their top five donors.[8] With few exceptions, multilateral donors (especially the World Bank, ASDB, and IADB) give the vast majority of environmental assistance to these countries. Over 8.1 billion of China's $10 billion in the 1990s is from three donors: the World Bank, ASDB, and Japan. The next three recipients—India, Brazil, and Mexico—have a similar group of major funders: the World Bank, Japan, and a regional development bank. Notably, the World Bank is the largest or second-largest donor for many countries, and its financial support often represents the vast majority of environmental aid received by a country. Of Brazil's $9.3 billion in environmental aid over the two decades, $4.9 billion came from the World Bank alone. More than a third of India's $8.7 billion total came from the World Bank ($3.1 billion).

---

[7] If receipts are calculated on a per capita basis, some of the smaller countries rise to the top.

[8] The last bar in Figure 3.1b for 'Least Developed Countries' does not indicate that this is the cumulative amount to all LDCs. Instead, some donors did not specify the recipient country and entered 'LDC' as the recipient. The total amount of money to all LDCs is certainly higher than it appears in this chart.

Indonesia was the fourth largest recipient with $7 billion in environmental aid receipts, and Mexico totaled $5.4 billion. Two more countries—Egypt and the Philippines—received more than $5 billion in environmental grants and loans over the period, and four more captured more than $3 billion: Pakistan, Turkey, Argentina, and Bangladesh. While it is not surprising to find China, India, Brazil, Indonesia, and the Philippines at the top of the list of world's largest recipients of environmental aid, Egypt, Pakistan, and Turkey are a bit more peculiar. US interests in the Middle East almost certainly explain its huge donation to Egypt's sewage system. A billion-dollar water supply loan from the Japanese government, which provided lucrative contracts to Japanese firms, accounts for Turkey's inclusion in the top ten list.[9] Argentina similarly received a number of large water supply and sanitation projects. Mexico garnered $563 million for air pollution in its capital city, almost half a dozen water supply and sanitation projects worth over $2 billion overall, and was promised $406 million for a (failed) 'Northern Border Environment Project' associated with NAFTA compliance.[10] The lion's share of Bangladesh's environmental funding focused on riverbank and flood protection, an area of desperate human and environmental need predicted to worsen with a changing global climate.

Three final points can be made. First, in the listing of 1990s projects, the 'Least Developed Countries' appear in tenth place, with over $2 billion in environmental aid allocated to this group of the world's thirty-five poorest countries. Unlike many other recipients, over 80 per cent of environmental funding to this group of mostly African governments is earmarked for green issues. This pattern of allocation is consistent with our conjecture that recipients with geopolitical leverage are better able to secure more highly valued types of assistance for brown issues. Second, Appendix B shows that in the 1980s, 143 countries and groups of countries received some environmental aid, while in the 1990s the number rose by 66 recipients, to 199. Finally, to return to our naïve observer, they were nearly half-right. Some of the largest and most bio diverse countries in the world are at the top of the list of major recipients of environmental aid. However, several other countries appear to be on the list because of the geopolitical support they offer to 'patron' states— most notably, the United States and Japan. In what follows, we seek clear

[9] The single largest environmental project in the 1990s was Japan's water supply loan to the government of Turkey. It included a weir on the Melen river, a 150-kilometre transmission pipeline, pumping stations, a water treatment plant, and a sea-bed crossing of the Bosporus. A consortium led by a Japanese company was awarded the large consultancy contract and another Japanese firm was contracted to build one of the water treatment plants.

[10] According to the Operations Evaluation Department of the World Bank, 'the Northern Border Environment Project...was a substantial failure. Designed hastily in response to environmental concerns among NAFTA opponents in the United States, the government assigned low priority to the project, especially after the 1995 [financial] crisis, and 80 percent of the loan was cancelled.' World Bank (2001b).

Table 3.1. Top ten recipients and their top five donors, 1980s (3.1a) and 1990s (3.1b)

Donor	Environmental Aid	Donor	Environmental Aid
(a) 1980s			
1. BRAZIL	$2,790,000,000	6. PHILLIPPINES	$1,480,000,000
World Bank	$2,020,000,000	World Bank	$472,000,000
IADB	$742,000,000	Japan	$448,000,000
West Germany	$21,000,000	ASDB	$414,000,000
Canada	$2,980,000	United States	$135,000,000
Japan	$1,200,000	Denmark	$6,230,000
2. EGYPT	$2,220,000,000	7. S. KOREA	$1,440,000,000
United States	$1,760,000,000	ASDB	$550,000,000
World Bank	$134,000,000	Japan	$474,000,000
EU	$119,000,000	World Bank	$412,000,000
West Germany	$52,300,000	OPEC	$6,780,000
United Kingdom	$46,800,000	Canada	$138,000
3. INDIA	$2,180,000,000	8. ALGERIA	$1,200,000,000
World Bank	$1,500,000,000	World Bank	$1,100,000,000
The Netherlands	$326,000,000	EU	$90,200,000
Denmark	$97,500,000	ISDB	$10,700,000
United States	$87,800,000		
Sweden	$77,100,000		
4. INDONESIA	$2,160,000,000	9. BANGLADESH	$1,170,000,000
World Bank	$1,050,000,000	United States	$362,000,000
Japan	$277,000,000	World Bank	$249,000,000
ASDB	$261,000,000	ASDB	$241,000,000
The Netherlands	$186,000,000	Japan	$105,000,000
United States	$144,000,000	West Germany	$79,900,000
5. PAKISTAN	$2,030,000,000	10. TURKEY	$1,093,945,354
ASDB	$1,250,000,000	World Bank	$869,172,495
World Bank	$257,000,000	W. Germany	$210,656,560
Japan	$184,000,000	France	$7,655,395
United States	$132,000,000	Italy	$3,619,361
United Kingdom	$68,200,000	UK	$2,778,871
(b) 1990s			
1. CHINA	$10,100,000,000	Japan	$464,000,000
World Bank	$3,710,000,000	Germany	$161,000,000
ASDB	$2,440,000,000	GEF	$139,000,000
Japan	$2,070,000,000		
Germany	$546,000,000	4. MEXICO	$5,210,000,000
Montreal Protocol	$314,000,000	World Bank	$2,090,000,000
		IADB	$1,650,000,000
2. INDIA	$6,590,000,000	Japan	$1,170,000,000
World Bank	$1,620,000,000	GEF	$103,000,000
Japan	$1,480,000,000	NADB	$101,000,000
ASDB	$1,440,000,000		
United Kingdom	$646,000,000	5. INDONESIA	$4,860,000,000
Germany	$394,000,000	Japan	$1,110,000,000
		ASDB	$1,020,000,000
3. BRAZIL	$6,540,000,000	Australia	$126,000,000
World Bank	$2,970,000,000	United States	$116,000,000
IADB	$2,660,000,000	Italy	$110,000,000

(cont.)

Table 3.1. (*Continued*)

Donor	Environmental Aid	Donor	Environmental Aid
6. PHILIPPINES	$3,930,000,000	EU	$122,000,000
Japan	$1,930,000,000	Japan	$95,400,000
World Bank	$676,000,000	Italy	$47,800,000
ASDB	$631,000,000		
United States	$291,000,000	9. TURKEY	$2,550,000,000
Italy	$88,100,000	Japan	$936,000,000
		Germany	$597,000,000
7. EGYPT	$3,200,000,000	World Bank	$524,000,000
United States	$1,430,000,000	EU	$297,000,000
World Bank	$262,000,000	France	$84,800,000
France	$255,000,000		
Germany	$243,000,000	10. BANGLADESH	$1,950,000,000
Japan	$208,000,000	World Bank	$647,000,000
		ASDB	$447,000,000
8. ARGENTINA	$2,920,000,000	United States	$275,000,000
IADB	$1,570,000,000	Denmark	$127,000,000
World Bank	$980,000,000	Germany	$115,000,000

Note: 'Least Developed Countries' would have been ranked tenth; however, due to its aggregate nature, the next single largest state recipient, Bangladesh, is included.

comparative descriptions of environmental conditions and policy within five key recipient countries, and a more complete understanding of how foreign aid assists, or might assist, in addressing environmental problems in each country. We begin by comparing the giants of China and India, and then two nations of obvious biological importance, Brazil and Kenya. The final case is Egypt, without exceptional needs for environmental aid but overall the sixth largest recipient, capturing $5.4 billion over the two decades. These five cases provide detailed and contextual insights into the allocation process, which we attempt to understand more rigorously with an empirical analysis in Chapter 4.

Five Major Recipients

China: 'China Will Play if the World Will Pay'

There are few countries of greater global environmental significance than China. It is the world's most populous country and has one of the fastest growing economies on the planet. China is home to roughly 10 per cent of global flora and fauna, a leading global contributor to ozone depletion, and the world's largest consumer of coal.[11] China has recently become responsible for more greenhouse gas emissions than any other country in the world, including the United States. China is also the source of numerous regional environmental problems: acid rain falling on Japan and South Korea,

[11] Bradsher and Barboza (2006).

sandstorms affecting large swathes of north-east Asia, and water pollution arriving on its neighbors' shores. China also faces extraordinary domestic environmental challenges. Seventy per cent of its seven largest rivers are severely polluted; 85 per cent of its wastewater goes untreated; two-thirds of its cities face crises of landfill management; one-third of the country suffers from severe soil erosion; and it is home to sixteen of the twenty most polluted cities in the world.[12] In the mid-1990s, the World Bank estimated that 7.7 per cent of China's annual GDP was lost to environmental degradation.[13] By 2006, the Chinese government itself revised that figure to 10 per cent of GDP, or $200 billion, a year.[14] The human toll is equally startling: an estimated 300,000–400,000 Chinese die prematurely every year due to air pollution.[15] Unsafe water and poor sanitation claim many more lives. Water scarcity and desertification are major problems, with water tables falling rapidly in the north, per capita freshwater availability at dangerously low levels throughout the country, and dust storms overtaking urban centers.[16]

While there are only mixed signs of improvement on the ground, there are early indications of policy changes to address many of these issues. Due to increased public demand for environmental protection, growing awareness of the economic costs associated with environmental degradation, and sustained international pressure, the Chinese authorities have begun to take environmental issues more seriously.[17] The National Environmental Protection Agency (NEPA) was given ministerial rank in 1998 and renamed the State Environmental Protection Agency (SEPA), and an impressive number of environmental protection laws and regulations have been passed in the

[12] Wonacott (2004); Chan (2004).   [13] Pei (2002). Also see World Bank (2001a).

[14] Fincher n.d. In 2001, the World Bank revised its earlier estimates, arguing that after one takes into account the effect of acidification on croplands, lost work and medical bills from waterborne disease and air pollution, unsustainable resource harvesting, and disaster recovery costs, the total economic cost of environmental degradation in China is likely somewhere in the range of to 8–12% of annual GDP (World Bank 2001a). Given these costs and China's average annual economic growth of approximately 10%, it is easy to understand why experts believe that 'China's environmental problems have the potential to bring the country to its knees economically ('A Great wall of Waste' 2004).'

[15] Fincher n.d. The cost of air pollution alone is 2–3% of GDP according to Bolt et al. (forthcoming).

[16] According to an American Enterprise Institute (AEI) report, 'groundwater has been badly depleted, and surface water sources are equally overused. The Yellow river, for example, has run dry every year since 1985 because of diversions; in 1997, it failed to reach the ocean for 226 days' Hayward (2006).

[17] French (2005); Cody (2005a, 2005b); Yardley (2005). Schwartz (2003: 72) cites a Horizon Market Research company survey, conducted in November 2000 in ten Chinese cities, which identified environmental protection as the highest priority of ordinary Chinese citizens. Ranking below environmental protection were the following issues: unemployment, children's education, social order, corruption, economic growth, and social security for the elderly.

last decade.[18] The government has successfully implemented a partial logging ban and a tree-planting initiative to address deforestation, shut down 60,000 pollution-intensive small enterprises, set stringent vehicle fuel-economy standards that surpass those in the United States, and built wastewater treatment plants at breakneck speed.[19] Energy efficiency has also improved markedly and the government has committed itself to continuing energy conservation efforts: it plans to reduce the energy intensity of its economic growth by 20 per cent over the next five years.[20] Public expenditure on environmental protection is also budgeted to skyrocket. Between 2001 and 2005, the authorities spent $17 billion a year on the environment. In July 2006, the Chinese government announced plans to ramp up environmental protection spending to $35 billion a year for the next five years—more than three times the amount of environmental aid given annually from the donor community to *all* countries, and more than twenty times the amount of environmental aid given to China each year.[21] The magnitude of these expenditures raises a fundamental question: what role can foreign aid play in environmental reform if the total amount is dwarfed by China's own spending on the environment?

A number of obstacles stand in the way of effective environmental protection in China. Most fundamentally, there is a lack of institutional capacity within SEPA and its local branches (called Environmental Protection Bureau or EPBs).[22] SEPA has relatively few full-time staff at its headquarters in Beijing, and generally lacks the institutional clout needed to effectively navigate interagency processes.[23] Many of the staff members within the local bureau lack the requisite environmental expertise. But more importantly, while SEPA has

---

[18] Economy (2004) argues that '[o]ver the past decade, however, the government has made great strides on the legislative side, passing upwards of 25 environmental protection laws and more than 100 administrative regulations, in addition to hundreds of environmental standards. While the quality of some of these laws certainly could be improved, China's environmental lawmakers within the Environmental Protection and Natural Resources Committee of the National People's Congress have demonstrated increasing sophistication in their understanding of how to negotiate and draft a technically sound and politically viable law. One of their relatively recent policy innovations has been to publish draft laws and regulations on their websites to invite public comment. This is a dramatic change in the level of transparency of the government.'

[19] Bradsher and Barboza (2006); Hao and Wang (2005) also show in a recent article published in the *Journal of the Air and Waste Management Association* that ambient air pollution declined between 1990 and 2002.

[20] Bradsher and Barboza (2006).

[21] BBC News n.d. Vaclav Smil, an expert on environmental issues in China, argues that 'the [Chinese] government pays more attention to the environment than was the norm in virtually all western countries at comparable stages of their economic development.' Smil (1997).

[22] Schwartz (2003); Economy (2004).

[23] According to Jorgen Erikson, Environmental Attaché for the Swedish International Development Agency, who works with the myriad government agencies that coordinate and implement policy on the environment in China, 'SEPA is weak compared to the National Development Reform Council... and there is a lack of implementation.' Watkins (2004: 77).

nominal authority to order local EPBs to enforce regulations on the ground (often at the expense of local governments), the EPB staff members are paid by these same local governments! As Chen and Uitto explain, EPBs have been placed 'in a position to sanction their own alms giver.'[24] Many EPB staffers are also subject to intense pressure from companies trying to avoid environmental regulation. Polluters offer bribes for lax enforcement, threaten regulators with subtle and not-so-subtle threats, and seek tax breaks and other forms of compensation for environmental fines. In addition, the incentives of local staffers are often not aligned with the environmental protection objectives being pursued at SEPA headquarters. With local governments placing great emphasis on economic growth and unemployment, EPB staffers often view strict environmental enforcement as limiting their opportunities for career advancement. According to Lieberthal, '[m]uch of the environmental energy generated at the national level dissipates as it diffuses through the multi-layered state structure, producing outcomes that have little concrete effect.'[25]

China is a powerful actor in global environmental politics.[26] It is a major contributor to many global environmental problems, and as such has the potential to be a key part of any solution. As importantly, its threats of non-cooperation are credible because of its natural inclination to pursue economic development, industrial growth, and the expansion of a consumer middle class at the expense of more regional or global environmental aims. During ozone negotiations, Chinese negotiators bargained hard for environmental assistance that would help them comply with their obligations under the Montreal Protocol. They also sent clear signals that they would not participate in an ozone regime without such compensation.[27] A Chinese SEPA spokesperson warned, 'The call for modernization is so irresistible that China will continue to produce these ozone depleting chemicals.'[28] He later cautioned that 'without the help of developed countries, [we] will continue to quickly expand the use of harmful chemicals.'[29] The large increase in green aid to China during the 1990s suggests that donors believed these warnings, and that China has successfully negotiated financial support for a wide range of

---

[24] While this book is not about principal–agent problems in China's regulatory regime, this example of incentive misalignment is striking and leads to predictable behavior of poor enforcement. Chen and Uitto (2002: 72).

[25] Lieberthal (1997). Kenji Someno, the Japanese diplomat charged with coordinating Japan's environmental aid to China, explains, 'On the local level officials still think that economic development is key, and they are willing to marginalize environmental issues. While the central government may think the environment is an important issue, this does not trickle down to the local government. SEPA is unable to monitor all of China because of its large size and due to the fact that EPBs are not directly responsible to SEPA.' Watkins (2004: 78).

[26] China not only ably represents its own interests; it also plays a central role in formulating, articulating, and negotiating the interests and strategies of the G-77.

[27] Sell (1996); DeSombre (2000a)   [28] Sell (1996: 101).   [29] Sell (1996: 103).

environmental issues (Figures 3.2a and 3.2b). In fact, between 1990 and 1999, China was the single largest recipient of environmental aid in the world.

Despite these large increases, China still received far more non-environmental aid during this time period. The IBRD, China's single largest donor between 1980 and 1999, lent a total of $26.7 billion, of which 87 per cent was dirty and 8 per cent was environmental. The Asian Development Bank and Japan, two of China's five largest donors, demonstrated a similar pattern: 11.9 per cent of Japanese aid was environmental, while 69 per cent was dirty; 24 per cent of ADB funding was environmental, while 67 per cent was dirty.[30] While this could be an indication of the donor community's environmental preferences, it may also reflect China's extraordinary bargaining power in global environmental politics and its ability to extract concessions when bargaining over the type of aid to be allocated. This is a point to which we will return in Chapter 4.

Despite these constraints, China has demonstrated that it is willing and able to implement many of its international environmental commitments. The ozone issue offers the clearest example. 'Once it committed to complying with the London Amendments to the Montreal Protocol,' writes Jimin Zhao, 'the Chinese government moved quickly to satisfy procedural requirements that called for China to establish institutions to organize protocol implementation.'[31] However, according to Zhao, 'China's willingness to ratify the agreement, and its eventual successful compliance, *hinged critically on the provision of financial assistance.*'[32] This is a key point on which there is almost universal agreement. Elizabeth Economy, author of *The River Runs Black: The Environmental Challenge to China's Future*, puts it this way: 'China will play, if the world will pay.'[33]

India: 'You Have the Capability and the Money to Restore What You Have Destroyed'

India, as the second most populous country in the world and one of just twelve 'mega-biodiversity countries,' is another major force in global environmental politics.[34] It is also the fourth largest producer of greenhouse gas emissions in the world, and these are expected to grow by 70 per cent over the

---

[30] Most bilateral donors followed Japan's lead. Germany, for example, gave almost $5 billion in total aid, of which 11% was for environmental projects and 78% for dirty projects.

[31] Zhao (2002: 332–3) continues, '[B]y 1998, China was already below the protocol's 2002 goals for freezing Halon production and consumption at average levels for the period 1995 to 1997; China also met the protocol's requirement to freeze consumption and production of CFCs beginning in July 1999 at the 1995 to 1997 average levels.'

[32] Zhao (2002: 333).   [33] MacFarquhar (1999).   [34] Rajan (1997).

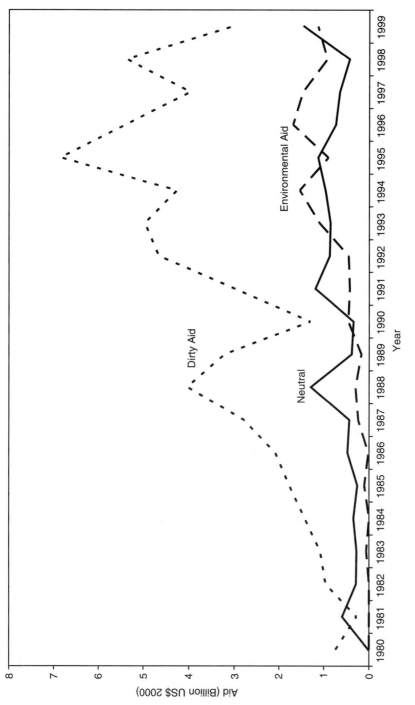

Figure 3.2a. Total aid across types to China, 1980–1999

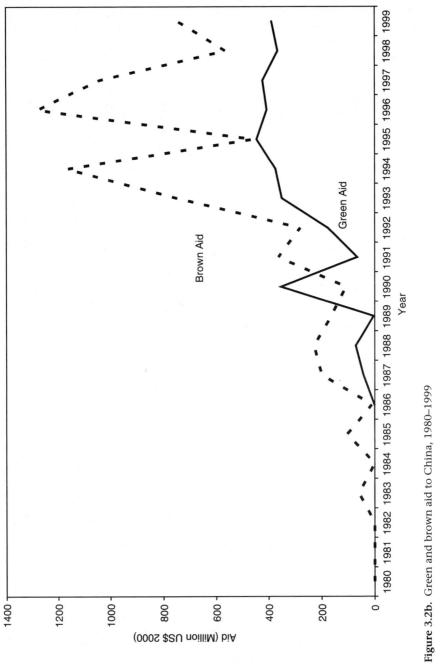

Figure 3.2b. Green and brown aid to China, 1980–1999

Note: Data show–utilizes only categorized aid data; see Appendix A for details.

next twenty years.[35] At the same time, India suffers from extremely high levels of local environmental degradation: the World Bank estimates that India loses roughly 4.5 to 8 per cent of GDP to environmental damage every year.[36] India bears some similarity to China with respect to its approach towards environmental aid, but there are also important differences between the two countries.

Like China, India's poverty, large population size, global environmental significance, and local environmental needs make it an attractive candidate for environmental assistance. Between 1980 and 1999, India was the largest recipient of foreign aid overall, and the second largest recipient of environmental aid. Its largest benefactors during this period included the World Bank, Germany, Japan, the ASDB, the United Kingdom, and the United States. India distinguishes itself from other recipient countries in that it closely monitors and coordinates all of the foreign aid that it receives, including environmental aid, and has a reputation for being quite discriminating in terms of the governments or international organizations it will work with. Major donors coordinate their assistance through the Aid to India Consortium, and the government will exclude donors that seek to reorient India's development priorities.[37] According to one World Bank staffer, 'the government made clear to [us], as well as to the International Monetary Fund, that it preferred to follow its own pace in reforming the economy and that it did not see a role for [us] in framing the agenda.' India is also known for being quite strategic in its relationships with donors. The Cold War is a case in point: when US aid began to decline, India compensated for the loss by accepting more assistance from the USSR.

India's policy priorities are governed by strongly statist 'Five-Year Plans,' which in turn have a significant impact on the environmental profile of its foreign assistance portfolio. Under the government's second Five-Year Plan (1956–61), it prioritized heavy industry and increased agricultural productivity through petrochemical-intensive farming, and donor funding fell closely in line with these priorities. Under the third Five-Year Plan, a similar pattern of cooperation was observed. The World Bank's IBRD gave 45 per cent of its aid for railway construction, 21 per cent for the steel industry, 15 per cent for broader industrial development, and 11 per cent for power generation. The United States allocated 56 per cent of its support for food aid, 25 per cent for industrial development, and 7 per cent to railway construction. The Soviet Union allocated 40 per cent of its aid to the steel industry, 19 per cent

---

[35] Hayward (2006).

[36] Ringskog and Chow (2002: iii). The World Bank estimates that 59% of the economic losses associated with environmental degradation are attributable to unsafe water and unsafe excreta disposal, 20% to soil degradation, and 13% to air pollution.

[37] Zanini (2001: 12).

to oil and gas development, and 18 per cent to the power sector.[38] In the 1980s, projects remained concentrated in heavy industry, agriculture, power generation, and infrastructure.

A major shift from dirty projects to more social and environmental projects occurred in the 1990s. 'Dirty' aid funding fell from 77 per cent of total aid in the 1980s to 54 per cent in the 1990s. The numbers plunged at the end of the decade. At the same time, environmental aid increased from 4 per cent to 13 per cent. During this period India made significant strides in protecting its own local environment and expanding access to environmental services. The Indian government reports that access to drinking water and sanitation services improved dramatically during the 1990s.[39] The government also committed itself to providing universal access to potable water and cleaning up the country's most polluted rivers by 2007. In addition, deforestation has been reversed and the government is implementing plans to increase forest and tree cover to 33 per cent by 2012.[40] Most recently, India committed to substantially increasing renewable energy as a share of total energy consumption.

India's environmental laws, regulations, and policies are linked in part to the 1984 Bhopal disaster. In December 1984, a Union Carbide plant leaked poisonous gas that killed and injured thousands of Indians. Estimates of immediate deaths ranged from 4,000 to 100,000 people. Shortly thereafter, the government upgraded the Department of Environment to ministerial status, renamed it the Ministry of Environment and Forests (MOEF), and granted it more expansive powers. The Environment Act of 1986—India's umbrella legislation on environmental protection—authorizes the central government to take all necessary measures to protect the environment. The MOEF works through the Central Pollution Control Board (CPCB) and the State Pollution Control Boards (SPCBs), which 'have the authority to cut off the electricity and water supplies of polluting industries, launch prosecutions, and initiate proceedings against top management so as to hold them personally liable.'[41] Nevertheless, the CPCB and SPCBs are widely regarded as ineffective.[42] They are underfunded and understaffed, and in

---

[38] Eldridge (1970: 11–22).

[39] Drinking water access reportedly rose from 82% to 90% in urban areas and from 65% to 90% in rural areas. Access to sanitation services also expanded: from 43% to 62% in urban areas and from 5% to 20% in rural areas. World Bank (2006).

[40] See National Development Council of India (2001) and Foster and Rosenzweig (2003). The government of India has placed stringent controls on the use of forestland, including a policy on compensatory afforestation, and this has resulted in a substantial increase in forest cover. However, aggregate forest cover data obscure the fact that while plantation forest cover has grown by an average of 6.2% a year between 1990 and 2000, natural forest coverage has declined by an average of 3.8% a year.

[41] Curmally (2002: 99).   [42] Pargal et al. (1997).

many cases lack the equipment necessary to do their jobs.[43] Despite the fact that SPCBs possess the legal authority to inspect enterprises at any time, local scholars and environmentalists complain that these Boards only act after complaints have been filed or accidents have occurred. More fundamentally, the SPCBs' threat of punishment for violations of environmental law is not credible. Implementation and enforcement of environmental legislation rests with the SPCBs, yet they have weak incentives to strictly enforce the law. Indian states compete for investment and states with lower levels of effective environmental regulation are typically viewed as more 'business-friendly.'[44]

India is among the most powerful developing countries in global environmental politics: its negotiators are tough, articulate, and not easily persuaded. For more than thirty years, India has strenuously argued that most of the responsibility for global environmental problems lies with the industrialized countries. During ozone negations, India's Environment Minister Maneka Gandhi was particularly blunt: 'We didn't destroy the layer. You did. I'm saying that you [the West] have the capability and the money to restore what you have destroyed.'[45] Like China, India refused to sign the Montreal Protocol until rich industrialized countries agreed to underwrite their transition from CFCs to non-ozone-depleting substances.[46] India's influence is evident in the data: CFC-conversion projects make up the single largest type of environmental aid transferred to India in the 1990s (Figures 3.3a and 3.3b). Two hundred and forty-two of the 1,012 environmental projects in India were related to the production and consumption of CFCs.

Large dams have been the focus of much of the debate in India on the impact of internationally funded aid on the environment. The Sardar Sarovar Project, one of several dams being constructed on the Narmada River, is one of the largest and most expensive projects ever to be initiated in India. It was designed to irrigate 2 million hectares of land and provide drinking water to over 40 million people in addition to supplying hydroelectric power. The government argues that it will eliminate droughts in the state of Gujarat and provide significant water resources to Madhya Pradesh and two other states.[47] The project was originally financed by the World Bank, with a ten-year credit of $450 million initiated in 1985. However, under pressure from local and transnational groups, the Bank conducted an Independent Review

---

[43] It is estimated that India spends roughly 0.5% of GDP on environmental protection each year. This is widely regarded as under-investment. In relative terms, India spends much less than most other countries in the Asia-Pacific region. Asia-Pacific Forum for Environment and Development (2002).

[44] Gupta (1995). Statistical analysis by researchers at the World Bank also suggests that there is no link between regulatory inspections in India and compliance with its environmental laws and regulations Pargal et al. (1997).

[45] Sell (1996: 104).   [46] Rajan (1997: 61).   [47] Ram (1995).

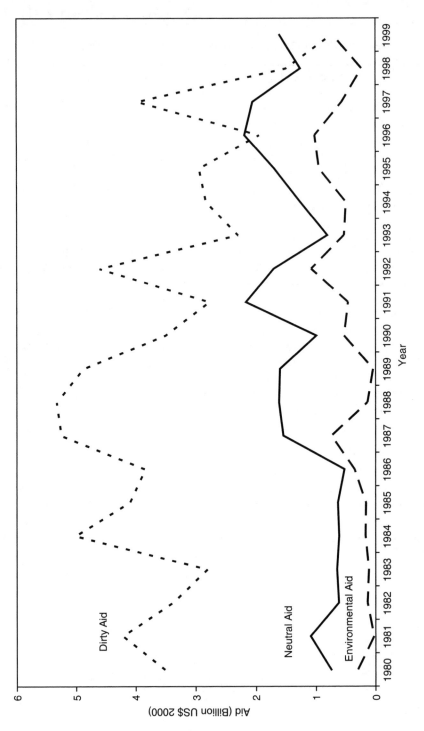

Figure 3.3a. Total aid across types to India, 1980–1999

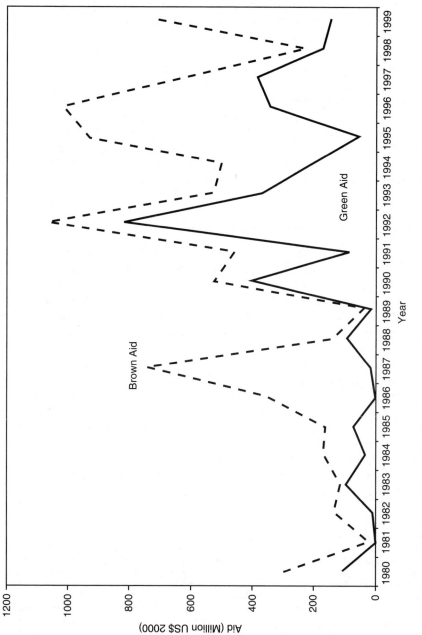

Figure 3.3b. Green and brown aid to India, 1980–1999

Note: Utilizes only categorized aid data; see Appendix A for details.

in 1992, which criticized the dam for not adhering to India's own 1987 environmental clearance standards and not adequately providing for resettlement and rehabilitation (R&R) of the affected population. As a response to this report, the Bank attempted to negotiate a new action plan for the dam, taking these criticisms into account. However, rather than succumbing to international pressure, India requested in March 1993 that the Bank end their funding of the Sardar Sarovar project.[48] The Indian government continued funding the project, though they did commit to continue the R&R and environmental policies recommended by the Bank.[49] It is not clear to what extent this policy shift is attributable to domestic and international pressure, but donor agencies have certainly played a role in raising public awareness and disseminating information about 'best practices', while local politics shape the final outcome.[50]

Whose Amazon? Brazil and Environmental Aid

Brazil is a high-stakes arena for environmental aid allocation, pitting external desires to protect some of the world's most unique natural environments against sovereignty claims and the economic interests of subsistence farmers, miners, ranchers, and agro-businesses. The Amazon is ground zero in this fight: 58 per cent of Brazil is covered by the largest tropical rainforest in the world, possessing two million species, or roughly half of the world's biodiversity. While governments and residents of wealthy countries argue that its preservation is vital to human kind, Brazil's government argues that these same donor countries were the instigators of ecological ruin in the past and have often failed to adopt similar environmental restrictions themselves.[51] Brazil's Department of State claims that developed countries impose an unfair burden on the country by demanding that the entire Amazon be preserved and untouched, despite the fact that it is a tremendous economic asset. Tied to that belief is the assumption that through exploitation of natural resources, Brazil will set in motion a process of economic development that will generate the financial resources needed to remediate environmental damage.

[48] Only $150 million had been disbursed by the World Bank when the funding ended, merely 0.23% of the $64.06 billion total estimated cost of the project.

[49] Since then, dam construction has continued at a much slower pace and many families have been resettled and economically rehabilitated, though there is continued dissatisfaction. The government has even funded several environmental measures, including compensatory afforestation, catchment area treatment, and preservation of cultural sites and protection of wildlife. Independent Evaluation Group (2006).

[50] International Environmental Law Research Center (2006). For instance, the local opposition group Narmada Bachao Andolan has achieved delays in construction and temporary restrictions on the dam's height, and even brought the case before the Indian Supreme Court in March 2005.

[51] Guimarães (1991).

There has been a long history of human habitation in the region, but until the 1960s, Brazil's massive Amazon Basin was protected by natural barriers to economic development—disease, temperature, heavy rainfall, difficult access, and its sheer size. However, in the 1960s, Brazil's new military government made securing the country's boundaries in the area a top national security priority.[52] Through building highways, colonization projects, and military installations along key parts of its Amazon borders and through its heart, Brazil began what became a continent-wide land and resource rush. To accelerate this initiative, Brazil sought external aid from the World Bank and regional development banks for five types of projects in the Amazon: roads, colonization projects, mines, lumber mills, and dams. In the mid-1980s, the huge Polonoroeste and Carajás projects became flash points for protests over the negative environmental impacts of foreign aid. The main strategy adopted by environmentalists and indigenous rights advocates was to attack these projects through their external financers, and the World Bank was their top target. To attack the Bank, they in turn targeted its largest financier: the US Congress.[53]

Years of sustained pressure have left a series of enduring legacies at the Bank: a Sustainable Development Network which includes its own Vice President, increased transparency, mandatory environmental assessments for projects, a ban on projects that finance logging, and years of a blanket ban on funding large dams. In the Amazon, the Bank shifted funding dramatically, providing support for environmental management projects, such as the Rondônia Natural Resource Management Project (PLANAFLORO) between 1992 and 1999, and the demarcation of lands for Indians, rubber-tappers, and natural parks.[54] The Bank also began working in 1997 with the World Wildlife Fund (WWF), and in 2002, it teamed up with both the WWF and the Brazilian government to make a dramatic announcement at the World Summit on Sustainable Development in Johannesburg, South Africa: the government, the Bank, and WWF would be partners in a crash program to triple the amount of protected

---

[52] Katzman (1975); Reis (1968).

[53] Stephen Schwartzman of Environmental Defense told readers of the Sierra Club's booklet *Bankrolling Disaster* that they should petition and protest against the US government's appropriation to the World Bank. The huge dams for the Carajás area included a series along the Xingú River, which cut through the center of the territory of the Kaiapó Indians. With support from the NGO group Cultural Survival, anthropologist Darryl Posey brought two Kaiapó Indians to testify to the US Congress about the likely consequences of this project. On the successful effort of the US Congress to rein in the Bank, see Nielson and Tierney (2003).

[54] For a quantitative review from that time, see Hecht and Schwartzman (1988: table 1); Keck and Sikkink (1998). Of course, the Bank had other reasons to reduce spending in the Amazon. In most colonization projects, more than half of the government-settled colonists had abandoned their land by 1988. World Bank-funded projects in the Brazilian Amazon worth $700 million reached only 16% of their original productivity targets by 1989. Ministerio de Fazenda, cited in Margolis (1989).

lands in the Amazon over the next ten years, setting aside 50 million hectares, an area roughly the size of Spain.[55]

The World Bank's increased focus on the environmental impacts of their loans has had a much wider impact, as the Brazilian government has become increasingly aware that it will not be able to access credit from official sources without the perception that it is a responsible steward of its lands. In a trip to Europe and the United States before taking office in late 1989, conservative President-Elect Fernando Collor de Melo was startled by how many heads of state were asking him about protecting the Amazon. His successor, Fernando Henrique Cardoso, said in 1995 shortly after assuming office that Brazil would not be able to obtain low-cost loans from such sources as the World Bank 'if we don't have a sense that we are responsible before the rest of mankind for preserving nature, for preserving indigenous culture.'[56] The Brazilian government has therefore had to walk a fine line in an effort to send at least three sets of tailored signals to different audiences. First, to appease environmentalists, it has tried to signal it is taking meaningful steps toward preservation. To investors, it has signaled that it is still very much 'open for business.'[57] And to avoid strident nationalist backlashes from critics who see external pressure as part of a plot to keep Brazil from becoming a developed country, the government has had to assert its sovereign right to control and manage its own natural resources.[58]

After another round of reports on deforestation and renewed campaigning by environmentalists in Europe, President Kohl of Germany launched a G-7 initiative in 1992 to 'maximize the environmental benefits of Brazil's rain forest consistent with Brazil's development goals, through the implementation of sustainable development approach...'[59] The Pilot Program to Conserve Brazil's Rain Forest (PPG-7) was designed to bridge the divide between Brazil and donor countries. It was the first major program aiming to prevent rainforest destruction by improving development practices, not just mitigating the aftermath or creating parks. Over the course of the 1990s, the PPG-7 funded 181 small projects: 45 million hectares of indigenous reserves were demarcated, four federal extractive reserves established, and

---

[55] Brazil et al. (2002).   [56] Reuters News Service (31 Mar. 1995).

[57] A 1983 report apparently prepared for the Brazilian government by consultants from the Japanese International Cooperation Agency noted that the region around the Carajás mine could draw investment, 'seeing as how the industrialized countries are facing growing costs of energy, labor, pollution, etc. and the conditions are extremely favorable to attract them.' One group of Brazilian academics saw the huge undertaking at Carajás as an attempt by the government to create the image of the country as open to foreign direct investment.

[58] For example, speaking to a meeting of the Amazon Basin's nine countries in 1989, senior Brazilian diplomat Paulo Flecha de Lima described accusations about Brazil's poor environmental record in the region as part of 'a campaign to impede exploitation of natural resources in order to block [Brazil] from becoming a world power.' *O Liberal* (Belém), (14 Nov. 1989).

[59] Indufor (2000).

new participatory methods for project implementation integrated university professors and NGOs as active participants.[60] These projects went far beyond technocratic management of forests: they sought to manage whole sets of people in civil society groups, the private sector, and the state. They sought to shift incentives and policies and build capacity to preserve biodiversity and provide sustainable livelihoods in the states, focusing on agro-forestry systems in suitable areas and 'agro-ecological zoning.' Stakeholders, including local, national, and international development and environmental groups, were invited to participate in the project reviews.[61] A new 'environmental control' system (satellite remote sensing, GPS, and GIS) for the Amazon provides a more accurate picture of undocumented destruction of the rainforest and has enhanced enforcement of development regulations.[62] Because of the complexity of the region and the ambitiousness of the project, the PPG-7 program was criticized for its reliance on multiple financing sources, which led to lengthy negotiations, complicated contracting procedures, complex cross-conditionalities, and significant disbursement delays.[63] However, the long-term engagement of a group of external funders ultimately resulted in a more constructive dialogue with the government of Brazil (and other relevant stakeholders) on the future of the Amazon.

Outside of the Amazon, environmental protection in Brazil has trod a bumpy path. Under military rule from 1964 to 1985, economic growth was nearly always favored over environmental conservation. While Brazil's leaders publicly stated that environmental decisions played a role in development, economic growth remained the principal objective. The creation of Brazil's first environmental agency, the Special Secretariat for the Environment (SEMA), was widely regarded as a token gesture. Brazil had previously passed many statutes and laws for environmental protection in the 1970s, but they were difficult for the smallest and poorest agency in the Brazilian government to enforce.[64] SEMA was never given the institutional tools to prevent

---

[60] Aparecida de Mello (2005); Redwood (2005).

[61] Redwood (2005: 103); Mancin (1998).

[62] World Bank (2005); Chomitz and Wertz-Kanounnikoff (2005); Fearnside (2002, 2003).

[63] PPG-7 could be seen as an example of 'donor domination.' PPG-7 was spearheaded not by Brazil but by Germany and its strong environmental NGOs. According to Hall (2005: 76) and Indufor (2000: 246), PPG-7's two most important objectives (reducing deforestation and biodiversity protection) were directly dictated by the German government. The largest foreign funders of PPG-7 are Germany (41%) and the EU (23%). Project design is provided through two channels: the Rain forest Trust Fund (RTF) operated by the World Bank, and bilateral co-financing projects. Funding from the bilateral side has been problematic: aid from Japan and the United States was significantly smaller than anticipated. Over the first seven years, only 25% of the overall commitment was actually used, and of this, 17% was related to World Bank administration costs. The World Bank (2005) reports that of the twelve projects identified in 1994, only five were actually launched. However the program was extended and later considered a relative success in changing the tone of debate in the region towards understanding the need for more careful development. See Killeen (2007); Redwood (2005).

[64] World Bank (2005: 164).

environmental degradation, only the power to respond to emergency environmental situations.[65]

PLAID data confirms that the donor with largest number of environmental projects in Brazil during the 1980s and 1990s was Germany. They not only led the PPG-7 initiative, but were the second largest bilateral donor in total monetary terms (the largest being Japan). The sharp increase in environmental aid commitments seen in Figure 3.4a coincides with the 1992 Rio Summit and the launch of PPG-7. Seeing the polluted Guanabara Bay that sits alongside Rio de Janeiro, delegates to the conference were reported to have promised over US$5 billion to clean up sewage in Brazilian cities. As Figures 3.4a and 3.4b show, this represented a huge increase in environmental funding to Brazil; yet after three years, amounts fell back to their pre-Rio levels. Donors appear to have focused their efforts elsewhere in the latter half of the 1990s.

Elephants Pull the Wagon: Environmental Aid to Kenya

Deforestation, soil erosion, poaching, population growth, and overuse and degradation of water resources, directly impinge upon national welfare in Kenya. Rapid population growth reduces the availability of resources; water scarcity, deforestation, and soil erosion limit agricultural productivity; and unregulated resource harvesting threatens the economic viability of the fishing, forestry, and mining sectors. These problems interact with each other to multiply their effects: deforestation destroys wildlife habitats, depleting the wood resources that provide 80 per cent of Kenya's energy, and undermining Kenya's water security since trees act as reservoirs for rainfall. Severely eroded lands drive ethnic violence, which sometimes plays into the hands of authoritarian rulers.[66] Biodiversity in Kenya also means big business in eco-tourism, earning $300 million from wildlife-oriented tourism in 2001 (5 per cent of GDP), $27 million in taxes, and generating one-tenth of formal jobs and a large portion of the country's foreign exchange.[67]

Kenyan environmental policy dates back more than a hundred years to when the British colonial authorities established reserves controlled by gamekeepers. While the gamekeepers promoted conservation, their purpose was to preserve game, not the entire ecology of their reserves. By the 1950s, Kenya had established national parks with more holistic preservation in mind. In 1965, newly independent Kenya passed environmental legislation. Kenya established the National Environmental Secretariat (NES) in 1974, under the Office of the President, and as of 2002, the office had a staff of 109.[68]

---

[65] World Bank (2005: 161).   [66] Bocchi et al. (2006).   [67] USAID (2007).

[68] In 1979, the NES was moved to the Ministry of the Environment and Natural Resources. The Kenyan government reorganized its environmental bureaucracy once more in 1999 with the Environment Management and Coordination Act of 1999. The National Environment Council has become the new top environmental authority under the EMCA. The EMCA

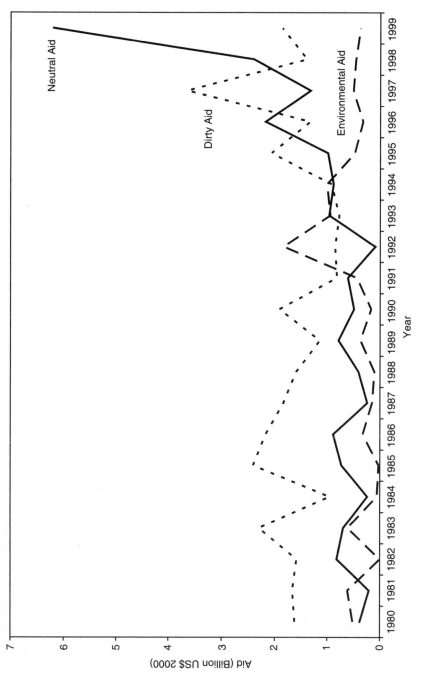

Figure 3.4a. Total aid across types to Brazil, 1980–1999

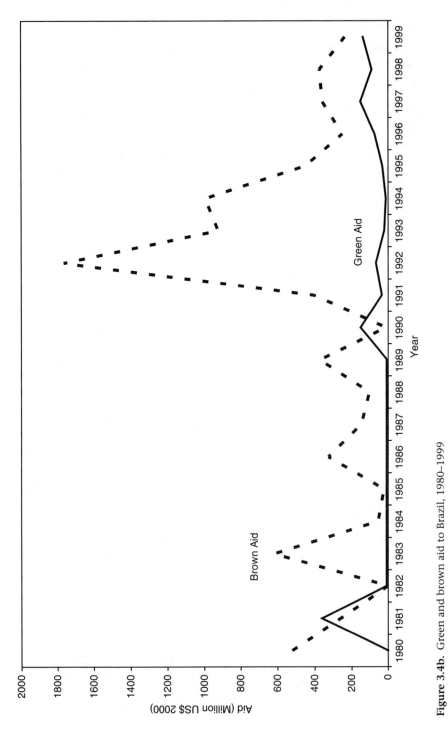

Figure 3.4b. Green and brown aid to Brazil, 1980–1999

Note: Utilizes only categorized aid data; see Appendix A for details.

The Environment Management and Coordination Act of 1999 (EMCA) also introduced several major reforms to the structure of Kenya's environmental bureaucracy and gave citizens the legal right to a clean environment and easier standing to sue those who violate that right.

Despite the many environmental problems that exist in Kenya, two issues in particular have attracted significant attention and funding from the donor community: population growth and biodiversity protection. Kenya's rapid population expansion seriously threatens the environmental sustainability of its development. By the late 1970s, Kenya had one of the highest fertility rates in the world, with each woman having an average of eight children and an annual population growth rate of almost 4 per cent per year. Kenya's population expanded from 8.7 million people in 1963 to 28 million in 1996. However, substantial progress in controlling population growth has been made over the past few decades: the fertility rate dropped from 8 children per woman in 1970 to 4.9 in 2005, and the annual population growth rate declined from 3.8 per cent in 1980 to 2.3 per cent in 2005. Foreign donors have claimed much of the credit: bilateral donors collectively provided $221 million in population assistance between 1980 and 1999.[69]

After populations of the African elephant fell from 167,000 in 1973 to 16,000 in 1989, Kenya became a strong advocate for implementing a total ban on ivory trading. Prior to the ban in 1989, the then head of the Kenya Wildlife Service (KWS), Richard Leakey, proposed raising funds by selling off ivory stocks that the KWS had confiscated from poachers and acquired by other preservation-friendly means. However, once a CITES (Convention on the International Trade in Endangered Species) group concluded that only a complete ban on the ivory trade could forestall the decline of the African elephant population, Leakey reversed course. Instead of selling off the stocks, Leakey burned a twenty-foot pile of ivory worth $3 million to highlight the importance of a blanket ban on the ivory trade. Leakey's ivory pyre and the CITES trade ban helped stem the tide in the African elephant's population decline. The trade ban effectively wiped out all legitimate demand for ivory

also established the National Environment Management Authority as the primary agent for implementing environmental policy. Along with organizational change, the EMCA has reshaped policy.

[69] Only one multilateral donor gave population aid to Kenya, the IDA, which gave $88.8 million, making the IDA the second largest population aid donor after the United States with its $102 million commitment. The other donors of population aid to Kenya were, in order of amount given, the United Kingdom, Sweden, Norway, Denmark, Canada, Finland, and Germany. Kenya actually received more population aid after the imposition of the 'Mexico City Policy' or 'global gag rule' in 1984. The Reagan era policy forced recipients of United States federal funds to choose between performing abortions or losing their American funding. For groups in Kenya, the policy's impact did not have as profound an impact as in other countries since abortion was banned by national law.

and caused the price to plummet from \$40–50 a kilo to \$2–3 a kilo in 1991.[70] Here again, donors played a key role. Biodiversity funding totaled \$125 million for Kenya in the 1990s, making up 4.4 per cent of total aid. The majority came in 1992 when donors funded biodiversity protection to the tune of \$83.2 million. Much of this funding was designed to strengthen the Kenya Wildlife Service.

In total, international donors channeled \$1.15 billion in environmental aid to Kenya during the 1980s and \$2.82 billion during the 1990s (Figures 3.5a and 3.5b). In per capita terms, this represents a substantial sum of money. Environmental aid constituted 13.6 per cent of total aid to Kenya in the 1980s, and 11.6 per cent in the 1990s. At the same time, the share of dirty aid declined from 44.8 per cent to 38.7 per cent between 1980 and 1999. In absolute terms, both types of aid increased by about 250 per cent. During the 1980s and 1990s, the top environmental aid donors included the IDA (\$402 million), Germany (\$306 million), and Sweden (\$249 million). However, the IDA also topped the list of dirty aid donors, giving \$1.38 billion, followed by Japan (\$1.06 billion) and Germany (\$506 million).

Aid to Egypt: Politics First, Economics Second, and Development Third

Egypt is quite a different case than Brazil and Kenya because of the high geopolitical stakes and relatively low global environmental stakes.[71] Egypt's geo-strategic importance is well understood and illustrated by US aid levels: from 1980 to 1999, the United States contributed 44 per cent of Egypt's total aid and the same proportion of Egypt's total environmental aid. In the 1980s, the United States gave ten times more environmental aid to Egypt than did the next donor, and in the 1990s, it gave four times as much (Table 3.1).

Egypt is not a country of great global environmental significance. It contributes to less than 1 per cent of global carbon emissions and it possesses a relative small share of global biodiversity. However, it does face very serious local environmental problems. Due in part to its weak environmental policies and institutions, Egypt loses an estimated 2.1 per cent of GDP to air pollution ever year. Cairo's air recently had the highest lead content in the world;[72] 90 per cent of Egypt's water continues to go untreated; 80 per cent of its industrial wastewater goes unmonitored; and a third of its solid waste ends up in uncontrolled landfills, canal banks, and drains. The Nile Delta faces widespread flooding if sea level rises from climate change.

---

[70] Leakey and Morell (2001).

[71] Egypt's contribution to global environmental problems is small. Its CO_2 emissions are something on the order of 0.5% of global emissions; CFC production and consumption is relatively minimal; it also houses a small fraction of global biodiversity.

[72] World Bank (2005: 11).

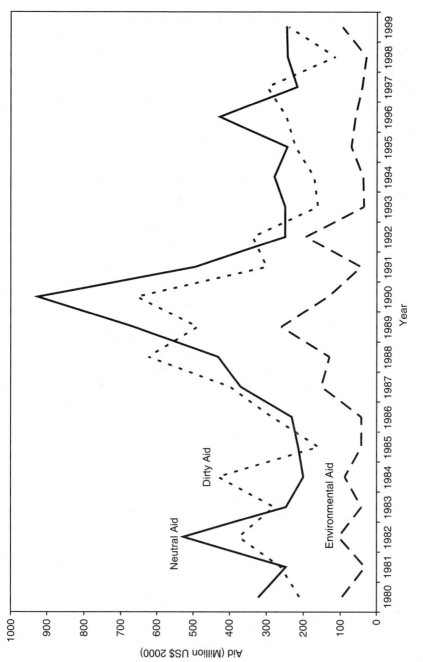

Figure 3.5a. Total aid across types to Kenya, 1980–1999

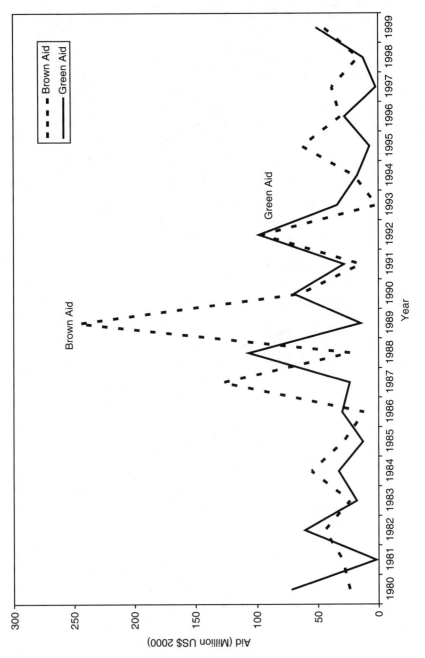

Figure 3.5b. Green and brown aid to Kenya, 1980–1999

As part of the 1979 Camp David peace accords, the United States agreed to provide approximately $1 billion a year in aid to Egypt. During the Cold War, Egypt was also the first Arab government to abandon its alliance with the Soviet Union and join forces with the West. However, in spite of the political benefits associated with this relationship, there is a consensus among foreign aid officials that this relationship has not been nearly as satisfying in terms of achieving concrete development results. Nazih Ayubi (1989) argues that the US government has had limited success with its foreign aid programs because of its inability to draw a clear distinction between political support and development assistance: 'The motives of [American] aid to Egypt are political in the first place, economic in the second and developmental third. Politically, American aid is in some ways a celebration of the end of Egypt's divorce with Israel. Economically, it helps to promote sales of arms and grain. Yet, mostly to preserve the image, it also has to pay some attention to Egypt's developmental needs.'[73]

US foreign assistance programs to Egypt have a long history of difficulty and frustration. In his testimony to the House International Relations Committee, Jon Alterman, the Director of the Middle East Program at the Center for Strategic and International Studies, put it this way: 'The U.S. relationship with Egypt has been mutually beneficial, but it has rarely been easy...It is hard to be a long-time donor and see so little progress on a wide range of issues into which we have been putting effort for decades. Similarly, it is hard to be a long-time aid recipient and not come to treat the aid as an entitlement.'[74] Taher (2001) argues that when donor and recipient countries have strong political ties, the recipient often dominates the relationship.[75] Alterman (2006) argues that US conditional aid contracts in Egypt are doomed to failure because 'there is just so much that the United States asks Egypt for on Arab–Israeli issues, counterterrorism, military transport through the Suez Canal, and so on, that American diplomats are unlikely to sacrifice near term needs for uncertain long-term reward.'[76]

Environmental assistance projects, like all other types of foreign aid, are enmeshed within this difficult political environment. However, there are several additional factors that limit the effectiveness of environmental aid programs in Egypt. The Egyptian public has historically exhibited low levels of awareness about environmental issues, and low levels of organized civic environmental activism have led to minimal domestic pressure on the

---

[73] Ayubi (1989). The huge global spike in neutral aid in 1991 is due to the United States rescheduling Egypt's official debt of $2.9 and $2.5 billion, respectively.

[74] Alterman (2006).   [75] Taher (2001).

[76] Alterman (2006). According to Weinbaum (1986: 132), 'With Washington committed to authorizing more than U.S.$ 1 billion yearly in economic aid, it effectively denies itself an important means of leverage over Egyptian economic policy. AID officials cannot with much conviction threaten to withdraw or withhold funds from the government.'

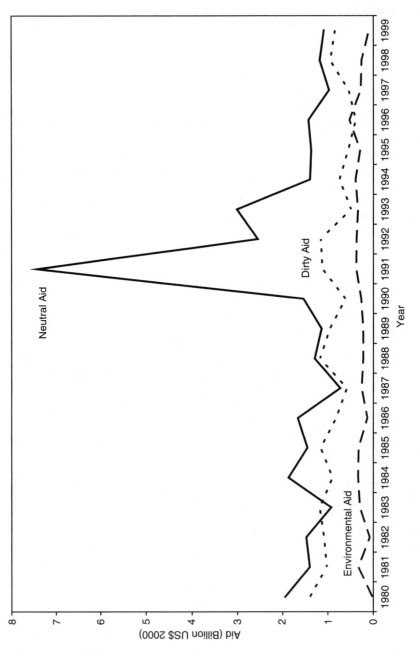

Figure 3.6a. Total aid across types to Egypt, 1980–1999

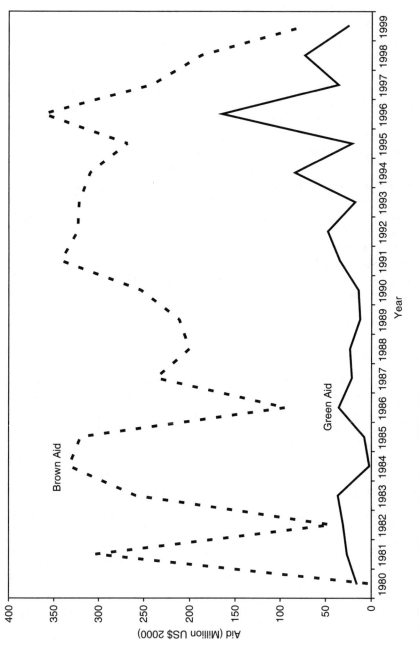

Figure 3.6b. Green and brown aid to Egypt, 1980–1999

government to reform its environmental laws and practice.[77] In 1982, the donor community and the government of Egypt agreed on the need for an environmental ministry and created the Egyptian Environmental Affairs Agency (EEAA). The EEAA was created to work alongside national and international development partners on designing and implementing environmental policies geared toward sustainable development.[78] However, the EEAA has had less autonomy and policy-making authority than other less environmentally friendly ministries, like the Ministry of Petroleum.[79]

Figure 3.6a shows the massive 'economic stabilization' loans the US gave Egypt in 1991, which dwarfs all other aid. The highest value green aid project from 1980–99 was a $39 million project from Germany for 'environmental policy and administration management.' Only 10 per cent of the United States' total aid to Egypt was environmental: 1 per cent green, and 9 per cent brown. The United Kingdom, however, gave 60 per cent of its aid to Egypt for brown environmental issues. Denmark's aid to Egypt was 30 per cent environmental, with 16 per cent green and 14 per cent brown. This evidence supports the conjecture that recipient countries with close geo-strategic ties to donor countries tend to receive more brown aid than green. Because of US political dependency on Egypt, Egypt appears to have more bargaining power to elicit support for local environmental issues over global ones (Figure 3.6b).

Conclusions

These broad trends and five case studies suggest some of the issues that the wealthy countries must address when sending environmental aid overseas. The list of largest environmental aid recipients conforms to what common sense would lead us to expect: countries with large populations and rainforests, and countries with major environmental problems that affect donor countries, top this list. Yet there are still anomalies. That Egypt was number two in the ranking of 1980s recipients of environmental aid, and still seventh in the 1990s, is best explained from a geopolitical perspective of the United

---

[77] As in Brazil, Egyptian activism initially tended to come from well-educated, higher socioeconomic classes who have less direct exposure to environmental hazards. Gomaa (1997).

[78] The EEAA currently receives funding from a wide array of sources: NGOs, bilateral and multilateral donors, and the Egyptian government. At the urging of outside donors, the EEAA's board of directors includes representatives from the public and private sectors, academic and scientific communities, and the NGO community.

[79] Bell (2000: 217); and Nandakumar et al. (2000). Under a 1994 law, the EEAA was restructured to give it more expansive powers, including the ability to draft laws, establish environmental management plans, create and enforce environmental regulations, regularly report environmental data, and serve as a central coordination point for environmental protection initiatives.

States attempting to exert influence in the Middle East. The appearance of Turkey and Pakistan in the top ten also appears to be driven by geopolitics rather than environmental need. That environmental projects are part of 'high politics' has not been well documented in previous literature, and we return to these issues in the chapter on bilateral donors and in our empirical analyses of who receives environmental aid and why. These points raise the broader question of whether geopolitically motivated aid is more prone to being wasted, as some critics contend.

China and India are central to the story of environmental aid's rise over the final two decades of the century. China's environmental aid rose steeply in the early 1990s, roughly five years after steep increases in dirty aid. While China did not appear in the top ten list of environmental aid recipients in the 1980s, it surpassed all the others by over 50 per cent in the 1990s. India's environmental aid nearly tripled over the period, from just over $2 billion to $6.5 billion. China and India's list of top donors is nearly identical: the World Bank, ASDB, Japan, and Germany. Our very preliminary analysis suggests that China is a country where foreign assistance is making an important difference in encouraging the government to put environmental issues on the agenda. Still, during the 1980s and 1990s, major donors such as the IBRD, the ASDB, and Japan gave China seven times as much for dirty projects as they did for environmental ones. 'Dirty' aid remained very significant in India until the late 1990s, when it dropped markedly. Binding promises of environmental aid have been critical to secure India and China's participation in global environmental treaties, and these countries' tremendous leverage in global negotiations will likely continue to grow. Whether aid promises will make as much difference in the future, especially in China with its growing economy and lending to Africa, remains to be seen. The question is especially salient on climate change, in which some participation by China and India in a global agreement is imperative.

For countries with precious environmental resources, such as rainforests (Brazil) or 'charismatic' wildlife (Kenya), the debate over environmental aid appears to be quite different. Westerners have responded to graphic images of burning rainforests by pressuring the World Bank to suspend major projects in the Brazilian Amazon. Still, Brazil has resisted efforts by outside agencies to 'solve' the Amazon problem. The PPG-7 program (funded by the G-7 nations and coordinated by the World Bank) marked a new direction in attempting to integrate development and environmental protection, and appears to have been a partial success partly because it spent much of its effort supporting civil society organizations and facilitating discussions about the future of the region. However, bureaucratic red tape from coordinating donors slowed each of the PPG-7 projects and the overall program significantly. Massive flows of aid are now being discussed under the Kyoto Protocol to compensate Brazil and other rainforest countries for preventing deforestation. We return to this issue in the concluding chapter of this book.

Kenya provides a striking case of environmental aid in Africa, where the environmental issues include the difficult task of protecting wildlife while addressing population growth and meeting human needs. The results are mixed, but environmental aid from a different set of donors (including many smaller European states) appears to be making a difference in addressing the leading environmental issues there.

Through this description of initial trends in who receives environmental aid and who does not, we have been guided by some expectations arising from social science theories. For example, we expected countries with large stocks of 'natural capital' (Brazil) and those whose development is most threatening to global atmospheric stability (China, and to a lesser extent, India) to receive more environmental aid and to be able to negotiate more effectively for the types of aid they want. The same can be said for countries that attract aid as allies in a volatile and strategic part of the world (Egypt). We expected countries with such political leverage to more effectively negotiate for greater amounts of environmental aid of the types that could support the needs of local politicians and the constituents of political leaders, such as water supply and sewage treatment projects. We can see some of these differences in these case studies, but to test these hypotheses more systematically, statistical analysis is needed. In the next chapter, we develop more formal hypotheses and quantitatively test these conjectures using the full set of aid projects. We also explain which kinds of recipient countries manage to secure more or less aid of various types.

4

To Areas of Need, Opportunity, or Strategic Interest? Explaining Which Countries Receive Environmental Aid and Why

Who receives environmental assistance and why? There are conflicting claims about why donors give environmental assistance to some countries and not to others. The annual reports and websites of donor agencies often emphasize the high levels of local environmental degradation experienced by their 'partner' countries. Recipient governments, in contrast, publicly or privately complain of a donor-dominated environmental agenda that focuses on regional and global environmental threats and the small sub-set of countries associated with them who reap the greatest share of donors' largess. As seen in the GEF story described in Chapter 3, many developing governments also take issue with donor efforts to limit the provision of environmental assistance to those countries with sound environmental policies, economic policies, and government institutions. Yet the opposite claim is often made as well: that donors use environmental aid to support nascent environmental institutions and develop sound environmental policies where none currently exist. Critics argue that environmental aid is no different from traditional foreign aid: like non-environmental funding, it is channeled to military allies, strategic partners, countries rich in natural resources to which donors seek access, past colonial possessions, and key trading partners.

In this chapter, we examine the central question of this book: how donors allocate development funds among recipient countries. The process of aid allocation is complex and varies tremendously between each donor and recipient; however, we believe there is much to be learned from an analysis of broad patterns across all donors, recipients, and sectors. Beyond the purely academic question of how aid is allocated, this research may help illuminate the conditions under which successful outcomes follow aid. Understanding why donors provide aid to some countries and not to others also informs our analysis of other links in the aid allocation chain—for example, how development funds are allocated within sub-sectors and channeled through either bilateral aid agencies or multilateral institutions. The financial and environmental stakes are enormous, and the implications for efforts to reform aid are clear.

Previous research on inter-recipient aid allocation has typically relied upon truncated sets of aid data, and/or datasets that pool all recipients in single-year cross-sectional analyses. We address these issues by creating a new database for all loans and grants from each donor to each recipient, plus a series of variables describing those recipient nations, for each year in the 1990s. Our statistical models in this chapter use up to 15,000 donor/recipient dyads and incorporate the total amounts of aid from all projects of a certain type in one calendar year. We break that universe of cases down into analyses of patterns for bilateral, multilateral, green, brown, environmental, and dirty aid. Our analysis allows us to test a series of hypotheses informed by different theories of why aid goes where it does.

Chapter 3 presented some descriptive statistics, a series of brief case studies, and introduced preliminary hypotheses that might account for observed inter-recipient aid allocation patterns. We saw that environmental aid amounts appear to be directed to the big developing countries and ones with globally important ecosystems, like the rainforests in Brazil or savannas that support megafauna in Kenya, or large populations as in China and India. But others, like Egypt, Turkey, and Pakistan, appear to receive large amounts of environmental aid for largely geopolitical reasons. The case studies revealed very different profiles in the use of environmental aid: some recipients tended to receive aid for climate change, biodiversity, and other global issues, while others received more aid for local issues like sewage, water, and desertification prevention.

In this chapter, we present a series of formal hypotheses on inter-recipient aid allocation, with a particular emphasis on environmental aid, and then report whether the results from our models conform to our predictions. To examine whether the various claims found in the literature carry over to environmental aid, we employ multivariate regression analysis on our project-level dataset that disaggregates development assistance into its constituent parts. This type of analysis allows us to hold constant a whole host of factors and measure the impact of single factors affecting allocation of aid across numerous donors and recipients. Based on the most comprehensive set of development projects in any study to date, we attempt to provide gener-alizable conclusions about how aid is allocated. We also examine whether these conclusions differ across types of donors (bilateral vs. multilateral) and environmental vs. non-environmental ('dirty') aid.

To give the reader a preview of our results, we find that each school of thought on environmental aid receives some support, but some findings do not support theoretical predictions. Some of the expectations based on 'eco-functional' theory—that environmental aid goes where it's needed most—are supported. But the impact of these variables is substantively small—rather national income, population size, UN voting affinity, and colonial history are far stronger predictors. Bilateral donors give more aid to the poorest countries than multilateral donors in the 1990s, and this pattern holds across all sectors, including environmental aid. Surprisingly perhaps, bilateral aid agencies also appear to do a better job targeting recipient countries with high levels of environmental need, and rewarding countries with credible environmental policies and institutions. As expected, bilateral donors tended to favor their neighbors, their former colonies, and their commercial interests, but not necessarily their close political allies, as measured by UN voting patterns. We also note that there are differences in how environmental aid and more traditional forms of assistance are allocated, but these differences are not huge. Our findings have significant policy implications, an issue we return to in the conclusion of the chapter.

Allocating Environmental Aid among Recipient Countries

The foreign aid literature—in political science, economics, and sociology—has for five decades attempted to explain why some recipients attract extraordi-nary amounts of aid and others receive nothing or relatively little.[1] Inter-recipient patterns of aid allocation are interesting because they provide some indication of donors' underlying motives and priorities. Allocation patterns also condition the effectiveness of aid. Burnside and Dollar (2000a, 2004), for example, find that aid allocated along political lines has not led to higher lev-els of economic growth.[2] Analysts also suggest that foreign aid is plagued by recurrent problems. Aid tends to increase risky behavior by recipients (moral hazard), favor poor performers (adverse selection), provide opportunities to siphon off aid funds for other purposes (fungibility), promote corruption (rent-seeking), weaken crebile threats by donors to withhold funds (credibil-ity), and create a bargaining situation where the recipient knows much more about the projects than the donors (asymmetric information).[3]

---

[1] Schelling (1955); Morgenthau (1962); Pincus et al. (1965); Huntington (1970); Waltz (1979); Baldwin (1985); Haggard and Kaufman (1995); Haggard and Moravcsik (1993); Keo-hane and Levy (1996); Milner (2003); Hattori (2001); Neumayer (2003b); Bornschier et al. (1978); Chase-Dunn and Rubinson (1978).

[2] Alesina and Dollar (2000); Dollar and Levin (2004); Knack and Rahman (2004); Easterly (2005); Heckelman and Knack (forthcoming); Knack (2004); Djankov et al. (2005); Boock-mann and Dreher (2003); Kilby (2005).

[3] In countries where there are good institutions and an 'enabling policy environment,' the conventional wisdom is that some of these problems can be overcome and aid can have a modestly positive impact on growth and other development outcomes Radelet et al. (2004).

After the Second World War, international relations scholarship generally treated foreign assistance as a quid pro quo, or an intergovernmental bribe (Morgenthau 1962; Baldwin 1985). International financial transfers, in the view of most scholars, were made for reasons of political loyalty and national security, rather than for economic development, poverty reduction, public health, education, and so on. Indeed, until the end of the Cold War, most money flowed to strategic military locations, areas rich in natural resources, newly independent colonies, and certain key trading partners. Yet soon after the fall of the Berlin Wall, existing models of aid allocation were unable to explain new types of aid that closely resembled voluntary interstate cooperation. As international financial transfers for collective good provision—particularly, debt relief, environmental protection, infectious disease control, and structural adjustment—figured more prominently in the portfolios of bilateral and multilateral donors, new patterns began to raise new questions concerning donor (and recipient) motivations. Had benefactors and beneficiaries moved toward pursuing broader shared interests that required and enhanced long-term policy coordination, unlike the earlier focus on more straightforward 'aid-for-loyalty'—or 'private good'—transactions? In the 1990s, new theorists—rational choice institutionalists—attempted to explain this shift by characterizing foreign assistance as an act of international cooperation that represented mutual policy adjustment on the part of recipients and donors.[4] Aid, they argued, could be understood as a 'contract in which funders trade concessional loans or grants for policy reforms in a recipient [country].'[5] Also crucial for these institutional theories was the presence of underlying rules, principles, norms, and decision-making procedures to govern such resources-for-reform swaps.[6] They emphasized that states could reduce transaction costs and uncertainty, discourage reneging, and advance the shared interests and absolute gains of all parties by establishing mutually acceptable 'rules of the game' that would stabilize expectations. Rational choice institutionalists therefore conceive of environmental aid transfers as inter-governmental contracts that promote collective good provision. Importantly, the implicit eco-functionalist assumption underpinning their causal logic is that donors who distribute environmental assistance are genuinely interested in environmental protection.

Nevertheless, many scholars continue to argue that political and commercial factors primarily drive allocation decisions. Among many possible examples, commentators point to the fact that Turkey was promised large-scale military and economic assistance in the run-up to the US invasion of Iraq in 2003. The US also generously rewarded Pakistan and Uzbekistan for assisting

---

[4] Keohane and Levy (1996); Kaul et al. (1999, 2003).   [5] Ross (1996: 186).
[6] Keohane and Levy (1996: 5).

their military efforts in Afghanistan. International financial institutions (IFIs), which are in principle designed to provide collective goods like international financial stability, are also routinely leveraged by their most powerful share-holders when the geo-strategic stakes are high.[7] In 1998, for example, Pakistan saw IMF loans disappear after testing a nuclear weapon in defiance of US wishes, and then suddenly reappear at the beginning of the war in Iraq. One leading analyst of international organizations has called the World Bank 'a source of funds to be offered to U.S. friends or denied to U.S. enemies.'[8] For these reasons, our analysis contrasts these big loan-providing international institutions with bilateral donors and smaller and more specialized multilateral granting agencies.

Many of these analysts also argue that aid targeting the increased provision of international public goods, such as global environmental protection, is no exception. For example, Haggard and Moravcsik suggest that the West's pri-mary motivation for distributing $30–40 billion of assistance to former Soviet bloc states after the Cold War was not democracy, economic growth, and environmental protection—the stated objectives—but 'privatizable' benefits advantaging special interests in donor countries. They also argue that 'the lack of any coherent justification for the creation of the EBRD . . . [suggests] . . . it was an act of political symbolism rather than functional necessity.'[9]

Yet curiously, foreign aid is also credited with a number of important successes: the post-Second World War reconstruction in Western Europe, the eradication of river blindness and smallpox, the Green Revolution, the intro-duction of family planning, and generalized improvements in life expectancy. Since the fall of the Berlin Wall, bilateral and multilateral aid donors have also strenuously argued that when aid is allocated and implemented properly, it can help the international community address some of its greatest interna-tional public good provision challenges: global and regional environmental threats, terrorism, drug trafficking, international financial instability, and infectious disease. From world leaders all the way down to the rank-and-file of USAID, DFID, and the World Bank, the aid community now enthusiastically embraces these dual goals of increased international public good provision and aid effectiveness.

For example, the 'Meltzer Commission,' established by the US Congress amidst heated debate in 2000 over $18 billion of additional funding to the International Monetary Fund, urged multilateral development banks (MDBs) to redouble their efforts to provide undersupplied international public goods.

---

[7] Thacker (1999); Stone (2002).   [8] Wade (2002).

[9] Haggard and Moravcsik (1993: 280), emphasis added. Marc Levy also 'accept[s] the argument made by Haggard and Moravcsik that the EBRD is a largely redundant exercise in political symbolism, and suspect[s] that the decision to extend participation in the European Environmental Agency to eastern governments was motivated in large part by a perceived opportunity to garner similar symbolic laurels' (1993: 332).

Its authors argued for a sharper focus on the 'treatment of tropical diseases and AIDS, rational protection of environmental resources, tropical climate agricultural programs, development of management and regulatory practices, and inter-country infrastructure.'[10] G-7 Finance Ministers also underscored the need for *ex ante* conditionality in 2000, calling upon '[MDBs to] emphasize a selective, quality-oriented approach rather than a quantity-oriented or profit-oriented one . . . [and] place [a] high priority on good governance.'[11] Again, at the Genoa Summit in 2001, G-7 countries stressed that '[MDBs'] main priorities . . . should be to fight infectious diseases, promote environmental improvement, facilitate trade, and support financial stability.' They also endorsed the idea that every MDB should 'define more explicitly its role in the provision of [IPGs] on the basis of its comparative advantages.'

The rise of these two objectives appears to be more than just talk. During the 1990s, especially, Western governments created a Montreal Protocol Fund to provide incentives for developing countries to help protect the ozone layer; a Global Environmental Facility that mobilizes funding to help developing countries address a range of global environmental issues; a Global Fund to Fight AIDS, Tuberculosis, and Malaria that seeks to combat disease through a variety of innovative aid delivery mechanisms; and, in the US, a Millennium Challenge Account that rewards poor countries based on their demonstrated commitment to good governance.

Donors have responded to this growing skepticism and public scrutiny about their underlying motives by shifting their focus toward 'measurable results' and 'experimentation.' The European Union and the UK's Department for International Development (DFID) have taken up outcome-based conditionality, which makes the disbursement of aid contingent upon the realization of certain outputs and outcomes—for example, the number of children immunized, the number of girls that complete primary school, or the achievement of certain public financial management benchmarks. Shareholders of the World Bank have made funding of the International Development Association (IDA)—the concessional lending arm of the World Bank—contingent upon it achieving measurable targets, such as reductions in the time and cost of business registration and increases in the number of functioning household water connections, through the IDA-14 results measurement system. The International Fund for Agricultural Development (IFAD), the Asian Development Bank (ASDB), the Global Environment Facility (GEF), African Development Fund (AFDF), the Caribbean Development Bank (CDB), and other multilateral institutions have implemented performance-based allocation systems, which reward countries with good macroeconomic policies, successful records of project implementation, and sound public sector management institutions. The Global Fund to Fight AIDS, Tuberculosis,

---

[10] Meltzer (2000).   [11] G-7 (2000).

and Malaria and the Global Alliance for Vaccines and Immunizations are also experimenting with a variety of innovative aid delivery mechanisms. In addition to these institutionalized mechanisms for international public good provision, increasing amounts of aid are channeled through traditional mechanisms to prevent drug trafficking, fight terrorism, resolve financial crises, foster democracy, promote peace in war-torn regions, and achieve a number of other interstate objectives.[12]

We are therefore faced with competing explanations of what motivates donors' provision of aid for international public goods such as environmental protection. On the one hand, many foreign aid experts insist that aid—in all of its different forms—is manipulated for strategic and commercial purposes and thus destined to not realize its stated objectives. On the other hand, donor rhetoric, and to some extent behavior, seems to reflect a genuine interest in putting aid dollars to their most effective use and addressing real world problems, particularly undersupplied international public goods. To adjudicate between these seemingly contradictory explanations, we take a closer look at what drives environmental aid allocation, and test whether these determinants differ at all from those of broader aid flows.

As a baseline, we offer a series of 'eco-functional' predictions against which donor behavior can be empirically evaluated. That is, we treat environmental aid as if it were being provided solely for the purpose of realizing its stated objective: environmental protection. At the same time, we control for the geo-strategic, commercial, and humanitarian motivations of donors, which supposedly cut across all of the various types of aid that are channeled to recipient countries. We first analyze what explains the inter-recipient allocation of environmental and non-environmental aid, and then among environmental loans and grants we test whether these theories are more effective in explaining green or brown aid (that addresses global or local public goods issues, see Chapter 2).

The process of testing these hypotheses is quite complex: for the 429,000 individual aid projects in the PLAID dataset, we sum amounts given from each donor to each recipient. Depending on the group of allocations we are attempting to analyze, there are approximately 1,000 to 15,000 donor–recipient–year observations. For each group of cases, we divide the policy-making process of allocating environmental aid into two separate decisions: Which countries get environmental aid? And of those countries who do receive environmental aid, which countries get the most? The first decision, which we call the 'gate-keeping' stage, raises the question of *whether* a country will receive aid at all and is modeled with a binomial probit. The second decision, the allocation stage, tracks the determinants of *how much* a recipient country will receive using linear regression techniques. The resulting picture is

---

[12] Kaul et al. (1999, 2003); Ferroni (2002).

quite complex.[13] We begin by attempting to build a theory of environmental aid allocation and deriving a series of testable hypotheses.

Hypotheses of Environmental Aid Allocation

To investigate the factors affecting the allocation of development finance, we offer a series of hypotheses drawn from a number of perspectives offered in the literature. We first outline seven 'eco-functional' recipient-level characteristics that might explain broad patterns in financial transfers to developing countries for environmental protection. These include a recipient country's potential to deliver to global and regional environmental benefits, its local environmental needs, the strength of its environmental policies and institutions, its commitment to environmental transparency, the strength of its democratic institutions, the quality of its economic policies, and the overall effectiveness of its government. We also test for the impact of population size and poverty, and the role of donors' geo-strategic, commercial, and historical interests. For each hypothesis, we discuss some theoretical motivation found in the literature and a proposed method of measurement. The actual measures we use to test these hypotheses are described briefly and listed in the summary hypothesis Table 4.1. A crucial point to be made at the outset is that many perhaps better variables were not available for the number of recipient countries and years we wished to examine.

Hypothesis 1A: The receipt of environmental aid will correlate positively with the global environmental significance of recipient countries.

Hypothesis 1B: The receipt of environmental aid will correlate positively with the regional environmental significance of recipient countries.

First, for an efficient environmental aid contract to be written, we argue donors and recipient must establish a shared interest. Their interests need not be naturally harmonious, but both parties must stand to gain from cooperation. Donor and recipient preferences, we argue, are less likely to coalesce around issues of local environmental concern since they often (though not always) lack the characteristics of a collective good. However, global issues such as climate change and biodiversity loss, and regional issues, such as acid rain and watershed management, yield significant benefits to both donors and recipients and require collective action, so we would expect the probability of a stable cooperative equilibrium to be higher for this sub-set of environmental issues. We would therefore expect more environmental aid dollars to flow

[13] The gate-keeping and amount distinction is more a statistical artefact for correctly modeling limited dependent variables truncated at zero and need not parallel formal decision processes by donors.

Table 4.1. Summary table of hypotheses, variables, and findings, recipient allocation

Hypothesis	Variable	Description, Source
H1a: The receipt of environmental aid will correlate positively with the global environmental significance of recipient countries.	Natural capital index	Natural capital score: 1225 (most natural capital), 0 (least natural capital) (World Bank)
H1b: The receipt of environmental aid will correlate positively with the regional environmental significance of recipient countries.	Distance from donor to recipient	Distance between donor and recipient country center points using great circle geometry (authors' calculations)
H1c: Donors will target recipient countries where environmental quality is poor, and recipients experiencing high levels of environmental stress will have a greater interest in securing environmental aid.	Water quality index	Organic water pollution intensity indicator, measured as kilograms of organic water pollutant (determined by bacterial biochemical oxygen demand) emissions per day per worker (World Bank, World Development Indicators)
H2a: Donors will reward countries based on the strength of their revealed environmental policy preferences, as reflected in how many major environmental treaties they have ratified.	Enviro. treaty ratifications	Percentage of the 9 major environmental treaties ratified by recipient nation, 1969–99 (Roberts et al. 2004)
H2b: Donors will provide more environmental assistance to governments that provide credible and verifiable information about their policies and performance.	CITES reporting	Percentage of requirements met under the Convention on International Trade in Endangered Species (CITES) (World Resources Institute)
H2c: Donors will favor countries with strong democratic institutions.	Democracy index	Institutionalized democracy: 10 (democracy), 0 (non-democracy) in recipient nation (POLITY IV)
H2d: Donors will target governments with a track record of delivering reliable public services.	Government effectiveness index	Government effectiveness estimate: 2.5 (highly effective), −2.5 (highly ineffective) (World Bank Institute)
H2e: Donors will reward recipient governments with 'sound' economic policies.	Regulatory quality index	Regulatory quality estimate: 2.5 (high regulatory burden), −2.5 (low regulatory burden) (World Bank Institute)
H3a: Donors will focus aid of all types on their greatest trade partners, including environmental aid.	Dyadic trade data	Total trade between donor and recipient in each year (Total trade: imports + exports) (Gleditsch 2002 and authors' calculations)
H3b: 'Loyal' recipient countries will receive more aid from bilateral donors.	UN voting data	Policy similarity of a given donor–recipient dyad, as measured by voting records in UN General Assembly (Erik Gartzke and authors' calculations)
H3c: Nations that were previously colonial outposts will continue to receive significantly more aid of all types.	Colonial recipient	Colonialism: 1 if recipient was a colony of donor in 1945 (CEPII), else 0
H4a: Environmental aid will target the poorest countries, since they face greatest needs.	GDP per capita	Gross domestic product (measured in purchasing power parity) per capita (World Bank World Development Report)
H4b: Large recipient countries will receive more aid of all types.	Population	Total recipient population for year (Global Development Network (GDN) database)

to countries of global and regional environmental significance. For example, Brazil and Indonesia may matter more to donors than Chad or Afghanistan for environmental aid, even when holding all other factors that might explain aid allocation patterns constant. We use the World Bank's 'natural capital index' for the first hypothesis, and we calculated the distance from each donor to each recipient country for the latter.

Hypothesis 1c: Donors will target recipient countries where environmental quality is poor, and recipients experiencing high levels of environmental damage will have a greater interest in securing environmental aid.

We further suggest that donors will target recipient countries where environmental quality is poor. There are no doubt a whole host of variables that condition the effectiveness of environmental aid—and thus a donor's willingness to give aid—but if donors are genuinely interested in improving environmental protection, they will target those countries where they expect their aid investment to yield the highest 'environmental rate-of-return.' Furthermore, recipients experiencing high levels of environmental stress will have a greater interest in securing environmental aid contracts than recipients with relatively undamaged environmental resources. Many variables were possible here, but all lacked quality data for these recipients and years. One of the most complete indicators of recipient environmental need was water pollution levels, so we used the World Resources Institute and World Bank's compilation of organic water pollution intensity. The problems with this indicator are discussed more fully in the concluding section of this chapter.

Hypothesis 2a: Donors will reward countries based on the strength of their revealed environmental policy preferences, as reflected in the number of major environmental treaties they have ratified.

The prospects for international cooperation also fundamentally depend upon the credibility of state commitments. If a state's willingness or ability to implement an international environmental policy is weak, or even in question, institutionalists would argue that cooperation is unlikely. Donors will therefore be less likely to enter into aid contracts with recipients who fail to demonstrate their willingness and ability to implement meaningful environmental reforms.[14] As Connolly suggests, 'recipient countries' political commitment to environmental reforms stands out as a major explanatory

---

[14] Kotov and Nikitina (1998) argue that the USSR was unable to secure external financing for environmental protection during the Cold War largely because of credibility problems: 'Unlike most other countries, the USSR had no agency devoted entirely to the environment with authority to issue and enforce regulations. Environmental quality was simply too low a priority for the government, which lacked the resources to invest in cleaner technology and could not provide incentives for plants to behave differently. Underlying these failings, of course, was the inability of a command economy to operate efficiently or to make significant technological progress. Limited information about the environment, low levels of public

factor for the success or failure of financial transfers.'[15] As an admittedly flawed proxy of revealed environmental policy, we use the percentage of major environmental treaties ratified by recipient countries, an index on which we have worked extensively in the past.[16]

Hypothesis 2b: We expect donors to provide more environmental assistance to governments that provide credible and verifiable environmental information about their policies and performance.

Also critical to a recipient's credibility is its willingness and ability to provide donors with reliable information about its own behavior.[17] Transparency is an important determinant of interstate cooperation because it allows demandeurs to assess the intentions, capabilities, and past behavior of potential cooperators and thus evaluate their trustworthiness.[18] Trust reduces uncertainty and transaction costs, enhancing the credibility of state commitments, making defection more costly, and promoting stable expectations. Though some states can certainly report false information, those who report less environmental information may be viewed with greater suspicion and thus receive fewer environmental aid dollars and contracts. Bad information is better than no information because self-reporting opportunistic actors run a higher risk of being detected and punished by donors, particularly in an era of high resolution satellite, spacecraft, and aircraft imagery, which on some environmental issues can provide 'objective, unbiased, and transparent data sources in a near real time basis.'[19]

The incentive to misrepresent one's intentions, capabilities, or level of need is also weaker in transparent countries since government officials are aware that donors are better able to assess the credibility. Raustiala and Victor offer anecdotal support for this hypothesis. In the Baltic Sea region, they report, 'donors have focused on countries where transaction costs are lower and domestic assurances are higher. Consequently, in the Baltic Sea regime donors have favored Poland over Russia; the fraction of resources sent to Russia has risen only slowly. In both the regime to limit dumping of radioactive waste and the regime to protect the Baltic Sea, programmatic commitments and activities, such as to report and analyze data, have improved knowledge about national situations and made it easier to target aid.'[20] Since it requires serious annual reporting to an international registry overseen by the independent World Wildlife Fund, the CITES treaty on endangered species trade has been

concern, and even lower responsiveness by the central government to these public concerns also contributed to this situation.'

[15] Connolly (1996: 330).   [16] Roberts (1996); Roberts et al. (2004).

[17] Mitchell (1998); Florini (2000); Tierney (2003).

[18] Abbott and Snidal (1998: 431) define demandeurs as 'states...that have worked to obtain commitments from others...in the face of strong resistance.'

[19] de Sherbinin and Giri (2001: 3).   [20] Victor et al. (1998: 675).

widely used as an indicator of transparency and commitment to environmental treaties. Again, this is a potentially flawed indicator, but provides a start in testing this proposition.

Hypothesis 2c: Donors will favor countries with strong democratic institutions.

The recipient country's political regime type may also be critical in aid allocation of all types. Several authors have argued that states with strong democratic institutions are generally able to make more credible international policy commitments than autocratic states.[21] Where open and responsive domestic political institutions are in place, domestic audience 'costs of defection' are higher,[22] and with re-election or consistency of party control weighing heavily on the minds of elected representatives, 'democratic leaders make only the commitments that they can keep, and once made will tenaciously attempt to comply with those commitments.'[23] Conversely, where there are no clear lines of political accountability, defection is relatively costless and therefore common. Indeed, there is evidence that democratic leaders are better able to carry out their military, trade, investment, aid, and debt commitments.[24] One alternative explanation of the positive relationship between democracy and environmental aid is that 'in democracies citizens are better informed about environmental problems (due to freedom of the press) and can better express their environmental concerns and demands (freedom of speech), which will facilitate an organization of environmental interests (freedom of association), which will in turn put pressure on policy entrepreneurs operating in a competitive political system to respond positively to these demands (freedom of the vote).' The team creating and updating the Polity IV dataset has developed and tested a ten-point index of democracy that we believe is a fair evaluation of this hypothesis.

Hypothesis 2d: Donors will target governments with a track record of delivering reliable public services.

If donors are genuinely interested in improving environmental protection, we would also expect them to favor countries with politically insulated,

[21] Lake (1992); Fearon (1994); Martin (2000). Also see Gaubatz (1996); Leeds (1999); Mansfield and Snyder (2002); Shultz and Weingast (2003); Jensen (2003); Tierney (2003). Lisa Martin's book *Democratic Commitments: Legislatures and International Cooperation* is perhaps the most thorough treatment of this popular hypothesis.

[22] Fearon (1994).

[23] Tierney (2003: 50). Implicit in the logic of this argument is that democratic leaders who take on treaty obligations are willing and able to implement their commitments. If this is indeed true and the empirical evidence matches up with theoretical expectations, there would be greater reason to celebrate the current push for democratization in the developing world.

[24] Lake (1992); Fearon (1994); Gaubatz (1996); Leeds (1999); Martin (2000); Mansfield and Snyder (2002); Shultz and Weingast (2003); Jensen (2003); Tierney (2003).

meritocratic bureaucracies that are capable of delivering public goods and sound policies. Government effectiveness is widely cited as a key determinant of effective environmental policy.[25] Therefore, from a donor's perspective, such countries represent safer investments than countries without such institutions. We utilize the World Bank Institute's Government Effectiveness Index, from Kaufmann, Kraay, and Mastruzzi's widely used 'Governance Matters' dataset. This index, used extensively by donors for allocation decisions, combines 'into a single grouping responses on the quality of public service provision, the quality of the bureaucracy, the competence of civil servants, the independence of the civil service from political pressures, and the credibility of the government's commitment to policies.'[26]

Hypothesis 2e: We expect that donors will reward recipient governments with 'sound' economic policies.

If donors are concerned about environmental rate-of-return on their aid investments, we would also expect them to favor countries with sound economic policies. In countries where the government regularly intervenes in markets and distorts pricing structures, there is a strong possibility that the selection and appraisal of public investment projects will be distorted. For example, in countries where excess demand has been artificially generated, donors may select inappropriate investments and overestimate the 'optimum attainable output capacity' of their projects.[27] Where trade, investment, and exchange rate restrictions are high, crucial project inputs may also be prohibitively expensive or unavailable.[28] Local firms seeking to provide complementary environmental goods and services will also do so more efficiently in the absence of state controls on capital goods and other imported inputs. From a more critical perspective, since the fall of the Soviet Union, the major aid donors are capitalist countries, and especially during the study decade of this chapter (the 1990s), 'sound' policies were widely seen as those which limited government 'distortions' of markets (called 'the Washington Consensus'). As Raustiala and Victor more moderately propose, 'when domestic regulatory and market institutions are poorly developed, it is especially difficult for recipients to assure donors that financial transfers will be spent as intended.'[29] Alternatively, Roginko argues that more environmental aid flows to Russia than other Baltic states because of the 'greater political and economic stability in the Baltic countries compared with the situation in Russia. Furthermore, enterprise and municipal facilities in Estonia, Latvia and Lithuania are better positioned to purchase foreign technology because their domestic currencies are convertible.'[30]

[25] Esty and Porter (2005); Kishor and Belle (2004); Léautier (2006).
[26] Kaufmann et al. (2003).   [27] Isham and Kaufmann (1999: 155).
[28] Kaufmann and Wang (1995); Burnside and Dollar (2000a).
[29] Victor et al. (1998: 675).   [30] Roginko (1998: 604).

These hypotheses comprise our 'eco-functionalist' and 'recipient credibility' baseline. If donor provision of environmental assistance were indeed motivated by a genuine concern to address real world environmental problems, we would expect the empirical evidence to conform to these hypotheses that aid flows to areas of environmental need and government competence. There is a rich literature, however, making claims about the more general determinants of foreign aid allocation, and we attempt to test some of these factors as well.

Hypothesis 3a: Aid will be correlated with trade between donor and recipient countries.

Donors may also use aid as an export promotion tool.[31] As we will see in Chapter 5 on donor countries, companies with contracts from donor agencies are a major domestic source of support for the foreign aid budget.[32] It therefore stands to reason that if legislators want to be re-elected they will make efforts to ensure that aid is channeled to the export markets of greatest interest to those contractors. Environmental aid is likely not exceptional in this regard. Robert Darst (2003) explains that at the European Bank for Reconstruction and Development 'efforts to take a "hard line" [with underperforming environmental aid recipients] have been regularly undercut by pressure from donor states with politically influential nuclear engineering industries, such as the United States and France.'[33] Bilateral donors also face these pressures. The US government is especially open about the link between aid and US exports. A former USAID deputy chief in El Salvador is reported as saying that 'the purpose of our aid is to get them to buy American products.'[34] According to a report from the Japan Economic Institute, Japanese companies have also been key players in the allocation of their country's aid budget. In 1998, for example, 'a Keizai Doyukai (Japan Association of Corporate Executives) report called for more grant and environmental funding, initiatives that would dovetail nicely with popular interest and support for environmental protection policies at home and abroad.' Critics of the report argued that the export of green technologies abroad was a major driver in the Keizai Doyukai push for environmental aid.[35] In the chapters examining bilateral donors (Chapters 5 and 6), we examine the strength and apparent impact of these 'coalitions of the green and greedy.' Here, however, we attempt to gauge whether they have an impact on which countries are targeted for environmental aid projects.

---

[31] Kanbur (2000).

[32] Contracts won from bilateral and multilateral donor agencies create significant employment opportunities and additional income for Western citizens. The evidence is mixed on whether this support for foreign aid affects the voting patterns of parliamentarians Fleck and Kilby (2001); Milner and Tingley (2006).

[33] Darst (2003: 20).   [34] Quoted in Chatterjee and Finger (1994).

[35] Altbach (1998). See also Chapter 5. Also see Dauvergne (2001b); Arase (1995); Evans (1994); Forrest (1991); Evans (1999); Taylor (1999); Dauvergne (1997).

Donors may also use foreign assistance to secure trade partners that can provide the raw materials needed for their domestic industries. Schraeder et al. argue that '[t]he top recipients of Japanese aid during the 1980s can be divided into three types of trade categories: (1) important sources of raw materials vital to Japanese industry, such as copper in Zambia and Zaire, uranium in Niger, and chromium in Madagascar; (2) potential future sources of such raw materials, including chromium in the Sudan and oil in Gabon; or (3) major economic markets, such as Kenya and Nigeria, capable of absorbing Japanese exports.' They continue to describe policy-making in Japan as a result of concern about future access to African raw materials.[36] The explosion of China onto the scene after 2002 in loaning funds for African mineral extraction appears to be a similar case. Aid-for-trade swaps of this type are believed to be especially common among donors with few domestic raw materials, such as Japan, but may also heavily influence countries with high domestic political costs to internal resource extraction. To test this key hypothesis, we calculate dyadic trade data between each donor and recipient nation for each of the ten years in this chapter's analysis.

Hypothesis 3b: 'Loyal' recipient countries will receive more aid from bilateral donors.

One common hypothesis is that donor governments use their aid to buy the political loyalty of other countries. The Reagan administration, for example, maintained a policy of limiting foreign assistance to those countries that supported US policy positions in the UN General Assembly.[37] A number of other donor countries, including Japan, Mainland China, and Taiwan, are notorious for exchanging aid in political quid pro quos. Indeed, in 2001, Japan was caught in a vote-buying scandal when the head of its fishery agency openly admitted that the government had bribed countries with promises of foreign assistance to support their pro-commercial whaling position at the International Whaling Commission (IWC). New Zealand's *Evening Post* reported: 'Client nations such as St. Kitts and Nevis, Grenada and the Grenadines...were wooed to IWC membership at Japan's behest. All are recipients of Japanese aid; to suggest they've any genuine interest in whales, whaling and the Southern Ocean sanctuary promoted by New Zealand and Australia stretches credulity.'[38] Other, albeit sometimes less blatant, instances of donor countries using aid to influence the positions of small or aid-dependent recipients have abounded since the 1970s, so we include a test of this important criticism in our allocation model. We often hear about some of the worst cases, but do not know if the pattern is generalized and whether

---

[36] Schraeder et al. (1998: 331).
[37] Kegley and Hook (1991). Also see Keohane (1967); Kim and Russett (1996); Neumayer (2003c); Lai (2003); Thacker (1999); Wang (1999); Wittkopf (1973); Gates and Hoeffler (2004).
[38] Eigen and Eigen-Zucchi (2003: 578–9).

it holds up when other factors are held constant. To test this hypothesis we used Erik Gartzke's UN General Assembly voting records and calculated some of our own for missing years.

Hypothesis 3c: Countries that were previously colonial possessions will continue to receive significantly more aid of all types.

Colonial countries retain connections with their former possessions long after these ties are formally severed, and so we predict a continuing relationship between donors and countries which were colonial possessions as recently as 1945. To test this we used a dummy variable (with values either 0 or 1) produced by CEPII, on whether the recipient was a colony in 1945.

Hypothesis 4a: Environmental aid will target the poorest countries, as they have the least capacity to respond to environmental crises.

Finally, we consider the possibility that donors are responsive to the human needs of recipients. The existing literature controls for the needs of recipients for at least three reasons. First, if donors are at least to some extent motivated by changing actual development outcomes, they can generally achieve a greater rate-of-return on their investment if they focus on countries with higher levels of need. Generally, the poorer a country is, and the more poor people there are living within that country, the more opportunities there are for donors to help. Many donors also have an explicit policy of systematically favoring countries with the highest levels of need, and these often preceded the drafting and acceptance of the Millennium Development Goals (which set concrete global targets for reducing poverty, disease, etc.). Sometimes this is self-imposed; other times it is externally imposed by overseers. The US Congress, for example, has 'tied the hands' of its new bilateral aid agency, the Millennium Challenge Corporation, by allowing it to only work with countries with a gross national income per capita of $3,465 or less.[39] The World Bank goes a step further, using a statistical formula to allocate IDA (International Development Association) funds that includes two variables that account for the depth and breadth of recipient needs: per capita income and population size.[40] It also stands to reason that recipient countries with

---

[39] MCC is also legislatively prohibited from spending more than 25% of its resources on lower-middle-income countries—those countries with a per capita income between $1676 and $3465. The remaining 75% must target low-income countries with a per capita GNI of $1675 or below.

[40] The IDA allocation formula is $(POP \times GNP_{pc}^{-0.125}) \times [(0.8CPIA + 0.2PORT) \times (GOV/3.5)^{1.5}]^{2.0}$, where POP equals population size, GNP_{pc} equals gross national product per capita, CPIA equals country policy and institutional performance assessment, PORT equals portfolio performance, and GOV equals the average of five public sector management indicators. The African Development Fund, Asian Development Fund, Global Environment Facility, Caribbean Development Bank, and International Fund for Agricultural Development all use similar allocation formulas.

greater needs generally have a stronger interest in securing aid contracts than those who are better off and able to access private capital markets without having to deal with the hassle of donor conditionality, paperwork, and oversight.

As we've alluded to in previous chapters, environmental aid is somewhat unique in that donors likely consider both human needs and more purely environmental needs. It is also unique in that donors and recipients will likely disagree about where the needs are greatest, as Chapter 2 explored in some detail. Global issues, like ozone depletion, habitat preservation, and climate change (what we call 'green aid'), are typically perceived by poorer countries to be much less pressing than providing safe drinking water, slowing soil erosion, treating sewage, and reducing urban air pollution (human environmental, local, or 'brown' issues).[41] Connolly notes that this wedge between Northern and Southern interests has put donor countries in the difficult business of 'persuad[ing] recipient countries...to take the environmental actions of [lowest] priority to them.'[42] This North–South divide has important implications for patterns of environmental aid allocation. On the one hand, donors have the money, and 'money talks.' But developing countries also possess unprecedented bargaining power through their ability to obstruct Northern efforts to protect the global environment. In this regard, we might expect the South to extract political concessions—in the form of more highly valued aid for economic, social, and local environmental issues—from donors in exchange for their cooperation on global environmental issues. This leverage can be strong because donors as a whole have formulated a mandate to fund the world's poorest nations. We test just how important this factor is by using the World Bank's standard indicators of gross domestic product per capita corrected for purchasing power parity.

Hypothesis 4b: Recipient countries with large populations will receive more aid of all types.

As an additional control variable, we test whether environmental aid tends to be focused on countries with large populations. On the one hand, population size captures another important dimension of recipient need since poor countries with more people pose larger-scale development challenges and have huge 'brown' social environmental issues. On the other hand, the largest developing countries (China, India, Brazil) have huge economies and

---

[41] Roberts and Thanos (2003); Roberts and Parks (2007a). As discussed above and again in Chapter 9, the Global Environmental Facility was founded to fund environmental projects in poorer nations, and has in its mandate a focus on issues of global importance. But increasingly, the line between local benefits and global ones has grown impossible to pin down. The ongoing conflict over what can be defined as 'adaptation to climate change' funding shows how this is still a contentious issue Muller (2007).

[42] Connolly (1996: 330). Additionally, on a number of key issues, rich nations have failed to honor their international policy commitments. Najam (2002a, 2004a, 2004b); Bernstein and Bluesky (2000); Baumert (2002); Porter et al. (2000); Jokela (2002).

often times a national pride which might make them less willing to accept international aid, especially when it comes with policy and programmatic conditions. Environmental aid may be somewhat different than traditional economic aid in this regard. In particular, environmental aid may be less associated with the demands that recipient countries undertake economic reforms under direction of IMF or other international lenders programs (widely known as 'structural adjustment' programs). Large countries are generally less willing to adopt these reforms than many smaller countries that have less leverage with multilateral development banks and large bilateral donors. We utilized the GDN database for population estimates for years between censuses.

The Empirical Aid Allocation Model

To help the reader understand our empirical aid allocation model, we will provide a brief description of the econometric approach taken in this chapter. Additional detail is provided in Appendix B and an online technical companion document.[43] To empirically examine how donor countries allocate their environmental aid and whether their allocation rules depend in part on environmental, economic, and political factors in the recipient country, we use a statistical model designed to deal with the peculiarities of aid finance data. A cursory examination of aid patterns over the last few decades reveals that a significant proportion of countries receive no aid in given sectors for long periods while others receive large amounts of aid consistently in the same sectors. This empirical pattern lends itself to thinking about aid allocation as a two-step process.[44] In the 'gate-keeping' stage, a donor country decides whether or not to give a recipient country some positive amount of aid. Once a recipient country has passed the gate-keeping stage, a donor country sets aside a percentage of their overall aid budget for that particular recipient country in the 'amount' stage.[45] Consequently, when one asks how donor preferences and recipient characteristics affect aid allocation, one needs to think about how both of these factors affect the gate-keeping and allocation stages of the process.

Using the PLAID database on international development assistance, for each donor, recipient, and year, we construct the share of a donor's aid budget for a given year and environmental or non-environmental aid given to each recipient country. This share of a donor's aid budget is the variable our model is attempting to explain. It is important to note that, by construction, this variable treats all donors as equal, since we are attempting to describe the

---

[43] See Appendix B.

[44] Poe and Meernik (1995); McGillivray and Oczkowski (1991, 1992); Tarp et al. (1998).

[45] One good example of this two-step process can be found in the Millennium Challenge Corporation's (MCC) annual country selection process, discussed above.

behavior of the average donor, not just the big ones. There are advantages and disadvantages to this approach. On the one hand, defining the dependent variable in this way does not allow the allocation decisions of large donors to swamp the allocation decisions made by smaller donors. On the other hand, because we do not assign different weights to donors based on the overall size of their aid budgets, the 'generalizable' conclusions that we attempt to provide do not account for the relative significance of different donors. We have examined the individual behaviors of donors in separate models when possible, but for this chapter we are examining the impact of average donor behavior on recipients. We test allocation patterns for all projects, environmental projects, 'dirty' projects with likely negative environmental impacts, environmentally neutral projects, and those addressing global 'green' issues and local 'brown' projects, separately and together.

Using these calculated shares, many donor–recipient–year pairs correspond to no aid given, since not all donors give money to all recipients every year. Our model treats these donor–recipient–years differently than those combinations receiving positive shares. In the gate-keeping model, we examine how variables in Table 4.2 influence the probability that a recipient receives a positive share of aid from a donor. In the amount stage, we examine how the same factors influence the amount a recipient receives, conditional on passing the gate-keeping stage.

Ultimately, we are interested in the combined effect of both the gate-keeping and amount stages of the model. It is instructive, however, to consider the interpretation of each. In the gate-keeping stage, the parameter estimates we present should be interpreted as influencing the probability that a recipient passes the gate-keeping requirement for each donor and year for that type of aid. Therefore, a positive (negative) coefficient on, for example, a democracy score indicates that as democracy increases (decreases) the probability of getting some positive aid share increases (decreases). In the amount stage, coefficients influence the amount of aid given. These coefficients are estimated only over those donor, recipient, type, and year combinations where a positive share is observed. For example, a positive (negative) coefficient on gross domestic product (GDP) per capita in the amount equation should be interpreted as increasing (or decreasing) the share of a donor's aid budget given to a recipient when its GDP per capita increases. To estimate the combined effect of *both* stages of estimation, we use both models to estimate an 'elasticity score' for each variable. This elasticity score evaluates how a change in that variable influences the share of aid a recipient receives by changing both the gate-keeping and amount stages of the model. This elasticity describes how a 1 per cent change in an explanatory variable (like gross domestic product) leads to an x per cent change in the share received.

An important innovation in our empirical work, and one we describe in detail in Appendix B and the technical companion to this book, is the use of multiple imputation techniques for handling the missing data that are a part of most international panel data studies. Recipient countries are by definition poorer, and many have extremely weak data-collection capabilities. Therefore, finding variables with complete time-series data can be quite difficult. Prior work has either performed listwise deletion, a procedure that removes observations with any missing values, using 'pairwise' deletion of cases which can make models uncalculatable or unrealistic, or has imputed missing data in unsystematic ways. While our work is less affected by the selection bias associated with listwise deletion and ad hoc imputation, the use of multiple imputation also introduces the uncertainty associated with missing data in the estimation process. Missing imputed data are unknown and therefore estimates and standard errors are subject to the researcher's uncertainty regarding the independent variable data. Recent research on the use of multiple imputation indicates it is likely the best research tool for the missing data problems abundant in most cross-national time-series analyses. Rather than being a weakness in our research, our estimates include this uncertainty over missing data and are therefore not overestimating the statistical significance of factors influencing aid.

Results

Which countries receive environmental aid and why do some countries receive more environmental aid than others? Is the allocation of environmental aid among recipient countries any different from the allocation of more traditional types of aid? How do bilateral and multilateral donors vary in the way they allocate environmental aid among recipient countries? In this section, we discuss the results from the two stages of our aid allocation model. In each case, we examine differences across donor types (e.g. bilateral, multilateral, MDB, MGA) and environmental aid types (e.g. green and brown). We also report models of 'dirty' aid allocation as a check on whether the drivers of environmental aid allocation are in fact unique to environmental aid.

We present three sets of results. Because we see this work as the core of this book's contribution to the study of aid, we present the analysis in substantial detail, some of which is avoided in future chapters. For each major donor type, we include results from the gate-keeping equations (Tables 4.2a, 4.2b, and 4.2c), the amount equations (Table 4.3a, 4.3b, and 4.3c), and elasticity results (Table 4.4a, 4.4b, and 4.4c). While the two-step model is designed to deal with limited dependent variable issues, we are ultimately interested in the net effect of both the gate-keeping and the amount models. In this regard, the elasticity results are the most useful results for interpreting the *overall* impacts of recipient country effects, and judging the relative impact

Table 4.2a. Gate-keeping stage predictors of allocation of environmental and 'dirty' aid to recipient countries, 1990–1999

Hyp.		Gate-keeping stage			
		Environmental		Dirty	
		Bilaterals	Multilaterals	Bilaterals	Multilaterals
	Number of cases	14,912	5,493	15,299	6,304
	Variable name				
H1	Ln (natural capital index)	0.05** (2.08)	0.07** (2.91)	0.04* (1.68)	−0.00 (−0.25)
	Distance from donor to recipient	−0.01* (−1.65)	—	0.00 (0.418)	—
	Water quality	−0.00 (−0.00)	−0.90* (−1.74)	0.33 (0.52)	0.27 (0.61)
H2	Enviro. treaty ratifs.	0.56** (2.59)	0.23 (1.26)	0.22 (1.20)	0.16 (0.85)
	CITES reporting	0.00** (2.17)	0.00 (−0.93)	0.00** (1.97)	0.00 (0.70)
	Democracy index for recipient	0.02 (1.57)	0.01 (0.81)	0.02* (1.81)	0.01 (0.85)
	Recipient gov't effectiveness	0.21** (3.28)	0.20** (3.22)	0.16** (2.50)	0.12** (2.03)
H3	Importance of recipient in donor trade	0.01 (1.58)	—	0.01* (1.85)	—
	Recipient UN voting with donor	−1.06** (−9.24)	—	−0.43** (−4.07)	—
	Recipient was colony in 1945	0.67** (6.71)	—	0.92** (7.06)	—
H4	Ln (GDP per capita)	−0.34** (−7.48)	−0.21** (−6.61)	−0.36** (−7.34)	−0.24** (−7.82)
	Ln (population)	0.15** (5.99)	0.05** (3.00)	0.14** (5.05)	0.08** (4.78)

Note: t statistics in parenthesis; ** significant at 5% level; * significant at 10% level.

of the hypotheses offered earlier in this chapter. The elasticity results have the added advantage of normalizing the size of the effect of a particular independent variable across all models and donor types considered. While we do present results of the gate-keeping and amounts stages of estimation in this chapter, we focus our discussion on the elasticity results in Table 4.4a, 4.4b, and 4.4c, referring back to the component parts of the overall model when appropriate.

It is important to note that the number of cases we model for the gate-keeping stage (roughly 15,000 donor–recipient dyads) is much greater than the share equation (between 1,800 and 5,000), since many countries did not receive any aid of a particular type in a particular year. Consequently, the number of observations falls below 5,000 for the share models in some sectors. For example, in the MDB green aid regression there are only 223 dyadic combinations of multilaterals and recipients actually committing to green projects in a given year. The impact of these smaller sample sizes is that statistical significance is more difficult to achieve in the share amount models of where aid flows.

Table 4.2b. Gate-keeping stage predictors of allocation of green and brown aid to recipient countries, 1990–1999

Hyp.		Gate-keeping stage			
		Bilaterals		Multilaterals	
		Green	Brown	Green	Brown
	Number of cases	14,100	14,912	6,146	5,468
	Variable name				
H1	Ln (natural capital index)	0.08** (3.20)	0.06** (2.19)	0.09** (4.02)	0.04 (1.44)
	Distance from donor to recipient	−0.01 (−1.38)	−0.02** (−3.04)	—	—
	Water quality	−0.85 (−1.44)	−0.12 (−0.19)	−0.79 (−1.45)	−1.80** (−2.92)
H2	Enviro. treaty ratifs.	0.83** (3.86)	0.16 (0.77)	0.39** (2.26)	−0.44* (−1.82)
	CITES reporting	0.00** (−2.05)	0.00* (−1.94)	0.00 (−0.87)	0.00 (0.41)
	Democracy index for recipient	0.02* (1.81)	0.01 (0.73)	0.01 (0.81)	0.00 (0.10)
	Recipient gov't effectiveness	0.24** (3.65)	0.22** (3.51)	0.18** (2.65)	0.21** (2.99)
H3	Importance of recipient in donor trade	0.01* (1.78)	0.01 (1.42)	—	—
	Recipient UN voting with donor	−1.21** (−10.57)	−0.54** (−5.01)	—	—
	Recipient was colony in 1945	0.39** (4.44)	0.66** (6.70)	—	—
H4	Ln (GDP per capita)	−0.31** (−8.31)	−0.34** (−7.12)	−0.22** (−6.91)	−0.22** (−5.20)
	Ln (population)	0.12** (6.12)	0.12** (4.57)	0.04** (2.18)	0.05** (2.24)

Note: t statistics in parenthesis; ** significant at 5% level; * significant at 10% level.

We first sought to test whether environmental aid tends to flow to the countries of greatest global environmental significance (H1a). Table 4.2a shows that, at the gate-keeping stage, a country's natural capital is positively related to flows of bilateral and multilateral environmental aid.[46] The natural capital elasticity scores are also striking. The elasticity estimate is significant and positive for *green* aid, but not for *non-environmental* aid. This suggests that (a) donors are genuinely interested in using foreign assistance to provide undersupplied international public goods, (b) not all aid allocation decisions are motivated by geo-strategic and commercial factors, and (c) the procedures used by donors to allocate aid for international public good provision are in some measure different from the procedures used to allocate more traditional types of foreign assistance. To interpret the relative importance of this finding, consider the green elasticity estimate in the bilateral models presented in Table 4.4a. A 1 per cent increase in a recipient country's natural capital score increases its share of green aid from an average bilateral donor by

---

[46] Dirty aid from multilaterals does not appear to flow to countries of global environmental importance.

Table 4.2c. Gate-keeping stage predictors of allocation of environmental, 'dirty', green and brown aid to recipient countries from Multilateral Development Banks (MDBs) and Multilateral Granting Agencies (MGAs), 1990–1999

Hyp.		Gate-keeping					
		Environmental		Dirty	Green		Brown
		MDB	MGA	MDB	MDB	MGA	MDB
	Number of observations	5,493	1,846	6,203	4,299	1,846	5,160
	Variable name						
H1	Ln (natural capital index)	0.04* (1.64)	0.12** (3.19)	-0.00 (-0.30)	0.07** (-2.91)	0.12** (-3.223)	0.04 (-1.436)
	Water quality	-1.19** (-2.220)	-0.39 (-0.36)	0.28 (0.64)	-1.42* (-1.76)	-0.36 (-0.39)	-1.81** (-2.94)
H2	Enviro. treaty ratifs.	-0.12 (-0.61)	0.86** (2.32)	0.10 (0.53)	0.12 (0.49)	0.87** (2.35)	-0.49 (-2.01)
	CITES reporting	0.00 (1.01)	0.00 (0.61)	0.00 (0.68)	0.00 (1.26)	0.00 (0.60)	0.00 (0.42)
	Democracy index for recipient	0.01 (1.16)	0.00 (0.22)	0.01 (0.85)	0.03** (1.99)	0.00 (0.19)	0.00 (0.04)
	Recipient gov't effectiveness	0.19** (2.66)	0.28** (2.78)	0.12 (2.09)	0.11 (1.10)	0.28** (2.81)	0.21** (3.05)
H4	Ln (GDP per capita)	-0.23** (-6.17)	-0.24** (-4.89)	-0.24** (-7.80)	-0.28** (-6.49)	-0.24** (-4.92)	-0.22** (-5.10)
	Ln (population)	0.05** (2.48)	0.08** (3.10)	0.08** (4.83)	0.0244594 (1.10)	0.08** (3.12)	0.05** (2.30)

Note: t statistics in parenthesis; ** significant at 5% level; * significant at 10% level.

Table 4.3a. Allocation amount stage predictors of allocation of environmental and 'dirty' aid to recipient countries, 1990–1999

Hyp.		Amount			
		Environmental		Dirty	
		Bilaterals	Multilaterals	Bilaterals	Multilaterals
	Number of observations	3,489	1,439	4,943	1,799
	Variable name				
H1	Ln (natural capital index)	0.03 (0.55)	−0.09* (−1.81)	−0.02 (−0.35)	−0.11** (−2.09)
	Distance from donor to recipient	−0.04** (−3.27)	—	−0.06** (−4.96)	—
	Water quality	−0.80 (−0.62)	−3.81** (−1.99)	0.04 (−0.034)	−0.69 (−0.424)
H2	Enviro. treaty ratifs.	−3.30** (−5.81)	−1.73** (−2.79)	−2.16** (−5.14)	−0.60 (−1.52)
	CITES reporting	0.00 (1.04)	0.00 (0.87)	0.01** (2.83)	0.00 (0.81)
	Democracy index for recipient	−0.03 (−1.42)	0.03 (1.30)	−0.02 (−0.90)	0.03 (1.26)
	Recipient gov't effectiveness	0.12 (1.10)	0.13 (0.81)	0.11 (0.88)	0.20 (1.25)
H3	Importance of recipient in donor trade	0.02** (2.63)	—	0.03** (4.92)	—
	Recipient UN voting with donor	0.12 (0.68)	—	−0.55** (−2.84)	—
	Recipient was colony in 1945	0.41** (2.54)	—	0.75** (4.69)	—
H4	Ln (GDP per capita)	−0.33** (−3.43)	0.45** (4.59)	−0.35** (−3.49)	0.12 (0.91)
	Ln (population)	0.28** (5.01)	0.54** (9.16)	0.32** (6.34)	0.59** (8.82)
	Constant	−6.69** (−4.77)	−16.40** (−10.96)	−7.40** (−5.42)	−14.79** (−8.97)

Note: t statistics in parenthesis; ** significant at 5% level; * significant at 10% level.

0.23 per cent. For multilaterals, the equivalent relationship is: a 1 per cent increase translates into 0.15 per cent more environmental aid.

It is also important to note that while the *green* aid elasticity estimate is significant and positive, the *brown* aid elasticity estimate is not. As we expected, green aid, which tends to target global public good provision, is systematically channeled to countries of regional and global environmental significance. The elasticity estimates reported in Tables 4.4a and 4.4b suggest that this positive relationship for green aid holds across bilateral and multilateral donors.[47]

Yet, when one looks at both the gate-keeping and amount equations, natural capital is a positive and significant predictor of the probability of receiving positive shares of aid from a donor in a sector, but is not significant and positive in any of the *amount* equations. For multilateral agencies, higher natural capital stocks actually lead to smaller aid allocations. Since the elasticities, however, combine both model results, Tables 4.4a, 4.4b, 4.4c, and 4.4d report the net effect of both influences on aid. This effect is consistently

[47] However, when we disaggregate multilateral agencies into the multilateral development banks and multilateral grant agencies, we observe estimates that are positive but not significant.

Table 4.3b. Allocation amount stage predictors of allocation of brown and green aid to recipient countries, 1990–1999

Hyp.		Amount green bilaterals	Amount brown bilaterals	Amount green multilaterals	Amount brown multilaterals
	Number of observations	2,094	2,386	979	543
	Variable name				
H1	Ln (natural capital index)	0.05 (1.16)	0.03 (0.44)	−0.02 (−0.40)	−0.06 (−0.73)
	Distance from donor to recipient	−0.04** (−2.56)	−0.04** (−3.13)	—	—
	Water quality	−1.28 (−0.92)	−1.49 (−0.86)	−5.73** (−3.20)	−2.74 (−0.75)
H2	Enviro. treaty ratifs.	−3.00** (−3.72)	−3.97** (−6.97)	−1.58** (−2.13)	−0.65 (−0.70)
	CITES reporting	0.00 (0.16)	0.00 (0.74)	0.00 (0.72)	0.00 (0.62)
	Democracy index for recipient	0.02 (1.04)	−0.06** (−3.03)	0.05** (2.34)	0.03 (0.99)
	Recipient gov't effectiveness	0.12 (1.08)	0.06 (0.38)	0.10 (0.50)	0.07 (0.24)
H3	Importance of recipient in donor trade	0.02** (2.09)	0.02** (2.20)	—	—
	Recipient UN voting with donor	0.22 (1.35)	0.03 (0.10)	—	—
	Recipient was colony in 1945	0.54** (3.77)	0.13 (0.64)	—	—
H4	Ln (GDP per capita)	−0.44** (−3.60)	−0.16 (−1.60)	0.33** (2.62)	0.46** (2.40)
	Ln (population)	0.26** (4.78)	0.20** (3.19)	0.51** (8.30)	0.40** (3.93)
	Constant	−5.36** (−3.22)	−5.78** (−3.44)	−15.16** (−8.27)	−13.26** (−4.87)

Note: t statistics in parenthesis; ** significant at 5% level; * significant at 10% level.

positive and significant. Therefore, our first hypothesis is broadly but not strongly supported: green aid allocation by bilateral donors is more responsive to recipient country's natural capital stocks than brown aid allocation and non-environmental aid allocation.

Hypothesis 1b sought to evaluate the potential impact of a recipient country's regional environmental significance. In the absence of a direct measure of regional *environmental* significance (such as being upwind or upstream of a donor), we employed a measure of physical proximity—the distance between a potential donor and potential recipient. Given that many bilateral donors have regional 'spheres of influence,' we expected to observe a 'regional effect' across all aid sectors; however, we also predicted a stronger effect on environmental aid because of the direct impact that regional environmental problems have on donor countries. While projects of an explicitly trans-boundary nature were coded as 'green' projects (e.g. regional air pollution), we are also mindful of the fact that many so-called 'local' environmental projects may have significant effects that spill across borders (e.g. water pollution projects in border towns and cities). The elasticity results in Table 4.4 show that the joint effect of being located close to a donor country leads to higher total aid flows. The magnitude of this effect is similar across the environmental, green,

Table 4.3c. Allocation amount stage predictors of allocation of environmental, 'dirty', green and brown aid to recipient countries, 1990–1999

Hyp.		Amount					
		Environmental		Dirty	Green		Brown
		MDB	MGA	MDB	MDB	MGA	MBD
	Number of observations	681	758	1,798	223	756	540
	Variable name						
H1	Ln (natural capital index)	−0.09 (−1.32)	−0.05 (−0.87)	−0.11** (−2.10)	−0.12 (−1.24)	−0.05 (−0.83)	−0.06 (−0.71)
	Water quality	−2.51 (−0.76)	−3.06* (−1.69)	−0.68 (−0.42)	−5.42 (−0.96)	−3.09* (−1.70)	−2.75 (−0.74)
H2	Enviro. treaty ratifs.	0.15 (0.20)	−2.34** (−3.53)	−0.60 (−1.51)	1.15 (−1.82)	−2.32* (−3.51)	−0.58 (−0.63)
	CITES reporting	0.00 (0.57)	0.00 (0.40)	0.00 (0.79)	−0.00 (−0.32)	0.00 (0.37)	0.00 (0.58)
	Democracy index for recipient	0.02 (0.66)	0.02 (0.73)	0.03 (1.28)	0.04 (1.21)	0.02 (0.73)	0.03 (0.99)
	Recipient gov't effectiveness	0.20 (0.80)	−0.00 (−0.02)	0.21 (1.34)	0.22 (0.73)	0.01 (0.03)	0.09 (0.31)
H4	Ln (GDP per capita)	0.48** (3.09)	0.64** (5.60)	0.12 (0.90)	0.35 (−1.357)	0.647** (5.55)	0.46** (2.35)
	Ln (population)	0.49** (5.35)	0.61** (10.20)	0.59** (8.84)	0.44** (3.60)	0.61** (10.12)	0.40** (3.91)
	Constant	−15.02** (−6.49)	−20.02** (−13.23)	−14.75** (−8.98)	−11.59** (−2.71)	−19.98** (−13.08)	−13.21** (−4.83)

Note: t statistics in parenthesis; **significant at 5% level; *significant at 10% level.

Table 4.4. Elasticity estimates of allocation of environmental 'dirty', 'green and 'brown' aid to recipient countries, 1990–1999; (a) Bilateral donors; (b) All multilateral agencies; (c) Multilateral development banks; and (d) Multilateral grating agencies

Hyp.	Variable name	Green	Brown	Environmental	Dirty
(a) Bilateral donors
H1	Ln (natural capital score)	0.23*	0.15	0.11	0.02
	Distance	−0.48*	−0.67*	−0.45*	−0.42*
	Organic water emissions	−0.65	−0.37	−0.18	0.07
H2	Treaty percentage	−0.10	−0.30*	−0.20*	−0.15*
	CITES reporting	0.42	0.49*	0.45*	0.51*
	Democracy Index	0.35*	−0.20	0.03	0.03
	Government effectiveness	0.31*	0.26*	0.19*	0.09*
H3	Trade importance	0.08*	0.08*	0.06*	0.09*
	UN voting affinity	−2.10*	−.89*	−1.32*	−0.78
	Colony in 1945	1.46*	1.55*	1.48*	1.67*
H4	Ln (GDP per capita)	−1.15*	−0.89*	−0.87*	−0.71*
	Ln (population)	0.54*	0.45*	0.51*	0.46*
(b) All multilateral agencies
H1	Ln (natural capital score)	0.15*	0.04	0.02	−0.12*
	Organic water emissions	−1.48*	−1.50	−1.09*	−0.08
H2	Treaty percentage	−0.07	−0.16	−0.11	−0.03
	CITES reporting	0.27	0.26	0.26	0.21
	Democracy Index	0.35*	0.18	0.21	0.20
	Government effectiveness	0.27	0.35	0.28*	0.19*
H4	Ln (GDP per capita)	−0.11	−0.10	0.08	−0.16
	Ln (population)	0.59*	0.52*	0.63*	0.68*
(c) Multilateral development banks
H1	Ln (natural capital score)	0.12	0.03	−0.01	−0.12*
	Organic water emissions	−2.06	−1.53*	−1.09	−0.08
H2	Treaty percentage	0.13	−0.17	−0.01	−0.04
	CITES reporting	0.32	0.24	0.33	0.21
	Democracy Index	0.68*	0.17	0.26	0.20
	Government effectiveness	0.35	0.36	0.35*	0.19*
H4	Ln (GDP per capita)	−0.58	−0.09	−0.06	−0.16
	Ln (population)	0.52*	0.53*	0.60*	0.68*
(d) Multilateral granting agencies
H1	Ln (natural capital score)	0.20		0.01	
	Organic water emissions	−1.61*		−0.68	
H2	Treaty percentage	−0.15*		−0.18*	
	CITES reporting	0.51		0.09	
	Democracy Index	0.52*		0.09	
	Government effectiveness	0.22		0.09	
H4	Ln (GDP per capita)	−0.29		0.52*	
	Ln (population)	0.68*		0.64*	

and 'dirty' sectors, and Tables 4.2b and 4.3b show that environmental gate-keeping and aid amounts are negatively and significantly related to distance from donor to recipient. It is much stronger, however, for the brown sector. Our results therefore suggest that Hypothesis 1b is only partly supported. Geographical proximity exerts a stronger effect on brown aid than on green aid, and this difference is largely influenced by the gate-keeping stage of the model. That is, donors were more likely to give brown aid to their neighbors, but not to give massively greater amounts of that aid to neighbors as opposed to other recipient countries.

Our final hypothesis related to the environmental characteristics of recipient countries (H1c) addressed the issue of local environmental damage. We predicted that donors would discriminate in favor of countries with more local environmental damage, and recipients would express greater interest in cooperating on such issues. We also predicted that brown aid would more closely target local environmental issues than green aid. Our proxy measure, given severe shortages of adequate time-series cross-national data, was water pollution levels, which has dangerous sampling bias problems. That is, countries addressing their water pollution are the only ones where samples are being widely taken and reported. In the end, our findings generally did not support the hypotheses: all significant elasticity results are negative. This effect is most striking for multilateral institutions. It appears that multilateral donors reward recipients with *low* water pollution intensity, and this is particularly true for multilateral development banks giving brown aid and for multilateral grant agencies giving green aid. One potential explanation for this negative effect is measurement error. While water pollution intensity is certainly related to *overall* levels of local environmental damage, it is an admittedly imperfect proxy. It is also possible that we observe this result because we are effectively measuring the strength of a country's environmental policies and institutions, and multilateral donors discriminate in favor of recipient countries with some degree of credibility.[48] Bilateral donors had trends in the same direction but which were not statistically significant. Again, the direction of causality can be problematic with this variable, since funding can lead to more testing and worse results.

The next set of hypotheses (H2a, H2b, H2c, H2d, H2e) addresses the issue of recipient credibility—in particular, the strength of government institutions, economic policies, environmental policies, and democracy. Much debate now centers on whether these factors should be a top consideration in aid allocation. Looking broadly at the findings, one important stylized fact that emerges from the models is that donors appear to screen for credibility more extensively at the gate-keeping stage than at the amount stage. That is, when choosing partner countries, donors do seem to favor those with reasonably effective governments, credible environmental policies and institutions, and to some extent, democratic values and institutions. At the gate-keeping stage, we also note that environmental treaty ratification is positively related to bilateral environmental aid, but not to multilateral environmental aid. Looking more closely, bilateral agencies especially target their *green* aid to countries

[48] The World Bank and several regional development banks explicitly evaluate the quality of a recipient country's environmental policies and institutions when allocating their assistance.

that have ratified international environmental treaties. For multilateral agencies, the lack of an overall effect is due to a significant positive relationship between green aid and environmental treaty participation that is canceled out by a significant *negative* relationship with brown aid. So, multilaterals seem to channel environmental aid for local issues like water and desertification to countries that have not ratified environmental treaties, but receiving green aid from them may require participation in international treaties. Once a recipient passes the gatekeeping stage, however, it appears that more funding of both types (green and brown) flows to countries that have ratified *fewer* treaties. This might be understood as an attempt to use environmental aid to bring these nations into the 'brotherhood of nations' addressing these global environmental problems. In an unreported set of models, we also tested for the effect of 'sound economic policies' by substituting the World Bank Institute's Regulatory Quality Index for its Government Effectiveness index (since they were highly correlated with each other). Countries with what donors consider to be 'sound economic policies' appear to have a better chance of receiving environmental aid.

This pattern should not be particularly surprising. Many donors publicly advertise that they screen for recipient credibility at the eligibility stage of the aid allocation process. Take for example the Millennium Challenge Corporation's (MCC) annual country selection process, which Parks was responsible for administering from 2005 to 2007. In its gate-keeping stage, the MCC selects countries as eligible for assistance based on their income level and their commitment to good governance, investments in health and education, and sound microeconomic and macroeconomic policies. However, at the amount stage, MCC allocates its funds based on a very different set of factors: the budget constraint, the recipient's population size, the quality of the recipient's proposal, and so forth.

Examining the elasticity estimates in Table 4.4, there are some important sectoral differences in how donors actually screen for recipient credibility. For example, bilateral donors as a group appear to be more responsive to recipient credibility, as measured by these indicators of their level of democracy, environmental transparency (CITES reporting) and government effectiveness. There also appear to be different criteria in allocating green and brown aid project funds. A country's level of participation in environmental treaties has a negative elasticity, indicating that environmental funds, and particularly brown projects, are being channeled to recipients who have ratified fewer environmental treaties. Interestingly, many of the findings for the environmental sectors carry over to the dirty sector as well. That is, bilateral dirty aid generally went to countries that ratified fewer treaties, even holding national GDP/capita constant. The results for multilaterals were not significant.

In addition to recipient-level factors, we tested for the role of donor self-interest. By definition, these factors are only relevant to bilateral donors.

While donors clearly use multilateral agencies to advance their national interests, these cannot be measured here. We predicted that donors would reward their geo-strategic allies, neighbors, trading partners, and former colonies with significant amounts of environmental and non-environmental aid. While many of these factors were influential as evidenced by the elasticity estimates, not every relationship existed in the direction we had predicted. The trade elasticity is positive and significant for all sectors, though it should be noted that the elasticity estimates are quite small compared to other explanatory variables. Neighbors received more bilateral aid of all types. Colonial ties also exhibited a strong and positive effect. The magnitude of this elasticity measure needs to be interpreted differently than other variables in our model, since a 1 per cent change in colonialism is a meaningless concept. Even with this caveat, the significance of our results does suggest that recent colonies receive large amounts of aid across all sectors, although the effect is strongest for dirty aid.

We also tested the hypothesis that donors reward recipients based on their political loyalty, using a measure of UN voting affinity. Voting in UN General Assembly with a donor was, to our surprise, *negatively* related to bilateral environmental aid and dirty environmental aid. This result does not correspond to many other studies of aid allocation, but may be a result of our time period analyzed. Again, our dependent variable is the share of funding to each recipient for the average donor, and so 'realist' theories of international relations, which perhaps apply most directly to large, influential Western countries, may be counterbalanced by the effect of smaller Western donors with major aid commitments to the poorest nations. Several studies have shown that in fact aid does not always buy loyalty in UN voting. For example T. Y. Wang has shown that US aid recipients only vote with the US 15–25 per cent of the time, but on votes of high importance to the donor the correspondence rises substantially.[49] Also, as the former Soviet Union dissolved in the early 1990s, the opposite effect may have taken hold as significant aid funds flowed to countries that did not traditionally vote with Western donor governments. Interestingly, the effect of UN voting affinity is not significant for the dirty sector and strongest in the environmental sectors. One possible explanation is that as environmental problems were uncovered in the former communist states, significant environmental funds were made available to those countries. Yet another is that since these are aid/vote annual correlations, donors seeking to bring future votes to their side might have sent aid to those countries whose votes they *did not* have. Still, these results were not as we predicted.

Finally, we included two variables that can be considered controls, but which represent important factors influencing the allocation of

---

[49] Wang (1999).

environmental aid. Hypothesis 4a predicts more environmental aid flowing to poorer countries, and Hypothesis 4b predicts that countries with large populations get more environmental aid. Both of these hypotheses are strongly supported in our models and there are some interesting differences across donor types that are worth noting. Bilateral donors overall give aid to poorer countries and this effect is stronger for environmental sectors than for the dirty sectors. By contrast, multilateral agencies as a group do not appear to systematically target poorer countries in any sector. When disaggregated into the two broad categories of multilateral agencies, we see that the multilateral grant agencies actually appear to target wealthier countries when giving brown aid. All donors give more of their aid to more populous countries (across all sectors).

Conclusions

In this chapter, we have uncovered some important findings: bilateral donors appear to be more responsive to a recipient country's global and regional environmental significance, policies and institutions, and poverty level. Additionally, we have shown that of all the environmental sub-sectors considered, bilateral green aid is the most responsive sector to factors signaling a project's likely success. These findings are important in light of the analysis to follow later in this book. If bilateral agencies are more responsive to the factors we believe should influence environmental outcomes, the question arises of why countries ever delegate to multilateral agencies.

We also identified some important differences in the allocation of environmental aid and more traditional types of aid. A country's natural capital stocks positively influence its probability of receiving environmental aid, but not its probability of receiving non-environmental aid. A recipient's regional significance also appears to be more relevant to the allocation of environmental aid than non-environmental aid. Yet, in spite of all of the differences that can be pointed out for any type of donor or sub-sector of aid, the weight of the evidence points to allocation rules that are similar when considering where, for example, to build a road versus an energy efficiency project. This could be a signal that recipients demand packages of multi-sectoral aid before agreeing to implement environmental projects. There is some anecdotal evidence that supports this idea, but we believe this is an important area of future research.

Several interesting policy implications emerge from these findings. First, for a citizen in a donor country that is interested in providing money for effective environmental projects overseas, whether they have the potential to deliver global environmental benefits or not, they may be more satisfied in their own bilateral aid agencies. To our surprise, we did not find that multilateral agencies were necessarily better at targeting environmental needs or institutional credibility during the 1990s. It could be that recipients have more influence over the allocation decisions (or formulas) in multilateral agencies, and have more leverage in resisting 'ex ante conditionality' (this issue comes up at length in Chapters 7 and 8). The big picture, however, is that for recipient governments, regardless of whether money is coming from bilateral or multilateral institutions, having sound environmental, economic, and government institutions pays off with respect to getting larger shares of the foreign aid budget. The impact is greater on one's chance of getting any bilateral aid (the gate-keeping stage). In addition, proximity to a donor on average leads to a higher likelihood of being the beneficiary of their environmental largess, and this is particularly true for water projects and other local environmental activities. Former colonial status and trade ties to donors also raise a recipient's odds of getting environmental aid.

Each school of thought on environmental aid, then, received some support with some qualifications. Some 'eco-functional' criteria were significant predictors of which countries receive environmental aid. They are relatively weak predictors, however, ranking well down the list behind national income, population size, UN voting affinity, and colonial history. Domestic and international institutions like government effectiveness and participation in environmental treaties were significant, but only modestly effective predictors of environmental aid flows. There was also evidence that bilateral donors were most responsive to democratic institutions in deciding where to allocate green aid.

In the next chapter, we turn the question around, to examine environmental aid from the donor side. Which countries give more environmental aid and why? We look at the broadest trends and then briefly examine five major donor countries to gain insight into the historical events and trends that might explain increased willingness to send tax money abroad to address environmental issues far from home. We then in Chapter 6 conduct additional analyses, building hypotheses to test what drives increases and cutbacks in bilateral aid budgets.

5

Which Donors Are the Greenest? Trends in Bilateral Aid and Key Donor Profiles

For decades, donor governments have trumpeted all they were doing to help the world's poor, while creating opportunities for their own companies to sell products and invest in recipient countries. The political coalition needed to support a policy of sending taxpayer funds abroad has brought together actors with very different interests: Cold Warriors seeking to pre-empt Soviet and Maoist expansion, business leaders seeking economic opportunities, farmers with surplus grain to sell, and a small army of development professionals who ranged from bush camp nurses to urbane consultants and bureaucrats.[1] For some in this coalition, improving the lot of the poor in developing countries meant building roads, dams, mines, power plants, pipelines, and airports; for others it meant building latrines, schools, and health clinics. Yet both groups supported the idea that their country's government should spend substantial sums of taxpayers' money in poor countries.

The budget for foreign aid is not stable: pressing domestic issues, wars overseas, and the changing opinions of taxpayers often prompt policy-makers to search through their budgets for something to cut. So when reports come back to government appropriators about corruption or environmental problems associated with their aid projects, foreign aid budgets often end up on the chopping block. Since the late 1980s, many Western voters and organized pressure groups have expressed a particular interest in slowing rainforest destruction, biodiversity loss, species extinction, ocean dumping, ozone depletion, and climate change, and do not want their tax money funding the dams, mines, and pipelines that have been targeted by NGO campaigners for their negative environmental effects. Both bilateral and multilateral donors have faced harsh critiques for promoting large

---

[1] The 'development project,' as Phillip McMichael called it, was supported by an evangelical rhetoric of bringing light to the darkness and rescuing the world's poor by bringing markets, modern infrastructure, and social development projects McMichael (1995). Also see Easterly (2007).

infrastructure projects. Sustained pressure has led to policy reforms within many aid agencies, greater project oversight, and a shift in resources towards neutral and away from dirty aid projects. The big infrastructure projects that are funded now undergo environmental impact assessments. Greater scrutiny has also led to increases in assistance for environmental protection and remediation.

As described in Chapter 1, donor countries at the Rio Earth Summit promised substantial financial resources for environmental aid. President George H. W. Bush declared, 'We come to Rio recognizing that the developing countries must play a role in protecting the global environment, but will need assistance in pursuing cleaner growth. So we stand ready to increase United States international environmental aid by 66 per cent above the 1990 levels, on top of the more than $2.5 billion we provide through the world's development banks for Agenda 21 projects.'[2] Leaders from other wealthy countries, facing similar domestic pressure to address international environmental problems, vied in the international media to appear more committed to environmental protection than their peers. Twelve members of the European Community promised a $4.3 billion environmental aid package.[3] Canada pledged $115 million,[4] and Japan attempted to outbid everyone by offering $7.7 billion in environmental assistance over the next five years.[5]

However, many donor governments failed to follow through on their promises. The reasons varied: recessions at home, new electoral coalitions in power, or executive commitments that legislatures refused to ratify or sustain. Other governments did a better job of honoring their promises. How can we explain this variation in compliance with prior promises? What explains the variation in the amount of environmental aid given by donor countries?

In this chapter, we document the broad trends in bilateral aid for environmental protection. Utilizing the PLAID dataset, we report which donors are greenest and where they target their assistance (sectorally and cross-nationally). To understand why national aid agencies sometimes appear so different in their approaches to environment and development issues, we then turn briefly to five case studies of bilateral donors. We begin with two consistently green donors: Denmark and Germany. We then examine two countries that have increased their spending on environmental aid, but still spend less than the average donors in per capita terms: the UK and the US. Finally, we analyze the case of Japan—a donor that has substantially increased its environmental aid commitments over the course of a decade

---

[2] Harris (2001: 59). According to Chatterjee and Finger (1994), the US promise amounted to $217 million above and beyond existing environmental assistance.
[3] Lewis (1992: A6).   [4] Weisskopf and Robinson (1992).
[5] Haas et al. (1992); Lewis (1992: A6).

to rise from one of the smallest to one of the largest environmental aid donors. This chapter is meant to complement our analysis in Chapter 6, where we develop and statistically test hypotheses that shed light on why governments might give relatively more or less bilateral environmental aid. Here, we explore the same terrain with qualitative evidence and descriptive statistics.

Which Countries Are The Greenest? Patterns in International Environmental Aid

Which governments are the most generous donors of aid for the environment? There are three obvious ways to measure the contribution of donors. First, which country gives the most money each year? However, with this measure, donors with large economies tend to dominate. Therefore, we also provide a per capita ranking. But here still there may be a problem: governments that give large amounts of environmental aid on a per capita basis may also be giving even larger amounts to non-environmental projects. So, our third list ranks donor governments by the *share* of their total funding earmarked for environmental projects. Using these various measures, we show how trends in the allocation of environmental aid vary across donors and over time.

Between 1980 and 1999, the PLAID dataset shows that bilateral donors committed $61.9 billion in environmental foreign assistance, out of $735.2 billion of all aid given bilaterally. That is 8.4 per cent of all bilateral aid given for projects with likely positive environmental impacts over the two decades. Table 5.1a shows the rise in bilateral environmental foreign assistance: from $5.8 billion for all donors in the early 1980s to $27.4 billion in the late 1990s, an increase of 371 per cent. At the same time, while environmental aid is clearly on the rise among bilateral donors, it is still a small fraction of most donors' aid budgets.

In terms of total dollars sent abroad to protect the environment, the United States was first in the 1980s, giving a total of $3.8 billion (Table 5.1a). That amount doubled to roughly $7.6 billion during the 1990s. However, the US fell to third in total environmental aid during the second half of the 1990s, as Japan's environmental funding increased fivefold: from $3 billion in the 1980s to nearly $15 billion in the late 1990s. By the end of the 1990s, both countries dedicated roughly 10 per cent of their funding to environmental projects (Table 5.2). Germany rose from third to second place with environmental aid increases of 379 per cent between 1995 and 1999.

Denmark had the greenest aid portfolio of any donor country, giving 13 per cent of all its aid for environmental projects in the five years of the

Table 5.1a. Environmental aid in real US$ 2000, major bilateral donors, 1980–1999

Rank	Donor	1980–1984	1985–1989	1990–1994	1995–1999	Percent change
1	Japan	$1,068,534,240	$1,943,895,506	$5,767,253,085	$8,852,993,035	728.5%
2	Germany	$1,407,349,821	$2,268,802,983	$3,970,845,601	$6,708,761,445	376.7%
3	United States	$1,865,238,929	$1,953,915,168	$3,144,500,663	$4,465,172,287	139.4%
4	France	$275,821,108	$462,815,792	$1,032,409,962	$1,424,144,506	416.3%
5	UK	$54,798,218	$241,554,890	$780,695,098	$1,112,516,103	1930.2%
6	The Netherlands	$282,000,049	$652,636,931	$730,305,296	$1,098,221,055	289.4%
7	Denmark	$170,270,057	$354,111,980	$556,344,040	$956,849,532	462.0%
8	Sweden	$209,762,228	$433,249,541	$567,821,915	$443,517,299	111.4%
9	Australia	$51,216,044	$48,754,756	$181,583,372	$422,282,656	724.5%
10	Norway	$114,528,825	$180,922,566	$211,874,746	$371,366,695	224.3%
11	Canada	$195,687,270	$357,989,307	$382,652,273	$345,352,192	76.5%
12	Switzerland	$46,770,340	$164,560,921	$201,505,574	$305,678,917	553.6%
13	Austria	$90,739	$72,357,156	$85,028,936	$238,542,054	262788.1%
14	Spain	$0	$9,881,932	$69,120,991	$213,666,409	2062.2%
15	Italy	$52,836,646	$512,082,093	$801,493,232	$198,936,864	276.5%
16	Finland	$12,427,507	$208,764,699	$235,884,206	$159,016,152	1179.5%
17	Belgium	$8,347,428	$4,232,094	$20,005,968	$94,879,459	1036.6%
18	New Zealand	$8,155,846	$3,334,062	$0	$3,151,332	−61.4%
19	Portugal	$0	$0	$0	$2,292,953	n/a
	Total	$5,823,835,294	$9,873,862,375	$18,739,324,959	$27,417,340,944	370.8%

Table 5.1b. Environmental aid per capita, major bilateral donors, 1980–1999

Rank	Donor country	1980–1984	1985–1989	1990–1994	1995–1999	$ Change over period
1	Denmark	$33.27	$69.10	$107.58	$181.26	$147.99
2	Norway	$27.83	$43.19	$49.42	$84.26	$56.43
3	Germany	$18.00	$29.08	$49.30	$81.86	$63.87
4	The Netherlands	$19.72	$44.50	$48.13	$70.32	$50.60
5	Japan	$9.02	$15.93	$46.42	$70.22	$61.20
6	Sweden	$25.20	$51.52	$65.50	$50.13	$24.94
7	Switzerland	$7.33	$25.14	$29.36	$43.11	$35.79
8	Finland	$2.57	$42.32	$46.81	$30.95	$28.37
9	Austria	$0.01	$9.54	$10.86	$29.93	$29.92
10	France	$5.07	$8.31	$18.04	$24.46	$19.40
11	Australia	$3.38	$3.00	$10.39	$22.80	$19.41
12	United Kingdom	$0.97	$4.24	$13.49	$19.02	$18.05
13	United States	$8.05	$8.06	$12.26	$16.38	$8.32
14	Canada	$7.77	$13.46	$13.43	$11.53	$3.76
15	Belgium	$0.85	$0.43	$1.99	$9.32	$8.47
16	Spain	$0.00	$0.26	$1.77	$5.39	$5.39
17	Italy	$0.93	$9.04	$14.09	$3.46	$2.53
18	New Zealand	$2.56	$1.00	$0.00	$0.84	−$1.73
19	Portugal	$0.00	$0.00	$0.00	$0.23	$0.23
20	Luxembourg	$0.00	$0.00	$0.00	$0.00	$0.00
	Total bilaterals	$7.79	$22.05	$23.57	$33.36	$25.57

late 1980s, and nearly 22 per cent during the 1995–9 period (Table 5.1b). By 1999, 42 per cent of Denmark's total aid portfolio was earmarked for environmental projects. This proportion was nearly three times that of the next three countries, Germany, Austria, and Sweden, whose environmental funding ranged from 12 to 15 per cent in 1999.[6] From the late 1980s to the late 1990s, Germany tripled its environmental giving in absolute terms, from $2.3 billion to $6.7 billion, which meant a doubling of the proportion of its total portfolio going to the environment, from 7.5 to over 15 per cent. New Zealand, meanwhile, was the only country to shift funds away from environmental aid: allocating 17.6 per cent of its aid for the environment in the late 1980s, but only 3.8 per cent in the late 1990s.[7] We have also witnessed large increases in environmental aid spending over the last twenty years by the Netherlands, France, Sweden, Italy, Austria, the UK, Canada, and Denmark. In annual totals between 1990 and 1999, the top environmental donors scaled up their funding from $2.9 billion to over $5 billion a year.[8]

In per capita terms, Denmark's $181 per capita is extraordinary: it is more than double the per capita spending of any other donor country. Denmark has led the pack in per capita spending since the early 1980s, and maintained that lead—by a significant margin—through the end of the 1990s. However, by the end of the 1990s, five other governments were giving over $50 per person for the environment abroad: Norway, Germany, the Netherlands, Japan, and Sweden. Eleven were giving over $20 per capita, nearly all in northern Europe. Bringing up the bottom of the table are two donors we discuss in more detail below: the UK and the US. The UK's per capita spending increased from nearly nothing in the early 1980s, while the US fell from seventh place to thirteenth place in the late 1990s. The next section will shed light on these two countries and three per capita leaders: Denmark, Germany, and Japan.

Another indicator of a government's commitment to environmental aid is the proportion of its total foreign assistance portfolio dedicated to environmental projects. Table 5.2 shows how this ranking differs from total or per capita spending. Again, Denmark, Germany, and Japan are at the top of the list, but others such as the United States move up the list, from thirteenth to seventh place. Looking at change over time, 17 of 19 donor countries allocated a greater proportion of their aid dollars to environmental

---

[6] We look more closely at Denmark and Germany's environmental aid portfolio later in this chapter.

[7] We note that for several years in the 1990s New Zealand did not report its annual aid figures.

[8] Beyond the bilateral funding, a similar amount was being pumped through multilateral agencies like the World Bank, the UNDP, and the EU TACIS fund. We discuss these trends in Chapter 7.

Table 5.2 Environmental aid as percentage of total aid portfolio, bilateral donors, 1980–1999

Rank	Donor	1980–1984	1985–1989	1990–1994	1995–1999	Change in %
1	Denmark	11.2%	12.8%	19.8%	21.9%	10.7%
2	West Germany	4.7%	7.8%	7.9%	15.6%	10.9%
3	Finland	5.7%	13.4%	11.8%	14.0%	8.3%
4	Japan	4.9%	5.0%	10.8%	13.8%	8.9%
5	Austria	0.0%	10.3%	8.1%	12.7%	12.7%
6	The Netherlands	6.7%	10.1%	10.4%	12.3%	5.6%
7	United States	5.3%	4.5%	7.9%	11.2%	5.9%
8	Switzerland	4.3%	9.2%	6.9%	10.1%	5.8%
9	France	3.4%	3.9%	7.0%	10.1%	6.6%
10	United Kingdom	1.3%	5.5%	11.1%	9.4%	8.1%
11	Australia	1.8%	2.0%	6.2%	9.3%	7.5%
12	Norway	10.1%	8.0%	7.4%	8.2%	−1.9%
13	Sweden	5.7%	4.6%	6.4%	8.1%	2.5%
14	Spain	0.0%	1.3%	2.3%	5.7%	5.7%
15	Italy	2.7%	4.9%	9.2%	5.5%	2.8%
16	Canada	4.1%	4.8%	5.9%	5.4%	1.3%
17	Belgium	1.5%	1.3%	1.6%	3.9%	2.4%
18	New Zealand	6.6%	17.4%	0.0%	3.7%	−2.9%
19	Portugal	0.0%	0.0%	0.0%	0.4%	0.4%

issues at the end of the century (New Zealand and Norway being the lone exceptions).

However, the increase in bilateral environmental aid over time tells only part of the story. Figure 5.1 shows the overall composition of bilateral aid, including not only environmental aid but dirty and neutral aid as well. In a relatively short period of time, bilateral donors have divested from development projects that damage the environment: from about 45 per cent of bilateral aid in the 1980s to about 20 per cent a year at the end of the 1990s.[9] Meanwhile, environmental assistance increased from less than 5 per cent of aid to over 10 per cent in the 1990s.[10] As for the 'Earth Increment' discussed in Chapter 1, we find that much of the increase in environmental aid indeed appears to be new funding, as the drop in dirty funding is almost a mirror image of the increase in neutral aid, particularly in percentage terms (Figure 5.2). Despite these clear increases in environmental funding, it seems that bilateral donors are moving away from infrastructure towards health, education, and other environmentally neutral projects more than they are substituting environmental aid for dirty aid.[11]

[9] The anomalous 'blip' in 1991 in 'neutral' aid was due to two huge grants from the United States to Egypt for balancing their payments during a financial crisis (see Chapter 3).

[10] See also Nielson and Tierney (2003, 2005); Gutner (2005); Keohane and Levy (1996).

[11] It is also possible that donors are increasingly 'marbling,' or 'mainstreaming' environmental concerns in the projects that we categorize as 'neutral.' See Nielson and Tierney (2003).

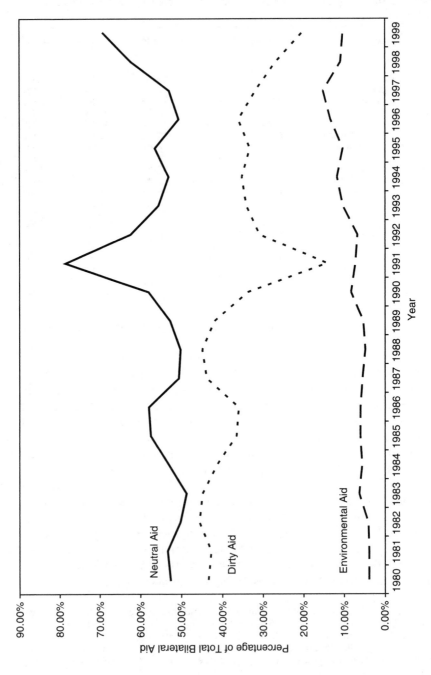

Figure 5.1. Percentage of total bilateral aid, 1980–1999

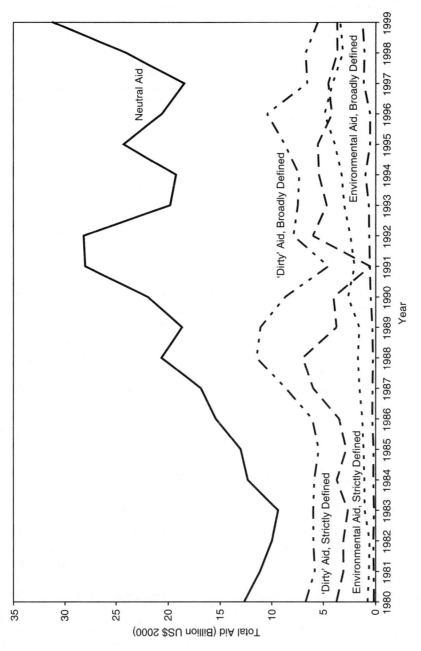

Figure 5.2. Bilateral aid by type, 1980–1999

131

The above figures and tables show that in general wealthy countries are spending four times as much on environmental assistance as they used to, and that much of the increase occurred in the early 1990s. Nearly every donor has increased their environmental funding from the early 1980s to the late 1990s, and most increased their spending very substantially. Perhaps more importantly, most donors scaled back their spending on projects that would directly harm the natural environment. Yet, donors vary substantially in terms of their overall commitment to environmental protection. We suggest two useful methods for illuminating such cross-national variation. First, we closely examine the policies and procedures of donor governments as they relate to aid allocation and project implementation. Second, in Chapter 6 we use statistical tools to account for a variety of factors that are hypothesized to explain cross-national variation in environmental aid allocation. Our case study research and statistical analyses complement each other to provide a deeper understanding of what influences increases and cutbacks in Western environmental aid budgets.

The case studies illuminate the particular histories of donor aid agencies in these five donor countries and discuss the peculiarities of their national political contexts. The countries we cover—Denmark, Germany, the United Kingdom, the United States, and Japan—represent four of the top five donors in terms of total funding, and five of the top ten governments that spend the highest proportion of bilateral assistance on the environment. Among the donors, there is substantial variation in per capita spending, varying from Denmark's $181 per person to $16 per US resident. Japan is a surprising case of turnaround. It began as an average environmental aid donor, but by the early 1990s, it was a leader in the environmental aid community.

Two Leaders, Two Laggards, and One Surprise

Tiny Leader: Denmark's Foreign Aid and the Environment

Denmark is the greenest donor government by almost any measure. Its environmental assistance is embedded within the most generous aid program among all the bilateral donors. Denmark is one of the only countries in the world to have achieved the OECD target of donating 0.7 per cent of GDP as Official Development Assistance by 1978.[12] Denmark's focus has shifted

---

[12] Since then it has consistently maintained one of the world's highest rates of ODA per GDP. According to OECD (2004: 11), it was the largest donor as a percentage of GDP from 1995–2002, giving over 1% in 2003, though in 2005 it fell to fifth, donating 0.81%. OECD

drastically over time: in earlier years, it funded many physical infrastructure and modern agriculture projects.[13] Railroad and road-building, electrification, factory development, industrial material supply, and fertilizer and insecticide projects dominated the Danish aid portfolio from the 1970s through the late 1980s. However, from 1989 through 1993, a marked shift can be seen in Denmark's approach towards social and environmental issues. Despite its tiny population and relatively small economy, Denmark's *total aid for the environment* was fifth in the world in both 1990 and 1999, rising from $199 million to $274 million. From 1995 to 1999, the Danish International Development Agency (Danida) allocated most of its resources for health and education programs, environmental improvement, women's rights, governance, and debt forgiveness, with very few physical infrastructure projects.

Overall, Denmark's environmental aid increased dramatically from 1980 to 1999. In the 1980s, about 12 per cent of its aid fell into the categories we coded 'environmental.' In the 1990s, that number increased to around 20 per cent. In 1992, the year of the Earth Summit in Rio de Janeiro, the number of Danish environmental projects doubled from 25 to 50. Denmark's dirty aid to environmental aid ratio averaged 8 : 1 in the early 1980s, but dropped to 1 : 1 in the early 1990s and fell far below that in the late 1990s (Figure 5.3a).

Denmark committed over $2 billion for 597 environmental projects from 1980 to 1999. Its environmental aid tends to be concentrated in the 'urban environments' category, reflecting a very human-oriented environmental strategy. The other areas receiving significant funding include natural resource management, sustainable energy, and 'cross-cutting initiatives'.[14]

When examining Denmark's environmental projects in terms of the local/global dimension, brown aid appeared to follow less of a defined trend than green aid. Brown aid fluctuated between $20 and $70 million in the 1980s, and then rose to over $100 million for five years during the 1990s. In

(2006). Another unique feature of Denmark's aid program is that it ranks first overall in terms of aid quality on the Commitment to Development Index (CDI). The CDI gives good marks on aid quality for low tied aid, selectivity (giving aid to countries with sound policies and institutions) and focusing on larger projects rather than overloading recipients with many small projects. Tarp et al. (1998: 4). Danish international development assistance emerged in the 1940s, shortly after the Second World War, mostly under the auspices of the United Nations. A formal Secretariat for Technical Co-operation with Developing Countries was not created until 1962, pushed by formation of the OECD's DAC, independence of former colonies, and pressure from Danish businesses and NGOs. Tarp et al. (1998: 2–3). In 1971, the Secretariat was renamed the Danish International Aid Agency, or Danida. Giving through multilateral agencies continues to be a major aspect of Danish aid, but it has shrunk from 80% of aid in the early years to 50% in 2005 (see Chapter 4).

[13] Tarp et al. (1998: 5).   [14] Danida (2005: 40; 2003: 60).

contrast, green aid, for issues like biodiversity and climate change, hovered around $20 million until 1993, after which it rose to $40–50 million a year. On average, the Danish government spent three times as much on brown issues as on green issues, and this relationship did not change much over the twenty-year time period (Figure 5.3b).

A major feature of Danish foreign assistance has been its focus on the least developed countries (LDCs)—those countries with a per capita GDP of $760 or less.[15] Almost all Danish environmental aid over the years has gone to poor countries in Sub-Saharan Africa and South-East Asia. Their main recipients until 1999 were Bangladesh, India, Egypt, Tanzania, and Uganda. After our study period in the mid-2000s, Denmark took an even sharper focus on poor countries.[16] In 2004, the biggest recipient of Danish environmental aid in Africa was Zambia, with US$6.95 million in 2004, and its largest recipient in Asia was Vietnam, with US$45.24 million.[17]

Environmental aid to Vietnam provides an example of Denmark's unique approach. One of Denmark's recent projects was a $6.4 million grant provided in 2000–5 to strengthen sustainable environmental and social management of marine resources. This was labeled a 'cross-cutting' project by Danida because it aimed to protect biodiversity of marine life and mitigate environmental damage, while at the same time focusing on 'sustainable livelihoods' by providing job training, micro credit, and community education in the aquaculture sector. In 2000, Danida partnered with the World Bank to fund a $65.6 million project in Vietnam to restore mangrove forests on the Mekong coast. This project is representative of Danida's programs because it was a joint venture with a multilateral agency and, while clearly environmental, a primary goal of the project was also to 'give a boost to aquaculture and improve quality of life.'[18]

In its attempts to 'mainstream' environment into all aid projects, Danida in December 2006 revised its Environment Guidelines and published a new 'Environmental Screening Note' to be completed for every project brought to its review committee.[19] The form includes a checklist on whether a program or project will damage the land, water, soil, or air, workers, or communities. It requires project developers to consider whether the project will be at risk from climate change in the medium or long term, and whether it will 'result in economic and sector policy initiatives including production subsidies with direct or indirect impacts on the use of natural resources and the environment.' It screens for a broad range of

---

[15] In 2002, 0.52% of Danish GDP was given to LDCs. From the PLAID database we calculate that between 1980 and 1999 $7.3 billion or 48% of their bilateral aid went to Sub-Saharan Africa. According to Danida reports, an even larger portion goes to that region today (US$554.38 million a year, or 54%). Danida (2005).

[16] Roodman (2006).   [17] Danida (2005: 40).   [18] Fistenet (2006).
[19] Danida (2006a).

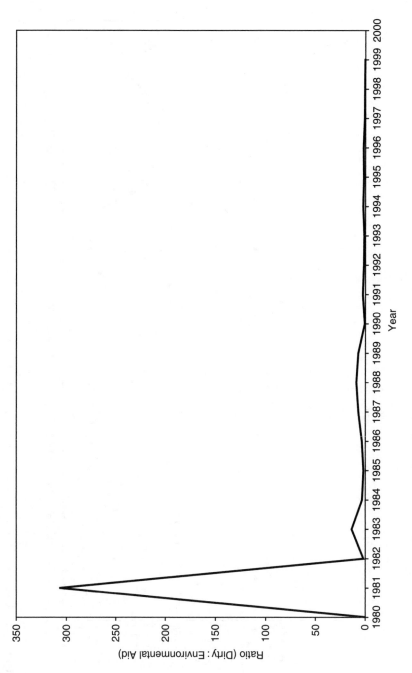

Figure 5.3a. Ratio of 'dirty' to environmental aid given by Denmark, 1980–1999

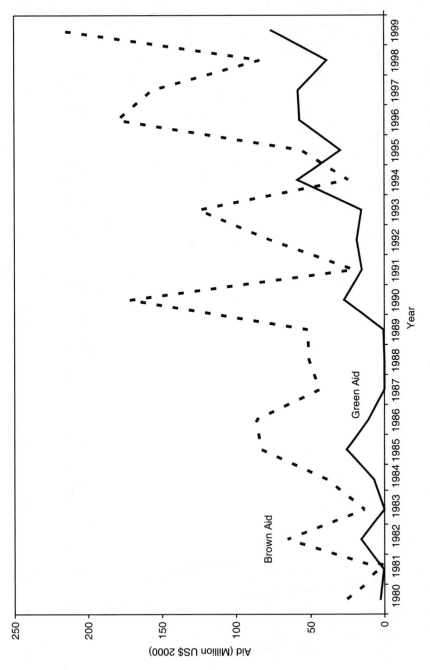

Figure 5.3b. Green and brown aid given by Denmark, 1980–1999

environmental impacts, and for whether recipient countries have adequate capacity for impact assessment, management, budget, policy, and planning. It also requires that Danida attempt to coordinate with other governments and multilateral agencies in assessing and managing the environmental impacts of the project. While the proof is in implementation, the Danida Environmental Screening Note represents a significant step toward the consideration of both direct and indirect environmental impacts of foreign aid.

The Green Party and the Greening of Aid in Germany

The Kreditanstalt für Wiederaufbau Bankengruppe (KfW), or the Reconstruction Credit Institute, is the organization through which Germany's Federal Ministry for Economic Cooperation and Development (BMZ) designs, executes, and monitors international development projects on behalf of the German government.[20] BMZ also contracts with the German agency for technical cooperation (GTZ). In the 1980s, Germany's aid portfolio was shaped by its Cold War position on the frontline of the Iron Curtain. Its original purpose was to give 'money to reconstruction projects,'[21] but President Adenauer of West Germany quickly realized the easiest way to shed 'Germany's pariah status after the Nazi atrocities and to rejoin the international community would be by utilizing the country's industrial capacity and economic potential' to benefit developing countries.[22]

Germany's aid portfolio has greened significantly over the past two decades. Environmental aid funding rose steadily between 1980 and 1995 (Figures 5.4a and 5.4b), and then dramatically increased in the second half of the 1990s from \$1.4 billion to \$6.7 billion (Table 5.1a). That represents an increase from \$18 to \$82 per person per year (Table 5.1b). As a fraction of Germany's aid portfolio, environmental aid also increased from less than 5 per cent to over 15 per cent (Table 5.2). Together, these increases and a corresponding drop in the funding of dirty projects led to a bumpy but persistent decline in the ratio of dirty aid to environmental aid: from over 10:1 in the early 1980s to less than 1:1 at the end of the 1990s (Figure 5.4a).

Until 1989, Germany channeled its environmental aid almost exclusively to brown environmental issues, like water pollution and land degradation (Figure 5.4b). Brown aid also increased steadily from 1982 to 1998, nearly tripling by the end of the period from less than \$100 million a year to more than \$400 million a year. Germany provided little assistance for green projects, like biodiversity protection and climate change, until 1990. However, by 1999, green aid rose to over \$200 million a year. Due to a significant decline in brown aid in the last two years of the 1990s, green aid had nearly overtaken

---

[20] Grübacher (2004).   [21] Grübacher (2004: 18).   [22] Grübacher (2004: 207).

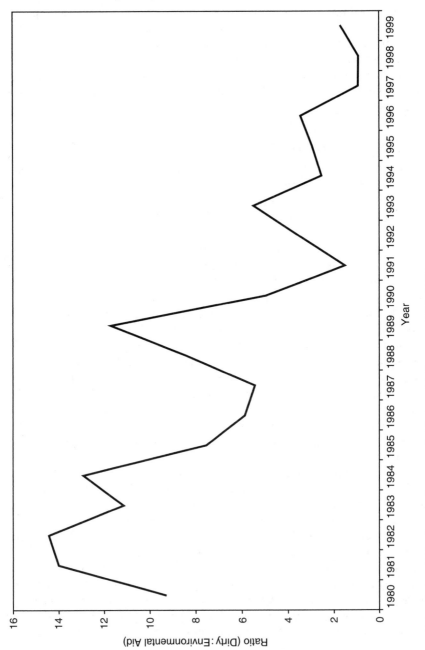

Figure 5.4a. Ratio of 'dirty' to environmental aid given by Germany, 1980–1999

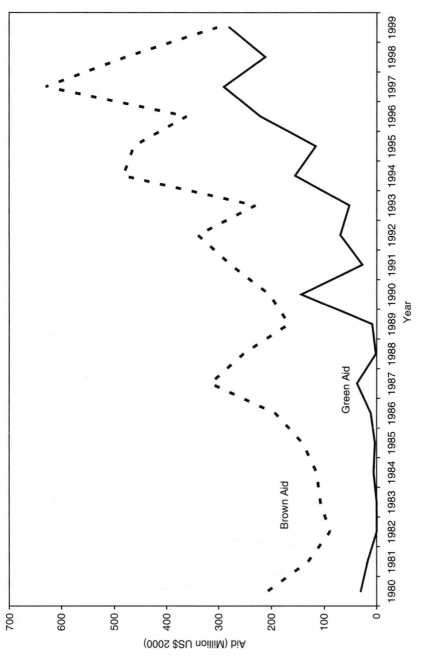

Figure 5.4b. Green and brown aid given by Germany, 1980–1999

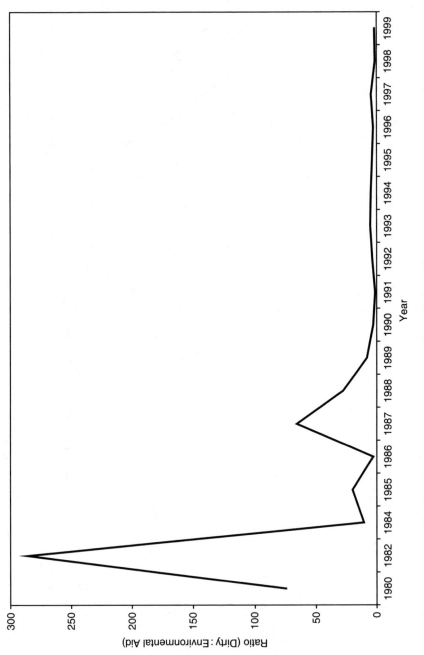

Figure 5.5a. Ratio of 'dirty' to environmental aid given by United Kingdom, 1980–1999

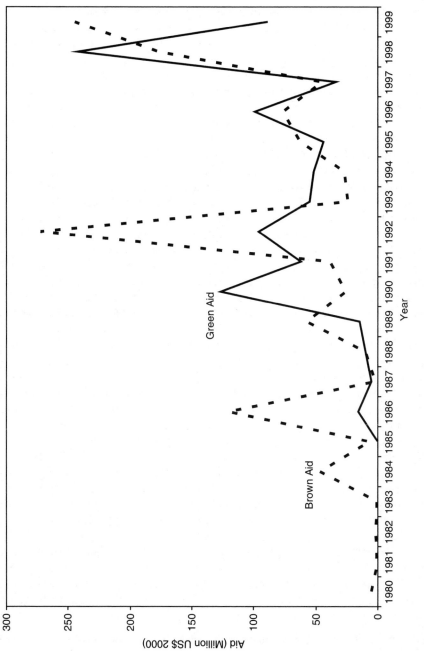

Figure 5.5b. Green and brown aid given by United Kingdom, 1980–1999

brown aid at the end of the decade. The total number of environmental projects funded by Germany increased from less than 100 in 1997 to more than 400 in 1999. However, most of these green projects were small compared to the large-scale urban brown projects financed by Germany during the same period.

Environmental NGOs and the rise of the Green Party under Joschka Fischer played key roles in this transition. When the Green Party joined the Social Democrats to form a coalition government in 1998, the BMZ adopted much stronger environmental rules and regulations. German environmental NGOs had always played an important role in German politics, but the election of 1998 gave them increased access and leverage. Environmental NGOs were instrumental in pushing the German government to take a leading role in the preservation of the Amazon rainforest (such as the PPG-7, discussed in the Brazil section of Chapter 3). Today, all projects within KfW Bankengruppe are subject to the agency's Environmental Guidelines, which were written at the height of Green Party power.[23] These rules have been institutionalized and have so far not been watered down by the more conservative government of Angela Merkel. While the number of environmental projects increased during the time when the Greens shared power in government, the total amount of money dedicated to pro-environment projects actually began to decline in 1998. This decline may be attributable to a growing number of pilot projects in new priority countries, or to KfW Bankengruppe's increased focus on local micro-development projects.

KfW Entwicklungsbank claims that approximately 30 per cent of its current loans are designed to protect the environment.[24] Special attention is given to countries with poor environmental track records through environmental impact assessments. The German government has also given KfW Entwicklungsbank the right to ease the repayment of loans for countries that meet the qualifications of Heavily Indebted Poor Countries (HIPC). This approach is an important innovation because KfW Entwicklungsbank can provide debt relief if the country in question has already committed the freed-up funds to environmental protection.[25] However, proving that freed-up funds were *actually* spent on environmental protection can be very difficult.

One of KfW Bankengruppe's five divisions is KfW Förderbank (KfW promotional bank), which has recently developed a Carbon Fund available for companies in Germany and the rest of Europe to purchase emission credits due to the demands set by the Kyoto Protocol, potentially from

---

[23] KfW Bankengruppe's Environmental Guidelines were revised and strengthened in October 2006.
[24] KfW Bankengruppe (2006).   [25] KfW Bankengruppe (2005a, 2005b).

developing countries.[26] In an effort to respond to criticism on the impacts of the projects they have financed, another branch called KfW IPEX-Bank includes environmental principles in its loan decision processes. The bank policies require that it deny loans—to projects it would have previously funded—due to adverse environmental impacts. It has also sought to finance projects that are environmentally friendly. Its new direction is based on KfW Bankengruppe's environmental principles that were created in a 2003 declaration on environmental protection and sustainable development.[27]

KfW Entwicklungsbank boasts that it ranks first in the world in the financing of renewable energies. It finances loans in 'wind power and hydropower plants as well as biomass, geothermal, photovoltaic and solar thermal power.'[28] Wind energy in China is a particular focus for Germany, which is not surprising given that German firms are among the world leaders in developing wind energy technology.[29] Fifteen projects from 1996 to 2000 were earmarked for renewable energy or energy efficiency projects, totaling $441 million. China has received the most environmental project commitments from Germany: 92 projects that account for just over $1 billion.

According to the German government, from 1997 to 1999 loans to recipient countries totaled €4.8 billion and included €1.3 billion for environmental and resource protection. PLAID data are consistent with this trend for German development assistance as a whole: in 1997 and 1998, Germany spent 26 per cent of its aid budget on environmental projects. In 1998, the BMZ changed their development loan strategy. Instead of assisting some 120 developing countries, the BMZ directed KfW Bankengruppe to focus on 70 so-called 'priority partner countries.' Selection as a partner country is based on economic, social, ecological, and political objectives and interests.[30] In sum, we observe a strong greening of Germany's bilateral aid programs over the past twenty years. Though never rising to number one on the list, Germany has remained at number two on the top environmental donors list for over twenty years.

Conservatives, Labour, and UK Bilateral Aid for the Environment

In the eyes of some observers, UK foreign assistance has come a long way in improving the overall quality of its aid programs. According to a 2005 assessment, '[t]en years ago, DFID was considered a middle-of-the-pack

---

[26] KfW Bankengruppe (2006).   [27] KfW Bankengruppe (2006).

[28] KfW Bankengruppe (2005a: 66).

[29] In Chapter 6, we test the hypothesis that domestic environmental technology lobbies increase the amount of environmental aid allocated by donor governments.

[30] Federal Ministry on Cooperation and Development (2006).

development agency. Today it is generally considered to be the best in the world.'[31] Indeed, the Department for International Development (DFID) is known for its transparency and coherence, its sharp focus on poverty reduction and evidence-based policy-making, and its track record in building country capacity.

But how did the bilateral aid agency of the UK come to earn such a reputation and what is its environmental profile? The historical origins of British foreign aid can be traced back to grants provided to British colonies in the 1870s and formalized with the 1929 Colonial Development Act. The British did not intend for colonial assistance to continue once colonies achieved independence. However, Harold Wilson's Labour government came to power in 1964 and, motivated by dire needs in the former colonies, pressure from commercial interests, and the perceived need to contain communism in the developing world, created the Overseas Development Ministry (the ODM). The goal was to bolster India and the newly independent African countries, which were important trading partners for Britain.[32] Wilson envisioned a high-profile agency, but his idea failed almost from the start. Budget cuts in 1965 targeted the ODM, and a 1972 study concluded, 'aid's poor performance was due more to Labour's political priorities than to economic difficulties.'[33] Foreign aid fell even lower on the priority list when the conservative Tory government came to power in 1979.[34]

In 1997, a Labour government was elected for the first time in eighteen years, heralding major changes in British foreign aid. Total aid and environmental aid increased significantly over the next decade. Between 1980 and 1996—the seventeen years in our study period under Conservative Party rule—average aid amounts totaled about $1.2 billion (370 projects) per year, with only $79 million (33 projects) a year in environmental aid (Figures 5.5a and 5.5b). In contrast, during the three years of Labour Party rule in our study period (1997–9), total aid averaged $2.78 billion (1,590 projects) a year with environmental aid accounting for $272 million (168 projects) annually.[35] This surge in funding suggests that party politics play an important role in environmental foreign aid decision-making.[36] Comparing the late 1990s to the early 1980s, the Labour government made the UK the donor country that greened the most quickly, with a nearly 2,000 per cent increase in both the total amount of environmental aid and in per capita terms in equivalent five-year periods (Tables 5.1a and 5.1b). For some years in the early 1980s the ratio between dirty aid and environmental aid is enormous: in 1982, the ratio was

---

[31] Greenhill, cited in Barder (2005).   [32] White (1998: 152).   [33] Seers (1972: 9).

[34] Morrissey (1998: 249); Hewitt and Sutton (1980: 5).

[35] As explained above, all these figures have been converted into constant 2000 dollars, which makes comparisons across time periods valid.

[36] In 2004–5, the UK's Official Development Assistance was $7.95 billion, a fivefold increase from the 1980s.

286 to 1; in 1981 and 1983, the ratio was undefined because zero projects were categorized as likely to have positive environmental impacts. However, after a few more years in the mid-1980s dominated by dirty projects, British dirty/environmental ratios fell to levels below 4 : 1 and never rose to a higher level.

The 1997 Labour government also made significant qualitative changes to its foreign assistance programs. A new, cabinet-level Department for International Development was created; poverty reduction was established as the number one goal of UK foreign aid; social sector funding was prioritized; and the government committed itself to focusing on fewer countries in order to improve aid quality.[37]

From 1980 to 1999, India received the largest amount of British environmental aid (18.6 per cent of the total), followed by Bangladesh, Ghana, and Tanzania. (It is also worth noting that all are former British colonies.) A 1997 White Paper also recommended that DFID should increase its environmental aid budget and conduct more environmental assessments at the project design stage.[38] In addition, all aid was effectively untied on 1 April 2001.[39] This was very significant because tied aid had reached 79 per cent in 1986 and British industrial interests had favored large projects like dams, power stations, and mining works, which were often in conflict with environmental objectives.[40]

DFID's Policy Information Marker System (PIMS) provides an informative comparison with PLAID-coded data. DFID claims that during the 1990s projects with positive environmental objectives accounted for roughly *one-quarter* of bilateral expenditure. Our project-by-project categorization indicates substantially lower numbers than PIMS, with closer to 10 per cent of bilateral British aid likely having positive environmental outcomes in the 1990s (Table 5.2). PIMS appears to overstate DFID's environmental aid: it counts projects across every sector with environmental improvement components, even those with other primary objectives. In the PIMS system, agricultural, forestry, and energy efficiency projects all automatically receive an Environmental Protection (EP) mark, regardless of their overall environmental impact. In Chapter 2, we explained why such coding rules by aid agencies are problematic.[41] Our re-analysis of OECD sector codes showed that forestry sector projects, for example, varied tremendously in their likely environmental impact. 'Forestry sector' projects range from clear-cutting to biodiversity reforestation projects. However, both PIMS and PLAID numbers do agree that environmental aid has increased; PIMS reports that environmental aid increased 2–3 times during the 1990s, and PLAID shows a similar trend, with a huge increase from the early 1980s.

---

[37] DFID (1997: 6–7). [38] DFID (1997: 50–8). [39] DFID (2001).
[40] Hayter (1989: 75). [41] Flint (2000: 13–14).

In the mid-1980s, DFID (then the ODA) began prioritizing environmental issues because of international and domestic public pressure.[42] Britain was channeling over 10 per cent of its overseas development assistance through the World Bank at that time, and tended to follow the Bank's lead in foreign aid matters, including structural adjustment (requiring poorer countries to reduce debt and inflation by sharply cutting government spending, including on social programs). However, domestic political pressure from citizens and lobbying by NGOs pushed DFID to focus more on environmental issues. DFID made a few small changes, such as the establishment of a Natural Resources and Environment Department, staffed by twelve advisers, in 1986. However, throughout the 1980s and mid-1990s, Britain's Conservative government was not as pro-environment as the US or the World Bank, insisting that environmental conditionality be approached 'with circumspection.'[43]

DFID reports from the early 1990s claimed that it was making strides in its environmental assessment procedure for all projects, though it remained 'lightweight and informal' when compared to the stringent policies of donors like the World Bank.[44] DFID's first Manual of Environmental Appraisal (MEA) was published in 1989. Under the MEA framework, only in the initial stages of a project would environmental impacts be evaluated, with the submission of an Environmental Screening Summary. If the screening showed that environmental impacts were significant, further action could in principle be taken. However, a 2000 Environmental Evaluation Synthesis Study (EESS) stated that '[none of the] project managers of the EESS sample projects [was] able to identify a case in which use of the MEA had affected the design or implementation of any DFID project.'[45] Much like broad allocation patterns, the policies regarding environmental assessment changed dramatically in the mid-1990s.

The UK is unusual in its dedication to green environmental projects, spending nearly as much on them as brown environmental projects. Brown aid saw two flush years in the 1980s, but then a sharp return to earlier levels until the entirely atypical spike in 1992 of over $250 million. Green aid, in contrast, rose in 1990 to over $50 million and remained at that level until rising sharply again in 1998 to levels above those of brown aid. Across different recipients of UK aid, the programs varied widely. For instance, in Tanzania, Kenya, and Brazil, most environmental projects (72 per cent) were green, involving forestry protection, biodiversity, and family planning. Brown projects in those countries focused primarily on community natural resource

---

[42] Several focus areas for DFID include humanitarian aid, of which the United Kingdom is the largest bilateral donor in the world, education, and debt relief.

[43] Hayter (1989: 91, 102).   [44] Hayter (1989).   [45] Hayter (1989: 18, 51–4).

management and water and sanitation projects.[46] However, in more recent years, there are initial indications that DFID's emphasis on the environment has been eclipsed by a focus on poverty reduction.[47]

The National Interest, Economic Growth, and Global Public Goods: USAID and the Environment

The US Agency for International Development (USAID) was launched soon after the Cuban Revolution in 1961, under President's John F. Kennedy's 'Decade of Development,' as the main instrument through which the US could influence developing country governments during the Cold War with non-military aid.[48] Since then, USAID has moved in and out of favor as a tool used by the President and the US Congress to conduct foreign policy or reward domestic constituencies. Under President Ronald Reagan, security interests dominated the US government's foreign aid strategy. To combat emerging communist threats, significant funds were channeled to countries like El Salvador, Guatemala, the Philippines, and Indonesia.[49] President Reagan also advocated an explicit policy of linking foreign aid disbursements to a country's level of compliance with US interests in UN voting.[50] As we saw in Chapter 4, aid flows and UN voting patterns are not correlated in the direction we predicted (that is, recipients vote against donors overall), so the overall success of such political conditionality is open to question.

[46] Yet in other countries, brown projects like 'rural livelihoods' and water and sanitation were the main focus, including in India (65%) and China (61%); green projects in these countries tended to fund family planning and sustainable agriculture. This sector concentration by country was deliberately designed to concentrate DFID's limited resources Hayter (1989: 15).

[47] For example, in the recent draft of India's Country Strategic Plan (CSP), the environment is not identified as a priority for the DFID program, as it was in the CSPs of the mid-1990s. The DFID environmental aid to India that did continue beyond 1999 tended to be marbled with poverty alleviation. For instance, approximately $30 million for the Karantaka Watershed Development Project (KAWAD) was disbursed from 1998 to June 2005. Final evaluations of the project stress its success in helping residents of the watershed to increase their incomes and construct their own houses, although the original purpose involved sustainable management of the natural resources and protection of the watershed upon which 70% of the residents depended. DFID (2003).

[48] During the early years of USAID, project design was loosely based on W. W. Rostow's theory of economic development, which postulated that initial industrial take-off was the key to development planning. Roberts and Hite (2007). In response to observations that economic growth was not reaching the poor, the focus later shifted to economic equity and basic human needs. Butterfield (2004: 315).

[49] USAID was not the only bilateral aid agency involved in aid allocation for geopolitical interests. For a discussion of the domestic politics of US aid to Central America allocated by an understudied agency of the US government (the Inter-American Foundation), see Lyne et al. (2006).

[50] Kegley and Hook (1991).

USAID addressed very few environmental issues before the 1970s.[51] However, the UN Conference on the Human Environment in 1972 prompted significant concern for environmental issues. Under President Carter's direction, USAID's forestry sector was tasked with leading the effort in environmental protection. As with much early environmental work in poor countries, initial projects during the 1970s mirrored domestic environmental concerns in donor countries. After a lawsuit was brought against the agency in 1975 to force environmental impact analyses on US investments, environmental compliance regulations were placed on USAID projects.[52] However, it was not until after the Rio Earth Summit that USAID changed its environmental programs to include sectors beyond natural resource management, such as urban pollution management and energy efficiency.[53]

The US sent $11.4 billion abroad during the 1980s and 1990s for environmental protection. Over $7.5 billion of that was in the 1990s (Table 5.1), but the US was an early leader in giving a substantial proportion of its aid to the environment in the 1980s. Environmental funding from USAID was near $400 million a year until 1994, when it spiked at over a billion dollars. Funding quickly fell back in 1995 and 1996, and only returned to its 1994 level after 1998 (Figure 5.6). The large decrease in 1995 corresponds with the return of a Republican Congress that sought to cut spending, especially in areas such as family planning and environmental protection.[54] US funding for green and brown projects (for global and local public goods, respectively) was almost even for the 1980s. Both totaled about $200 million a year, which was very unusual at that time (Figure 5.6b). After 1991, however, green aid increased much faster than brown aid. Brown aid rose to roughly $320 million through the 1990s, while green aid increased sharply (except during the 1995 funding crisis), tripling to $1 billion in 1999. This increase in the late 1990s made the US by far the world's largest funder of green projects.

USAID's justification for environmental aid reflects the importance of national self-interest in US foreign aid policy. As Tom Barry explains,

---

[51] Butterfield (2004: 315).

[52] Ivory (1992); USAID (2005). While environmental consequences must be identified and considered for every USAID project, no one environmental consequence will ultimately exclude a project from being funded. While USAID has strong environmental assessment procedures, the high number of 'opt out' opportunities makes it easy for those who know the details of the compliance mechanisms to get around the long decision process. Aid for disasters, emergencies, and sensitive foreign policy issues are automatically exempt from environmental compliance regulations. Only heavy industrial projects are required to go through the entire environmental regulation compliance procedures, which involve environmental impact assessments done both by USAID and independent contractors.

[53] Harris (2001: 276).

[54] Family planning also reaches its highest percentage of total environmental aid in 1994 (7.6%—$525,697,354) to drop again as well in 1995.

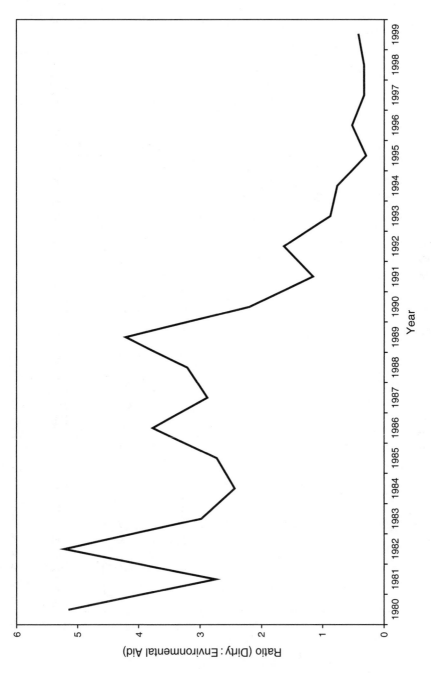

Figure 5.6a. Ratio of 'dirty' to environmental aid given by United States of America, 1980–1999

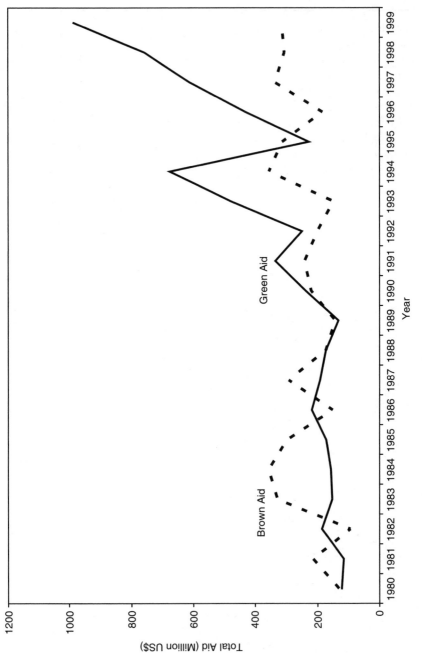

Figure 5.6b. Green and brown aid given by United States of America, 1980–1999

'[e]nvironmental degradation and inefficient use of natural resources pose a growing threat to the interests of the United States... The global challenges of climate change and loss of biodiversity, combined with the consequences of local environmental mismanagement, such as social instability and conflicts over resources, threaten America's own economic and national security interests.'[55] Former USAID administrator Brian Atwood also made a case for US environmental assistance by reaching out to commercial interests. He once remarked, 'Does it make any sense for America to turn away from a $300 billion annual market in environmental goods? Without US support for environmental programs, American firms will be losing their comparative advantage. It makes no sense at all to drastically cut these funds and shoot our own businesspeople in the foot.'[56] The next chapter allows us to test whether allocation decisions of donors track with domestic economic interests, or whether other factors highlighted in these case studies are more important (such as political parties, the strength of environmental NGOs, or geo-strategic interests).

From Laggard to Environmental Leader? Japan

Japan is one of the few donor countries that actually started out as an aid recipient. While its economy was in ruins after the Second World War, its recovery (aided by Western assistance) was so rapid that twelve years after the war's end, in 1957, it was prepared to begin giving aid itself. From its inception, Japanese aid was significantly different from much Western aid in its intent and implementation. While most Western aid has been justified largely in altruistic terms—to raise living standards in less developed countries—Japanese aid has not historically had this objective. Its own agency reports suggest as much.[57] Some observers attribute this difference to Japan's lack of a religious tradition that emphasizes charity towards the poor.[58] For whatever reason, aid is conceived as a tool to help achieve Japan's foreign policy aims. Among these aims were acceptance by other donor countries, mending political ties broken in the Second World War, and fostering pro-Japanese attitudes in countries that exported raw materials to Japan or offered investment or export opportunities to Japanese manufacturers.[59]

This difference in intent also manifested itself in the type of aid given by Japan. In 1957, when Japan first began to disburse aid, it focused on south Asia as a region with large potential markets. From 1957 to 1964, 16 out of Japan's 21 loan agreements were with India and Pakistan, provided at a fairly high interest rate of 6 per cent, and tied directly to purchases from Japan.[60] This set a precedent for the next few decades. During this period,

---

[55] Barry (1996).   [56] Barry (1996).   [57] Rix (1989: 15).   [58] Rix (1989: 16).
[59] Rix (1989: 93, 17, 135); Arase (1995: 9).   [60] Rix (1989: 137).

Japan became one of the world's top donors. Foreign aid paralleled its rise as an economic superpower.[61] However, Japanese aid became notorious for being composed mostly of loans instead of concessional grants, securing access to raw materials, being tied to purchases from Japan, focusing heavily on strategic areas of Asia, and serving Japan's self-interest rather than the needs of less developed countries.[62] Japan argued that its vulnerability forced it to use development assistance as a means to strengthen its international economic capacity. Its aid agencies frequently report that as a recently industrialized non-Western country Japan can share important lessons with other developing countries and forge stronger links between the North and the South.[63]

More than any other major donor country, Japan has historically required recipients to spend its funds on Japanese products or services in an arrangement known as 'tied aid.'[64] From 1978 onward, Japan pursued a general policy of untying loans, but in 1986 Japanese companies were still winning 67 per cent of the 'untied' loan contracts.[65] Faced with continuing criticism over this practice, Japan's Ministry of Foreign Affairs (MOFA) made efforts in the 1990s to open up Japanese aid contracts to companies from other countries. By that standard, the effort was successful: in 1999 Japanese companies won only 19 per cent of untied loan contracts.[66] However, it had the unintended consequence of weakening support for development assistance within the Japanese legislature. The loss of aid contracts for Japanese companies reinforced the sense among the Japanese business community that ODA was no longer important to their interests.[67] This, combined with the economic crisis of the late 1990s, contributed to an unprecedented (for Japan) reduction in ODA that began in 1998 and continued throughout the first half of this decade.

Japan's concern for environmental aid dates from the mid-1980s, and was a response to international and domestic criticism that its aid—focused as it was on heavy industry—contributed seriously to global environmental

---

[61] Arase (1995: 1). [62] Arase (1995); Rix (1989: 20).

[63] However, some would argue that partly due to Japan's near-complete inattention to the needs of the LDCs that received its aid, this envisioned role never materialized. Rix (1989: 31).

[64] Japan is also notorious for its complex and opaque system of aid administration. It has never had a centralized aid agency or ministry; aid today is coordinated between some thirteen cabinet-level bureaucratic actors, and technical cooperation, grant aid, and loan aid are handled by separate organizations. The Japan Bank for International Cooperation (JBIC, which was created in 1999 from the merger of the OECF and the Japan Export-Import Bank JEXIM), currently funds aid that responds to Japanese commercial and political interests. JICA, on the other hand, is responsible for aid that is more in line with international norms and expectations. Arase (1995: 273).

[65] Rix (1989: 109). Contractors for all grant projects had to be Japanese nationals, who were likely to purchase Japanese goods for the project.

[66] Arase (1995: 4). [67] Arase (1995: 4).

degradation, especially the destruction of tropical forests.[68] In 1986, Japan's Overseas Economic Cooperation Fund (OECF) published a report recommending that aid include environmental impact assessment measures, a recommendation that was echoed one year later by Japan's Environmental Protection Agency. This translated into diplomatic action at the Paris G-7 summit in 1989, where Japan made a major commitment to environmental aid of ¥300 billion (about $2 billion in 1990 dollars) over the next three years. In September of 1989, Japan hosted an international conference on environmental protection in Tokyo. Japan identified its priorities as forest protection, urban air pollution mitigation measures, and assisting LDCs in managing their own environmental problems, in keeping with the Japanese emphasis on 'self-help.'[69] Before 1989, there was little mention of the environment in the annual reports of the Japan International Cooperation Agency (JICA). Reports after this date, however, all contain strong language on the importance of sustainable development and environmental priorities. The Rio Earth Summit in 1992 reinforced this trend, with Japan identifying the environment as a central consideration in policy formulation and making a very significant new commitment to spend ¥1 trillion ($8 billion in 1992 dollars) on environmental projects over the next five years. Japan also pledged to finance large-scale projects, such as a $500 million loan in 1990 for air-quality improvement in Mexico City, and aid middle-income countries that were the worst hit by environmental degradation.

Yet, even when environmental assistance was at its peak, it was dwarfed by the massive amount of Japanese aid allocated for dirty projects. Dirty aid did see a gradual decline over the twenty-year period, from 71 per cent of total lending in 1980 to 50 per cent in 1999, but even in the mid-1990s dirty aid made up almost two-thirds of Japan's total aid portfolio (Figure 5.7a).[70] One fluctuation came in 1991, when dirty projects comprised just 19 per cent of the total Japanese aid budget. However, the next year they were back at a normal level of about 56 per cent dirty aid. Annual reports from JICA, while consistently emphasizing the need for environmental action throughout the 1990s, never once mention the idea of cutting back on lending to environmentally harmful projects. Japan did make attempts to mitigate the destructive effects of projects such as dams, roads, and power plants by sending teams of environmental experts to judge their impacts and ameliorate some of their effects, but such economic infrastructure projects were too

---

[68] Rix (1989: 124); Dauvergne (1997); Kim (2006).

[69] JICA (1993: 20); Rix (1989: 124); Kim (2006).

[70] In this respect, Japan is still less environmental than European and American donors. While Japan has dramatically increased its allocation of environmental aid, it has not reduced dirty aid to the same extent as most other bilateral donors.

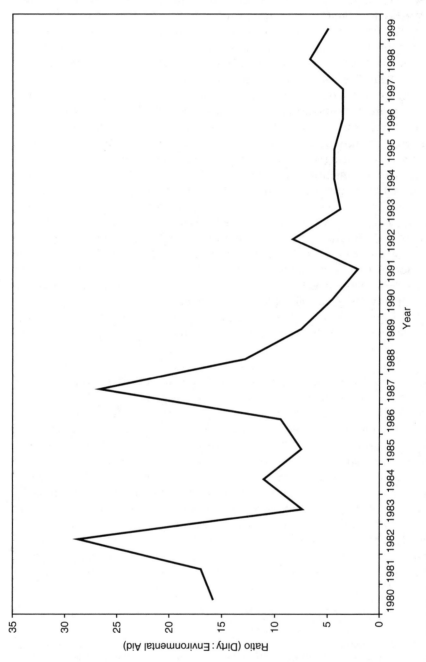

Figure 5.7a. Ratio of 'dirty' to environmental aid given by Japan, 1980–1999

firmly entrenched in Japan's aid philosophy to substantially reduce them as other bilateral donors have done.[71]

Of the $17.6 billion in environmental aid given by Japan over these two decades, about 2.5 times as much was given for brown projects as for green ones (Figure 5.7b). The economic crisis in the late 1990s led to deep cutbacks: environmental aid received less total funding and received a smaller percentage of the funds that were available. Japanese aid organizations were so overwhelmed with the Asian financial crisis that environmental issues were not even mentioned in JICA's 1998 annual report, despite having a designated section for environmental issues in the previous nine years. Given these trends, Japan's position as a permanent leader in environmental aid is not at all certain.

Conclusions

This chapter lays the groundwork for the formal hypothesis-building and testing that we perform in Chapter 6. There we seek to explain the cross-national patterns in environmental behavior that we have described here. Some general trends are apparent, but the cases make clear that donors are different in important ways. The five major bilateral donors described in this chapter illustrate the importance of Second World War reconstruction in their founding and structure. In the cases of Japan and Germany, the reconstruction of their international standing as members of the global community was a primary motivation. Japan's foreign aid was for decades self-described as securing access to resources and markets, especially in South-East Asia. The importance of the Cold War in driving aid decisions for four decades (the 1950s to the 1980s) by all five donors cannot be underestimated, especially since US Funding often flowed to frontline states and to projects that were designed to demonstrate the advantages of capitalism and slow the spread of Soviet and Chinese influence.

These cases also suggest the importance of domestic politics within donor countries. As left and right parties gain control of the legislative or executive branches and bring their particular visions and coalition of supporters, they often change the amount and direction of aid. The long rise and influence of Germany's Green Party created political pressure for its five main aid agencies to fund environmental projects, and its aid is now among the greenest in the world. In the UK, Labour's election in 1997 brought significant increases in environmental aid funding. After the study period of this book, Denmark's ruling Liberal Party's long tenure ended in 2005, and both environmental and development efforts now face sharp cutbacks. These cases suggest that to understand green aid's past and likely future, serious research is needed on

[71] JICA (1996: 24); Kim (2006).

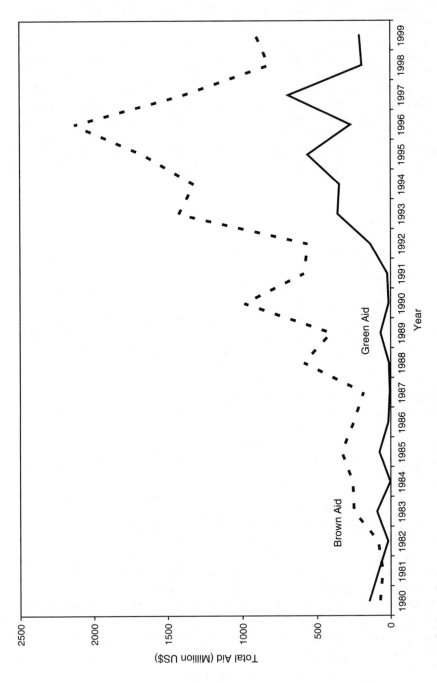

Figure 5.7b. Green and brown aid given by Japan, 1980–1999

the political coalitions that support and oppose the appropriation of taxpayer money for foreign environmental assistance. In the next chapter, we seek to develop and test a series of hypotheses on the role of environmental technology sectors and environmental NGOs in creating the political conditions for environmental aid to increase—what have been dubbed 'coalitions of the green and greedy.'

The sudden shift in Japan's aid in 1986–9 bears careful study, since it jumped to the top of the list of environmental aid donors in a comparatively short time period. Long a strategic donor that tied its aid to geopolitics, resource extraction, and the purchase of Japanese products and services, Japan's 1989 pledge of billions of yen in environmental aid at the G-7 summit in Paris marked a huge shift in priorities. That Japan chose the Rio Earth Summit in 1992 to announce another even larger goal suggested to some observers that Japan was responding to outside criticism that its aid was mostly focused on heavy industry and was a main cause of environmental degradation in developing countries. However, the sudden reduction of environmental projects in the late 1990s suggests that neither the Japanese government, nor any supporting coalition, has institutionalized the idea of sustainable development within the Japanese aid regime.

The overall trends and the five donor cases in this chapter demonstrate that environmental aid has grown sharply in importance for bilateral agencies over these two decades. In each case, the ratio of dirty project funding to environmental project funding plummeted over these twenty years, marking a significant reorientation of aid. Dirty aid was relatively flat in total dollars spent over most of the period, but then dropped sharply in the early 1990s and again in the late 1990s (Figures 5.1 and 5.2). The data also suggest the immense impact of the 1992 Rio Earth Summit, bringing short-term bumps in environment aid (including billions for sewage projects in Rio itself) and longer-term increases. Indeed, environmental aid in the 1990s was three times that of the 1980s.

The comparison of Britain's internal accounting system for environmental aid (PIMS) with our PLAID categorization suggests that we should be cautious about accepting aid agency reports on what percentage of their aid is 'environmental.' In Britain's case, projects whose main goals were not environmental and whose overall impacts could actually be environmentally damaging were counted as 'environmental.'[72] Pressure on agencies to show

[72] A serious measurement problem that we discuss in this book and in previous articles has to do with marbled or mainstreamed environmental aid—where a traditional project has environmental components, usually to mitigate some expected damage that will result from the primary purpose of the project. Neither the PLAID database, nor any other empirical effort of which we are aware, has definitively solved this measurement problem. This problem almost certainly leads us (and other analysts) to undercount the amount of development assistance that is spent on environmental protection or remediation. See Chapters 2 and 9 of this book and also Nielson and Tierney (2003, 2005). Also see Powers (2008).

they are 'doing something about the environment' (combined with relative difficulty in monitoring agency claims) suggests why over-reporting might be so prevalent. If donor governments have political incentives to convince others that they are having a positive impact on the environment, then they will be tempted to over-state their contributions. This reinforces the need for independent and systematic reviews, like this one.

The current trend in foreign aid is to focus on Africa and to 'make poverty history' by meeting the Millennium Development Goals (reducing poverty and other social ills by half by 2015). British foreign aid remains focused on poverty reduction, but there is growing pressure for the agency to consider climate change and other environmental issues. The former head of DFID, Clare Short, gave a blistering speech to environmentalists at the World Wildlife Fund's Washington, DC, office in 2003. She argued that environmentalists must move away from lobbying against individual development projects to advocating sustainable development for the world's poor. Nevertheless, DFID's funding profile has shifted in a way that is quite similar to most other bilateral donors': increasing attention to both green and brown environmental issues.

Looking to Chapter 6, we test a series of hypotheses derived from the most relevant theories about what might cause certain donor countries to spend more or less on foreign aid for the environment. Chapter 6 is essentially an exercise in comparative foreign policy analysis. To what extent are large commitments to environmental aid in countries like Denmark and Germany a reflection of strong preferences for environmental protection at home? To what extent is it the reflection of wealth and post-materialist values? How much variation is explained by coalitions of the 'green and greedy'— environmental technology firms and environmental NGOs? Is some of the pattern simply explained by the way budget decisions are made and whether social groups are incorporated into corporatist decision-making structures? Do geopolitical considerations shape environmental aid allocation in the same way that they shape other allocation decisions? Informed by the trends and brief case studies described in this chapter, we turn now to the development of formal hypotheses and statistical tests of these alternative explanations.

6

The Political Market for Environmental Aid: Why Some Donors are Greener Than Others

Chapter 5 highlighted the significant variation in donor countries' commitment to environmental protection. Some donors, such as Japan, have dramatically re-aligned their aid portfolios in the span of a decade to be more responsive to environmental objectives. Other donors, such as Denmark, have historically given large amounts of aid (as a percentage of GDP) and consistently allocated a large proportion of their aid budgets to social and environmental projects. Still others, such as the UK, have made significant changes following an election. In this chapter, we use systematic evidence to examine the issue of why some donor governments are more willing than others to spend taxpayer funds on environmental protection in developing countries.

We test four sets of possible explanations for why countries give bilateral environmental aid, and for why they give relatively less aid with likely environmentally harmful impacts ('dirty' aid). First, we test whether environmental aid as a proportion of donor portfolios reflects their broader environmental preferences, as revealed in domestic environmental policy, ratification of international environmental treaties, and their compliance with these treaties. Second, we test theories claiming that people change their values when they have satisfied their basic human needs. In particular, we examine the effects of wealth and 'post-materialist values' on the share of a donor country's aid portfolio earmarked for environmental and dirty projects. Third, we explore a political economy approach to aid allocation that suggests the relative strength of environmental NGO and industry lobbies in shaping the environmental profile of aid portfolios. Fourth, we test propositions from new institutionalist theory by examining whether environmental aid is influenced by the number of checks and balances in government and whether there is a corporatist or pluralist decision-making structure within a donor polity.

In addition to examining institutions independent of societal preferences, we explore the impact of left-wing and right-wing parties within legislative institutions. Is the reputation for environmentalism among left-wing parties reflected in the aid portfolios of their governments when in power? Do left-wing governments allocate more money for environmental projects and relatively less money to dirty projects than do right-wing governments?

The first set of hypotheses build upon the logic of principal–agent theory, which suggests that voters in democratic states are ultimately empowered to remove politicians that do not follow their policy preferences. In this view, there is a 'political market' for environmental aid in wealthy countries, and this market is shaped by the preferences of voters within each country. We empirically evaluate two alternative hypotheses about aid allocation that highlight very different political logics. In the first, developed country citizens authorize and financially empower their elected officials to resolve specific regional and international environmental problems that affect them. The preferences of citizens for their government to spend relatively large or small amounts on a clean environment should be revealed in the strength of domestic environmental policy. So, governments with robust environmental protections at home will be rewarded electorally for distributing foreign aid that is beneficial to the natural environment or minimizes environmental damage. Conversely, governments with lax environmental regulations at home will not face the same constraints when allocating foreign aid abroad.

In the second hypothesis, governments provide environmental aid in order to reflect the post-materialist values of their citizens, even if those citizens receive no direct benefit from the allocation. Ronald Inglehart has argued that the world's wealthier nations are increasingly 'post-materialist' in that they value services and experiences over material products, and that demand for an improved quality of life (including a clean environment) is superseding demands for more material goods.[1] The basic post-materialism argument is that when standards of living increase to levels where concerns for material needs are diminished, citizens pay more attention to social and environmental issues (at least when it comes to voting). Inglehart and his colleagues have conducted a number of cross-national surveys that allow us to explore this idea empirically.

What drives and sustains Western environmental aid budgets? If Western citizens are primarily motivated by post-materialist values, we would expect their governments to promote environmental values abroad in an altruistic and non-discriminatory manner. However, if Western support for environmental aid is tied to specific trans-boundary environmental threats that affect the interests of voters within donor countries, we would expect a more selective allocation of environmental assistance—both among implementing

---

[1] Inglehart (1990).

agencies and recipient countries. Are wealthier donors only willing to pay for projects that address global public goods such as climate change, ozone, and biodiversity that might affect them, or are they willing to fund more local environmental projects, like the construction of drinking water and sewage treatment systems or preventing erosion in poor countries? The analysis in this chapter provides some evidence about how income and distinct national preferences shape the aid allocation priorities, and thus disbursements, of different donor governments.

We also test for the impact of interest group influence by environmental advocacy, environmental technology, and industry lobbies. Here again, there are implications for the geographic distribution and effectiveness of environmental aid. Recall from Chapter 1 that we model the aid allocation decision as a series of nested principal–agent relationships where voters in donor countries delegate authority to elected officials who then delegate to aid agencies (either multilateral or bilateral). These aid agencies are then authorized to negotiate aid contracts with recipients in developing countries. If Western environmental NGOs play a determinative role at the agenda-setting stage, then green environmental projects targeting global or regional public good provision will likely be funded at the expense of locally focused brown environmental projects favored by recipient governments. If social justice or global poverty groups are more influential, or if industry groups have more influence, then different trends should result. There is a new 'green products and services' branch of industry which stands to benefit from the types of spending that environmental aid projects bring: wind turbines, energy efficient technology, lower-input agricultural systems, sustainability consulting and so on. Some estimates of the current and likely near-future size of this industry are huge. These environmental industry groups may join with mainstream environmentalists to create 'coalitions of the green and greedy,' strengthening domestic support for environmental aid budgets.

However the impact of these social groups on actual policy, budgeting, and implementation depends on how their preferences and demands are aggregated and mediated by domestic institutions within the state. Therefore, our fourth set of hypotheses examines whether the domestic institutions— party structures, institutional veto gates, and the corporatist/pluralist nature of the policy-making process—structure the political market and therefore measurably promote or hinder appropriations of 'dirty' aid and environmental projects of different types.

The analysis in this chapter empirically examines the impact of these factors on aid shares of seventeen bilateral donors over the twelve years when the data were best, 1988 to 1999. As it turns out, we were far more effective at explaining the decrease in environmentally damaging aid, developing models that account for up to two-thirds of that 'dirty' aid. To preview what lies ahead, we found that as wealth increases in donor countries, dirty aid decreases as a fraction of that country's total aid portfolio. To a lesser degree, the more prevalent post-materialist values were found to be in national surveys, the less dirty aid donors gave. As political economy theories suggest, environmental/green industry lobbying groups tend to reduce the share of aid allocated to dirty projects, but only increase funding for global goods projects, not local environmental projects. The factors influencing the environmental, green, and brown sectors were not as clear overall, and our models were not as effective in predicting aid shares. When we use a broad measure of revealed government preferences for (domestic and international) environmental protection, our results suggest that having better environmental policies at home correlates *negatively* with spending on environmental aid projects abroad. However, more direct measures of a donor's *international* environmental policy appear to correspond to *increases* in the share of aid earmarked for environmental purposes. We also find that the strength of a donor country's environmental advocacy and technology lobby tends to increase the share of aid allocated to *green* projects and decrease the share of aid allocated to *brown* projects. We conclude by discussing the implications of these findings and outlining a number of avenues for future research.

Hypotheses: Aid Reflects National Policy, National Wealth, and Post-Materialist Values

We begin with a discussion about how voter preferences interact with donor institutions to create a political market for environmental aid, building on principal–agent theory. Citizens entrust their governments with many day-to-day operational and oversight responsibilities, among them international environmental concerns.[2] Citizens authorize and financially empower their elected officials to resolve specific regional and international environmental problems that affect them. Therefore, citizens and politicians do not 'contract' on the issue of environmental aid. Rather, their focus is on stabilizing the

---

[2] To understand the 'political market' for environmental aid, one must consider both the supply side and the demand side of the electoral marketplace. According to Douglass North (1981), Barry Weingast (1995), and Mancur Olson (1993), the state is a functional response to social needs of individuals living in a particular territory. Individuals would benefit from things like law and order, justice, national defense, and environmental protection, but these types of goods possess non-rival and non-excludable characteristics and are prone to market failure. Thus, in the absence of verifiable and enforceable individual commitments to contribute to these collective goods, each individual has an incentive to free-ride on the efforts of others. Under these circumstances, 'political markets' often emerge. Citizens demand public goods, but since they themselves are unable to provide them voluntarily, they collectively 'hire' an agent (Leviathan) to coerce the contributions of others through the mechanism of contract enforcement. Such a delegation of authority promotes public good provision. In the language of agency theory, principals (or citizens) require an agent (or state) with a 'comparative advantage in violence' to reduce their short-term incentives for defection North (1981: 21).

atmosphere, conserving biodiversity, protecting international waters, reducing acid rain, halting ozone depletion, and so forth.[3] Within these larger negotiating sets, citizens grant their elected officials the formal authority to transfer aid overseas when doing so advances their interests. In this framework, foreign aid is conceived as one of many potential policy tools that an elected leader might employ in pursuit of these interests.

This framework, which employs what we call the 'revealed environmental policy preference' approach, departs from Milner's (2006) aid allocation model in an important way. Unlike Milner's model, in this view the electorate's core motivation in distributing environmental as well as other types of international public goods is not altruism. Instead, citizens are assumed to be concerned about their own welfare, which may be directly affected by international environmental problems. Citizens have good information about the environment and have clearly defined preferences over environmental goods and services, whether local, national, or global. Specifically, they demand international environmental protection and authorize international financial transfers in the interest of maximizing their own material welfare.[4] Again, environmental aid is unique in that its explicit purpose is often regional or global public good provision, which means that rich country citizens gain or lose utility based on the effectiveness of the international financial transfer.[5]

This distinction is important because voters don't get immediate feedback when someone or some country is not contributing to environmental goods, but eventually they will experience change if the global commons is damaged. Much of the foreign aid literature assumes that there is a 'severed feedback

---

[3] Hassler (2002), Lofstedt (1994, 1995), Lofstedt and Sjostedt (1996), and Lewis (2003) all suggest that specific trans-boundary environmental issues motivate citizens to pressure their elected officials to use aid as a positive incentive to induce compliance with international environmental agreements.

[4] When delegating authority to politicians and government institutions, citizens are of course not always able to get what they want. The politics of development assistance is a series of multi–principal–multi-agent relationships in which the voters cannot fully contract due to information asymmetries and high transaction costs. Therefore, the revealed patterns of aid allocation may shed light on the preferences of the electorate, but differ significantly depending on the nature of the good being pursued (international public goods vs. non-IPG) and the potential aid delivery channel.

[5] It is not surprising that environmental aid programs often ride on the coattails of public concern—particularly when public perceptions of vulnerability to global and regional environmental threats build to a sharp crescendo. For example, toward the end of 1988, *Time Magazine* ran an important issue on global environmental crises and awarded Planet Earth the dubious distinction of 'Planet of the Year.' The release of this issue coincided with one of the worst heat waves and droughts ever to hit the United States, ominous reports about a growing hole in the ozone layer, the release of satellite images of a burning Amazon, and James Hansen's famous congressional testimony on global climate change Bowles and Kormos (1999). A year later, OECD parties to the Montreal Protocol acknowledged a need for environmental assistance to developing countries. Shortly thereafter, wealthy countries also requested that the World Bank consider establishing a separate funding facility for global environmental problems, which eventually evolved into the GEF Keohane and Levy (1996).

loop' which separates the taxpayers who fund aid projects and the people who benefit from them. Milner (2006), for example, argues that 'voters in the donor countries have *an impossible time* evaluating how aid is being used in [recipient countries].... [T]he feedback loop is broken and the public paying taxes for aid has little knowledge to use to reward or punish their agents for foreign aid outcomes.'[6] Similarly, Martens et al. (2002) argue that 'the most striking characteristic of foreign aid is that the same people for whose benefit aid agencies work are not the same as those from whom their revenues are obtained; they actually live in different countries and different political constituencies.' Thus, unlike say taxpayer-supported local services like policing or the postal service, 'this geographic and political separation between beneficiaries and taxpayers blocks the normal performance feedback process: beneficiaries may be able to observe performance but cannot modulate payments as a function of performance.'[7]

One could argue that unlike traditional foreign aid interventions, the outcomes associated with global public good funding are more observable and thus more vulnerable to public scrutiny. If a World Bank construction project in north-east Brazil is undermined by corruption or a USAID education project in Malawi turns out to be a spectacular failure, for example, citizens of Western countries have a limited ability to acquire such information and thus no reason to hold their politicians accountable and demand better service delivery. Politicians and donor agencies also have strong incentives to conceal failures and showcase successes, creating even more 'noise' for ordinary citizens in rich countries.[8] Yet, if a USAID project in Russia designed to eliminate the production and consumption of ozone-depleting substances fails, Western citizens—who themselves will eventually experience the effects of ozone layer depletion—should be in a relatively better position to assess whether the policies implemented by their government officials have been effective (in the longer term and subject to international monitoring and Earth System cycles). They certainly should care more.

However, financial transfers for international environmental protection (and other international public goods) are different from traditional forms of aid in that rich country citizens possess more and higher-quality information about the impact of their giving. The informational environment that elected officials and citizens have is better because citizens themselves are eventually directly affected by damage to global and regional public goods, and they want to know whether future disruptions are likely. If the international financial system becomes unstable, global terrorism increases, or the ozone layer continues to decay, Western citizens suffer a direct utility loss and they often know it. Even if they don't perceive a change in the public good, scientific and policy networks, NGOs, and the media will loudly announce the failure and

---

[6] Milner (2006), emphasis added.   [7] Martens et al. (2002: 14).   [8] Milner (2006).

the coming disaster they fear. Therefore, voters are able to make more reliable assessments about whether the aid policies pursued by their elected leaders have been successful, and reward or punish them accordingly.[9] For instance, Swedish and Finnish citizens possess a significant amount of information about the effectiveness of their acid rain reduction programs in neighboring Baltic countries because they directly experience the effects of trans-boundary air pollution.[10] From this logic, we derive our first two hypotheses about countries acting in foreign affairs as they do at home:

Hypothesis 1a: The intensity of a donor country's *domestic* environmental policy preferences will be positively reflected in the share of its foreign aid budget dedicated to environmental issues.

Hypothesis 1b: The intensity of a donor country's *international* environmental policy preferences will positively correlate with the share of its foreign aid budget dedicated to 'green' issues.

Cross-national, longitudinal measures of national environmental policy preferences are surprisingly difficult to obtain, even for the two dozen environmental aid donors considered in this chapter. To measure a country's revealed preference for environmental protection, we use the Environmental Policy Index (EPI), which ranks donor countries on twenty-two measures of domestic and international environmental policy.[11] The overall score is an average percentile ranking of these measures; a higher score on the EPI signifies a stronger revealed preference for environmental protection. We also include two measures that more directly capture the intensity of a donor country's *international* environmental policy preferences. The first is a measure of national ratification of a series of major environmental treaties over the twelve-year period (treaties%; H1c). Higher scores indicate higher levels of participation. The second indicator, developed from annual survey data of business leaders on their perception of whether their government is serious about complying with environmental treaties, is from the World Economic Forum's Global Competitiveness Report (wefagr). A higher score on this seven-point metric indicates a stronger revealed preference for international environmental protection.

Voter preferences could also be motivated by a broader set of post-materialist values. The strength of these values varies over time and across countries. As incomes rise and survival become less of a concern, the relative worth of market goods declines relative to scarce environmental commodities,

---

[9] This assumption is quite similar to the assumptions made in models of retrospective voting where the electorate uses information about aggregate outcomes in order to make judgements about incumbent officials Fiorina (1981).

[10] Levy (1993); Hassler (2002, 2003); Albin (2003); Lofstedt and Sjostedt (1996); Lofstedt (1995).

[11] Nielson and Tierney (2003).

leisure, the arts, and other non-market goods. The rise of post-materialism may also signal a 'value shift' away from egoism and instrumental rationality toward altruism, equality, and redistribution for its own sake.[12] Alternatively, it can be seen as another layer of wishes and concerns layered upon survival and materialist ones. Again, Inglehart's post-materialism hypothesis has been criticized on many grounds,[13] but it allows some insight into whether attitudes are changing on value-based issues that might influence voter willingness to fund environmental aid. If post-materialism affects voter preferences in this broader way, we would expect elected governments to respond to citizens' environmental values abroad in a more altruistic and non-discriminatory manner, as opposed to using environmental aid as a coercive policy instrument or as a tool to reward political allies.[14] Inglehart distinguishes between environmentalism deriving from 'subjective cultural factors' (i.e. post-materialism) and environmentalism that grows out of responses to specific environmental threats that reduce material utility. We are able to observe the allocation patterns made by donors for global public good aid and more localized environmental aid (and other types of aid), so we can gain some insight into this question.

Hypothesis 2a: The more post-materialist the median voter's preferences, the more environmentally friendly the donor country's foreign aid budget.

Hypothesis 2b: Wealthier countries will be more willing to spend aid money on environmental aid.

As an indicator of the prevalence of post-materialist values, we use Inglehart's World Values Survey. However, significant data limitations restrict our ability to disentangle the post-materialist values of citizens from other fixed effects associated with donor countries.[15] Since Inglehart (1990) points out that post-materialism and GDP per capita are highly correlated, and the Environmental Kuznets Curve (EKC) literature argues that the intensity of environmental preferences rise beyond a certain income threshold, we also settled on GDP per capita (in PPP terms) as an admittedly imperfect second test.[16]

---

[12] The term 'post-materialism' was coined by researchers employing the World Values Survey. See Inglehart (1990); Brechin (1999); Rohrschneider (1988). Inglehart (1995: 63–4).

[13] See e.g. Dunlap et al. (1993); Dunlap and Mertig (1995); Brechin (1999); Guha and Martinez-Alier (1997); Bell (2004).

[14] See Meyer et al. (1997) and Boli and Thomas (1999).

[15] The limited periodicity of World Values Survey data is a severe constraint. The inclusion of such data would effectively capture all fixed effects within a country and would not reveal a reliable estimate of voter preferences for environmental concerns.

[16] These data were taken from the World Bank's World Development Indicators dataset. The lack of good longitudinal data is part of the reason we use GDP per capita to test the effect of post-materialist values.

Alternative Explanations: Political Economy and the Importance of Lobbies

The principal–agent framework is, of course, a radically simplified version of complex social reality. There are many alternative channels through which citizens articulate their interests: environmental and pro-industrial lobby groups, political parties, protests, bribes, and market power. Donor governments also possess different institutions that structure the political market and determine how individual preferences are aggregated and revealed.

While the linkages between special interest groups, the electorate, and elected officials have been explored within a principal–agent framework, we believe that treating lobbying groups as agents for citizens in donor countries is problematic because interest groups have no authority to demand behavioral changes or to remove elected officials under any circumstances. We therefore conceive of interest groups as actors in their own right (third parties), but not principals.[17] However, given the considerable debate in the literature on the influence of special interest groups on environmental policy and environmental aid, we consider them in our empirical models of donor aid portfolios.[18]

[17] To be clear, principal–agent theorists do not deny that other forms of interest articulation 'matter.' They merely suggest that election (or re-election) is the primary constraint facing politicians. In the real world, politicians are rent-seekers and their utility functions are not defined exclusively in terms of votes. In fact, Milner and Tingley (2006) demonstrate that third parties have a substantive and statistically significant effect on the voting behavior of elected officials in the US Congress. These third parties (campaign donors, unions, firms, etc.) have no authority to remove elected officials, but they can certainly shape their calculation of costs and benefits.

[18] In attempting to explain the relationship between interest groups and politicians within donor governments, many foreign aid analysts have drawn upon the insights of agency theory Grossman and Helpman (1994, 1996); Fredriksson (1997); Damania and Fredriksson (2003); Damania (2001); Bernheim and Whinston (1986). Murshed (2003) models competing NGOs as multiple principals of a common agent—the executive, who is responsible for aid policy. Damania (2001) similarly conceives of environmental lobbying groups as principals of a single 'government' agent. Lahiri and Raimondos-Møller (2000) also model ethnic lobbying groups as principals in their own right and try to explain how these actors affect the distribution of aid across the population of potential recipients. Each of these articles examines important aspects of the political economy of aid-giving. However, the analytic assumption common to all of these papers—that all actors with political influence should be modeled as principals—is inconsistent with the core assumptions of agency theory. Much of the rigor in agency theory stems from the fact that analysts can identify principals as those (individual or collective) actors who possess the 'residual rights of control' within a hierarchical contract with some agent that has been conditionally granted authority to act on behalf of the principal Williamson (1979); Lake (1996). While industry lobbyists and environmental NGOs may well influence the behavior of the US President, and it makes sense to document and analyze such influence, it does not follow that these actors have delegated authority to the President to make policy. In the US context the constitution specifies the contract between voters (we the people) and the President. Voters have the authority to elect the President through the Electoral College and they also have the authority to periodically terminate that contract. In economics, the principal is the actor that has the ultimate right over some piece of property.

The authors of the seminal book *Institutions for Environmental Aid* suggest that the political market for environmental aid is dominated by environmental lobbying groups and (environmental) industry groups. Borrowing a concept called 'coalitions of the green and the greedy,' first coined by Kenneth Oye and James Maxwell, Barbara Connolly and her colleagues argue that 'strong political coalitions of environmentalist and industry groupings within donor countries... tend both to justify environmental aid budgets and drive the selection of remedies for environmental problems.'[19] The authors insist that, above all else, governments are responsive to interest groups: 'Without strong political constituencies invested in the mitigation of trans-boundary environmental problems or the export of goods and services made possible by aid programs,' writes Connolly, 'competing priorities within donor countries would eclipse environmental aid budgets.'[20] General public concern is discussed as a potentially important variable at various points throughout the 1996 Keohane and Levy volume; however, when the policy preferences of citizens are discussed, it is only in conjunction with interest group influence. As Connolly puts it, environmental aid can materialize in ' "Stiglerian situations," where the public's desire to improve the environment converges with the self-interest of actors who gain tangible benefits from regulation.'[21]

Of course, interest group influence in Western industrial democracies is not limited to environmental lobbyists. One must also account for the potential role played by groups representing industries that contribute to what we've defined as 'dirty' environmental outcomes. Many corporations are directly involved in the extraction, production, distribution, and consumption of natural resources and therefore vigorously oppose environmental

In domestic politics, a large literature starts by identifying political property rights within various political systems (typically enshrined in a constitution or some other role-defining document). For example, see Romer and Rosenthal (1979); Cox (1987); Carey and Shugart (1992); Pollack (1997); Lupia and McCubbins (1998); Lyne (2008). All these scholars take the formal rules of accountability within the polity at face value and assume that voting citizens possess such residual rights of control in liberal democracies. Roeder (1993), Shirk (1994), and Bueno de Mesquita et al. (2003) make analogous claims regarding the delegation of authority in non-democratic regimes. However, as all major donors of environmental aid are established democracies, we are concerned only with the behavior of elected democratic governments. Voters collectively can offer, abrogate, or rescind any contract they offer to politicians, and they (or other agents they designate) possess the formal authority and discretion to 'fill in' the unspecified parts of contracts offered to their agents Lake (1999); Grossman and Hart (1986). Interest groups, by contrast, have no authority to demand behavioral changes or to remove elected officials under any circumstances. We therefore conceive of interest groups as actors in their own right (third parties), but not principals.

[19] Connolly (1996: 331). See also Vogel (1995).

[20] Connolly (1996: 330). In the case of the ozone layer, the prospect of government regulation prompted key companies—for fear of shrinking profit margins and loss of market share—to invest in chemical substitutes that would not exacerbate the problem Rothenberg and Maxwell (1997); Levy and Prakash (2003). Also see Sonnenfeld (1999).

[21] Connolly (1996: 331).

regulation.[22] For example, *The New York Times* refers to Exxon and Mobil as 'rich in cash, aggressive in style...[and] effective in pursuing their agenda...at the highest level of government and through arm-twisting in Congress.'[23] Corporate actors also channel influence through think tanks and lobby groups like the US Chamber of Commerce the Competitive Enterprise Institute,[24] and public relations firms. In the run-up to global climate change negotiations, US and EU energy firms waged a massive campaign to kill all proposals for aggressive environmental reform.[25] Mitchell (1993) has also carefully documented how various corporate interests inserted themselves into international oil pollution negotiations to ensure that the regime would lack 'teeth.' 'IMCO [the Inter-*Governmental* Maritime Consultative Organization]...immediately fell victim to "regulatory capture,"' he writes, 'and it became commonplace to think of the IMCO as a "shipowner's club."'[26] From the above discussion, we derive two predictions:

Hypothesis 3a: The stronger a country's environmental lobby, the larger the proportion of its aid budget that will target environmental protection (and less to 'dirty' projects).

Hypothesis 3b/c: The stronger a country's industrial lobby, the smaller the proportion of its aid budget that will target environmental protection (and more to 'dirty' projects).

The number and strength of lobbies are difficult concepts to measure. For data on the number of environmental non-governmental organizations in each country, we relied on Binder and Neumayer's 2005 study, whose primary data source is the World Environment Encyclopedia and Directory. Additionally, we gathered data on the size of each donor country's environmental technology market from 2001 OECD data. To capture the relative strength of these lobbies in each donor country, we divided the total number of environmental NGOs by the total population and multiplied that by the size of the environmental technology market divided by the size of the economy. Potentially more important than the environmental advocacy groups and environmental technology lobbyists are the industrial lobbyists who would like to minimize environmental aid, and see funding re-allocated from environmental projects to dirty projects where they have a market advantage. As an indicator of dirty industry lobbying strength, we use Henisz and Zelner's (2006) 'industrial

[22] Rowlands (2001). Crenson's landmark 1971 study *The Un-Politics of Air Pollution* was one of the earliest attempts to document how entrenched corporate interests can suppress the environmental 'voice' of the electorate.

[23] Cited in Bruno et al. (1999: 6).

[24] e.g. CEI has been reported to have received $2 million from Exxon-Mobil for climate change 'public education' over seven years. Mufson (2007).

[25] Paterson (1996); Levy and Egan (1998).

[26] Mitchell (1993: 227). Also see Clapp (1998).

representation' variable, which is measured as industrial consumption of electricity as a fraction of total electricity consumption. Higher scores indicate greater industrial representation. These indicators better approximate the size of industry as a percentage of the national and global economy, but are not particularly good at representing whether industry is well organized into influence-peddling groups, an important avenue for future research.

How Institutions Shape Environmental Aid

Though not articulated in the environmental aid literature, deviations from the preferences of the electorate may also follow from country-specific political institutions that promote or hinder the passage of environmental reforms. To tie this to the current discussion, the impact of lobby groups depends upon the rules and norms of national political systems of what behavior is allowed. The list of political institutions that could matter is potentially endless. We concentrate on just three institutions that are likely to be especially salient: political parties, veto gates/players, and corporatist policy-making processes.

Political parties, as institutional mechanisms of aggregating groups of voter's interests, can generate powerful forces that 'pull' policy away from the preferences of the median voter. There are a number of reasons why this may be the case. Depending on the electoral rules and the constitutional rules within a polity, candidates may have strong incentives to seek support from the party base rather than the median voter. For example, in winner-take-all electoral systems, candidates who are located at the median for their party may be electorally advantaged during primary elections. This leads to nominees who are some distance from the median voter in the electorate. If this happens in both parties, then the elected leader can shift policy toward his or her ideal point to the degree that there are opportunities for slack (hidden action and hidden information) that cannot be credibly punished. Substantively, a defining characteristic of left-wing parties across advanced industrialized democracies has been a stronger preference for environmental protection and environmental regulation.[27] These preferences are typically codified in party platforms. Hence, when left-leaning parties are in power, we would expect to see a policy shift in a direction that leads to greater spending on environmental protection and more stringent environmental regulations. The traditional electoral coalitions that support such policies will also favor spending a larger share of the foreign aid budget on environmental protection. To measure the relative strength of liberal political parties, we rely on the *Leftgs* variable from Swank's (2002) Comparative Parties Data Set,

---

[27] Neumayer (2003a).

which measures the number of left governing party seats as a percentage of all legislative seats.

Hypothesis 4a: The more left governing party seats in the donor country's legislature, the larger the proportion of its aid budget that will target environmental protection.

Donor governments also differ in terms of the number of checks and balances that govern their policy-making processes. In political systems where there are many veto players and veto gates, it is widely agreed that environmental reforms—and reforms, more generally—are more difficult to implement.[28] More veto players imply greater preference heterogeneity, so as the number of veto players rises, environmental policy becomes more dependent on political compromise and tends to drift toward a 'lowest common denominator.' Multiple veto players and veto gates also provide additional points of access through which anti-environmental lobby groups can prevent, dilute, or completely capture environmental regulation. Anti-environmental interest groups are relatively more effective in this respect, since they tend to be small, concentrated, and capable of overcoming collective action problems among themselves. They also can generally garner larger pools of funding, and can mobilize extremely persuasive corporate leaders, who can testify about the severe costs associated with new regulations and their potential decisions to relocate or close their operations.[29] Environmental interest groups, in contrast, tend to be large, diffuse, and fragile in the face of collective action problems.[30] Therefore, anti-environmental groups appear to wield relatively more influence than environmental groups in political systems with many checks and balances. Further, since more veto gates will favor the status quo policy, which is less environmentally friendly as we move back in time, then veto gates should inhibit enactment of new environmental regulations.

At the same time, checks and balances should not exert an unambiguously negative effect on environmental policy. Multiple veto gates and veto players may also have the effect of 'locking in' environmental policy reforms that have already been approved and implemented. A robust system of checks and balances may insulate environmental reforms from politicians with short time horizons who seek to roll back prior commitments for political gain. This point is especially important in Western democracies where many of the most ambitious environmental reform programs occurred prior to 1988. Although our analysis in this chapter does not begin until 1988, we would expect donor countries to vary significantly over the 1990–2000 period in

---

[28] Strøm et al. (1998); Tsebelis (2002); Scruggs (2003).
[29] e.g. Schnaiberg and Gould (1994); Kazis and Grossman (1990).   [30] Scruggs (2003).

terms of their ability to shield existing reforms from political manipulation.[31] When it comes to aid funding and agencies' futures, we also expect significant bureaucratic inertia and resistance to cuts and major reform. Following the idea that the median voters should want environmental aid, especially to protect global public goods, we hypothesize that:

Hypothesis 4b/c: The fewer checks and balances (or veto players) in the donor country's government, the larger the proportion of its aid, budget that will target environmental protection.

For an indicator of the checks and balances that restrain government behavior, we employ the *checks* measure from Beck et al.'s (2001) Database of Political Institutions, which ranges from 1 to 18 (1 indicating few veto players; 18 indicating many veto players). The number of veto players is also tested in Hypothesis 4c using Tsebelis's index of the number of veto players in the political system.

A third institutional variable of potential significance is the presence and strength of corporatist policy-making processes. Corporatist countries, such as Austria, Norway, Sweden, Denmark, Finland, Germany, and the Netherlands, are characterized as having 'consensual' policy-making processes that promote the dissemination of reliable information, provide institutionalized channels of interest expression upwards through large structures like unions and business organizations, compensate losing firms, sectors, and social groups, encourage government flexibility (and, by implication, policy efficiency), and discriminate against particularistic interests. In contrast, countries with more pluralistic, or 'adversarial' policy-making processes, such as Canada and the United States, lack many of these attributes and therefore may have weaker environmental policies. Crepaz (1995: 393) argues, 'the success or failure of environmental policies is intimately connected to whether the system of interest representation is consensual and accommodative (corporatism) or whether it is adversarial and competitive (pluralism).'

There are three possible causal mechanisms through which corporatism may have a positive impact on environmental policies. First, in the consensual style of corporatist decision-making, firms may voluntarily transmit valuable and private information about their abatement costs to the government. Scruggs (2003) and Crepaz (1995) argue that more reliable information will then lead to more efficient environmental regulations, as policies are continually updated on the basis of new information, avoiding much of the deadweight loss associated with 'one-size-fits-all' solutions. By comparison, in pluralist systems, where the policy-making process is more adversarial, every

---

[31] Strøm et al. (1998) suggest that countries with more checks and balances have more effective environmental legislation. For environmental legislation to have any real effect, they argue, it must be applied consistently and implemented over the long term.

actor has an incentive to withhold valuable information and disseminate false information in order to disadvantage competing actors and hamper the state's efforts at regulation. Corporatist institutional arrangements may also promote environmental protection through a 'conflict management' function. As with many other reforms, environmental policy improvement can generate 'winners' and 'losers,' and according to Scruggs (2003), 'corporatist arrangements are noted for facilitating compensation for losers in economic adjustment, thereby socializing some of the distributional costs of policies.' These hypothesized corporatist advantages lead us to our next prediction:

Hypothesis 4d: Corporatist states will spend proportionally more of their aid budget on environmental protection than non-corporatist states.

To address the corporatist/pluralist nature of the policy-making process, we use Kenworthy's (2003) indicator of corporatism, which measures the degree of centralization in the wage-bargaining process. It ranges from 1 to 5, with 5 representing highly centralized wage bargaining and 1 representing highly fragmented wage bargaining. This is an imperfect indicator of corporatist policy-making, and risks being more adequate for understanding labor issues than other regulatory issues—such as environmental protection.

The Empirical Model

To investigate how countries allocate aid across environmental, dirty, and neutral sectors, we categorize all aid projects from seventeen bilateral donor countries during the period 1988–99. Our model examines the determinants of these sectoral allocations for each bilateral donor and year. We examine the relative performance of each hypothesis outlined in this chapter in explaining sectoral aid allocation patterns. As before, we refer the interested reader to Appendix C and the online companion document for more details regarding the modeling.

As with other models reported in this book, we measure environmental aid as the sum of projects categorized as environmental strictly defined (ESD) and environmental broadly defined (EBD). Likewise, we take dirty aid to equal the sum of projects in the dirty strictly defined (DSD) and dirty broadly defined (DBD) categories. Any project that received an ESD or EBD designation was also coded as either green or brown. While the descriptive statistics in earlier chapters cover more than twenty years of aid projects, the quality of data for our independent variables limits us to the later half of that time series for these econometric models. Therefore, in the results that follow we are investigating the behavior of seventeen bilateral donor countries for twelve years (1988–99). Data are lacking for some donors–years so the final N was 160 donor–year cases. Given this short time series and difficulties in finding donor-specific variables that explain sectoral aid shares, our results are hardly definitive. However, they do provide an important initial test of theories on why donors favor certain sectors in their aid portfolios.

Our models use multivariate regression techniques to isolate the individual effect of each variable listed in Table 6.1. We have estimated elasticities directly, so a parameter estimate on gross domestic product of .5, for example, indicates that a 1% increase in GDP leads to a 0.5% increase in aid in a given sector for an average donor country. It is important to note that these estimates control for all of the other factors in the model that might impact sectoral aid allocations. We offer several different modeling methodologies and discuss how robust our estimates are across differences in model specification.

Results

In this section, we first evaluate why some bilateral donors are more willing to fund dirty projects than others, and then evaluate why some donors spend more money on environmental projects. The first major and unanticipated finding is that our models explain much more of the variation in funding for 'dirty' projects than they do for environmental projects. We explain with these proxy measures of our four main hypotheses 40–65 per cent of the variance in which countries have reduced their aid likely to damage the environment, and 17–40 per cent of the variance in environmental aid. To summarize the four somewhat differently specified models in Table 6.2, they reveal the importance of national wealth, 'coalitions of the green and greedy,' and post-materialist values within donor countries. In Table 6.3, our hypotheses on the revealed environmental preferences of voters, as reflected in national environmental policies and international environmental treaty ratification and compliance, do seem to explain some of the environmental aid allocations donors make. Surprisingly, many of the institutional variables included in the model were not significant factors. Finally, holding everything else constant, the 'time trend' variable confirms that there is a significant negative trend over time in the proportion of aid given to projects likely to cause damage to the environment, and positive but not statistically significant trend in environmental aid (see descriptive trends in Chapter 2).

It is worthwhile, however, to systematically examine each of our hypotheses in turn. The overall hypothesis of voters having preferences that are revealed in actions of states as they dole out foreign aid gets some support (Hypothesis 1). The Environmental Policy Index developed by Nielson and Tierney (2003) had quite contradictory effects in two different techniques of examining allocation of aid, but contrary to the hypothesis, most of our models showed a strong and *negative* effect. One could interpret this as evidence for strong substitution effects between in-country and international

Table 6.1 Summary table of hypotheses, bilateral donor models

Hypothesis	Variable	Description, source
H1a: The intensity of a donor country's environmental policy preferences will positively correlate with the share of its foreign aid budget dedicated to environmental issues	Environmental policy index EPI	Environmental policy index: donor percentiles in twenty-two measures of domestic and international environmental policy outcomes. Nielson and Tierney 2003.
H1b: The intensity of a donor country's *international* environmental policy preferences will positively correlate with the share of its foreign aid budget dedicated to 'green' issues	Ln (percentage of treaties ratified)	Percentage of environmental treaties ratified by donor in a given year (calculated over Vienna, Kyoto, Heritage, UNFCC, Ramsar, Law of the Sea, CITES, Cartagena, Biodiversity)
H1c: The intensity of a donor country's *international* environmental policy preferences will positively correlate with the share of its foreign aid budget dedicated to 'green' issues	Compliance with enviro. treaties (Wefagr)	Government compliance with international environmental agreements (z-score). Environmental sustainability index 2001/World Economic Forum Global Compet. Report
H2a: The more post-materialist the electorate's preferences, the more 'environmental' the donor country's foreign aid budget	Ln (world values)	International survey of four items on attitude to consumption, Inglehart, World Values Survey
H2b: Wealthier countries will be more willing to spend taxpayer money on environmental foreign aid	Ln (GDP per capita)	GDP measured in purchasing power parity divided by population. World Bank World Development Indicators
H3a: The stronger a country's environmental lobby, the larger the proportion of its aid budget that will target environmental protection	Ln (relative size of enviro. lobby)	(Number of environmental NGOs/population) times (size of the environmental technology market/size of the economy). Neumayer and Binder 2005; OECD 2001
H3b: The stronger a country's 'dirty lobby,' the smaller the proportion of its aid budget that will target environmental protection (and more to 'dirty' projects)	Ln (IGC—industrial lobby)	Industrial lobby strength (Henisz and Zelner 2006)
H4a: The more left governing party seats in the donor country's legislature, the larger the proportion of its aid budget that will target environmental protection	Ln (LEFTS)	Measures the number of left governing party seats as a percentage of all legislative seats. Swank (2002) Comparative Parties Data Set
H4b: The fewer checks and balances in the donor country's government, the larger the proportion of its aid budget that will target environmental protection	Checks	Checks and balances that restrain government behavior: 1 indicates few veto players; 18 indicate many veto players. Beck et al. 2001
H4c: The fewer veto players in a donor country's government, the larger the proportion of its aid budget that will target environmental protection	Veto players	Number of veto players in political system. Tsebelis 2002.
H4d: Corporatist states will spend proportionally more of their aid budget on environmental protection than non-corporatist states	Corporatism	Corporatist/pluralist nature of the policy-making process: centralization in the wage-bargaining process. Kenworthy 2001.

Table 6.2. 'Dirty' aid (projects likely to have negative environmental impacts) as a share of bilateral donor portfolios

Hyp.	Variables	Dirty aid			
		1 OLS	2 OLS	3 fixed effects	4 fixed effects
H1	Donor environmental policy index [ln(EPI)]	—	−0.35** (−5.25)	—	0.51 (1.45)
	Percentage of environmental treaties ratified [ln(Treaty %)]	0.09 (0.67)	0.08 (0.56)	0.11 (0.71)	0.03 (0.21)
	Compliance with environmental treaties (WEFAGR)	0.01 (0.15)	—	—	—
H2	National wealth [ln(GDP per Capita)]	−0.33** (−2.18)	−0.35** (−3.95)	−0.49** (−2.50)	−0.21 (−1.04)
	Post-materialist values [ln(World Values)]	−0.80 (−1.47)	−0.46 (−1.13)	−1.56 (−1.39)	−2.29** (−2.58)
H3	Strength of environmental lobby [Ln(Enviro Lobby)]	−0.07 (−1.97)	−0.03 (−1.57)	−0.29** (−2.25)	−0.19* (−2.06)
	Strength of industrial lobby [ln(IGC)]	0.03 (0.16)	0.15 (0.95)	0.10 (0.08)	−0.88 (−1.02)
H4	Power of left in legislative branch [ln(LEFTS)]	−0.06 (−1.11)	0.02** (7.25)	−0.05 (−0.81)	−0.05 (−0.91)
	Checks and balances [ln(Checks)]	—	0.20** (2.73)	−0.03 (−1.02)	0.14** (2.26)
	Corporatism	—	−0.05 (−1.31)	—	0.06 (0.62)
	Veto players	0.07 (1.57)	—	—	—
	Time trend	−0.04** (−2.98)	−0.03** (−2.50)	−0.03 (−1.59)	−0.04** (−2.62)
	Constant	83.84** (3.16)	59.1** (2.60)	58.70* (1.81)	78.15** (2.82)
	R^2	0.39	0.51	0.59	0.65
	N	160	160	160	160

Notes: OLS and fixed effect models, 17 donor countries, 1988–1999 (** and * denote significance at the 5% and 10% levels respectively).

environmental problems. That is, as more money is spent locally, less is allocated to international problems. Participation in international environmental treaties, whether in ratifying them or in complying with them, was not at all important in whether countries used their foreign aid to support projects in developing countries with likely negative environmental impacts. However, in OLS regressions, it was an important predictor of aid earmarked for environmental protection in some of our models. This supports H1b, and shows a link between aid flows and international environmental diplomacy. Finally, the one equation in which we tested the World Economic Forum index of national compliance with international environmental treaties (wefagr) was not effective at predicting lower levels of dirty aid, but does nicely correspond to greater levels of environmental aid.

The wealth and post-materialism variables were consistent and strong predictors of an aversion to fund dirty projects (Hypothesis 2). These effects were strong regardless of the way the model was specified and computed. Wealthier countries allocate less money to dirty projects. Post-materialist values also had strong and consistently negative effect on the proportion of aid a donor country gives to dirty projects. This effect only rose to statistical significance in one of the models, but the consistency of the negative relationship suggests that there is some indication that countries with more prevalent post-materialist values have bilateral aid agencies that avoid dirty projects more than those with less prevalent post-materialist values. As for green, brown, and environmental projects as a whole, there is little evidence that donors are behaving in altruistic ways irrespective of material gains to voters in donor countries. National wealth, interestingly, was positively related to green aid shares, and negatively related to brown aid as a proportion of total aid. Thus it could be that lower income donors are more sympathetic to the needs of recipients, while wealthier ones want global issues addressed. (This has been argued recently for the case of China as an emerging donor, which is funding more of what recipients want without major conditions.) As a result, the two cancel each other out in the total environmental aid category. Post-materialism never rose to statistical significance in any of our environmental models reported in Table 6.3.

Turning to our hypotheses on the impact of lobbying groups (Hypothesis 3), one central idea was that 'coalitions of the green and greedy,' consisting of environmental advocacy groups and environmental technology suppliers, would push for more environmental aid, and especially for more green aid. The rather complex indicator we used to test this multiplied a population-adjusted index of the number of environmentalist groups in a country by the relative size of the country's environmental technology market. As predicted, the size of these lobbies was associated with reductions in their country's dirty aid as a proportion of their total aid portfolio. While these coalitions had little influence on increasing the overall environmental aid portfolio,

Table 6.3. Environmental projects as a share of bilateral donor portfolios

Hyp.	Variable	Environmental aid				Green aid	Brown aid
		1 OLS	2 OLS	3 Fixed effects	4 Fixed effects	5 OLS	6 OLS
H1	Donor enviro. policy index (ln)	—	-0.31** (-5.98)	—	0.18 (0.41)	—	-0.36* (-2.15)
	Ln percentage of environmental treaties rat'd.	0.27 (1.74)	0.29** 2.42	0.15 (0.89)	0.16 (0.81)	0.31 (1.47)	0.23 (-.94)
	Compliance w/environmental treaties (wfagr)	0.17** (2.32)	—	—	—	0.08 (0.65)	—
H2	National wealth [ln(GDP/cap)]	-0.06 (10.45)	-0.08 (-0.79)	0.01 (0.05)	0.02 (0.05)	0.40** (2.24)	0.30** (2.48)
	Post-materialist values (ln)	0.16 (0.30)	0.65 (1.31)	-0.72 (-0.42)	0.20 (0.12)	-1.32 (-1.47)	-0.13 (-0.17)
H3	Strength of environmental lobby (ln)	-0.62** (-2.32)	0.01 (0.35)	-0.02 (-0.11)	-0.04 (-0.18)	0.24** (2.98)	0.26** (2.88)
	Strength of industrial lobby (IGC)	-0.31 (-1.28)	-0.36 (-1.21)	-1.60 (-1.56)	-0.76 (-0.50)	0.35 (0.96)	0.11 (0.27)
H4	Left party strength (ln)	-0.01 (-0.18)	-0.00 (-0.30)	0.04 (0.37)	0.06 (0.47)	0.13* (1.84)	-0.02** (-2.83)
	Checks and balances (ln)	—	0.17 (1.38)	—	0.06 (0.58)	—	-0.14 (-0.83)
	Veto players	0.06 (1.62)	0.06 (1.04)	-0.18** (-3.16)	—	0.10 (0.96)	—
	Corporatism	—	0.00 (0.02)	—	-0.08 (-0.65)	—	0.08 (0.68)
	Time trend	-0.00 (-0.03)	-0.00 (-0.08)	-0.00 (-0.08)	0.00 (0.02)	-0.02 (-0.97)	-0.02 (-0.75)
	Constant	-1.55 (-0.05)	-3.24 (-0.12)	0.03 (0.00)	-4.65 (-0.11)	38.30 (0.84)	30.2 (0.64)
	R^2	0.18	0.17	0.37	0.36	0.28	0.25
	N	160	160	160	160	160	160

Notes: OLS and fixed effects models, 17 donors, 1988–1999 (** and * denote significance at the 5% and 10% levels respectively).

they do appear to have different effects on whether the environmental aid is targeted at green or brown sectors. Coalitions of the 'green and greedy' exert a positive effect on the share of aid allocated to green projects and a negative effect on the share of aid allocated to brown projects. We expected Western environmental NGOs to favor 'green' projects, but did not have a clear expectation about how environmental technology lobbies would influence allocation patterns *within* the environmental sector. On the one hand, water and sanitation projects and other brown issues can provide lucrative government contracts. On the other hand, many donor countries have environmental technology firms that specialize in things like scrubbers for industrial power plants, wind farms, and other emission control technologies characteristic of green projects.

Our admittedly flawed indicator of the size of the anti-environmental industrial lobby produced unexpected results. Industrial lobby strength, (IGC), was positive in one model and negative in another on the share of dirty projects in donor aid portfolios (neither significant statistically), and for all types of environmental aid it lacked significance but tended to have a negative impact. There is little evidence that dirty industrial lobbies, as we are measuring them, are playing a large role in sectoral aid allocation across countries. Again, this area requires further research.

We also tested four institutionalist variables as part of Hypothesis 4, with the idea that the way states are governed and organized will partly explain sectoral aid allocation patterns. There is very little evidence from this analysis that these particular and imperfect institutionalist variables are important drivers of the sectoral aid allocations we consider. Leftist party strength in the legislature had little impact on dirty aid allocation in three of the four models. (The fourth was in the opposite direction to the others, which is troubling.) Nor was there much of a discernible pattern in its effect on environmental portfolio size (with one exception). Surprisingly, funding for 'green' projects is significantly *lower* with left-leaning legislatures in power, and brown aid barely increased. One possible explanation is that these parties are under more pressure from labor and local environmentalists to spend their money at home. Given the qualitative evidence from Chapter 5, we were surprised by these results.

Countries with more checks and balances allocated a larger proportion of their aid to dirty projects in two models, but the index of the number of veto players was not a significant predictor of dirty aid allocation. In the environmental sectors, more veto players led to lower levels of aid in one model, while checks and balances had little effect on the proportion of aid dedicated to environmental projects (there was more brown and less green aid, but neither was significant statistically). Finally, our (labor-based) indicator of corporatism showed no impact on either dirty aid or environmental aid shares as a proportion of donor portfolios.

The time trend variable shows that, all else equal, dirty aid is consistently decreasing over time, while the share of funding for environmental projects is positive but necessarily increasing steadily, holding all else equal. These results support what we saw in the data in Chapter 3, and reinforce the notion that one of the most important stories related to aid and the environment is the displacement of dirty aid projects by social, educational, and civil society projects (our neutral sector).

Summary and Conclusions

Our examination of bilateral aid trends in Chapter 5 showed a seismic change in the total amount of aid and proportion of aid being re-allocated away from 'dirty' and towards environmental projects over the twenty-year period examined in this book in donor after donor. Environmental aid budgets increase from between 100 to 700 per cent or more over just twenty years in countries as diverse as Japan, the UK, Australia, and Spain. On average, governments spent almost three times as much of their foreign aid budgets on environmental projects in the late 1990s as they did in the early 1980s. Some spent upwards of 12 per cent, while others spent less than 6 per cent. Meanwhile, the proportion of funding spent on dirty projects dropped sharply, from over 45 per cent a year in the early 1980s to near 20 per cent in the late 1990s. Each of the five case studies showed massive changes in donors' aid portfolios over the twenty-year period.

In this chapter, we adapted and built a series of plausible explanations for why donor governments might fund more environmental projects and fewer dirty projects. Our hypotheses centered on whether sectoral allocations follow voter preferences, whether 'green and greedy' coalitions or anti-environmental lobbies are affecting the nature of bilateral aid, and whether leftist or corporatist governments would give relatively more for environmental protection. Some of our results were surprising. While we readily admit that our models, with short time series and some weak proxy measures, are far from definitive, they do provide some insight into how aid is channeled across sectors and may present some mysteries for future research to sort out. Most importantly, we found that the variables we tested were far more effective at predicting the amount of aid countries allocate for *dirty* projects than the amount allocated for environmental projects. It is worth recalling which factors reduced dirty aid the most. National wealth, environmental advocacy and environmental technology lobbies, and post-materialist values among donor country populations were the most consistent factors reducing the share of bilateral aid earmarked for projects likely to damage the environment.

There is a growing consensus in the literature that 'green and greedy' coalitions drive environmental aid financing. As Connolly puts it, 'Without strong political constituencies invested in the mitigation of trans-boundary environmental problems or the export of goods and services made possible by aid programs, competing priorities within donor countries would eclipse environmental aid budgets.'[32] By testing competing theories head to head, we find that such lobbies are only a partial explanation for the decline in dirty aid and the rise in environmental aid. Further, our findings reveal some important qualifications to the 'green and greedy' hypothesis. Table 6.2 showed that coalitions of the 'green and greedy' were associated with declines in dirty aid; however, their lobbying efforts may have contrasting effects on the two types of environmental aid we identified. They were associated with a rise in green aid, but a *decline* in brown aid. This suggests that it may be more difficult to build a strong domestic coalition in wealthy donor countries for the environmental problems of greatest importance to the developing world (local issues like sewerage and erosion control). It is also important to note that the overall impact on environmental aid was negative (but not statistically significant): the green and greedy lobby has not secured more funding overall for environmental projects in developing countries. But where they are strong, they have increased funding for foreign aid projects that benefit the *global* environment. Our measure of industrial lobbying strength (IGC) showed little impact on aid sectoral allocation.

Though our results in the second set of analyses were weaker overall, our hypotheses on the revealed environmental preferences of voters—as reflected in national environmental policies and international treaty ratification and compliance patterns—were more consistently effective at explaining the rise of environmental aid. Ratifying environmental treaties and compliance with those treaties does predict the proportion of a country's bilateral aid budget that goes to environmental projects. However, attention by governments to domestic environmental policy appears to actually *reduce* the amount spent abroad on environmental projects, especially those assisting developing countries in addressing local issues like water quality. How should we interpret this result? One possibility is that spending on environmental protection abroad is seen wholly as an issue of foreign relations, entirely detached from national environmental protection. For example, environmental aid might be given solely to secure the participation of poorer countries in environmental treaties (as has often been observed). It also could be a zero-sum game, where some total amount is available in national government accounts for environmental protection, and if more is spent domestically, then less can be sent abroad to address issues there.[33] Both of these interpretations are consistent with the

---

[32] Connolly (1996: 330).

[33] While this interpretation is logically plausible, it is not consistent with what we know about the budget process for development assistance in the largest foreign aid donors. In those countries, aid allocation decisions are taken by different legislative committees and bureaucratic agencies than are allocations for domestic environmental protection.

findings that robust domestic environmental regulations are correlated with lower allocations of environmental aid abroad.[34]

A final interpretation of this finding is possible if one thinks about issues like climate change: cutting emissions at home might be seen as reducing the need to help poor countries curb their own emissions. In fact, many citizens in developed countries see it as immoral to ask poor countries to clean up their environment when citizens of wealthy countries have not cleaned up their own act. This moral argument buttressed opposition to carbon permits trading in the negotiations for the Kyoto Treaty, and is still being debated. If this argument has any impact on foreign aid for the environment, then doing more at home should mean that there is less of a need to send that particular type of aid abroad.[35] If the normative mechanism is the operative one here, then these same countries may be delivering a disproportionate amount of social aid as well.[36]

Increasing national wealth did account for some of the rise in green aid, but had little impact on the size of environmental aid overall. But as mentioned above, both national income and, to a smaller extent, post-materialism correspond with a decrease in dirty aid. This drop in bilateral dirty aid, and wealthier populations blocking dirty projects more effectively over time, may have substantial impacts on poor countries. Developing countries generally want more dirty aid, since it funds the key facilities they need for improving their level of economic development: roads, power lines, power plants, mines, factories, and so on. The prospects for such finance from official development agencies in the West are increasingly dim given the preferences of donor country citizens. The findings from the green/brown/environmental side of the analysis have similarly grave implications for poor countries hoping to address issues like land degradation and water supply. The rise of environmental lobbying coalitions will reduce the bilateral funding available to address these issues; protected parks and climate change will be better funded.

These findings raise a series of other questions, such as whether donor governments will turn to multilateral agencies to fund projects unpopular at home, or contrarily, to implement their commitments to fund more environmental projects in poor countries. This issue is examined in the next

---

[34] Unlike the results reported here for bilateral donors, Nielson and Tierney (2006) show that robust domestic environmental policies in donor states are associated with increased voting for environmental aid in multilateral development banks. As Milner (2006) suggests, perhaps these contrary findings can be explained by the notion that governments use their bilateral aid agencies in order to pursue particular interests, but they attempt to realize different goals through delegations of authority to MDBs and other multilateral agents.

[35] Some economists argue that it is immoral to reduce carbon emissions at home, if doing so somewhere else could be done much cheaper while improving human well-being there.

[36] For a similar argument see Lyne et al. (2006). A new shift in the debate has been an emphasis on aid for adaptation to climate change that we discuss in Chapter 9.

two chapters, where we first describe trends in multilateral environmental and dirty aid (Chapter 7) and then evaluate a series of hypotheses about why countries give these agencies particular types of aid allocation tasks (Chapter 8). Though dismissed by some authors as of marginal importance, multilateral agencies offer national governments solutions to many of the contradictions inherent in addressing global environmental issues in a world without a global state.

7

Have the Multilaterals Been Greened? Major Trends and Cases

Why Would Countries Delegate Authority to Multilateral Agencies?

Multilateral aid agencies are lightning rods for criticism. Some Western NGOs have suggested that international organizations are unaccountable and engaged in activities that destroy the natural environment and impoverish developing countries.[1] Government officials and grass roots organizations from less developed countries complain about intrusive conditions placed on projects and their own lack of control over what aid they receive and who gets to run the projects. A growing number of policy-makers, academics, politicians, and citizen activists also see multilateral aid agencies as 'institutional Frankensteins' that have run amok and escaped the control of sovereign countries.[2] Jonathan Cahn, writing in the *Harvard Human Rights Journal*, characterizes the World Bank as 'fundamentally unaccountable.'[3] Another US commentator refers to World Bank funding as 'a black hole into which taxpayers pour billions of dollars for bad projects and pork-barrel contracts for a few American firms.'[4] US Congressman Ron Paul has complained that multilateral aid agencies like the World Bank are 'a socialist giveaway that hands out American taxpayers' money to foreign dictatorships.'[5]

Despite these complaints, in terms of sheer volume multilateral development finance overshadows bilateral aid. $1.3 trillion was distributed by multilateral agencies between 1973 and 2001, while $1 trillion was spent

---

[1] The role of NGOs is discussed at length in Fox and Brown (1998); Park (forthcoming, 2005).

[2] Nielson and Tierney (2003); Hawkins et al. (2006).

[3] Cahn (1993). Also see Krauthammer (2001); Thibodeau (1996). Wade (2002a: 217). Joseph Stiglitz and William Easterly have also complained of the lack of accountability within the Bretton Woods institutions, see Stiglitz (2002); Easterly (2001, 2002). As for the international relations theorists, see Barnett and Finnemore (1999); Barnett (2003); Barnett and Finnemore (2004); Babb (2003).

[4] Thibodeau (1996). [5] US Congressman Ron Paul cited in Caplen (1999: 177).

bilaterally during the same period. $25 billion in environmental aid was channeled through multilateral agencies in the 1980s, and this amount more than doubled in the 1990s. These facts raise an obvious question: why would countries give money to agencies they may not be able to fully control, and which members of their own governments openly criticize? Which countries are more likely to hand over this control? Are there types of aid that governments are particularly interested in funneling through multilateral agencies rather than allocating it themselves?

In the next section we present descriptive statistics on environmental aid funds that are allocated by multilateral agencies. We specify which of these International Organizations (IOs) deliver the most money, and which governments give the most to these organizations. We then present brief case studies of four multilateral agencies which are major distributors of environmental aid: the World Bank, the Asian Development Bank, the Global Environmental Facility, and the OPEC Fund for International Development. We spend some extra time on the World Bank, examining the struggle between the Bank and the US Congress over environmental impacts of its funding, since these were some of the most influential battles in the 'greening' of the multilaterals. Our goal in examining the broad trends, rankings, and the qualitative cases is to provide some historical context, to give readers a sense of the organizations that are currently delivering the majority of environmental aid, and to raise questions that we will address more systematically in Chapter 8. But first, we turn to the broad patterns in who delegates and to whom.

Multilateral Environmental Aid: Major Trends

Multilateral aid agencies have made dramatic changes to their grant and loan portfolios over the past two decades. The PLAID database allows us to get a broad, systematic picture of the environmental implications of their work. The first notable pattern, as described in Chapter 2, is that the environmental profile of multilateral donors has shifted significantly over our study period (Figures 2.1 and 7.1a). Dirty funding as a percentage of total multilateral funding dropped almost in parallel to bilateral funding between 1980 and 1999. In the early 1980s, nine to fourteen times as much funding was spent on dirty projects as environment projects. This ratio dropped quickly and by 1992 was near four to one (Figure 7.1b).

This is a substantial change, but critics point to an incomplete transformation.[6] Figure 7.1b shows that there has been almost no change in the ratio of 'dirty strictly defined' (DSD) projects to 'environmental strictly defined' (ESD) projects (see Appendix A for definitions). Looking more closely at the

---

[6] Salim (2004).

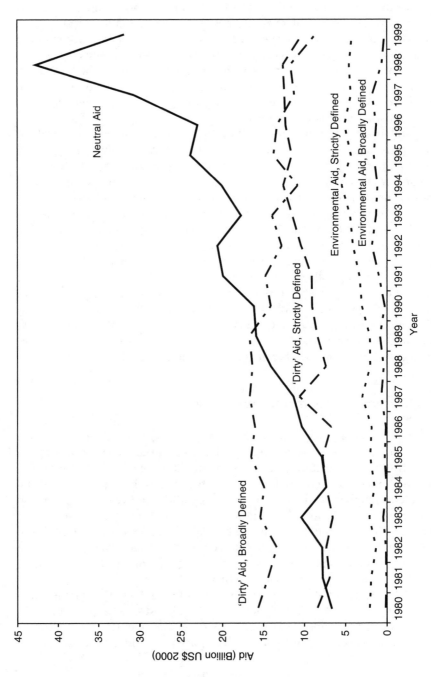

Figure 7.1a. Trends in multilateral project allocation, 1980–1999

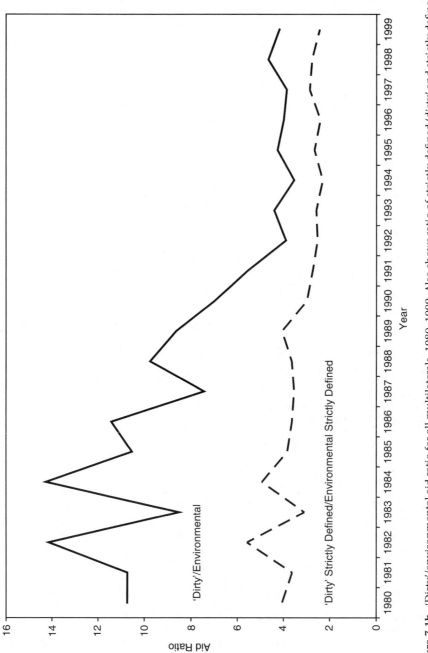

Figure 7.1b. 'Dirty'/environmental aid ratio for all multilaterals, 1980–1999. Also shows ratio of strictly defined 'dirty' and strictly defined environmental projects

Table 7.1a. Environmental aid in US$ 2000, multilateral donors, 1980–1999

Rank	Donor	1980–1984	1985–1989	1990–1994	1995–1999	Percentage change
1	WORLD BANK	$5,588,058,943	$7,691,709,585	$14,665,802,797	$10,559,892,812	89.0%
2	ASDB	$1,418,972,547	$1,803,241,680	$3,973,993,891	$5,033,251,647	254.7%
3	IADB	$1,658,189,655	$2,613,754,366	$4,732,681,067	$4,339,777,893	161.7%
4	EU	$592,459,001	$495,267,204	$995,055,607	$4,123,109,786	595.9%
5	GEF	$0	$0	$818,695,919	$1,980,591,705	141.9%
6	MONTREAL PROTOCOL	$0	$0	$274,694,634	$656,025,872	138.8%
7	EBRD	$0	$0	$101,654,758	$618,509,455	508.4%
8	AFDB	$422,462,928	$609,387,276	$161,009,033	$241,587,314	−42.8%
9	NIB	$0	$0	$49,018,272	$197,848,148	303.6%
10	ISDB	$53,209,058	$52,169,509	$82,503,924	$194,256,056	265.1%
11	NADB	$0	$0	$0	$101,306,311	N/A
12	OPEC	$84,213,428	$27,421,009	$35,112,420	$85,711,732	1.8%
13	NDF	$0	$0	$34,744,155	$70,874,418	104.0%
14	CDB	$21,789,333	$39,000,028	$42,467,714	$57,403,201	163.4%
15	IFAD	$0	$0	$17,826,414	$32,328,561	81.4%
	Total	9,839,354,894	13,331,950,657	25,985,260,602	28,292,474,911	187.54%

Notes: Percentage change is calculated from earliest to latest five-year period.

composition of dirty aid, multilateral DSD aid rose slightly over the period, from about $7 billion a year to about $10 billion a year (Figure 7.1a). 'Dirty broadly defined' (DBD) project funding was nearly flat over the two decades at about $15 billion a year, falling somewhat in the late 1990s.

Table 7.1b. The greenest multilateral donors: donors with the highest percentage of total aid classified by PLAID as environmental, 1980s and 1990s

Rank	Donor	1980–1984	1985–1989	1990–1994	1995–1999	Percentage change
1	GEF	0.0%	0.0%	100.0%	99.9%	−0.1%
2	MONTREAL PROTOCOL	0.0%	0.0%	97.7%	99.6%	2.0%
3	NADB	0.0%	0.0%	0.0%	91.7%	n/a
4	NDF	0.0%	0.0%	13.7%	19.4%	41.7%
5	EU	4.6%	0.0%	6.0%	16.8%	266.7%
6	ASDB	8.4%	7.5%	12.6%	12.8%	53.0%
7	NIB	0.0%	0.0%	7.4%	12.7%	71.0%
8	ISDB	4.7%	3.7%	7.5%	10.8%	128.6%
9	OPEC	4.7%	5.0%	4.2%	9.3%	98.8%
10	IADB	7.1%	14.6%	14.7%	8.8%	24.1%
11	AFDB	13.7%	5.8%	4.7%	8.8%	−35.9%
12	CDB	6.4%	8.4%	8.7%	8.6%	34.4%
13	EBRD	0.0%	4.3%	2.9%	7.4%	70.3%
14	WORLD BANK	5.7%	6.0%	10.0%	6.4%	13.9%
15	IFAD	0.0%	0.0%	1.4%	1.7%	21.2%
	Total	6.12%	6.80%	10.85%	9.48%	54.98%

Note: Totals do not include first three agencies; the specialized environmental funds.

Meanwhile, multilateral environmental aid nearly tripled, from $9.8 billion in the first five years of the 1980s to over $28 billion in the late 1990s (Table 7.1a). Both strictly and broadly defined environmental aid rose markedly during the period.[7] The most significant finding is the massive increase in what we categorized as neutral aid: funding for health, education, and other forms of support without direct environmental impacts. Multilateral neutral aid rose from $8–10 billion a year in the early 1980s to over $20 billion a year in the early 1990s. By the late 1990s, multilateral neutral aid had exceeded $30 billion a year, and by 1998, it topped $40 billion a year.

In the case studies that follow, we argue that pressure from IO member states and environmental campaigners has dramatically reshaped the funding profiles of multilateral agencies. Funding to projects with likely negative environmental impacts has been scaled back, while support for environmental projects has increased.

We found that multilateral environmental aid is an extremely concentrated sector: 90 per cent of it comes from just five major multilateral agencies—the World Bank, the Asian Development Bank (ASDB), the Inter-American Development Bank (IADB), the European Union (EU), and the Global Environment Facility (the GEF). This underlines the importance of understanding (and potentially reforming) these five agencies. The World Bank's environmental projects totaled over $13 billion in the 1980s, and then nearly doubled to $25 billion in the 1990s (Table 7.1a). This 89 per cent increase was far surpassed, however, by the next ten or so major multilateral agencies. The EU increased its environmental aid by nearly 600 per cent, the Nordic Investment Bank (NIB), Islamic Development Bank (ISDB) and ASDB by 300, 265, and 255 per cent, respectively. The IADB, Caribbean Development Bank (CDB) and Nordic Development Fund (NDF) increased their environmental aid contributions by 164, 162, and 104 per cent, respectively. Only the African Development Bank (AFDB) reduced its funding for environmental projects. Of the top twenty donors of environmental aid at the end of the 1990s, eight were multilateral agencies: the World Bank (allocating $38 billion over two decades), the IADB ($13.3 billion), the ASDB ($12.2 billion), the EU ($6.2 billion), and the GEF ($2.7 billion) topping the list (Table 4.1a). The greening of the EU, whose environmental funding increased by a factor of seven over the two decades, is generally underappreciated and ill understood. More surprising still is the Islamic Development Bank, whose environmental funding increased from $105 million to $276 million, a 265 per cent change.[8] This apparent 'greening'

---

[7] At the same time, environmental aid accounted for only one-tenth of total multilateral funding at the end of the period, and the largest funder, the World Bank, gave only about 6% to environmental projects (Table 7.1b).

[8] This result is 'surprising' because most member states of the Islamic Development Bank are not known for pushing environmental issues within international forums and the people

189

of the major multilateral agencies took place more or less at the same time as a series of new specialized environmental funds were being created: the GEF, Montreal Protocol Fund, and the North American Development Bank (NADB). The rise of the Global Environment Facility and the Montreal Protocol Fund to $3.5 billion in the 1990s accounts for a substantial portion of the absolute increase in environmental aid.

Four Major Multilateral Environmental Aid Donors

We now turn to four major multilateral aid agencies, and attempt with brief case studies to highlight key points in their histories and outline some of the broad trends in their grant and loan portfolios. We focus especially on the World Bank, which accounts by itself for more than a third of all multilateral environmental aid. We then move on to the second largest environmental aid agency—the Asian Development Bank—and the highly specialized Global Environment Facility, which was created in the early 1990s to deal specifically with global environmental problems like biodiversity loss and climate change. For a contrasting case, we also briefly examine OFID, the aid arm of the Organization for the Petroleum Exporting Countries (OPEC).

Two Decades of Environmental Reform at the World Bank

The World Bank is by far the world's largest environmental donor, allocating some $13.3 billion to environmental projects in the 1980s and increasing that funding to $25.2 billion in the 1990s, over a third of the total environmental assistance from multilaterals. As such, the stakes are enormous and this explains some of the controversy surrounding environmental aid at 'The Bank,' to which we will turn again shortly.

But first, understanding the Bank's importance and its recent greening requires a bit of history. With Europe in ruins after the Second World War, the International Bank for Reconstruction and Development (IBRD) was constructed to help the Western European countries rebuild and avoid further conflict. With Europe well on its way to recovery by the late 1950s, the Bank reoriented its mission towards helping developing countries stabilize and build their economies. A concessional lending arm was created in 1960 to complement the IBRD: the International Development Association (IDA). Together, the IBRD and IDA constitute the largest of the five parts of the World

living in those member states do not rate the environment as highly as their counterparts in Western countries. Hence, a norm-diffusion theory, rather than a principal–agent one, might help to account for this case as in Simmons (2005); McNamara et al. (2005). Clearly, more work needs to be done on this interesting case. For one promising start see O'Keefe and Nielson (2006).

Bank Group. For decades, World Bank projects brought medicines, food, and school supplies to the neediest countries. They also provided even greater financing for infrastructure and production due to the belief that sustained economic growth would be needed to treat more than the symptoms of 'underdevelopment.' The World Bank loaned millions of dollars to developing countries to build basic infrastructure: enormous hydroelectric dams which flooded whole river valleys to create electricity, mines and plantations to generate products which could be sold overseas, and roads, railroads, and airports to facilitate market transactions. The World Bank continues to be a major player in international aid, standing at the center of a complex universe of dozens of bilateral and multilateral agencies that lend and grant billions of dollars a year. These other donors often wait for the World Bank to commit to a project as an initial credibility check before they offer their support. This means that World Bank funding decisions often have far-reaching effects.[9]

In the early 1980s, for example, Brazil received $300 million in financing from the World Bank to develop a huge mining region in the Amazon rainforest called Carajás.[10] The iron was to be shipped by a new 600 km railroad directly to a huge port, and along the way there were to be two dozen smelting plants that would use charcoal from rainforest trees to turn some of the iron into a semi-processed product called pig iron. The iron was to be alloyed with bauxite from mines nearby using energy from a huge dam called Tucuruí, the construction of which flooded an enormous area of rainforest. Critics called the Tucuruí project 'pharoic,' and tied the dam to Brazil's unsupportable international debt and ongoing financial breakdown.[11] The $300 million from the World Bank for Carajás catalyzed $1.5 billion initial funding in loans from private banks and prospective iron buyers around the world.

The Carajás project was quickly dubbed one of the five greatest environmental disasters in the world by environmentalist critics, and a crush of attention fell on Brazil and the World Bank. At the time, the Brazilian state-owned company that developed the mine (CVRD) implemented a series of measures to deal with its immediate environmental impacts. They carefully 'hydroseeded' and replanted all the areas which were disturbed in the construction of the mine and railroad to minimize erosion. Every day, water trucks constantly

---

[9] Foreign aid broadly—and environmental aid in particular—has been the subject of a bitter struggle between environmentalists and the World Bank, with the US Congress serving as the arena where much of the battle has raged. Two influential articles by Bowles and Kormos (1995, 1999) have gone so far as to claim that 'it is not an overstatement to say that all major environmental reforms at the World Bank find their roots in an activist U.S. Congress.' While this statement overlooks decades of activism by European environmentalists and legislatures, briefly revisiting the key moments in the struggle between Congress and the Bank shows a clear relationship between the directives of the former and the promised reforms of the latter.

[10] e.g. Bunker (1985); Hall (1987); Roberts (1992); Roberts and Thanos (2003).

[11] Pinto (1982); others.

circled and sprayed the mine to keep dust pollution down, and a 0.5 million hectare nature preserve was established entirely encircling the mine. What was not foreseen was the land rush and massive deforestation that occurred all along the railroad and around the nature preserve, which critics said was driven by the mine and should have been identified in the World Bank's initial environmental impact analysis, and addressed.[12]

Leading environmental organizations such as Friends of the Earth UK, the Environmental Defense Fund, Conservation International, and the Natural Resources Defense Council brought some disturbing details to the attention of the European Commission and the US Congress about a series of World Bank-funded projects, including Carajás, and a major settlement project in the south-western Brazilian Amazon called Polonoroeste. The EC threatened to boycott the Carajás iron if the charcoal-burning pig iron smelters were built. An 'odd coalition of environmentalists and fiscal conservatives' in the US Congress also took up the issue.[13] The Subcommittee on Foreign Operations of the Senate Appropriations Committee in the mid-1980s, whose chair called a series of hearings on multilateral bank lending, threatened to withhold funding for the Bank's 'replenishments' unless it addressed detailed concerns about its projects' environmental impacts.[14] In 1985, the Bank followed through on its threat by suspending disbursements to the Polonoroeste settlement project in the Amazon,[15] and on 19 June 1986 the United States became the first country ever to vote against a Bank project on environmental grounds.[16]

In the late 1980s—at a time when the media was filled with images of the burning Amazon forest and concern about global warming was rising—the US Congress became even more interventionist and began to pressure the World Bank to overhaul its forestry and energy policies.[17] The 1989 International Development and Finance Act (the IDFA) required US representatives to the multilateral development banks to abstain from voting in favor of 'proposed loans with potentially significant environmental impacts, unless an environmental impact analysis has been made available at least 120 days in advance.' In the IDFA was a critical amendment offered by Nancy Pelosi from California. Under the 'Pelosi Amendment,' the environmental impact

[12] The gold rush at nearby Serra Pelada certainly could not have been foreseen, but many of the other features of population growth around a mega project could have been.

[13] Nielson and Tierney (2003).

[14] Bowles and Kormos (1999); Nielson and Tierney (2003).

[15] Nielson and Tierney (2003) note that after a five-month suspension, disbursements resumed, but with minor modifications intended to mollify Congress.

[16] Hugh Foster, Alternate Director from the US government, asked the Bank's board a pointed question on environmental protection before casting his negative vote on a massive Brazil Power Sector loan: 'How much confidence can we have that it will be carried out conscientiously when the same Brazilian government institutions will be implementing a series of environmental disasters at the very same time?' Despite US opposition, the loan was approved by the board Nielson and Tierney (2003); Bowles and Kormos (1995).

[17] Bowles and Kormos (1999).

statement had to be made widely available and US representatives had to push for the creation of 'Environmental Departments' in all of the multilateral development banks.[18] A 1991 World Bank Forestry Policy resulted, which entirely prohibited lending for commercial logging in rainforests.

The US Congress took an even more heavy-handed approach with respect to energy sector lending, with detailed guidelines in 1988 and then benchmarks against which to measure progress in 1990 and 1992. The goal was to move MDBs away from large-scale energy supply projects and toward lending designed to promote energy efficiency and 'demand side management.' Then World Bank President Barber Conable promised significant changes. By 1992, the Bank had a new policy on energy lending designed to promote efficiency and reform energy pricing to reduce consumption. But the Bank's efforts to implement the policies were openly questioned. A 1992 Senate report concluded that renewable energy and energy efficiency projects did not figure prominently enough in the Bank's energy lending portfolio and that the Bank continued to bankroll large-scale infrastructure without 'adequate concern for environmental and social consequences.'[19] A 1993 study by the Natural Resources Defense Council and the Environmental Defense Fund concluded that the Bank had complied with its own energy policies only two out of forty-six times.[20]

Matt McHugh, who was once a Democratic Congressman and later an adviser for World Bank President James D. Wolfensohn, argues that the US Congress has been particularly involved in foreign assistance debates because it 'is probably the least popular part of the budget politically... It's always a tough sell, especially when domestic programs are in danger for one reason or another.'[21] As hard as it is to gain constituent support for sending money to help people overseas, the disclosure that this money might be harming the environment or indigenous people can make such spending politically impossible. These dynamics catalyzed an unusual coalition in the US of spendthrift budget hawks, isolationists, environmentalists, and human rights groups. As a result, extremely detailed requirements for 'the greening of foreign aid' were forced on the Bank and other multilateral agencies through the 1980s and 1990s.

---

[18] Bowles and Kormos (1995). The Pelosi Amendment's passage pushed the Treasury Department to take a strong stand on the environmental assessment issue, and in October 1991 the Bank announced a major revision to its statement on environmental policy Bowles and Kormos (1999). World Bank President Barber Conable promised in 1987 that there would be a 150% increase in forestry lending by 1989, and then in 1989 he announced that forest lending would increase by an additional 300%. After a controversy over a forest sector loan in Ivory Coast in 1990, which NGOs claimed would open 500,000 hectares of rainforest to logging, the US representative and others on the World Bank board called for a moratorium on all new forestry lending until a more environmentally minded policy was in place. Bowles and Kormos (1999).

[19] Bowles and Kormos (1995).   [20] Bowles and Kormos (1999).   [21] Phillips (1999).

As the largest shareholder, the US government learned very quickly that the most effective way to influence the Bank's behavior is to threaten the flow of its money.[22] In 1992, the US Congress made $30 million of Global Environment Facility (housed at the World Bank) funding conditional upon reforms that would allow for public access to the GEF's project documents. They also explicitly threatened to redirect the funds to USAID if the World Bank did not institute the reforms by 30 September 1993. When the World Bank failed to implement the reforms within the given timeline, funding was re-programmed to USAID.[23] Not surprisingly, the first US contribution to the GEF was made contingent upon the new organization adopting specific institutional reforms.

A second notable trend at the World Bank has been the rise of environmental projects. This funding often accompanied the negotiation of Multilateral Environmental Agreements (MEAs) signed during the 1980s and 1990s. Funding was provided to developing countries so that they would adhere to new rules set forth in treaties like the Montreal Protocol on ozone-depleting substances, the Convention on Biological Diversity, and the Convention on the International Trade in Endangered Species (CITES). However, it is not clear whether this funding was used as an *inducement* or a *reward* for participation in global environmental accords. This is an issue that we return to in Chapter 8. Even as some countries like the US resisted signing these treaties, they were sometimes major contributors to voluntary funding facilities.

Three of the top five Bank recipients of environmental aid were the same during the two decades, but there have also been some important changes over time. In the 1980s, Brazil was first with $2 billion in environmental aid, followed by India ($1.5bn), Algeria ($1.1bn), Indonesia ($1.0bn), and Turkey ($0.9bn). In the 1990s, China was first with $3.7 billion, followed by Brazil ($2.9bn), Mexico ($2.1bn), Indonesia ($1.7bn), and India ($1.7bn). The largest recipients of World Bank environmental aid suggest the importance of a country's natural capital stocks and local environmental needs (Brazil, India, China).

Through the 1980s, the World Bank almost exclusively funded brown projects to address local environmental problems (Figure 7.2b). These include major water supply and sewage projects, local air pollution projects, and projects to help control erosion and flooding with better land management. For a few years in the early 1990s, the Bank spent significantly more on green projects addressing climate change and biodiversity protection. But this green

[22] As we write this book, the UK is threatening to withhold £50 million from the World Bank due to some of the conditionalities it places on countries who receive its funding.

[23] Bowles and Kormos (1995). This example illustrates the fact that policy-makers do weigh the pros and the cons of supra-national delegation and allocation funds along bilateral/multilateral lines. In Chapter 8, we model the decision to channel aid bilaterally or multilaterally.

wave did not last long. The Bank quickly scaled back its support for global environmental issues and increased its brown funding.[24] Later in this chapter we describe the rise of the Global Environmental Facility.[25] One possible explanation for the World Bank's declining support for green environmental projects is that the creation of the GEF to address global environmental issues has allowed the Bank to return to its traditional focus on dirty and neutral aid.

Another possible explanation is the increasing use of trust funds. Since its inception, the World Bank has allowed its members to create trust funds. Generally, if the Bank cannot reach a consensus on a certain project, then a single member country, and often a few countries, will bypass normal voting procedures and create a trust fund. These trust funds are financed directly by the shareholder countries, skirting the Bank's budgetary process, but carried out with World Bank resources. World Bank data suggest that individual member countries are using the trust fund function more than ever. In 2004, the Bank reported that it was supporting 903 different trust funds worth over $3 billion. In 2005 the Bank recorded an increase in trust funds to over $4 billion, while the total number of programs that it supported through traditional mechanisms dropped to 840.[26] Trust funds range in value from $200,000 in smaller funds to $2.2 billion for the largest fund.[27] In a sense, they offer donor countries the best of both worlds. Donors can earmark funding for their pet projects, while dumping the hard work of planning and implementation onto multilateral agencies and insulating the funding from domestic political pressures. Currently, the biggest donors to these funds are the United States, Japan, UK, European Commission, and the World Bank Group itself. The scope of the funds ranges from certain countries, regions (Africa receives 33 per cent of trust funds), or global public goods (20 per cent of total funds). There appears to be an emerging trend within the Bank to choose trust funds when a coalition is unlikely to form in favor of specific initiatives. Devesh Kapur argues that this system of bypassing the Bank's budgetary process is essentially 'off balance sheet financing.' He argues that, while effective, this system undermines the structure of governance in the World Bank.[28]

The World Bank's increases in environmental funding have been accompanied by a relative decline in dirty funding (Figure 7.2a). The broadest indication of institutional greening, the dirty aid to environmental aid ratio shown below, averaged 13 : 1 in the early 1980s, but dropped to around 5 : 1 in the mid-1990s. This is a substantial change, but the same ratio is far lower for most bilateral agencies (Chapter 5), and dirty funding

[24] However, even funding for brown issues has been unstable, rising to over $3 billion a year after the Rio Earth Summit in 1992, but falling to just $1 billion in the last two years of the decade.
[25] The GEF has its Secretariat housed at the World Bank in Washington, DC, but remains organizationally distinct from the Bank.
[26] Financial Times (2004).   [27] Powell (2005).   [28] Kapur (2002a).

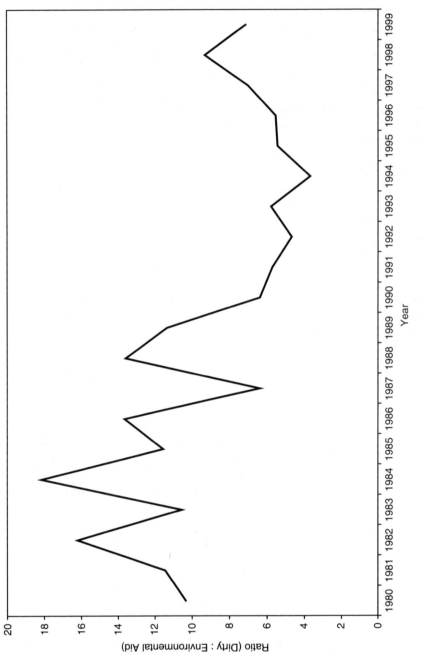

Figure 7.2a. World Bank aid: ratio of 'dirty' to environmental project funding (D/E ratio), 1980–1999

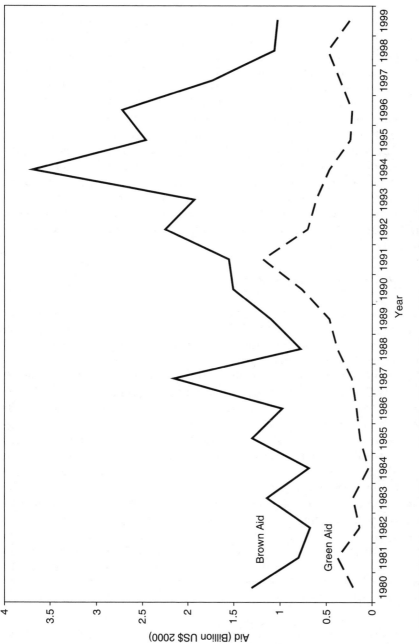

Figure 7.2b. World Bank green and brown (global and local public goods) funding, 1980–1999

appears to be increasing as a share of Bank funding at the end of the 1990s.

In the mid-2000s, there was some indication that the pendulum of environmental concern at the Bank and aversion to infrastructure and extractive industry projects was swinging back the other way. An independent Extractive Industries Review suggested in late 2004 that the Bank phase out all investments in oil and gas within just five years and switch to renewable energy.[29] However, the Bank's management strongly criticized the report, calling its recommendations unhelpful to poor countries, which they believed would be better off if their resources were responsibly extracted. There is also growing concern that developing countries will simply identify financiers with less stringent environmental requirements to bankroll their dirty projects. In 2005 and 2006, under the leadership of Paul Wolfowitz, it appeared that the Bank was placing a renewed emphasis on traditional infrastructure projects. The Extractive Industries Review suggested that even with decades of safeguards and reviews, the most modern extractive projects will create serious environmental problems.

The Asian Development Bank

As the regional development bank for the Asia-Pacific region, the Manila-based Asian Development Bank (ASDB) has historically focused on agriculture, rural development and infrastructure, and more recently poverty reduction.[30] The main operating principle of the ASDB is to finance specific projects or lend money to other development entities which in turn finance individual projects.[31] Like the World Bank, the ASDB's funding comes from bond issues, member contributions, earnings from lending, and repayments of loans. In 2005, it lent a total of $5.26 billion.[32]

The origins of the ASDB lie in a 1963 resolution passed by the United Nations body now known as the Economic and Social Commission for Asia and the Pacific (ESCAP). It began operations in 1966 with an initial membership of thirty-one countries.[33] Unlike other regional development banks, the ASDB chose to involve developed countries from the start, in order to secure the needed funding.[34] Developed countries had their own incentives for forming the bank: Japan saw developing countries in Asia as potential trade partners who could supply raw materials to the Japanese economy and buy its goods. Despite initial hesitation to join the ASDB, the United States wanted to use the ASDB to channel funds into the region to balance its military presence in Vietnam.[35] Unlike the African Development Bank and

[29] Balls (2004c); Salim (2004); IFC webpage.
[30] Guerrero (2003: 8).   [31] Kappagoda (1995: 15).
[32] Asian Development Bank (2007).   [33] Asian Development Bank (2006).
[34] Kappagoda (1995: 14).   [35] Kappagoda (1995: 14).

the Inter-American Development Bank, the ASDB avoided social lending and emphasized productive sector loans from the very beginning.[36]

However, between the 1980s and 1990s, the ASDB's environmental profile changed substantially. According to our systematic coding of the PLAID dataset, its environmental project funding tripled—from $2.56 billion in the 1980s to $7.54 billion in the 1990s—at a time when its total funding doubled to $58.6 billion (Figure 7.3a). Dirty aid declined as a proportion of ASDB funding over the period, from 76.3 per cent to 46.5 per cent.[37] Neutral aid also rose markedly, from 14.5 to 34.3 per cent, with peak levels of 70 per cent during the 1997 financial crisis.[38] Through 1991, dirty projects averaged ten times the funding that environment projects received, but this ratio fell below five from 1992 onwards. Since then, the ASDB has shown a remarkably consistent ratio of three dollars for dirty projects for every one spent on an environment project (Figure 7.3a). The ASDB increased its share of environmental funding from 9 per cent of total lending to 13 per cent in the 1990s. Distinct trends can be observed in different environmental aid sectors, with a noticeable rise in green aid in the years following the Rio Earth Summit in 1992, while brown aid has increased more consistently and currently makes up a larger share of aid (see Figure 7.3b).

The ASDB is a major funder of water projects. In the 1980s, 73.6 per cent of the ASDB environmental aid went to water sector projects. Climate change and land degradation projects received 9.2 per cent and 9.3 per cent of environmental aid in the 1980s, respectively, and until 1992, the ASDB did not fund any biodiversity projects. In the 1990s, the share of environmental aid earmarked for water projects declined to 43 per cent, while climate funding increased to 30 per cent. Land degradation and biodiversity remained low priorities (10 and 3 per cent, respectively).[39] The largest recipients of ASDB environmental aid 1980–99 were China (receiving 29 per cent of the ASDB's environmental aid), India (19 per cent), Indonesia (8 per cent), the Philippines (19 per cent), and Pakistan (13 per cent). Environmental aid paralleled overall aid from the ASDB: these were also the largest recipients of total aid from the ASDB. In the past, ASDB aid was biased toward middle-income countries, but with South Korea, Taiwan, and many other 'Asian Tigers' having 'graduated' from the lending program, a larger share of money now goes to the least

---

[36] Pascha (2000: 170).

[37] In absolute terms, dirty project funding rose from $18.9 billion in the 1980s to $29.8 billion in the 1990s.

[38] The ADB gave $9.93 billion in aid that year instead of its usual five to six billion, of which $6.98 billion went to environmentally neutral projects, including a $4.22 billion loan for restructuring the South Korean financial sector. In the two years before, the bank had only given about $1.6 billion for environmentally neutral projects.

[39] In absolute terms, climate change aid increased 877% to $2.30 billion, land degradation increased 211% to $739 million, and water aid went up by 73.5% to $3.25 billion.

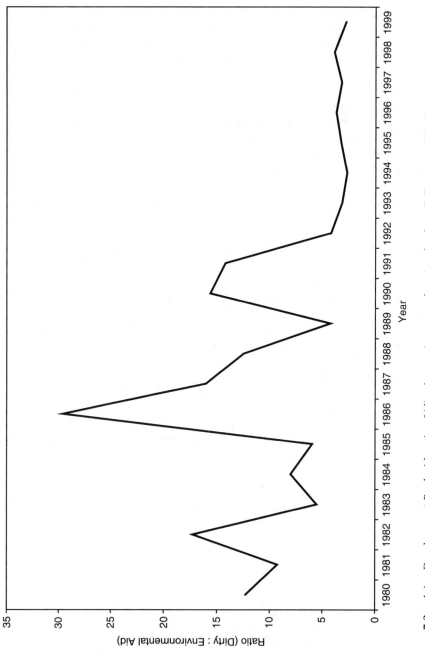

Figure 7.3a. Asian Development Bank aid: ratio of 'dirty' to environmental project funding (D/E ratio), 1980–1999

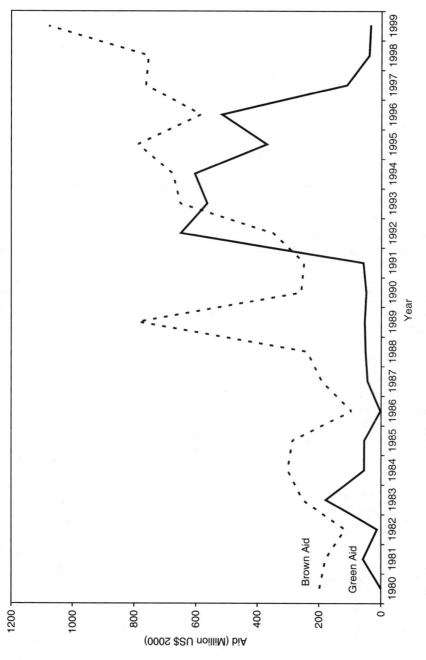

Figure 7.3b. Asian Development Bank 'green' and 'brown' (global and local public goods) funding, 1980–1999

developed countries in the region.[40] Membership and voting structures show a tension between large donor interests and developing country members, as well as between countries from inside and outside Asia.[41] The United States and Japan have the most votes, each with 12.85 per cent of the voting share.[42] Japan has a traditional policy of maintaining parity with the US in terms of shares, and they adjust their budgeting accordingly.[43]

The first proposal to consider environmental issues when approving ASDB loans came in the form of a 1980 working paper titled *Environmental Considerations in Banking Operations*.[44] The paper was supported almost entirely by developed countries, while recipient countries expressed fear that environmental concerns would become too strongly emphasized, leading to the cancellation of important projects. One regional director said, 'the critical issue for developing member countries . . . is survival, and poor people in these countries do not object to pollution if it means more jobs.'[45] Japan was the only donor not solidly in favor of creating a strict environmental assessment policy. They tried to broker a compromise between the donor countries and recipient countries by praising the paper but encouraging a cautious, moderate policy.

Like most multilateral development banks, the ASDB has been targeted by protests from environmental and social interest groups. The 'NGO Forum on ASDB' is an Asian-based network of civil society groups that has criticized several aspects of the ASDB, including its environmental impact.[46] The 'Forum' has partnered with another ASDB critic, Greenpeace, in protesting the ASDB's perceived lack of commitment to fighting climate change. Greenpeace held several protests against ASDB policies, including one where

---

[40] Pascha (2000: 167).

[41] The ASDB now has 65 member countries, 47 of which are located in the Asia and Pacific region. These countries control 65% of the votes and subscribe to 63% of the ASDB's capital; in fact the charter specifies that regional countries must always control at least 60% of the voting power, maintaining the 'Asian' character of the bank. But each country receives a vote for every bank share they hold, so larger donors have more influence.

[42] Asian Development Bank (2006).

[43] Bøas (2000: 38). ASDB members are directly represented in the Board of Governors, the ASDB's highest authority; but since this body only meets once a year, most powers are delegated to the Board of Directors. See Bøas (2000: 15). There are twelve seats on this board, four allocated to non-regional and eight to regional members. The United States, Japan, and China each have their own directors, while many other countries in close proximity share the same director as shown on the ASDB Board of Directors webpage. A few large donors including the United Kingdom, New Zealand, and the Scandinavian countries do not have representation on the Board of Directors. See Strand (1999). The ASDB President, elected by the Board of Governors, serves as the Chair of the Board of Directors, according to the ASDB Organization webpage. Under an unspoken rule, the president has traditionally been Japanese. See Guerrero (2003: 5). Thus, Japan and the United States have even higher influence in the ASDB than their voting shares imply. A quantitative study by Krasner in 1981, for example, showed the correlation between Japanese interests and aid allocation was high, between .5 and .88. Also see Kilby (2006).

[44] Kappagoda (1995: 141).   [45] Bøas (2000: 20).   [46] Withanage (2006: 3).

activists dressed as smokestacks blocked the exit gate at the ASDB's Manila headquarters.[47]

The ASDB continued to expand its environmental infrastructure throughout the decade. It hired its first two environmental specialists in 1981, created a framework for environmental policy in 1986,[48] and in 1987 established an environmental administrative unit. In 1990, the ASDB elevated this unit to a higher status and made it the Office of the Environment; however, five years later the office had only ten professionals.[49] The language of the ASDB's current Environmental Policy, adopted in 2002, is framed in the context of poverty reduction, which reflects regional recipient interests. One section of the policy reads, 'Economic growth alone is no longer considered sufficient to reduce poverty. The economic, social, and environmental policies that shape the process of growth and development must also address the needs of the poor and must ensure the sustainable use of resources on which continued growth depends.'[50] The 2002 Environmental Policy led to an increase in the number of environmental specialist positions in the organization's 2,000-person staff: from fifteen to eighteen.[51]

The Global Environment Facility

In 1989, in response to growing concern about environmental degradation, Western governments charged the World Bank with creating an international facility dedicated solely to environmental aid. The Global Environment Facility (GEF) was established in 1991 to financially assist developing countries in four main focus areas: global warming, biodiversity loss, pollution of international waters, and ozone layer depletion. The GEF began as a three-year pilot program with $1 billion from donor governments to support the implementation of major treaties like those on ozone, biodiversity, and climate change.[52] Its start-up was plagued by intense 'political, organizational, and administrative conflicts among its major stakeholders—developed and developing governments, implementing agencies, and interested nongovernmental organizations.'[53] These conflicts stemmed from disagreements over the GEF's charter, the voting power of developed and developing countries, and the role of NGOs.

---

[47] Greenpeace (2006).   [48] Bøas (2000: 19); Kappagoda (1995: 141).

[49] Kappagoda (1995: 148); Bøas (2000: 18). The agency reports that its 'Environmental Community of Practice' has seven members. Asian Development Bank (2006); Guerrero (2003: 28). The Regional Sustainable Development Department (RSDD) now handles the enforcement of the Environment safeguard policy.

[50] Asian Development Bank (2002).   [51] Asian Development Bank (2002).

[52] Fairman (1996: 59).   [53] Fairman (1996: 55).

Due to the eagerness of member states to 'demonstrate the viability and financial benefits of the GEF prior to UNCED' (the Rio Earth Summit in 1992), pressure was put on the GEF implementing agencies to 'accelerate the process of identifying and proposing GEF projects.'[54] The resulting 'rapid pace of portfolio development' led to the creation of projects before the planned selection criteria and 'facility's strategy' could be incorporated into the process.[55] The scientific and technical advisory panel (STAP) 'did not convene until the spring of 1991, and did not complete its criteria development work until after the third party participants' meeting, when the majority of pilot phase projects and funding had already been committed.'[56] This explains the major spike in funding and number of projects in 1991, levels that were not experienced again until 1996/7.

The quality of GEF projects varied greatly as a result of 'ad hoc' project development procedures, and some focal areas were worse than others. Fairman has analyzed water projects in some depth and concluded that 'The GEF's international waters portfolio was particularly deficient in strategic thinking. Many projects were marginal modifications' to World Bank projects.[57] Not only were projects poorly designed, he argued, but many did not even address the cause of the problem.[58] In an effort to keep the GEF alive, its member states restructured it in 1992 as the interim financial mechanism for the conventions on climate change and biodiversity, and in 1994, after intense negotiations, it was established as its own permanent facility.[59] The concerned parties reached the following stipulations for governance rules of the GEF: membership would be completely voluntary for both developed and developing countries, with only a 'de minimis financial contribution'.[60] There would be no reporting obligations beyond those necessary for project proposals.

The gruelingly complex administrative structure of the GEF was set up to incorporate three international organizations. The World Bank would be responsible for managing the finances of the GEF and implementing its large environmental investment projects.[61] The United Nations Development Programme was charged with providing 'technical assistance projects and coordinat[ing] GEF activities with national environmental programs in recipient countries.' Finally, the United Nations Environment Programme would serve as a bridge between the GEF and the 'UNCED [Rio 1992 Earth Summit] and

---

[54] Fairman (1996: 62).   [55] Fairman (1996: 62).   [56] Fairman (1996: 62).
[57] Fairman (1996: 63).   [58] Fairman (1996: 63).
[59] Fairman (1996: 55, 65). In 1990 the World Bank, representatives of potential donor and recipient countries, as well as UNDP and UNEP representatives agreed on four 'core institutional features of the GEF,' which address each of the following: 'status as a pilot program, governance rules, administrative structure, and the GEF's relationship to nongovernmental actors.'
[60] Fairman (1996: 60).   [61] Fairman (1996: 61).

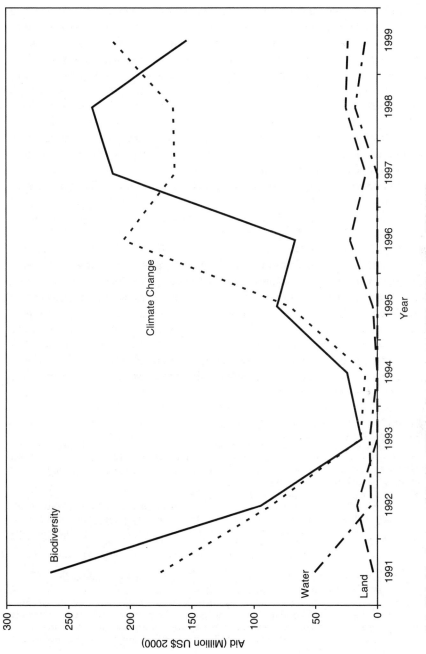

Figure 7.4. Global Environmental Facility (GEF) funding by sector, 1990–1999 (million US$ 2000)

convention processes; it would also organize and support an independent scientific and technical advisory panel (STAP).'[62] Seven other international organizations, known as GEF Executing Agencies, were designated to 'contribute to the management and execution of GEF projects.'[63] The GEF itself is managed by a central governing council, comprised of member governments who 'represent 32 constituencies (16 from developing countries, 14 from developed countries, and two from countries with transitional economies).' The constituencies operate as an 'independent board of directors, with primary responsibility for developing, adopting, and evaluating GEF programs.'[64] However, the GEF council only convenes biannually for a three-day period, and handles some affairs by email and mail. Most decisions by the council are reached by consensus.[65] If a formal vote is required, it is taken by a double weighted majority of the total membership count and 60 per cent of the total contributions.[66]

Another important point of contention within the GEF is 'additionality': projects must be shown to be ones that would not have been undertaken without GEF funding support. GEF grants have historically only covered the 'incremental' or added costs of 'transforming a project with national benefits into one with global environmental benefits.'[67] In essence, the difference in cost between a cheaper, dirtier project and a cleaner, more expensive alternative is the 'incremental' cost. The 'incremental cost' values are also used in project selection. When choosing between similar projects, those with the lowest incremental cost are favored.[68] The GEF's implementing agencies initially had difficulty producing a 'coherent methodology for calculating incremental cost,'[69] which slowed the rate at which the implementing

---

[62] STAP was to be responsible for refining the GEF's 'proposed overall strategy' and for suggesting project selection criteria.

[63] These executing agencies include the African Development Bank, the European Bank for Reconstruction and Development, the Inter-American Development Bank, the International Fund for Agricultural Development, the UN Food and Agriculture Organization, and the UN Industrial Development Organization.

[64] Global Environment Facility (2006).

[65] The process of reaching a consensus is explained in paragraph 25(b) of the Instrument: 'Decisions of the Council shall be taken by consensus. In the case of the Council if, in the consideration of any matter of substance, all practicable efforts by the Council and its Chairperson have been made and no consensus appears attainable, any Member of the Council may require a formal vote' Global Environment Facility (2004).

[66] Global Environment Facility (2004: 16).   [67] Global Environment Facility (1996).

[68] Global Environment Facility (1996). The GEF offers the following explanation of the significance of incremental cost value in determining which projects to fund. 'In general, incremental cost is an important—but by no means the only—consideration in project selection. Other considerations would be the program priority for projects of that type, national goals, equity considerations, the likelihood of success, and the environmental and social acceptability of the project.'

[69] Fairman (1996: 62).

agencies were able to develop the early projects.[70] Countries still argue about the near impossibility of determining whether the global environmental elements of a project would have been pursued in the absence of GEF funding.[71]

Figure 7.4 shows that after an initial round of funding for protecting international waters, very little funding has materialized for similar projects. Since then, the lion's share of the GEF's funding has gone to climate change and biodiversity projects. Each of the environmental sub-sectors received about $200 million in each of the last four years of the 1990s (Figure 7.4). By comparison, land degradation and water projects were negligible in their total funding amounts. Still, the GEF remains a crucial part of the overall greening of foreign aid. In its first fifteen years, the agency provided $6.2 billion in grants, $20 billion in co-financing from outside partners, and has funded over 1,800 environmental projects.[72]

The OPEC Fund for International Development (OFID)

For our last case, we sought a major multilateral aid agency with a different profile and history than most of the others. The OPEC Fund for International Development (OFID) is such an agency. It was created in 1976 by the member states of the Organization of Petroleum Exporting Countries (OPEC), following its conception at the Conference of the Sovereign and Heads of State of OPEC member governments held in Algeria in 1975. At the conference, the Solemn Declaration of the Sovereign and Heads of State was issued calling for economic development in all developing countries. Today, membership in the Fund is open to all OPEC member countries and currently all twelve members of OPEC contribute to the Fund. The United Arab Emirates chairs the Governing Board, while Saudi Arabia (35.0 per cent, over $1 billion), Venezuela (17 per cent, over $0.5bn), and Kuwait (13 per cent, over $370 million) have given 64.5 per cent of OFID funds.[73]

---

[70] 'The wide variety of problem and project types, and the pressure to produce project proposals quickly, led to great variation in the use of the incremental cost criterion.' Fairman (1996: 62); Global Environment Facility (1996).

[71] The GEF council in July 2006 implemented the Resource Allocation Framework (RAF), a 'new system for allocating GEF resources to recipient countries to increase the impact of GEF funding on the global environment.' Global Environment Facility (2006). Allocation for resources under the RAF seeks to direct funds to 'countries based on each country's potential to generate global environmental benefits and its capacity, policies and practices to successfully implement GEF projects.' See Chapter 3.

[72] Global Environment Facility (2006).

[73] The others are Nigeria (8%, $244 million), Iran, UAE, and Libya (all around 5–6% with donations between $160 and $170 million), Algeria, Qatar, and Iraq (each around 3%, donating about $90–100 million), and finally Indonesia, Gabon, and Ecuador all give less than 1% of the fund. OPEC Fund for International Development, 2006. Each member of the board has one vote under the stipulation that they have met 70% of their pledged funds. According to OFID, in 2005, Iraq and Iran had only given 48.7% and 33.0% of their

Generally speaking, the environment has not figured prominently in OFID's history. Environmental aid constituted only a small fraction of the total aid given by OFID. Over the 1980s and 1990s, PLAID coding shows that roughly 600 times as much was spent on environmentally damaging projects as on environmentally beneficial projects; only in the 1990s is there any indication of a gradual upward trend in environmental aid. The largest OFID-funded environmental project was a sewage treatment project for Yemen in 1995 for $14 million. There also appeared to be no simple relationship between the price of oil and environmental aid-giving by the OPEC Fund. Environmental aid did fall with the price of oil in the early 1980s, but then after five low years, it rose again after the Rio Earth Summit in 1992 with some very high but intermittent years. This was in spite of the continued low price of oil (under $30 a barrel).

The programmatic focus of the OFID has shifted over time. Early in its existence, development of energy and agriculture was the Fund's primary focus: developing domestic energy was a stated priority for OFID so that recipient countries could cut back on imports.[74] OFID gradually diversified its portfolio, with transportation projects gaining greater funding in the 1990s. Agriculture also remained a high priority. The 2000 Caracas Declaration by the member countries of OPEC was a reaffirmation of the goals outlined at the founding conference in 1975. It stated that the 'biggest environmental tragedy facing the globe is human poverty.'[75]

While OFID is primarily interested in economic development and poverty reduction, it does recognize the positive environmental impacts that their projects could have for recipient countries. For example, an OPEC promotional video clearly outlines how improving energy efficiency in Sudan will preserve trees and help prevent erosion by reducing firewood harvesting. In another case, it recognizes the impact that soil erosion has on farming yields in Guatemala. Yet, its focus is clearly on people rather than the environment itself.[76] The Caracas Declaration also 'asserted OPEC member countries' concern for the well being of the global environment and their readiness to continue to participate effectively in the global environmental debate.'[77]

pledged donations respectively and consequently these two countries did not enjoy a vote in OFID (ibid.). There is only one non-OPEC country contributing to the Fund, Gabon. OFID has three administrative bodies, the Ministerial Council made up of member governments' Ministers of Finance or other representative, the Governing Board with one representative of each member country, and the Director-General, appointed by the Ministerial Council for five years. The Council meets once a year and has supreme power over the Fund's general activities. The board is charged with the general operations of the Fund while the Director-General 'conduct[s] the business of the Fund under the direction of the Governing Board' and appoints the Fund's staff (OPEC 1981).

[74] OFID (1981).   [75] OFID (2001a).   [76] OFID (2001a).   [77] OFID (2001a).

Conclusions

This chapter has shown how multilateral agencies provided developing countries with more than $75 billion in environmental aid between 1980 and 2000. Five agencies were responsible for over 90 per cent of the funding, and the World Bank alone was responsible for one-third to one-half of all multilateral environmental aid. Every multilateral agency made major increases in their environmental funding over the period, and together they nearly tripled their environmental funding. Still, they spent over four times as much on projects with likely negative environmental impacts from 1980–99.

Our four case studies shed light on some of the history behind how these agencies were formed, how they operate, and how they are considering (or not considering) environmental issues. There are many areas of contention, including how much they *should* spend on the environment, and what types of environmental issues to fund. There is also endless wrangling and posturing over national contributions to these funds, and who is keeping up with their pledged donations. Nevertheless, the multilateral system still provides $3–4 billion in environmental aid each year.

Why do wealthy countries give substantial amounts of funds to agencies they may not be able to control? The cases presented in this chapter suggest some of the issues to be addressed in the hypothesis-testing part of our study in Chapter 8. First, some founding donor countries may seek to institutionalize voting arrangements that give them greater decision-making power on major policy and project-level funding decisions. The case of the Polonoroeste colonization project in the Brazilian Amazon suggests that donor countries can impose reforms on multilateral aid agencies by using the 'power of the purse strings.' We also saw in the case of the GEF that member states favored a policy of 're-delegation,' whereby implementing agencies with different types of expertise are mobilized to perform specific tasks. As we discuss in Chapter 8, this may reflect an underlying desire to exploit scale and scope economies.

However, the fragility of multilateral efforts periodically shows through. In 2005, for example, the Nordic Development Bank was closed when one member government could not agree with the others about major policy issues. This tension was also seen in the Global Environmental Facility case study, when a poorly planned pilot phase led to substantial disbursements without clear consultation and approval from donor and recipient governments. The years of negotiation over procedure and voting rights have led to a far different agency.

Finally, it is difficult to over-state the importance of the World Bank in a summary of multilateral environmental aid. The ASDB, and other regional banks like the IADB or AFDB, follow the World Bank's lead on many policy issues, including the environment. The crisis of confidence in the World Bank over President Paul Wolfowitz and his eventual resignation in May 2007 has led to broader soul-searching about whether the mandate and governance of the agency is outdated. The case studies and summary statistics in this chapter confirm that regional and issue-specific multilateral aid agencies depend upon the World Bank's leadership. In the next chapter, we attempt to explain why donor governments delegate to multilateral agencies.

8

Outsourcing the National Interest? Delegating Environmental Aid to Multilateral Agencies

Why do donor governments delegate some funding to multilateral institutions rather than distributing it through their own bilateral aid agencies? When delegating funds, why are some multilateral institutions preferred over others? In this chapter, we investigate these two questions to further illuminate the aid allocation process. The issue of supra-national delegation is particularly relevant to global and regional environmental issues because coordination is an essential part of addressing collective goods problems. As shown in earlier chapters, international public goods entail problems where need far exceeds the financial resources of even the wealthiest donor. This makes unilateral solutions impossible. In addition, if a significant amount of biodiversity or climate change aid were channeled through one donor's bilateral aid program, other donors could free-ride on those preservation efforts. So there are prima facie reasons to coordinate aid allocation by delegating to a multilateral agent. However, once a donor commits to disbursing aid through a multilateral mechanism, that donor has far less authority to determine where those funds are allocated and what type of aid will be delivered. So, delegation to a multilateral agent implies both costs and benefits to individual donor countries.

In this chapter, we identify and empirically evaluate hypotheses about why and under what conditions donor governments delegate the task of environmental aid allocation to multilateral granting and lending agencies. Building upon earlier analyses in this book, we suggest that donor governments authorize and financially empower multilateral agents to perform certain tasks that they cannot perform, or at least cannot perform as efficiently as multilateral agents. Claims about multilateral aid agencies are numerous but rarely subjected to empirical tests because of a lack of systematic, reliable, and detailed data on the aggregate amount, sources, and destinations of aid.[1] As we have argued in previous chapters, environmental aid examined at the project level provides an opportune testing ground for propositions that span the fields of international relations, development economics, and sociology. To investigate the decision to delegate to a supra-national agent, we again use the PLAID database to discern which countries favor multilateral institutions over their own bilateral aid agencies. Further, given the decision to delegate, we examine which multilateral agencies receive more delegated authority (in the form of more money) by donor governments. We examine these questions empirically by evaluating a large set of multilateral and bilateral agencies in our econometric models.

This chapter unfolds much like the two previous chapters with econometric models (4 and 6). We first describe the substantial variation in the behavior of donor governments. Some donor governments delegate the vast majority of their environmental aid to multilaterals; others delegate very little. We then articulate and test a series of potential explanations for why sovereign states might task multilateral agents with allocating and implementing international environmental assistance.

Why Delegate?

Despite the billions of dollars entrusted to multilateral development agencies every year, many commentators and scholars doubt the beneficial effects of delegation to multilateral funding agencies and other international organizations (IOs). For many, multilaterals either don't matter or they waste money that could be better spent through bilateral aid programs. Four criticisms are most prominent: that multilateral allocation decisions follow smoothly from the preferences of the most powerful member states;[2] that multilateral development banks and aid agencies are strategic tools of economically powerful groups and are used to benefit Western corporations and banks at the expense of recipient countries;[3] that multilateral behavior is pathological and largely the product of 'bureaucratic inertia' or 'organizational culture;'[4] and that

---

[1] See e.g. Kardam (1993); Kapur (2003); Boehmer-Christiansen (1999); Young (2003).

[2] Robert Wade summarizes this realist view: 'International organizations are like billiard balls that move along the vector of the forces applied to them. They do not have preferences, interests, authority of their own...autonomously of those of the powerful states.' Wade (2004b). For exemplars see Krasner (1983) and Grieco (1988).

[3] Gowan (2001); Parenti (1989); Pion-Berlin (1984); Payer (1982); Rowe (1978); Farnsworth (1972). For similar perspectives on environmental aid, see McCully (1991); Chatterjee and Finger (1994).

[4] Weaver and Leiteritz (2002); Barnett and Finnemore (1999); Miller-Adams (1999); Kardam (1993); Babb (2003); Nelson (1995). Barnett and Finnemore (2004) argue that 'international organizations are often repositories of expertise in their functional areas, and expertise is often an important source of autonomy, authority, and legitimacy for these organizations. There was no detailed knowledge about how to fix balance of payments problems before the [IMF] was created; Fund staff created the basic flow model that is still used. So international

multilateral aid agencies are inherently dysfunctional, due to the so-called 'multiple principals' problem, whereby principals (member governments) with disparate preferences task their common agent with a wide variety of objectives, and, in doing so, promote 'mission creep,' 'organized hypocrisy,' and low levels of staff morale.[5]

These arguments have merit, but they overlook three critical issues that we believe should be considered when analyzing multilateral aid allocation. First, many of these arguments discount the demand among states for collective goods, such as international financial stability, global environmental protection, infectious disease control, and the development of specialized knowledge. As with the fight against polio or terrorism, piecemeal or unilateral efforts to address global environmental problems are comparatively ineffective. Knowing this, some governments may attempt to coordinate their behavior and/or delegate some decision-making authority to multilaterals.[6] Second, and perhaps more importantly, these approaches overlook the possibility that member states have created institutions to resolve collective action problems among themselves while they are delegating authority to a multilateral.[7] That is, while coordination among 'multiple principals' is difficult, especially when their interests diverge, Multilateral Development Banks (MDBs) and Multilateral Granting Agencies (MGAs) are formally accountable to what may be more accurately characterized as 'collective principals.' Multilaterals have a single contract with a group of member states, rather than multiple delegation contracts with each member state.[8] These collective principals often develop formal decision rules that help states to coordinate their authoritative instructions and direct their multilateral agents to pursue shared goals. Third, other political actors such as activist NGOs and recipient governments have the power to shape choices about the allocation of development aid and the implementation of development projects. NGOs and other third parties shape outcomes by providing information to like-minded principals, by lobbying

---

organizations over time reshape the preferences of rich and poor states. They also have a direct impact on borrowing countries. The Board has historically served as a de facto rubber stamp for staff proposals precisely because decisions are being based on economic expertise.'

[5] On 'organized hypocrisy,' see Wade (2004a); Weaver (2008). On declines in staff morale, see Fidler (2001); Rich (2000). On the multiple principals problem, see Easterly (2002); Einhorn (2001); Pincus and Winters (2002). Wade (2001d) describes the World Bank as 'a great ship of the seas being pulled by tugboats in every direction at once.' Former Head of the World Bank Environment Department Kristalina Georgieva also uses a boat metaphor to describe the World Bank, but unlike Wade underlines the importance of bureaucratic inertia, which speaks to the previous point. In a 2003 lecture at the London School of Economics, she likened the Bank to the great *Queen Mary*: 'You can turn the wheel really hard, but the boat may not turn for a while.' Georgieva (2003).

[6] Hawkins et al. (2006); Bradley and Kelley (2008).

[7] On this topic, see Lyne et al. (2006).

[8] For more on the distinction between collective and multiple principals see Lyne et al. (2006); Copelovitch (2006); Lake (2006); Tierney (2008).

governments within member states, and, increasingly, by serving on oversight boards designed to enhance IO accountability.[9] Recipient governments matter both as members of the collective principal that votes on development projects and as actors that bargain directly with IO staff on the nature of specific projects that will be implemented (or not) in their own territory.[10] All three of these factors encourage donor governments and multilateral agencies to behave differently than the conventional wisdom often assumes.

Multilateral aid agencies, we argue, allow donor governments to reap certain gains that would otherwise be unavailable through bilateral aid work. Multilateral agencies often offer larger and better-trained staffs, greater technical expertise, lower administrative and coordination costs, more competitive procurement rules, and attractive cost-sharing opportunities that enable international public good provision. Multilaterals (especially the World Bank) also collect, interpret, and disseminate costly information about the credibility of recipient (and sometimes donor) governments. In many cases, they also have the formal authority to act upon that information in their substantive operations.[11] Therefore, in principle, multilateral aid agencies offer states important opportunities to allocate aid money and implement aid projects more efficiently than bilateral agencies. Since Western governments are subject to a wide variety of geo-strategic, commercial, bureaucratic, and domestic political constraints, multilateral agencies may provide a way for like-minded donors to issue credible threats that are necessary, but difficult or impossible to implement bilaterally.[12]

There are a large number of potential reasons why a donor country may choose to delegate allocation authority to a multilateral agent, and different states likely delegate for different reasons under different conditions. Sorting through these potential causes requires empirical testing of the competing propositions. The empirical work in this chapter establishes which actors delegate most and illuminates the general conditions under which Western countries favor supra-national delegation. We specify a multivariate model that attempts to explain why governments delegate environmental aid to multilateral agencies based on several core postulates, which we have formalized into a series of testable hypotheses. These arguments and hypotheses can be sorted into three basic groups:

[9] On accountability mechanisms that include NGOs see Park (2006); on third party information see Raustiala (1997b); Lake and McCubbins (2006); on NGOs as lobbyists within domestic politics see Fox and Brown (1998); Keck and Sikkink (1998); Udall (1998).

[10] Lyne et al. (2006); Nielson and Tierney (2001).

[11] Stone (2002) makes a similar argument about the role of the IMF in enforcing conditionality.

[12] While they may not agree on the reasons, the overwhelming majority of IR scholars in the US (73%) believe that multilateral development assistance is more effective than bilateral aid in realizing its stated objectives. Among scholars who specialize in International Political Economy, 86% believe that multilateral aid is more effective Maliniak et al. (2007).

1. Delegation solves problems of scale and efficiency, especially for smaller donors.

2. Delegation increases information provision.

3. Delegation to international organizations enhances the credibility of donors whose 'hands are tied' at home.

Following this exercise, we attempt to explain whether and why governments channel more of their aid through Multilateral Development Banks (MDBs), which give development loans at concessionary rates, or Multilateral Granting Agencies (MGAs), which give development funds without expectation of repayment. The former group includes the large multilateral agencies, like the World Bank, and the regional development banks (ASDB, AFDB, EBRD, and the IADB). The latter group of MGAs includes some specialized agencies like the Global Environmental Facility (GEF) and the Montreal Protocol Fund. When explaining whether donor governments channel money through MDBs or MGAs, we test hypotheses that fall into three groups:

1. Donor governments delegate to multilaterals in which they have a high voting share or capital subscription to maximize their influence over agency allocation decisions.

2. In the interest of exploiting scale economies, donor governments favor IOs with substantial technical experience and a demonstrated track record of performance.

3. To strengthen their own credibility and increase environmental aid effectiveness, donor countries delegate more authority to multilateral institutions that discriminate in favor of recipient countries that both have the potential to deliver global/regional environmental benefits and are capable of effectively implementing environmental aid programs.

Some of the findings that follow are quite logical and predictable: donors give more often and more funds to multilateral agencies with more technical experience, more years in existence, and to multilaterals in which they have greater voting shares. Those donor governments that focus their bilateral environmental aid on countries with high natural capital give less to multilateral agencies for green aid, but more for brown aid. Donor countries give brown aid bilaterally more often than green aid, which may allow them to take direct credit with recipients and gain the geopolitical leverage in the developing world from the former, while reaping PR benefits at home for the latter. But many other findings are not so clear or obvious. The chapter ends with a summary of the findings and a discussion of how 'governance' indicators became powerful conditions in the allocation of foreign aid. We begin, however, by very briefly examining which countries delegate their aid allocation to multilateral agents, and which keep it in house.

Who Delegates Environmental Aid to Multilateral Agencies?

Who provides environmental aid to multilateral agencies and why? There is tremendous variation in the proportion of donor governments' environmental aid portfolios channeled through multilateral agencies. Some governments choose to allocate and implement aid projects themselves, while others 'outsource' nearly all their environmental funding to multilateral agents. In the first group are Japan, Denmark, Switzerland, the Netherlands, and Germany—countries that give less than 40 per cent through multilaterals (Figure 8.1). At the opposite end of the spectrum are countries like Belgium, New Zealand, Spain, and Italy, which provide over 70 per cent of their environmental aid through multilaterals. Nine other donors lie between these extremes. But what is most notable here is the lack of international consensus on how much environmental aid to allocate through multilaterals.

In the broadest sense, governments that tend to delegate funds to multilaterals tend to delegate all types of aid to them: both dirty aid and environmental aid. The percentage of aid through multilaterals given for dirty aid explains roughly two-thirds of the aid from countries through multilaterals for environmental aid (bivariate correlation =0.65). In nearly every case, governments delegated more dirty funding than environmental funding, and chose to give a larger share of their environmental funds through bilateral agencies. Yet this aggregate relationship hides interesting variation within environmental aid. The delegation of dirty aid moves closely with aid for local 'brown' environmental issues (bivariate correlation =0.66), but not nearly as much of 'green' aid for global environmental projects (bivariate correlation =0.39). This is an important finding: national preferences for supra-national delegation are reflected closely in dirty and brown aid, but not in green aid. This suggests that a different logic is potentially motivating the delegation of green aid to multilaterals.[13]

Hypotheses on Delegation: Scale Economies, Information Provision, and Credibility

One hypothesis on supra-national delegation is that groups of states agree to contract with multilaterals to provide collective goods that they are themselves incapable of supplying (or could only supply at higher cost or less fully

---

[13] In a complementary finding, Nielson and Tierney (2001) argue that brown aid (like dirty aid) is more divisible and thus easier to use for the purpose of paying off domestic political allies. Perhaps a similar dynamic is at work here. If donor governments are using foreign aid to pay off their domestic constituents (contractors, construction companies, etc.) then brown aid is a more effective tool for doing so, and giving it bilaterally imposes fewer constraints on the government.

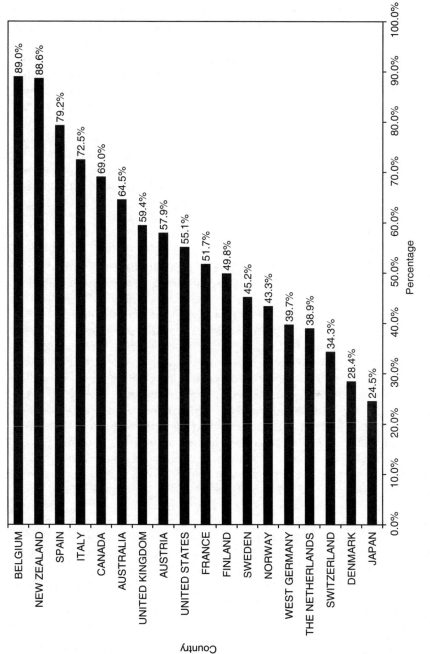

Figure 8.1. Percentage of environmental aid from bilateral donors given through multilateral organizations, 1980–1999

217

than their multilateral agent).[14] Collective action problems refer to situations where a group of rational actors seek to provide a collective good (like global security, disease control, or protecting the ozone layer), but no single actor is capable of doing so on its own.[15] Many states typically benefit from such a good, whether or not they contribute to its provision; thus, the classic free rider problem arises and the good tends to be undersupplied.[16] In the absence of a centralized authority that can enforce contracts or enhance trust of the individual states, every state faces a strong incentive to rely on the contributions of others. One way to overcome this problem is to hire a semi-autonomous agent with the 'expertise, time, political ability, [and] resources to perform [such] a task.'[17] Below we focus on three benefits that might motivate state delegation to aid-allocating and aid-implementing multilaterals: scale economies, information provision, and credibility. From these general propositions follow a number of observable implications.

Economies of Scale

Donor governments seeking to realize their international environmental policy objectives may task a multilateral agent with allocating and implementing environmental aid in order to capture scale economies. If the cost of delivering a unit of environmental protection is higher for a new entrant in the environmental aid allocation regime (like a bilateral aid agency with no experience or bureaucratic capacity in this issue area) than for a large extant agency, then the government can save money by delegating to such an agent. Increasingly, there does appear to be a pattern of delegation to specialized multilateral agents with expertise in environmental issues. The World Bank, for example, has at its disposal nearly 270 environmental staff professionals—something no bilateral aid agency can offer (in terms of quality or quantity) to donor country legislators interested in international environmental protection.[18] The GEF also draws on a wide array of environmental experts, and re-delegates its authority to implementing agents, like the United Nations Environment Programme (UNEP), the United Nations Development Programme (UNDP), and the World Bank (WB). These agencies are chosen on the basis of their expertise in implementing small-scale and large-scale environmental investment projects, developing ecosystem and resource management 'action plans,' and providing other forms of technical assistance.[19] These agencies, in turn, delegate most project implementation to NGOs, and consulting firms.

Multilateral aid agencies can also enable Western governments to more efficiently realize their international environmental policy objectives by

---

[14] Maizels and Nissanke (1984); Rodrik (1996); Parks and Tierney (2004); Martens (2005); Milner (2006).
[15] Ostrom (1990).   [16] Olson (1994); Hardin (1982).   [17] Hawkins et al. (2006).
[18] Georgieva (2003).   [19] Fairman (1996); Gerlak (2004b).

lowering their administrative costs and coordination costs. For example, states may seek a multilateral mechanism that allows them to pool resources through a common agent to economize on administrative overhead costs. Case study research on the activities of UNDP, the World Bank, USAID, the EU, the Asian Development Bank in Kyrgyzstan, UNHCR in the Democratic Republic of Congo, the UN Protection Force (UNPROFOR), and the European Community Monitoring Mission (ECMM) in Bosnia suggests that 'donors...seek to fund projects, not administrative overhead, hoping that this will push...contractors to rationalize procedures, demonstrate effectiveness, and slash overhead...as a way to curb waste, improve professionalism, and enhance project implementation.'[20] This concern for efficiency in the delivery of development assistance leads us to our first set of hypotheses about the factors motivating delegation to multilateral agencies.[21] We expect this impulse to delegate will be greatest where the local costs are highest. Our indicator of these local costs is the OECD's measure of the percentage of bilateral aid budget spent on administrative cost overhead.

Hypothesis 1: Donor governments with higher administrative costs in their bilateral aid agencies will give more aid through multilateral channels.

Second, high coordination costs among bilateral donors may encourage supra-national delegation. Asher argues that donor coordination around the Indus and Mekong River Project required 'a mechanism for reaching agreement about who will do what.'[22] Multilateral agencies have historically

---

[20] Cooley and Ron (2002: 11–12). Martens (2005), Radelet (2003: 10), Sandler (2002), Seabright (2002), Kaul et al. (2003: 353), and Cassen (1994) come to similar conclusions.

[21] That the efficiency of aid delivery is endogenous to policy-maker decisions concerning aid amount, aid type, and the recipient of aid is clearly illustrated by the US government's creation of the Millennium Challenge Corporation (MCC). In this case the Bush administration (and, to a lesser extent, Congress) performed an 'end-run' around USAID—an organization criticized often for its high administrative costs, low staff-to-aid-dollar ratios, huge overhead requirements, and general bureaucratic inefficiency. Citing USAID's reputation for wasteful spending, Senator Jesse Helms said, 'If I had my druthers, I would reform AID out of existence' Auer (1998). Helms subsequently proposed legislation to cut USAID's staff size in half and fold USAID into the State Department. His foreign relations spokesperson suggested that the rationale behind these changes was simple: 'We've got a proliferation of agencies that have duplicative functions that waste millions and millions of taxpayer dollars every day' cited in Yeoman (1996). Concern for high administrative costs was also expressed in the Meltzer Report and other documents that shaped the institutional design of the GEF and shaped the debate about how to design the MCC. Radelet (2003: 10) argues that this concern for efficiency is not limited to American legislators. Western policy-makers, more generally, are concerned about the bureaucratic costs of delivering aid. According to a 1998 OECD report on public opinion towards foreign aid, citizens are 'typically more aware of its failures than its successes...and concerned that aid is being wasted' Smillie et al. (1998: 23). In a more recent survey taken in October 2006 56% of Americans claimed that foreign aid should be cut, while only 23% believed it should be increased Maliniak et al. (2007).

[22] Asher (1962: 702).

provided such consultative and informational functions.[23] Centralizing the additional tasks of allocation and implementation within multilaterals may yield further efficiency gains. Many development professionals complain about the scale diseconomies that arise with the proliferation of small, bilateral projects.[24] In the absence of delegation, each bilateral agency must pay for its own staff salaries, travel, publications, facilities, project appraisals, data collection, financial audits, and environmental and social assessments, thus imposing higher delivery costs on recipient governments and Western taxpayers. Attendance at donor coordination meetings also introduces significant opportunity costs for government officials in recipient countries and for staff members from the many development agencies.[25] Centralizing authority for aid allocation can eliminate some of these redundant costs.

Finally, multilateral agents can play a catalytic role in that they are able to mobilize additional domestic and international funds.[26] Levy points out that 'it is standard operating procedure for a development bank to serve as lead institution for a particular project and then solicit co-financing from other institutions.'[27] Over the past thirteen years, the GEF claims to have leveraged almost three and a half times its total contributions in additional co-financing from multilateral agencies, regional development banks, NGOs, the private sector, recipient governments, and charitable foundations.[28] Between 1991 and 2003, the GEF received just under $4.5 billion in direct government contributions, and during the same period, the organization mobilized $14.4 billion in co-financing. The same catalytic logic may apply to the World Bank, the IMF, the regional development banks, the Montreal Protocol Fund, and the newly created Global Fund to Fight AIDS, TB, and Malaria (GFATM). Collier et al. have termed this the 'crowding-in' effect of multilateral aid. They argue that for every development dollar channeled through the World Bank's IDA division, nearly two additional private investment dollars are catalyzed.[29]

---

[23] For instance, faced with the task of improving water management in the Aral Sea Basin in 1994, the World Bank, UNDP, and UNEP helped coordinate the behavior of all the relevant aid actors tackling the $470 million environmental protection task Weinthal (2002: 144).

[24] As William Easterly puts it, 'When you choose where to eat lunch, the restaurant next door usually doesn't force you to sit down for an extra meal. But things are different in the world of foreign aid, where a team from the U.S. Agency for International Development produced a report on corruption in Uganda in 2001, unaware that British analysts had produced a report on the same topic six months earlier. . . . Even small bilateral aid agencies plant their flags everywhere. Were the endless meetings and staff hours worth the effort for the Senegalese government to receive $38,957 from the Finnish Ministry for Foreign Affairs Development Cooperation in 2001?' Easterly (2002a). Also see Acharya et al. (2004); Knack and Rahman (2004); Roodman (2006).

[25] World Bank (1999). A recent report from the World Bank's Operations Evaluation Department (OED) indicates that government officials believe the burdensome task of constantly attending coordination meetings prevents them from doing important work on the project or sector under consideration.

[26] Congleton (2003: 21).   [27] Levy (1993: 329).   [28] GEF (2003).

[29] Collier et al. (2001).

One rationale for delegation, then, is that Western governments can 'punch above their own weight' by pooling their environmental aid resources within a multilateral.[30]

We expect this concern to be especially strong among small donor governments, where bilateral aid bureaucracies possess little bargaining power vis-à-vis recipient governments due to the relatively small size of their projects and programs. A similar argument can be made with respect to a donor country's relative geopolitical power. Milner (2006) suggests that 'a country's relative power, as measured by the size of its GDP as a percent of U.S. GDP, may indicate how much influence a country can wield on its own. Countries with less relative power . . . may be more likely to use multilateralism for giving aid since this may increase their influence over recipient countries' (Milner 2006: 27). From this principal–agent logic, we derive the following hypothesis:

Hypothesis 2: The smaller the donor country's population, the greater the proportion of its environmental aid budget will be spent multilaterally.

Information Provision and Credibility

The allocation of development assistance and the implementation of development projects entail a series of relationships in which no *complete* contracts exist between the actors to the agreement. No donor can specify every condition and contingency in a contract with an implementing agent or with a recipient government. Instead, some discretion is always inherent in such contracts because of information asymmetries, high transaction costs, and decision rules that usually require agreement among some group of states within a collective principal.[31] This makes the task of assessing recipient intentions, capabilities, and behavior extremely costly for donors.[32] Imperfect and incomplete information creates three significant problems for well-intentioned donors: moral hazard, adverse selection, and fungibility.[33] While these problems cannot be eliminated, they can be ameliorated through delegation to a multilateral agent.

Moral hazard refers to the fact that insurance can promote riskier behavior.[34] In the context of international environmental aid, moral hazard means that recipient countries—especially those who are conscious of the intensity of Western preferences for environmental protection—may face weak incentives to undertake meaningful environmental reform on their own. Knowing that donors will disburse environmental funding regardless of their behavior,

---

[30] Olsen (2002).

[31] Martens et al. (2002); Nielson and Tierney (2003); Lake (1999); Ostrom et al. (2002).

[32] Svensson (2000c). Reliable information should be especially important to *eco-functional* donors since recipients face a number of incentives inimical to environmental improvement.

[33] Boone (1996); Svensson (2000c, 2003).   [34] Pauly (1968, 1974); Shavell (1979).

recipients may delay reform as long as they can.[35] Since recipients possess private information about their own willingness and ability to implement meaningful reforms, donors also face a problem of adverse selection.[36] Since donors are incapable of fully monitoring their effort level, these information asymmetries make it rational for recipient governments to exaggerate their needs, bluff about their intentions to reform, and shirk after disbursement.[37] Therefore, it is impossible to 'contract on the quality of a good' (in this case, development project outcomes) due to information asymmetries.[38]

Finally, there is a third problem of fungibility, which means that recipients may use funds for some purpose other than that which was agreed by the donor. If a donor provides a recipient country with money for environmental protection, this money may free up domestic resources currently spent on environmental protection to be spent on something else—in the worst case, say, a new palace for the ruling despot, a ballistic missile, or a highway through a fragile ecosystem. In the end, even if a donor's environmental project is successful, there may be no net environmental benefit.[39]

Given these perverse incentives, donors genuinely interested in improving environmental outcomes in recipient countries may choose to empower a multilateral agency to collect, analyze, and distribute costly information about developing countries on their behalf. By centralizing this task, donors can eliminate redundant monitoring efforts and reap significant efficiency gains. The Montreal Protocol Fund, for example, includes a single oversight mechanism that helps member governments to decipher who has 'cheated' by over-consuming or exporting ozone-depleting substances. Governments report data on their production, consumption, and trade of ozone-depleting substances to the Montreal Protocol Fund's Secretariat, which in turn verifies whether the information is correct and then distributes this information to all member governments and the public.[40] The World Bank performs a similar 'watchdog' function. Anne Krueger, former Chief Economist of the World Bank, argues that one of the Bank's central functions is 'to differentiate carefully between countries where reforms are serious and stand a reasonable prospect of success and those in which window dressing is used as a means of seeking additional funding.'[41] In this regard, many argue that the World Bank

---

[35] Rodrik (1996: 31); Svensson (2003); Ranis and Mahmood (1992); Knack (2001, 2004); Martens et al. (2002); Dollar and Svensson (2000).

[36] Pauly (1974).   [37] Dollar and Svensson (2000).   [38] Azfar (2002).

[39] Feyzioglu et al. (1998); Boone (1996); Pack and Pack (1990); Tierney (2003b); Petterson (2004). As Paul Rosenstein-Rodin, former Deputy Director of the World Bank's Economics Department, explained in 1949, 'When the World Bank thinks it is financing an electric power station, it is really financing a brothel.' More colloquially, the authors of the World Bank's *Assessing Aid* report suggest that 'what you see is *not* what you get' World Bank (1998: 60).

[40] Barrett (1999, 2003b); DeSombre (2001).

[41] Krueger (1998: 31); also see Rodrik (1996); Bird and Rowlands (1997, 2000, 2001b); Tierney (2003).

and other international financial institutions provide a 'good housekeeping seal of approval,' or confidence signal, to the foreign aid and investment 'market.' According to this logic, sovereign governments value multilaterals for the informational functions they serve.[42]

The need for a central information repository is directly related to the question of how donors issue credible threats to recipient governments that abrogate, backslide, or otherwise fail to implement their policy commitments. But multilateral organizations do much more than provide reliable information. The World Bank, for example, 'finances massive development projects, borrows on world capital markets, reviews state investment proposals, provides technical assistance and training in many disciplines, generates extensive research and publications, and performs other substantive activities.'[43] What explains these additional operational tasks that these international organizations perform? One plausible proposition is that states delegate aid allocation and implementation authority to international organizations to enhance the credibility of their policy commitments.

Indeed, states may seek to 'tie their own hands' *ex ante*—by delegating to a multilateral agency—in order to insulate bilateral foreign aid commitments from their own short-term interests or expected weakness of will in the future.[44] Such 'hand tying' may be driven by at least three related causal mechanisms with distinct observable implications: insulation against domestic pressures within donor states, inability to credibly threaten withdrawal of bilateral aid funds, and the Samaritan's Dilemma.

First, donor governments may be interested in providing collective goods within recipient countries—like development, growth, transition to a market economy, environmental protection, or even the protection of human rights—but face domestic pressure to support geopolitical allies, ethnic homelands of voters, or to open export markets with their bilateral aid programs. Often one branch of government seeks to protect its budget priorities from another. In the presence of strong domestic constraints, governments may financially authorize IOs with the task of distributing aid with an eye toward collective good provision.[45] Since states' geo-strategic and commercial interests often interfere with their ability to make credible threats to withdraw bilateral aid, they may additionally delegate discretion to suspend financial transfers when recipient governments renege or otherwise fail to comply with their policy and programmatic commitments. As Connolly explains,

---

[42] Multilaterals may also send important confidence signals to corporate non-state actors. Bird and Rowlands explain that '[b]y negotiating an agreement with the Fund it is supposed that countries can increase the credibility of policy reform and increase the willingness of private capital markets to lend' Bird and Rowlands (2001b).

[43] Abbott and Snidal (1998: 12).

[44] Milner (2006); Balogh (1967); Martens et al. (2002); Stone (2002); Martens (2005).

[45] Tierney (2003).

'intense competition among Western nuclear suppliers over major retrofitting contracts and lucrative commercial contracts for the expansion of nuclear power in the East undermines the resolve of Western governments to stick to common conditionality policies.'[46]

This is consistent with the idea that states take the multilateral route when 'the preferences of the agent [are] more extreme than those of the state itself, so that left to its discretion the agent will adopt a policy that moves the outcome in the direction the state knows it "should" go but cannot implement itself.'[47] In other words, if enforcing conditionality contracts comes at a high domestic political cost, governments interested in collective good provision may empower an international organization with the complementary tasks of information provision *and* contract enforcement.[48] Monitoring is important, but so is policing, and issues like global climate change and biodiversity loss require the participation of a large number of actors with highly heterogeneous preferences and strong incentives to free-ride. By hiring a single 'police department' that enforces prior commitments, donors may be better able to impose their collective will upon uninterested or opportunistic parties (recipient countries) more efficiently than any single actor could individually.[49]

It follows that if donor governments have the domestic 'policy space' to invest in recipient countries that offer a good return on their environmental (green) aid investment, they will do so bilaterally.[50] This will give them full credit with their own constituents for funding such public goods. However, if they are highly constrained at home due to geo-strategic, commercial, or other politically salient factors, donor governments will delegate the task of environmental (green) aid allocation and implementation to a multilateral agent. These considerations lead us to our next two hypotheses, both of which force us to create new indicators of donors' bilateral behavior based on the analyses in earlier chapters.

Hypothesis 3a: Donor governments that are able to target bilateral (environmental) aid to recipient countries with sound institutions will give less (environmental) aid through multilateral channels.

Hypothesis 3b: Donor governments that are able to target bilateral environmental aid to recipient countries of regional and global environmental significance will give less environmental aid through multilateral channels.

Both of these hypotheses are tested using 'elasticity' scores from our analyses in Chapter 4.

---

[46] Connolly (1996: 340).   [47] Hawkins et al. (2003).

[48] While such delegations are not permanent, they are politically costly to change. As many principal–agent analysts suggest, principals can 'lock-in' a particular policy bias by delegating to an agent with distinct preferences. Haggard and Moravcsik (1993); Hawkins et al. (2006).

[49] Calvo (1995); Haggard and Moravcsik (1993).   [50] See Radelet (2003).

Second, multilateralism may also be attractive to donor states that are unable to credibly threaten aid withdrawal from recipient countries because of a 'privileged [bilateral] relationship.'[51] Consider for example the relationship between the United States and Egypt, described in Chapter 3. For simplicity, assume that the US has two foreign policy goals vis-à-vis Egypt. It would prefer to see Egypt at peace with Israel and see the government improve its environmental policies. Egypt receives environmental assistance from the US, but this amount pales in comparison to the aid package awarded by the US for security purposes. Now, if, for one reason or another, Egypt is uninterested or unable to fulfill certain environmental policy commitments, the US government faces a dilemma. On one hand, it could threaten to withdraw environmental aid unless Egypt fulfills its commitment to reform its environmental policies. But because Egypt knows the nature of its 'privileged' relationship with the US (and the slim chance that its funding will be cut off), it will probably bargain strategically and issue its own threat. By linking its compliance with specific security commitments to the suspension of meddlesome 'green conditionality' policies, Egypt can weaken the bargaining leverage of the US. So long as US security concerns overwhelm environmental preferences, any threat to suspend or cancel a project on environmental grounds will not be credible and a successful environmental aid transfer will be unlikely. More than twenty years ago, Weinbaum correctly observed that '[USAID] officials cannot with much conviction threaten to withdraw or withhold funds from the government... [T]he US desire to assure Egypt's cooperation in [matters of international security] limits the demands the United States can impose.'[52]

Egypt is one illustrative example, but the inefficiency of bilateral aid allocation and implementation is a phenomenon that afflicts many OECD governments.[53] Western legislatures and executives regularly earmark large portions of their bilateral aid budgets for non-developmental reasons, which severely limits the ability of bilateral aid agencies to reward recipient governments on the basis of their performance.[54] The OECD's development assistance oversight committee (the DAC) argued in 2002 that the practice of earmarking in the United States 'limit[s] developmental specialists in Washington and in the field from exercising their best judgment to influence the allocation of scarce aid funds.'[55] Indeed, US Congressional appropriations committees decide where 70 to 80 per cent of USAID money will go before financially

[51] Martens (2005); Stone (2002); Abbott and Snidal (1998: 18).

[52] Weinbaum (1986: 64).

[53] In 1969, the Pearson Commission concluded that '[a] good deal of bilateral aid has indeed been dispensed in order to achieve short-term political favors, gain strategic advantages, or promote exports from the donor' Pearson (1969: 152).

[54] In the early 1990s, President George Bush referred to USAID as an 'institution born in the Cold War [that] needs to be fundamentally and radically overhauled' cited in Radelet (2003: 107).

[55] OECD (2002: 33).

empowering their bureaucratic agents.[56] Senator John McCain voiced his strong disapproval of widespread earmarking in the Fiscal Year 2002 Foreign Appropriations Bill: 'Peanuts, orangutans, gorillas, neotropical raptors, tropical fish, and exotic plants... receive the committee's attention, though it's unclear why any individual making a list of critical international security, economic, and humanitarian concerns worth addressing would target these otherwise meritorious flora and fauna.'[57] On the one hand, these domestic political constraints provide a strong rationale for supra-national delegation. On the other hand, governments confronting such constraints may find it difficult to delegate to a multilateral agent precisely because their hands are tied at home. Here we argue that donors will be more likely to delegate aid that is geared towards collective good provision because the stakes are high with such issues. This line of reasoning leads us to our fourth set of hypotheses that focus on tied aid, trade partnerships, and the geo-strategic importance of particular recipients. Again, assuming that donor governments seek to realize the collective good of environmental protection:

Hypothesis 4a: Donor governments that tie more aid to purchases of their products will prefer to channel environmental (especially green) aid multilaterally.

Hypothesis 4b: Donor governments that target bilateral aid to trading partners will prefer to channel environmental (especially green) aid through multilateral agencies.

Hypothesis 4c: Donor governments that target bilateral aid to geo-strategic partners will prefer to channel environmental (especially green) aid through multilateral agencies.

Our measure of tied aid comes from OECD data on the percentage of bilateral aid budgets which are tied to purchases from the donor country. These data are notoriously questionable, but are the only international data available over these years. The trade and UN affinity hypotheses are tested using elasticity measures created in our Chapter 4 models.

Finally, governments may delegate authority to a multilateral agent when their domestic constituents are *too* interested in providing a collective good. That is, if a donor country possesses intense preferences for a collective good like global environmental protection, it may find itself unable to credibly threaten environmental aid withdrawal from countries of global or regional environmental significance. Intense preferences such as these may actually be self-damaging because the receipt of environmental aid could provide an incentive for recipients to delay environmental reform or even further

---

[56] Bering-Jensen (1994); Lancaster (2000).   [57] McCain (2001).

degrade the environment and attract more aid![58] In Indonesia, for example, 'donor governments were so pressed to find projects to appease strong "save the rainforests" movements within their own countries that they were unable to coordinate their efforts to bargain collectively with the Indonesian government for macropolicy changes. Already deluged with aid projects for rainforest protection, the Indonesian government could afford to reject loans with conditionality aimed at reforming commercial logging policies.'[59] To avoid this type of 'Samaritan's Dilemma,' Robert Darst suggests states 'must delegate enforcement of [the] rules to an agent with less incentive and/or authority to override [the rules in the event of a] breach.'[60] Following this logic, we postulate:

Hypothesis 4d: Donor governments with strong preferences for international environmental protection will give a higher proportion of their environmental (green) aid budget multilaterally.

As a proxy for how serious donor governments are about their international environmental treaty compliance, we used the World Economic Forum's Global Competitiveness Report. The WEF conducts an annual survey of business leaders who are asked how serious they believe their government is about complying with these treaties. The 'WEFAGR' survey index has several disadvantages, including the subjectivity of the queried response, but it is one of the only indicators available on the issue.

Table 8.1 summarizes these predictions. It is important to note that there is a tension between Hypothesis 4d and Hypotheses 3a and 3b, but these predictions are not necessarily irreconcilable. Hypothesis 4d suggests that strong preferences for international environmental protection lead to higher levels of supra-national delegation because multilateral mechanisms insulate donors (that are *too* interested in environmental protection) from recipient country opportunism. Hypotheses 3a and 3b suggest that donors with strong preferences for international environmental protection, *and* the ability to maximize allocative efficiency through bilateral channels, will delegate less to multilaterals. Our empirical tests that follow suggest that some of these mechanisms are operative, while others are not.

---

[58] Following Buchanan's original logic for the so-called 'Samaritan's Dilemma,' Robert Darst (2003) argues that ' "altruistic" behavior—a proffered resource transfer, or a pledge of self-restraint—generates an incentive for exploitation on the part of the "beneficiaries" of that behavior. The "altruists" are unable to respond by punishing this exploitation, as this would lead to an increase in the very outcome that they seek to avoid, be it poverty, starvation, transboundary environmental degradation, or "collateral damage." The "beneficiaries" are aware that the "altruists" will find themselves in this bind, and thus rationally anticipate that exploitation will not lead to a permanent decline in resource transfers or the revocation of unilateral self-restraint.'

[59] Connolly (1996: 339).   [60] Darst (2003).

Table 8.1. Summary table of hypotheses, multilateral donor models

Hypothesis	Independent variable	Description, source
H1: Donor governments with higher administrative costs in their bilateral aid agencies will give more aid through multilateral channels.	Administrative cost	Percentage of bilateral aid budget spent on administrative overhead costs (source: OECD)
H2: The smaller the donor country, the greater the proportion of its environmental aid budget that will be spent multilaterally.	Ln (Population)	Size of national population (source: Global Development Network)
H3a: Donor governments that are able to target bilateral (environmental) aid to recipient countries with sound institutions will give less (environmental) aid through multilateral channels.	Government effectiveness elasticity	Bilateral allocation score on government effectiveness indicator. Variable calculated as elasticity score from Chapter 4 model
H3b: Donor governments that are able to target bilateral environmental aid to recipient countries of regional and global environmental significance will give less environmental aid through multilateral channels.	Natural capital score elasticity	Bilateral allocation score on Natural Capital. Variable calculated as elasticity score from Chapter 4
H4a: Donor governments that tie more aid to purchases of their products will prefer to channel environmental (especially green) aid multilaterally.	Tied aid	Percentage of bilateral aid budget that is tied to purchases from donor country (source: OECD)
H4b: Donor governments that target bilateral aid to trading partners will prefer to channel environmental (especially green) aid through multilateral agencies.	Trade elasticity	Bilateral allocation score on trade flow value. Variable calculated as elasticity score from Chapter 4 model
H4c: Donor governments that target bilateral aid to geo-strategic partners will prefer to channel environmental (especially green) aid through multilateral agencies.	UN affinity elasticity	Bilateral allocation score on affinity of UN voting patterns. Variable calculated as elasticity score from Chapter 4
H4d: Donor governments with strong preferences for international environmental protection will give a higher proportion of their environmental (green) aid budget multilaterally.	Creditibilty of recipient gov't on enviro. treaty compliance (WEFAGR)	Government compliance with international environmental agreements (z-score) (source: Environmental Sustainability Index 2001/World Economic Forum Global Competitiveness Report)

To *Which* Multilateral Agencies Do Donor Governments Delegate Environmental Aid Allocation?

After testing whether donor governments send more or less environmental aid through multilateral channels, we attempt to explain *which* multilateral agencies donor governments target when they want to give aid of different types. We develop three sets of hypotheses to test different logics from the principal–agent literature.

In principle, creating and funding multilateral agencies that serve no domestic political or economic masters should allow Western governments to collectively enforce environmental conditions upon disinterested or opportunistic developing country governments. But the ability of multilateral agencies to *actually* do so depends upon the formal rules governing that institution. In multilateral development banks (MDBs), where votes are generally distributed according to the 'one-dollar-one-vote' criterion, rich donor governments with strong environmental preferences have disproportionate influence over their multilateral agents, and thus greater leverage in implementing environmental conditionality. However, in multilateral grant agencies, where voting structures—such as 'one-country-one-vote' and double majority voting—favor developing countries, authoritative marching orders from the governing bodies of these IOs are less likely to reflect a strong interest in environmental protection or reform. Therefore, MDB agents ought to be more responsive to Western environmental concerns than multilateral grant agencies like the United Nations Development Programme. Specialist agencies such as the Global Environment Facility and the UN Environment Programme are tailored to address only environmental issues, but give more voting power to their developing country members. This leads us to a first hypothesis on which multilateral agencies donor countries will favor when delegating environmental aid allocation and implementation authority:

Hypothesis 1: Donor governments will favor multilateral agencies in which they have greater voting power.

In order to test this hypothesis we developed three variables which need to be tested separately: a continuous variable on the donor's share in voting, a dummy variable on other 'hybrid' voting rules, and a second dummy variable indicating whether the agency has any recipient governments represented on its voting Board of Directors. The details of these operations are explained below in the section entitled, 'A Note on Modeling.'

We also test two hypotheses on whether donor countries channel environmental aid to multilateral agencies with higher levels of technical experience. Delegating environmental aid allocation and implementation authority to a multilateral agent with significant environmental expertise may be favored because of the scale diseconomies associated with every bilateral agency hiring a large environmental staff. Therefore, donors contemplating the possibility of delegation may choose multilateral agents with a track record of performance to minimize the problem of 'adverse selection.'

Hypothesis 2a: Donor governments will delegate more environmental aid to multilateral agencies that are specialized on environmental issues.

Hypothesis 2b: Donor governments delegate more environmental aid to multilateral agencies with a track record of performance.

The first hypothesis is evaluated using a simple dummy variable on whether a multilateral agency is specialized on environmental issues; the second utilizes a continuous variable of the number of years a multilateral agency has been in existence.

Consistent with prior hypotheses, we also test whether donor governments favor multilateral agencies that allocate environmental assistance among recipient countries in ways that will best advance their interests in collective good provision. If a particular recipient government is unwilling or unable to use the assistance in the way that it was intended or if the government is simply less effective at implementing projects than an alternative recipient, then such assistance for global public goods could be better spent within a different country. Similarly, if government effectiveness is held constant, then the best return on an environmental aid investment will be in countries that have significant natural resources to protect. A dollar spent on rainforest protection will do more good in Brazil than in Chad, because Brazil has rainforests and Chad does not.

Hypothesis 3a: Donor countries will delegate more authority to multilateral institutions that discriminate in favor of recipient countries that score highly on government effectiveness ratings.

Hypothesis 3b: Donor countries will delegate more authority to multilateral institutions that discriminate in favor of recipient countries of global and regional environmental significance.

As with several others earlier in the chapter and explained further in the next section, these two hypotheses were tested using elasticity scores calculated from the models we developed in Chapter 4.

A Note on Modeling

This chapter examines two key delegation decisions made by donor governments. First, a government must decide how much of its total aid portfolio in a given sector should be delivered through multilateral channels. Conditional on this decision, the donor government must then decide which of the many multilateral agencies should disburse the 'multilateral' portion of its aid. In effect, donor governments can 'shop' among the various MDBs and MGAs (and/or discuss with other donors the need to create new multilaterals) in search of a multilateral agent that will maximize the government's interests while minimizing its agency losses.[61] In the preceding section, we outlined a number of hypotheses. To test these hypotheses, we continue to maintain the simplifying assumption that aid allocation is separable across sectors, given the choices made by bilateral donors described in Chapters 5 and 6. It is also important to note that we are modeling the choices of donor governments which, in all cases, have imperfect control over the multilateral allocation process.[62]

The first step towards estimating the multivariate regression models for this chapter is the calculation of each donor's funding to bilateral and multilateral institutions. Aggregating up from the individual bilateral project amounts allows us to measure total (environmental, green, brown, and dirty) aid flows through bilateral channels. But how much of a multilateral development bank's outlays should be attributed to each member government? Using PLAID data, we first constructed sectoral (e.g. environmental, green, brown, and dirty) aid amounts for each individual multilateral organization in each individual year. We then calculated the share of each multilateral development bank's funding that is 'owned' by individual donors, using capital subscription/voting power data.[63] For example, the United States contributed 16.4 per cent of the World Bank's basic share capital in 2006, so if the World Bank provided $1 billion in environmental financing in 2006, we would credit the US with giving $164 million in multilateral environmental aid to the World Bank for that year. For multilateral grant agencies and other agencies that do not rely on capital subscriptions, we used direct financial contributions from donor countries to the multilateral agency to calculate the share of funding 'owned' by a given national donor.[64] After calculating total flows of bilateral environmental aid and multilateral environmental aid from individual donor countries, we constructed our dependent variable: the

---

[61] On forum shopping see Jupille and Snidal (2005) and Hawkins and Jacoby (2006). On minimizing agency slack see Hawkins et al. (2006).

[62] For example, all donors to the World Bank's IDA window, with the exception of the US, provide three-year contributions to the institution. The US disburses its three-year commitments in annual tranches that must be approved by the US Congress.

[63] This assumption is restrictive since direct donor contributions are often leveraged on private capital markets and transformed into a loan portfolio that is much larger than the sum of all direct donor contributions. We were able to construct the shares for the following multilateral institutions: Asian Development Bank, Asian Development Bank Special Fund, the European Bank for Reconstruction and Development, European Union, the European Investment Bank, the Council of Europe Bank, the Global Environmental Facility, the International Fund for Agriculture and Development, the Nordic Development Fund, the World Bank IBRD, the World Bank IDA, the World Bank MIGA, the Rainforest Trust Fund, the International Finance Corporation, the African Development Bank, the African Development Fund, the Caribbean Development Bank, the Inter-American Development Bank, the Inter-American Development Bank Special Operations Fund, the MIF, the IIC, the Montreal Protocol Fund, and the Nordic Investment Bank.

[64] These data were collected directly from the multilateral institutions and imported into the PLAID database.

Table 8.2. Summary table of hypotheses: which multilateral agency will be utilized to distribute environmental aid?

Hypothesis	Variable	Description, source
H1a: Donor governments will favor multilateral agencies in which they have greater voting power (vote share).	Vote share	Donor government's vote share in each multilateral agency with one-dollar-one-vote decision-making rule (source: annual reports of individual multilateral aid agencies)
H1b: Donor governments will favor multilateral agencies in which they have greater voting power (hybrid voting rules).	Hybrid voting	Dummy=1 if aid allocation decisions are governed by a rule other than the one-dollar-one-vote rule (e.g. double majority voting, qualified majority voting)
H1c: Donor governments will favor multilateral agencies in which they have greater voting power (recipient on board).	Recipient on board	Dummy=1 if the multilateral agency includes one or more recipient countries to sit on the Board of Directors
H2a: Donor governments will delegate more environmental aid to multilateral agencies that are specialized on environmental issues.	Technical experience	Dummy=1 if the multilateral agency is a specialized environmental agency (source: PLAID Database; Yearbook of International Organizations)
H2b: Donor governments will delegate more environmental aid to multilateral agencies with a track record of performance.	Years in existence	Number of years the multilateral agency has been in existence (source: PLAID Database)
H3a: Donor countries will delegate more authority to multilateral institutions that discriminate in favor of recipient countries that score highly on government effectiveness ratings.	Government effectiveness elasticity score	Underlying variable (government effectiveness), value calculated as elasticity score from Chapter 4 model
H3b: Donor countries will delegate more authority to multilateral institutions that discriminate in favor of recipient countries of global and regional environmental significance.	Natural capital score elasticity	Underlying variable (score), value calculated as elasticity score from Chapter 4 model

share of bilateral environmental aid from an individual donor country as a percentage of total environmental aid from that donor country. We also performed the same calculation for all of the other aid sectors considered in this book: green, brown, neutral, and dirty.

In the first model we considered the decision of whether to delegate aid or not. Using the 'bilateral share' variable described above, we evaluated the hypotheses represented by the variables in Table 8.2. As in the other analyses in the book, the statistical approach we take allows us to isolate the individual effect for each of the variables by holding constant the other factors. This model includes 'performance scores' created from the donor-specific allocation models in Chapter 4.[65] These performance scores, which measure how responsive donors are to recipient-level factors, such as sound institutions (Government Effectiveness), global and regional environmental significance (Natural Capital), political allegiance (UN Affinity), and commercial significance (Trade), were estimated from a series of bilateral donor-specific allocation models similar to those reported in Chapter 4. These elasticity measures do not vary through time; they represent the average responsiveness of each multilateral donor for the 1990s.[66] Again, we hypothesized that the more efficiently a country allocates its bilateral aid, the less likely it will be to channel its funding multilaterally, holding all other factors constant.

In the second model, we examined how development funds are allocated by each donor across multilateral agencies. Here we constructed the annual share of a donor's multilateral environmental aid budget allocated to each multilateral institution.[67] We then examined how these shares are influenced by the variables listed in Table 8.3 using multivariate analysis. Since many multilateral institutions do not receive any money from certain donors, we estimated the Cragg model described in Appendix B and the online Technical Companion to this book. This model accounts for the parameter bias problems that arise when a high proportion of observations of the dependent variable mass at zero.[68] In practical terms, we modeled the probability of a country allocating money to a multilateral organization as a two-step process. First, a multilateral agency must pass the gate-keeping stage, and, conditional on that, it receives some positive amount of money.

Like the multilateral/bilateral model described above, the MDB/MGA model includes donor performance scores recovered from donor-specific models. However, unlike the bilateral/multilateral model where performance scores were taken from bilateral models, the scores included here are the performance scores for each *multilateral* organization. Elasticity scores are recovered from the government effectiveness and natural capital variables. These elasticity measures do not vary through time—they represent the average responsiveness of each multilateral organization for the 1990s. We hypothesize that donor countries will delegate more authority to multilateral institutions

---

[65] For the sake of brevity these country-specific results are not reported either in this chapter or in Chapter 6, but are available from the authors or online in a Technical Companion to this book at http://www.win.edu/irtheoryandpractice/plaid/.

[66] Fixed effects regression was not possible because the elasticity variables, which are donor-specific, do not vary through time. Fixed effects regressions which omit these elasticities are available in the online Technical Companion to this book at http://www.win.edu/irtheoryandpractice/plaid/.

[67] We also calculated the same variable for the green, brown, and dirty sectors.

[68] The problem of zeros is larger for donors that do not have annual (or multi-annual) replenishments and who have wide geographical memberships, such as the World Bank Group.

that discriminate in favor of recipient countries that have the potential to deliver global/regional environmental benefits and are capable of effectively implementing environmental aid programs. The caveats noted above concerning the use of these elasticity estimates apply here as well.

Findings: Multilateral or Bilateral Aid Channels?

Table 8.3 reports the bilateral/multilateral findings for the dirty, environmental, green, and brown categories of aid we documented.[69] We begin with our statistically insignificant results. To our surprise, the administrative cost of delivering aid bilaterally was not a statistically significant predictor of multilateralism. For the 1990s, governments with high administrative costs were not more likely to delegate aid allocation to multilateral organizations. However, it is notoriously difficult to measure *total* administrative costs with any degree of precision, so our lack of any statistically significant relationship should be taken with a grain of salt.[70] In addition, our indicator of 'tied bilateral aid,' which is plagued by its own measurement problems, did not attain conventional levels of statistical significance in any of our models.[71]

As expected, we find that smaller countries tend to give more multilateral aid. This is consistent with our prediction (H2) that small states use multilateral mechanisms to increase their influence and reduce the overall cost of delivering assistance. Interestingly, small states strongly seem to favor multilateral approaches when it comes to allocating and implementing *green* aid. This finding supports the notion that small states can maximize their bargaining leverage vis-à-vis recipient countries and overall impact on collective good provision when they channel international public good aid through multilateral mechanisms.

In an unreported set of models, we also found (somewhat unexpectedly) that revealed voter preferences for international environmental protection—as measured by international environmental treaty compliance (wefagr)—are not positively associated with a donor country's multilateral orientation. In

[69] The number of observations is equal to 17 donor countries × 10 years minus rows with missing data. Attempts to impute the missing data using MCMC simulation methods described in Appendix B did not converge to a stable distribution.

[70] Total administrative costs are difficult to capture because donors often classify administrative expenses as project costs. For example, if the US Government sends an adviser (and his or her family) to live and work on a bilateral aid project in a developing country, the total cost of that adviser (e.g. salary, moving costs, housing costs, education allowances for children, etc.) could range anywhere between $250,000 and $500,000. However, these expenses are often classified as 'technical assistance' and therefore counted as project costs.

[71] The US and some other donors have very incomplete records on reporting tied aid. In addition, the OECD DAC has periodically suspected donors of under-reporting tied aid even when they did provide an annual figure.

fact, the opposite is true: as a donor country's international environmental preferences increase, it appears that they tend to allocate more green aid through their own bilateral channels.[72] This is not consistent with our original hypothesis that environmental aid donors may delegate to multilateral agencies to escape the so-called Samaritan's Dilemma. One possible explanation for this result is that donor governments with a strong domestic mandate to solve international environmental problems, by extension, have granted their own bilateral agencies the authority to allocate environmental aid efficiently and enforce conditionality contracts without meddling by political principals (though we have no evidence to support this alternative logic). Another possibility is that donors under intense domestic pressure to 'do something' about international environmental problems may favor bilateral environmental projects because of the 'attribution problem' associated with delegation to a multilateral organization. Specifically, if a donor chooses to delegate its environmental assistance to a multilateral agent, it may be able to solve the problem more effectively, but it will not necessarily reap the domestic political benefits that come with being exclusively responsible for providing environmental projects.[73]

As there may be significant variation in how donor countries make bilateral/multilateral funding decisions with respect to their own ability to reward recipient countries according to eco-functional, commercial, and geopolitical criteria, we also included elasticity measures from the inter-recipient models of Chapter 4 as explanatory variables. Our original prediction was that donor governments would choose multilateral channels when the goal of public good provision could not be as efficiently pursued through bilateral means. Therefore, donor countries with 'tied hands' (e.g. bilateral aid agencies that target recipients where aid is less likely to be effective) may be more likely to channel green aid through multilateral agencies. Similarly, we predicted that where global public good provision was the explicit goal (e.g. green aid), states facing significant geopolitical and commercial constraints at home would favor multilateralism.

To test these hypotheses, we rely on point estimates of elasticity measures for four predictors of a country's bilateral aid allocation approach: responsiveness to sound institutions (Government Effectiveness), global and regional environmental significance (Natural Capital), political allegiance (UN Affinity), and commercial significance (Trade). Therefore, positive coefficients in Table 8.3 should be interpreted as follows: as elasticity scores increase,

---

[72] It is also important to point out that while stronger environmental preferences increase all reported sector allocations through bilateral channels, there is a much larger effect for the green aid sector.

[73] Attribution problems are the flip side of 'blame avoidance' arguments. Some analysts suggest that states will delegate authority to an IO in order to avoid blame in the event that a policy fails. Buthe (2006).

Table 8.3. OLS regressions: share of environmental aid channeled through bilateral agencies (bilateral environmental aid/total environmental aid)

	Green	Brown	Environmental	Dirty
H1				
Administrative overhead cost by donor country	.13 (1.26)	.06 (.94)	.07 (.92)	−.03 (−.83)
H2				
Ln (population)	.64* (2.11)	.25** (2.23)	.45 (1.26)	.19 (1.56)
H3				
Donor target 'effective governments' in bilateral aid (elasticity)	−1.69** (−2.20)	.96 (1.66)	.20 (.38)	−.52 (−.68)
Donor targets high natural capital index in bilateral aid (elasticity)	−.59 (−1.19)	.82* (1.96)	−.18 (−.67)	−.06 (−.58)
H4				
Percentage of bilateral aid budget tied	.02 (1.59)	.01 (1.65)	.01 (1.69)	.01 (.99)
Donor targets its major trade partners in bilateral aid (elasticity)	−.48 (−.52)	−.07 (−.13)	−1.75 (−1.34)	−.50 (−.51)
Donor targets loyal UN voters in bilateral aid (elasticity)	−.04 (−1.71)	−.04* (−2.09)	−.01 (−.48)	−.01 (−.42)
Constant	−14.66** (−2.39)	−7.53** (−3.63)	−10.89 (−1.54)	−5.37** (−2.23)
R^2	.32	.17	.14	.35
N	112	112	112	112

countries are more likely to channel funds bilaterally. Our findings suggest that the choice between bilateral and multilateral agents is generally not very responsive to the underlying elasticity scores of the country's own bilateral agencies. However, there are some exceptions. Donors, on average, give more green aid multilaterally when their own bilateral agencies are able to work with recipient countries that are capable of effectively implementing environmental aid programs. To a lesser extent, this is also true for donor countries with bilateral agencies that are able to discriminate in favor of recipient countries that have the potential to deliver global/regional environmental benefits.[74] These unexpected results beg an important question: Why would donors delegate green aid to a multilateral agency if their own agencies are relatively effective at allocating all types of assistance? One possibility is that donors with the domestic political 'space' to allocate their own aid efficiently also have an electorate that understands the efficiency gains associated with supra-national delegation. So, strategic politicians in such states do sincerely pursue global environmental goods through bilateral channels, but they also

[74] Surprisingly, we also found that brown aid tends to be channeled bilaterally when donor's own bilateral agencies target recipients of global and regional environmental significance. However, this is not the case with green aid, which flows in the opposite direction.

coordinate their efforts through multilateral organizations when those venues are perceived to be more effective or efficient.[75]

Bilateral responsiveness to the geopolitical significance of recipient countries, while generally not a statistically significant predictor of multilateralism, did obtain negative signs consistently and reach statistical significance in several unreported models. This is consistent with our prediction that donors insulate a portion of their foreign aid budget by delegating authority to multilateral agencies. Similar results were observed with our measure of bilateral responsiveness to the commercial significance of recipient countries.

These results, while interesting, are hardly definitive on the issue of whether governments are sensitive to the expected allocation decisions of potential agents for two reasons. First, our time series is short (ten years), and we estimate only one elasticity for each donor country for that time period, when it could change over those ten years. Consequently, there is potentially an endogeneity problem with the bilateral/multilateral allocation decision and our use of the elasticity estimates from the models reported in Chapter 4. That is, it could be that donors are allocating more money via multilateral channels to influence the sectoral aid mix of the multilateral donors. It should also be noted that we found very few statistically significant donor-specific elasticity estimates from the bilateral inter-recipient models. Hence, the results reported in this chapter should be treated as a starting point for further research rather than the definitive word on the subject.

Findings: Which Multilateral Institution do Donors Choose for Delegating Environmental Aid?

The findings for the multilateral allocation model are reported in Table 8.4. For each aid sub-sector, we report results for the gate-keeping and amount stages of the Cragg model. As we expected, donors tend to favor multilateral institutions in which they have greater say about where and how the multilateral should spend its money. However, this effect is only observed at the amount stage. At the gate-keeping stage (where donors are screening and selecting multilateral agents), the evidence is more ambiguous. While there does not appear to be a systematic bias toward multilateral institutions with one-dollar-one-vote decision-making rules, multilaterals with hybrid voting systems (double majority voting, qualified majority voting, etc.) are less likely to receive all types of multilateral aid, including environmental aid.

---

[75] Alternatively, this result could be driven by the data issue we discussed earlier—a substantial fraction of the green aid for the 1990s was delivered by two MGAs (GEF and MPF) that were designed *exclusively* for the allocation of green aid. The spotty data from more general donors, like UNDP, could be masking the effects suggested in Hypotheses 3a and 3b.

Table 8.4. Probit regressions of which multilateral agencies receive support and OLS regressions of why some multilateral agencies receive more support than others

	Green	Brown	Environmental	Dirty
(a) Gate-keeping stage				
H1				
Donor's vote share	−1.23 (1.19)	.24 (.43)	.58 (1.14)	−.91 (−.69)
Hybrid voting system	−1.22** (−4.05)	−1.04** (−2.64)	−1.23** (−3.12)	−1.75** (−3.59)
Recipient on Board of Directors	.36 (1.55)	.48 (1.33)	.75* (1.89)	.91 (1.55)
H2				
Multilat.'s technical experience	3.06** (8.87)	−.16 (−.35)	2.59** (7.17)	−2.18** (−4.01)
Multilat.'s years in existence	.03* (1.88)	.04** (2.15)	.04* (2.91)	.01 (.42)
H3				
Government effectiveness score (elasticity)	−.69 (−0.67)	.03 (.04)	−.28 (−.41)	−1.51** (−2.37)
Natural capital index (elasticity)	−.27 (−.40)	−.26 (−.62)	−.05 (−.06)	−1.18* (−1.80)
Constant	−.31 (−.72)	−.38 (−.66)	−.26 (−.51)	1.34** (3.88)
R^2	0.232	0.290	0.314	0.513
N	2939	2939	2939	2939
(b) Amount (OLS)				
H1				
Donor's vote share	4.85** (3.45)	2.48* (1.99)	2.50* (2.03)	5.95** (3.84)
Hybrid voting system	1.60 (1.15)	1.24 (.82)	1.17 (1.00)	.65 (.47)
Recipient on Board of Directors	−1.52* (−2.00)	−.90 (−1.05)	−1.29* (−1.77)	1.26 (1.38)
H2				
Multilat.'s technical experience	2.36* (1.94)	.43 (.34)	2.41** (2.26)	−4.28** (−3.17)
Multilat.'s years in existence	.06** (3.09)	.06 (1.69)	.07* (2.90)	.09** (3.47)
H3				
Government effectiveness score (elasticity)	−2.23 (−1.28)	1.41* (1.83)	1.38* (1.77)	−.11 (−.08)
Natural capital index (elasticity)	−3.15** (−3.77)	1.07 (1.42)	1.93 (1.20)	−.19 (−.07)
Constant	−4.42** (−5.46)	−5.39** (−3.88)	−5.71** (−5.95)	−6.94** (−6.86)
R^2	.485	.452	.445	.407
N	1682	1711	2110	2209

We also find that recipient country representation on a multilateral organization's Board of Directors exerts different effects at the gate-keeping and allocation stages. When donors are deciding whether or not to delegate any environmental aid to a multilateral, they seem to systematically favor those multilateral agencies that grant formal decision-making power to recipient countries. However, when donors are deciding *how much* environmental (and green) aid to give to a multilateral agency, they seem to favor institutions without formal recipient country representation. One way to interpret this finding is that donors acknowledge the importance of eliciting developing country buy-in in principle, but they find it difficult to resolve their differences with recipient countries in practice and therefore favor 'donor-dominated' multilateral institutions.[76]

As we expected, a multilateral agency's environmental expertise is a statistically and substantively significant predictor of donor willingness to channel environmental assistance through an international organization. Our results also suggest that agencies with significant environmental expertise are entrusted with significantly less authority to allocate and implement dirty aid. This supports our broad hypothesis that donors seek to exploit scale (and scope) economies by delegating authority to multilateral agents. In this case, it appears that donors understand the benefits of establishing a division of labor among multilateral agents. At both the gate-keeping and amount stages, we also find that a multilateral agency's prospects for receiving aid are significantly higher when it has established a track record of performance (proxied in our models with the number of years it has been in existence). This supports our hypothesis that donors screen and select multilateral agents based on concerns about potential 'adverse selection' problems.

Finally, the evidence on whether donors systematically favor multilateral agencies that invest in recipient countries with good institutions and the potential to deliver global environmental benefits is inconclusive. At the gate-keeping stage, multilateral responsiveness to these recipient-level factors does not appear to have a significant impact upon whether they receive support from their donors.[77] However, at the allocation stage, donor states provide more funding to multilateral agencies that allocate environmental assistance among recipient countries in ways that will enhance collective good provision. That is, multilateral agents that discriminate in favor of recipient countries with effective governments receive more support. We attempt to sum up these complex findings below.

---

[76] While much has been written about how the World Bank, the European Investment Bank, and the European Bank of Reconstruction and Development are dominated by donor governments Guntner (2002), an even more extreme case is the Nordic Development Fund, which had only five members—all of them wealthy donors.

[77] Donors do appear to delegate more dirty aid to multilateral agencies that favor recipient countries with weak institutions and little potential to deliver global environmental benefits.

Summary and Conclusions

Western democracies are quite diverse in their environmental aid policies. While some pursue environmental protection in developing countries through their own bilateral agencies, others choose to delegate such aid allocation to multilateral agencies. New Zealand and Belgium delegated nearly 90 per cent of their environmental aid in the 1990s to multilaterals, while Japan and Denmark delegated less than 30 per cent. In this chapter we sought to explain why countries delegate aid in general and environmental aid in particular to multilateral agencies. First, we reviewed different arguments from previous work, and attempted to extend and systematize these arguments into a series of hypotheses that we were able to test against one another. Some hold that delegation of environmental aid allocation varies with the preferences of donor country populations for environmental protection, others that delegation solves problems of scale and efficiency, especially for smaller donors. Alternative views held that delegation addresses issues of effective governments and eco-functionality, or contrarily, that delegation will be a less preferred option when donor interests like tied aid, trade facilitation, or political loyalty are on the line. So the first half of our task in this chapter was to predict how much of aid budgets of different types (dirty, environmental, green, and brown) would be given through bilateral or multilateral agencies.

Our findings in Table 8.3 showed that all four types of aid were given more bilaterally when national governments were perceived as more serious about complying with environmental treaties. Contrary to our predictions, donors overall were not more likely to channel funds multilaterally when their own bilateral overhead costs were high. Consistent with our hypothesis, larger countries appear to be more likely to give through bilateral channels, and this was especially true of environmental and green aid. National wealth made no difference, except in leading donor countries to give more dirty aid through multilaterals. This finding reinforces the point raised in Chapter 6, where populations in wealthier countries appear to be more interested in blocking dirty aid projects than in funding environmental aid projects. Donors who targeted recipients with effective governments were more likely to give green aid through multilaterals, but other types of aid showed no marked difference.

Governments who target their bilateral environmental aid to countries with high 'natural capital' (natural resources and biodiversity) channel more of their green aid through multilateral agencies, but more brown aid through bilateral agencies. As recipients overall appear to prefer brown aid, donors can gain more politically from giving that aid bilaterally. Conversely, funding specialized international environmental agencies may be seen as the best way to address global environmental concerns and much of our evidence supports this logic. Donor governments prefer to distribute green aid, which is designed to provide international public goods, through multilateral organizations and they have set up new multilateral agents (GEF and MPF) exclusively for that purpose. As seen in the second stage of this chapter's analysis, donors do indeed give more green aid through specialized agencies than they do brown aid.

Governments that give bilateral aid based in part upon national interests like tying aid pay-outs to the purchase of donor country equipment or services also gave more of their environmental aid through bilateral agencies. Contrary to realist predictions, donors giving more bilateral aid along geopolitical loyalty lines gave more green and brown aid through multilateral agencies. Finally, donors who focused their bilateral aid more on trade partners did not give more to bilateral agencies for brown, green, environmental, *or* dirty aid.[78] Many of these models were relatively weak in their predictive power, explaining only 14–36 per cent of the overall variance, but dirty aid was 2.5 times more adequately explained by these factors than was environmental aid. This is consistent with the logic articulated in the hypothesis section. Still, this empirical analysis is far from definitive in explaining the delegation decision due to the relatively small number of observations at our disposal and some difficulty in finding ideal measures for our explanatory variables, and in some cases missing data. However, we do believe our models speak to the observable implications deduced from the competing theories on why donors delegate the allocation of foreign aid for the environment.

We concluded our analysis with a study of why governments select particular types of multilateral agents, whether they are Multilateral Development Banks (MDBs, which give loans at concessionary rates) or Multilateral Granting Agencies (MGAs, which give funds without expectation of repayment). We expected donors to delegate to agencies in which they have a high voting share, and therefore relatively greater influence over the agency, that donors would give more to IOs with credibility, including high technical experience and years in existence, and that donors who target their bilateral aid to recipients according to environmental need or importance would also give more to specialized multilateral granting agencies set up specifically to dole out environmental aid (like the GEF). Our findings were straightforward on these points: donors give more often and more money to multilateral agencies with greater technical experience, more years in existence, and to multilaterals in which they have greater voting shares, which for some multilaterals is tied directly to capital subscriptions.

However, as we said above, the evidence on whether donors systematically favor multilateral agencies that invest in recipient countries with 'good

---

[78] We do not have an explanation for these findings but note that neutral (especially telecoms and balance of payments assistance) aid constitutes the remaining portion of the aid in these cases.

institutions' and the potential to deliver global environmental benefits was inconclusive. Looking backwards in time, this is somewhat surprising, since so much aid is now being allocated on this basis. But the epistemic consensus around 'aid selectivity' really only took hold at the end of our time series, which ran from 1990 to 1999. So the analysis here allows us to examine whether an informal selection of aid recipients was going on before that time.

In the late 1990s, bilateral and multilateral donor preferences largely coalesced around the idea that aid should be distributed more selectively. The World Bank's Research Department played a particularly influential role in this regard, producing and disseminating econometric 'proof' that foreign aid works only in good policy and institutional environments. In 1997, Craig Burnside and David Dollar published a working paper with the World Bank Research Department entitled 'Aid, Policies, and Growth.'[79] Using time-series panel data, they found that aid given to countries with 'good fiscal, monetary, and trade policies' had a positive and statistically significant effect on economic growth. By contrast, aid channeled to 'bad policy environments' had no observable effect on growth.

In the same paper, Burnside and Dollar also examined aid allocations over a thirty-year period and concluded that the vast majority of concessional funding distributed to the developing world had not been based upon 'good policies.' Rather, donors—particularly bilateral agencies—had focused their attention on recipients of geopolitical and commercial interest. A year later, Burnside and Dollar (1998) published a second World Bank working paper seeking to determine whether foreign aid had any effect on poverty reduction. Using infant mortality reduction as a proxy, they came to the same conclusion as the year before: development assistance given to countries with 'good policies' reduced poverty. That same year, the World Bank's External Affairs Department released the highly influential 'Assessing Aid: What Works, What Doesn't, and Why' report.[80] In it, the World Bank's Research Department built upon Burnside and Dollar's findings by adding an 'institutional quality' variable to earlier regressions. Finding a positive and statistically significant coefficient, they argued that the strength of a recipient's domestic institutions strongly conditioned the effectiveness of aid. The policy implication of this research was that donors would get more 'bang for their buck' if they discriminated in favor of recipients with strong institutions and good economic policies.

With the help of a well-financed public outreach effort, the World Bank's findings spread quickly throughout the development community. The report

---

[79] Burnside and Dollar (1997) was later published in *American Economic Review* as Burnside and Dollar (2000a).
[80] Dollar and Pritchett (1998).

offered an 'appealing blend of realism and optimism,'[81] and the World Bank seemed to tap into something deeper.[82] The policy community seized on their findings. In 2000, the G-7 Finance Ministers called upon 'MDBs [to] emphasize a selective, quality-oriented approach rather than a quantity-oriented or profit-oriented one on the basis of clear definition of their roles as public institutions and their development mandates.'[83] The UK's Department for International Development (DFID) cited the report as evidence that 'development assistance can contribute to poverty reduction in countries pursuing sound policies.'[84] *The Economist* argued that 'there is now a strong body of evidence, led by the research of David Dollar, Craig Burnside and Paul Collier, all economists at the World Bank, that aid does boost growth when countries have reasonable economic policies.'[85] In March 2002, President George W. Bush also proposed a $5 billion-a-year 'Millennium Challenge Account' that would selectively reward countries that 'rule justly, invest in their people, and encourage economic freedom.'[86]

Among others, econometricians immediately attacked the Burnside and Dollar conclusions, finding serious weaknesses in their methods and measures.[87] Hansen and Tarp in 2001 presented one of the earliest critiques, finding that aid had a positive and statistically significant effect on economic growth in both good and bad 'policy environments.' By varying the econometric estimator and assuming diminishing returns to aid, they not only disconfirmed Burnside and Dollar's (2000a) findings, but found strong support for the opposite relationship. In 2004 William Easterly and his co-authors published a study (2004b) showing that when one extends the Burnside and Dollar 2000a study's dataset to cover more countries and a longer time period, using the same model specification, the 'aid only works in a good policy environment' finding no longer holds. Regardless of whether the Burnside and Dollar results are robust to different econometric specifications, their findings did have a major impact on the way donors think about aid effectiveness. Without the weight of the World Bank's public outreach machine, the Burnside and Dollar detractors have not had the same policy impact. But the point here is that if donors are getting more selective over time on the

---

[81] Roodman (2003: 1).

[82] One could place these points in a larger historical context. After the collapse of the Soviet Union, foreign aid policy was rudderless: its geo-strategic justification—rewarding friends and punishing enemies—became significantly less compelling. As a result, foreign aid lost an important source of domestic support and came under attack from left and right. The Burnside and Dollar work provided a new justification that refuted the severe critiques about aid's near total ineffectiveness.

[83] G-7 Finance Ministers (2000: 31).   [84] UK DFID (2000).

[85] 'Help in the Right Places' (2002).   [86] Bush (2002); Radelet (2003).

[87] Dalgaard and Hansen (2001); Hansen and Tarp (2001); Easterly et al. (2003); Guillaumont and Chauvet (2001); Lensink and White (2001); Lu and Ram (2001).

basis of these indicators, our hypotheses may be ahead of our data (1990–9), which may not fully capture this effect.[88]

In our final chapter we take a broad view of the evidence and draw some conclusions about whether aid is being greened, why it is being greened, and what we should expect going forward. We briefly review our findings, acknowledge their limitations, and articulate some potential policy reforms and directions for future research. We focus on the case of aid for climate change, which may have a significant impact on the entire aid and development agenda. We step back and reconsider the sum of the evidence from the four descriptive and three analytical chapters. In particular, we evaluate whether environmental aid overall appears to be eco-functional, dysfunctional, geopolitically driven, commercially driven, or a side payment for participation in treaties to address global environmental public goods.

---

[88] See Dollar and Levin (2004) on this point.

9

Looking to the Future of Environmental Aid

The natural resources of the earth, including the air, water, land, flora and fauna and especially representative samples of natural ecosystems, must be safeguarded for the benefit of present and future generations...Resources should be made available to preserve and improve the environment, taking into account the circumstances and particular requirements of developing countries and any costs which may emanate— from their incorporating environmental safeguards into their development planning and the need for making available to them, upon their request, additional international technical and financial assistance for this purpose.

Over three and a half decades ago, the idea that wealthier countries should pay the poorer countries to address environmental protection was articulated in Articles 2 and 12 of the Declaration of the United Nations Conference on the Human Environment, in Stockholm in 1972. These principles were echoed in Nairobi in 1982, Rio de Janeiro in 1992, Johannesburg in 2002, and seem to resurface at nearly every major international conference on the global environment. But the central tradeoffs articulated in the 1972 UN declaration still confront both developed and developing countries. The vast majority of unprotected and endangered species, pristine natural habitats, and other environmentally significant resources exist in the world's poorer countries, but preserving them may not directly benefit and could even harm the people living in those same countries. With continued warnings of environmental crisis and repeated promises of action, many observers have become cynical about the prospects for significant North–South coop-eration on the environment. However, we maintain that the international community had it right back in Stockholm: development assistance has promise as a tool to help realize the goals they articulated. Realizing those goals will require international cooperation. A necessary condition for such cooperation is the transfer of resources from those with enough to those that lack the financial wherewithal to implement effective environmental protection.

The potential importance of development assistance in catalyzing and underwriting such cooperation highlights the need for systematic analysis. In this book, we have taken the most comprehensive inventory to date of official North–South assistance flows to evaluate whether environmental aid promises have been met, how that aid is being allocated, and whether funds are flowing in ways that will prevent or repair damage to the environment. This is the first book to take stock of aid patterns before and after the watershed 1992 Rio Earth Summit—to describe who gave how much aid that is likely to have negative or beneficial impact on the environment, to whom, and toward what specific ends. Addressing these questions may help us answer some of the most vexing problems facing modern society—how to live well and within our ecological means in an unequal world.

In the preceding chapters, we analyzed how and why billions of dollars flow every year from rich countries to poor countries for the purpose of addressing environmental problems. We explored several potential motivations of donors (both bilateral and multilateral) and recipients through descriptive case studies and statistical analysis of their actual behavior. Some donors target environmental aid according to environmental needs, even when the conditions for success in recipient countries—in the form of good institutions and policies—do not exist. Other donors favor their neighbors, trading partners, strategic allies, and former colonies. Still others focus on recipient countries that have signaled a credible commitment to environmental protection. We also explored whether and to what extent donor governments finance environmental projects because of domestic political pressure, and why they might forgo the political benefits of implementing high-profile environmental projects bilaterally in favor of delegating responsibility to an international organization. In this final chapter, we review these findings and discuss some of the implications for effectively addressing local, regional, and global environmental problems.

After reviewing our findings, we discuss the limitations of our study and outline directions for future research. We then evaluate some recent proposals for redirecting climate change aid, which could potentially bring billions of dollars in new North–South financial flows and reshape the entire development agenda. By way of conclusion, we explore the policy implications of our findings, and outline ten principles to guide future reforms of the development assistance regime and to make environmental aid more effective.

Two Decades of Environmental Aid

For years, environmental campaigners argued that the overall impact of foreign aid was disastrous for the environment. Constructing dams, paving highways, draining marshes, straightening rivers, and building airports damaged the environment, and also opened frontier areas to settlement and further environmental degradation in previously inaccessible places. Yet, in many of these same cases, the impact of aid has been positive in human terms—in helping poorer countries cultivate new crops for export; in providing technical expertise and more basic infrastructure like electricity, refrigeration, transport, and storage to get higher-value products to markets halfway across the world; and by strengthening health and education systems that allow individuals to realize their full potential. Aid, in no small sense, has reshaped the world.

We began our analysis by examining overall trends in environmental aid and non-environmental aid. From 1980 to the end of the twentieth century, environmental aid increased substantially (from roughly $3 billion to about $10 billion a year), while dirty aid remained relatively unchanged at around $30 billion a year. Most bilateral and multilateral aid agencies have responded to the critiques of environmentalists and legislative overseers by conducting mandatory environmental impact assessments on large infrastructure projects and financing more stand-alone environmental projects. We also documented an important, but underappreciated trend: a massive increase in projects that are neither environmental nor dirty—projects we categorized as environmentally neutral. While some 'neutral' projects have environmentally positive and negative elements, most are simply not directly related to environmental outcomes. Therefore, three of the most important trends are the increase in environmental assistance, the rise of 'neutral' aid, and the (relative) decline in funding for projects that are likely to harm the environment. In this sense, aid has been greened substantially. However, dirty projects still attract about four times as much funding as environmental projects.[1]

Breaking down environmental aid into four major sectors revealed that water supply and sewage treatment projects attract the most environmental funding, with climate change and biodiversity project commitments increasing substantially (in numbers and amounts) only in the late 1990s. Funding to assist poor countries in combating desertification and other types of land degradation was largely neglected throughout the two decades, despite continued warnings from the scientific community and staggering estimates of need. Water and sanitation projects remain popular among recipient countries, perhaps because of the direct economic and social benefits and the high visibility of such projects among large numbers of potential urban voters.

---

[1] There is also interesting variation along the bilateral/multilateral dimension. Bilateral funders more thoroughly 'greened' over the 1980–2000 period. However, they also gave as much or more financing at the end of the 1990s to projects that were likely to cause serious environmental damage.

Chapter 2 also revealed that the first half of the 1990s was the period of greatest growth for both green and brown environmental aid. Largely because of water projects after the 1992 Rio Earth Summit, brown aid increased from roughly 5 per cent of all aid to 9 per cent in the mid-1990s. However, it returned to earlier levels in the last two years of the decade. Financing for green projects, what some readers might consider to be 'true environmental aid,' increased from just 1 per cent of total aid during the whole 1980s to around 3 per cent in the 1990s. Green aid is continuing to become a larger proportion of environmental aid, growing from a fifth at the beginning of the 1980s to about a third in the last years of the 1990s. Together, green and brown projects constituted about 12 per cent of all foreign assistance for about six years: from 1993 to 1997. In all other years during our study period, environmental aid represented less than a tenth of foreign assistance. So has aid been 'greened?' While it has not come close to reaching the levels promised at Rio or the levels that scientists argue are needed to address global commons problems, by all three of our measures discussed above, aid has indeed become 'greener.'

Chapter 3 reported broad cross-national patterns in environmental aid and attempted to explain why some countries receive more than others. There were several unsurprising countries on the list of top recipients, such as Brazil, India, China, Indonesia, Mexico, and Bangladesh.[2] However, there were also some unexpected large recipients of environmental aid: Pakistan, the Philippines, South Korea, and Algeria. China and India are central to the story of environmental aid's rise over the final two decades of the twentieth century. China's environmental aid rose steeply in the early 1990s, about five years after it received sharp increases in infrastructure funding and other types of dirty aid. Although China did not appear on the list of the top ten environmental aid recipient countries in the 1980s, it surpassed all the others by over 50 per cent in the 1990s, receiving more than $10 billion 1995–9 alone. India's environmental aid nearly tripled (to $6.5 billion) in the last five years of the 1990s. Both countries have a similar list of top environmental donors: the World Bank, the Asian Development Bank, Japan, and Germany. Yet, major donors such as the World Bank, the Asian Development Bank, and Japan gave China seven times more funding for dirty projects than for environmental projects. While promises of environmental aid have been critical to securing India and China's often reluctant participation in environmental agreements in the past, it is unclear whether concessionary loans and grants will continue to be useful in catalyzing cooperation in the future. Both countries are experiencing significant economic growth—suggesting the amount of aid in the

---

[2] If receipts are calculated on a per capita basis, some of the smaller countries with populations under one million rise to the top, but with some tiny countries receiving huge amounts per person these are nearly insignificant parts of the environmental aid picture.

form of a side payment will have to increase proportionately.[3] Further, China itself is emerging as a major donor.

We also analyzed two recipient countries that have large stocks of natural capital: Brazil, with its tropical rainforests, and Kenya, with its 'charismatic' wildlife. For these countries, the debate around environmental aid is quite different. In the 1980s, environmentalists raised alarm in America and Europe about burning rainforests, and managed to put enough pressure on the World Bank and the EU to halt funding for major projects in the Brazilian Amazon. Kenya's environmental aid has been coming from a different set of donors (including many smaller European states) who have attempted to protect wildlife while addressing population growth and meeting human needs with better water resource management and assistance to farmers and herders.

In Chapter 4, we analyzed environmental aid allocation patterns across recipient countries and found mixed evidence for different theories of aid allocation. The most powerful predictors of bilateral environmental aid include a recipient country's population size, poverty level, and tendency to vote with its donor in the UN General Assembly. We expected that large, poor countries would receive more environmental aid, but the fact that donors assist countries that vote *against* them in the UN was a great surprise, and we offered some plausible but largely speculative explanations for this finding. We also found that the receipt of environmental aid was positively related to the effectiveness of a recipient country's government institutions, the transparency of its environmental policies, and whether it was once a colony. The size of a recipient country's natural capital stocks was of minor but positive importance, as was the level of trade with a given donor country. Unexpectedly, environmental aid was negatively correlated with participation in environmental treaties. This suggests that bilateral donors may use environmental aid as an inducement, rather than a reward, for participation in global environmental accords. Donors also seem to discriminate in favor of recipient countries within close geographic proximity—perhaps a signal that donors are particularly focused on solving regional environmental problems that directly impact their national welfare.

Multilateral environmental aid appears to be targeted somewhat differently than bilateral aid. IOs favor recipient countries with lower levels of environmental need, larger human populations, more effective government institutions, and significant stocks of natural capital. Democratic institutions and environmental treaty participation did not explain which countries received multilateral environmental aid. On balance, our results suggest that bilateral donors are more selective than multilateral donors with respect to a recipient country's poverty level, quality of governance, environmental needs, and

---

[3] On the role of side payments inducing international cooperation see Martin (1992).

environmental policy regime. This was surprising given the consensus in the economics and political science literature that bilateral aid is targeted toward geopolitical allies and former colonies.

These models raise important questions about how to define 'eco-functionalism.' Is an eco-functional ('environmentally-friendly') donor simply a donor that channels its environmental assistance to countries with the greatest environmental needs? What if many recipient countries have degraded environments because they are plagued by weak government institutions, low levels of domestic accountability, institutionalized networks of official corruption, and poor economic and environmental policies? Would it not then be 'eco-functional' for a donor to take a hard-nosed look at where the *opportunities for change* are greatest? This suggests a more complex mix of eco-functional criteria, including a recipient country's commitment to good governance, sound economic policies, credible and transparent environmental policies, and perhaps even level of economic need. Figuring out where an individual aid dollar can have the greatest environmental impact requires an understanding of political economy, as well as ecology and biology.

The behavior of individual aid donors has been shaped by the legacies of the Second World War and the Cold War (Chapter 5). Ranking among the most generous donor countries are Japan and Germany, who saw aid as crucial to rebuilding their standing as members of the global community after the Second World War. After decades of using foreign aid to secure access to natural resources and markets, Japan switched gears in the late 1980s with huge pledges of environmental aid in 1989 and 1992. Taking a very different tack than northern Europe, which has increasingly focused on the poorest countries, Japan targeted middle-income countries. Japan saw environmental crises in rapidly developing countries, especially those with urban pollution problems close to its own territory, as potentially impinging upon its own national welfare. Facing severe resource and oil supply uncertainties, Japan has also developed extremely efficient equipment for industry and residences, and growing environmental concern in developing countries has opened up important markets for these products. In the other cases, we saw the effects of electoral shifts in driving increases and cutbacks in environmental aid budgets: in Germany's Green Party, Labour's election in the UK, and Denmark's Liberal Party. For all five major donors studied in Chapter 5, the ratio of dirty aid to environmental aid plummeted in the 1980s and never rose again, marking a true reorientation of aid. The cases also highlighted the significance of the 1992 Rio de Janeiro Earth Summit, which brought short-term increases in environmental aid (including billions for sewage projects in Rio itself) and longer-term changes. Bilateral environmental aid increased by a factor of three, and several major bilateral donors also shifted towards funding global environmental issues in the late 1990s.

Taken as a whole, the changing composition of bilateral aid portfolios is striking. On average, donor governments spent almost three times as much of their foreign aid on environmental projects in the late 1990s as they did in the early 1980s. Some spent upwards of 12 per cent, while others spent less than 6 per cent. Meanwhile, the share of funding allocated to dirty projects dropped sharply, from over 45 per cent a year in the early 1980s to near 20 per cent a year in the late 1990s. In Chapter 6, we attempted to explain these patterns more systematically. Our models were far more effective at predicting the share of aid that donors earmarked for dirty projects than they were at predicting the share of environmental funding. Wealth, post-materialist values, and the strength of a donor country's 'green and greedy' coalition (made up of environmentalists and green technology firms) all exerted a negative influence on the share of bilateral aid dedicated to dirty projects. The revealed environmental preferences of voters—as measured by international environmental treaty ratification and compliance patterns—were more consistently effective at explaining the rise of environmental aid. Yet interestingly, the strength of a donor country's domestic environmental policy appears to actually *reduce* the amount spent abroad on environmental issues. Finally, 'green and greedy' coalitions were positively correlated with green (global issues) aid shares, but negatively correlated with brown (local issues) aid shares, which suggests that it is difficult to build a strong domestic coalition in wealthy donor countries for the environmental problems of greatest importance to the developing world. Where 'green and greedy' coalitions are strong, they appear to have increased funding for regional and global environmental issues (green aid), but not for local environmental issues (brown aid).

Chapter 7 showed how multilateral agencies granted or loaned developing countries over $75 billion in environmental aid in the 1980s and 1990s, and five of those agencies were responsible for over 90 per cent of the funding. Every multilateral agency saw major increases in their environmental funding over the period, and together they nearly tripled their environmental funding. Yet, at the end of our study period, multilateral agencies spent over four times as much on projects with likely negative environmental impacts. We evaluated the relatively recent 'greening' of the Asian Development Bank, and briefly examined OPEC's development fund (OFID). It is no surprise that the multilateral organization with the greatest representation of developing countries is also the one that focuses most heavily on brown aid. The World Bank, which we examined in a more extended case study, was responsible for one-third to one-half of all multilateral environmental aid. Our case studies suggest that shareholders of the World Bank and other MDBs have institutionalized voting arrangements in ways that give them significant influence over major policy and even project-level funding decisions. Unlike the OFID executive board, the governments disproportionately represented on the World Bank board are the wealthy donor countries of the West, and the portfolio of the Bank reflects this different distribution of preferences with a much greater emphasis on green aid. The Global Environment Facility case also illustrated the importance of funding 'replenishments.' Donor countries often use the power of the purse strings to implement institutional reforms that may be unpopular among IO staff and recipient countries. Multilateral development banks, like the World Bank, are insulated from this pressure to a greater extent because they can replenish some of their own funding with loan repayments from recipient countries. But the GEF is entirely dependent upon periodic replenishments.

The final research questions addressed with multivariate analyses are found in Chapter 8. First, we examined why some countries delegate more of their environmental aid to multilateral agencies than others. To our surprise, the administrative cost of delivering aid bilaterally was not a significant predictor of multilateralism. We also found that small donor countries seem to favor multilateral mechanisms, perhaps to increase their influence and reduce the overall cost of delivering assistance. Interestingly, small donors seem to particularly favor multilateralism when allocating and implementing *green* aid. This finding supports the notion that small states can maximize their bargaining leverage vis-à-vis recipient countries and overall impact on collective good provision when they channel aid for global public goods through multilateral mechanisms. Counter-intuitively, our models also suggest that revealed voter preferences for international environmental protection—as measured by international environmental treaty compliance—are *negatively* associated with a donor country's multilateral orientation. This does not support our original hypothesis that donors delegate environmental aid to multilateral agencies to escape the so-called Samaritan's Dilemma. However, it is possible that donors with a strong domestic mandate to solve international environmental problems also have the authority to allocate their environmental aid efficiently and enforce conditionality contracts through bilateral channels. We also speculated that donors facing strong domestic pressure to 'do something' about international environmental problems may prefer to reap the domestic political benefits associated with being responsible for high-profile bilateral environmental projects. Finally, contrary to our prediction, bilateral donors that are relatively effective at allocating their assistance were *more* likely to delegate to multilaterals. While it is possible that donors with the domestic political 'space' to allocate their own aid efficiently also have an electorate that understands the efficiency gains associated with supra-national delegation, we believe more research is needed in this area.

In Chapter 8, we also examined why some multilateral institutions are preferred over others. As we expected, a multilateral's environmental expertise was a statistically and substantively significant predictor of whether donors will channel environmental assistance through it, which lends support to the idea that donors try to capture scale and scope economies by delegating authority to multilateral agents. Our models also suggested that a multilateral agency's prospects for receiving aid are higher when it has established a track record of performance, which supports the hypothesis that donors screen and select multilateral agents based on concerns about 'adverse selection.' The evidence on whether donors systematically favor multilateral agencies that invest in recipient countries with good institutions and the potential to deliver global environmental benefits was inconclusive.

While donors generally favor multilateral institutions in which they have more formal decision-making power, they also systematically favor those IOs (at the gate-keeping stage) that grant *some* formal decision-making power to recipient countries. Yet, when donors are deciding *how much* environmental (and green) aid to give to a multilateral agency, they strongly favor institutions without formal recipient country representation and institutions in which they have substantial formal decision-making power. One way to interpret this finding is that donors acknowledge the importance of eliciting developing country buy-in, but they find it difficult to resolve their differences with recipient countries in practice, and therefore favor 'donor-dominated' multilateral institutions.

In Roberts and Parks (2007a), we argue that North–South inequality makes it harder for developed and developing countries to trust each other and establish mutually acceptable 'rules of the game' in global environmental negotiations.[4] As such, demandeurs (in this case, donors) may try to send 'costly signals' to prove their trustworthiness and bridge the North–South divide.[5] For example, the (reformed) GEF gave developing countries more say in the institutions' decision-making processes (including environmental aid allocation) through 'double majority' voting rules.[6] However, as a practical matter, it has been exceedingly difficult for donor and recipient governments to work together and agree upon key issues at the GEF. The controversy surrounding the GEF's performance-based aid allocation system is a case in point (see Chapter 3).

---

[4] Mutually acceptable 'rules of the game' are crucial because they reduce uncertainty, stabilize expectations, constrain opportunism, and increase the credibility of state commitments. On the role of international regimes enhancing cooperation see Krasner (1983); Young (1989); Ruggie (1992).

[5] Andrew Kydd (2000) defines costly signals as 'signals designed to persuade the other side that one is trustworthy by virtue of the fact that they are so costly that one would hesitate to send them if one were untrustworthy.'

[6] Woods (1999); Streck (2001). Rich countries agreed to institutionalize decision-making rules that substantively favor developing countries because of the generalized mistrust that 'one-dollar-one-vote' multilateral institutions, like the World Bank and IMF, generated. In the context of climate change negotiations, developed countries have also invited developing countries to participate in the 'Compliance Committee' (without having to adopt scheduled emission reduction commitments) and treated them as 'equal' partners through the double majority voting mechanism Roberts and Parks (2007a).

Limitations of our Study and Directions for Future Research

We believe it is important to acknowledge the limitations of this study and consider how future research could improve our understanding of the links between the environment and development. First, while we have explored global environmental aid allocation patterns by multilateral and bilateral official donors, there were many financial flows that we did not study. Increasingly, developing countries finance their development through foreign direct investment, revenue generated by trade, commercial bank loans, private remittances, and development assistance from private foundations and NGOs. While the absolute amount of official assistance has increased over the past twenty-five years, the share of resources coming from donor governments and IOs has declined relative to private sources. So, while official aid has surely greened, this does not necessarily mean that the development policies of poor countries have greened. Western taxpayers and voters may take solace in the fact that their governments are doing less harm to the environment in developing countries, but if these 'dirty' projects are now simply being financed with commercial bank loans or foreign direct investment, then the environmental impact of 'greened' aid may be largely cancelled out. The case studies of dirty projects in both China and Brazil are instructive in this regard. When official Western donors pulled out of these projects, other financiers sometimes stepped in to replace them. Future research should address this issue of substitutability. The first (and very challenging) step in such research should be the systematic collection of data on alternative sources of development finance.[7]

Second, in this book we described and analyzed the allocation of dirty, neutral, and environmental assistance, but aid effectiveness was left unstudied. Assessing the effectiveness of environmental aid projects has to date been mostly ad hoc, inconsistent, and not comparable across countries or sectors.[8] So, the long-term impacts of environmental projects remain understudied and poorly understood: it is certainly possible that the funding for the environmental projects documented in this book may ultimately have very little positive environmental impact. Hence, we need

---

[7] The PLAID research team hopes to collect comparable project-level data on NGO and private foundation giving in developing countries.

[8] Biodiversity funding is a case in point. A recent evaluation of the GEF's biodiversity program suggests that 'it is not possible to determine the GEF's cumulative impact on ... global biodiversity conservation at this time' GEF (2005: 19). A separate evaluation found that 'there are still no clear guidelines, standardized procedures, or measurable program-level targets or indicators to assess the impacts of the GEF portfolio on biodiversity status.' The same report recommended that 'links between project-level indicators of outcomes and impacts and their relationships to indicators of the program goal (that is, changes in the status of global biodiversity) must be more clearly established and dedicated work on this topic should be undertaken' GEF (2004c).

more research on the actual impact of dirty, neutral, and environmental aid projects.[9]

Of course the mere presence of environmental damage from a project is not a reason to automatically exclude it from funding. The environmental impacts need to be weighed against social and economic benefits of the project. As such, there is a serious need for rigorous impact evaluation. The PLAID database could play a useful role in this regard. While the existing literature on aid effectiveness has focused on the relationship between total aid flows—including support for military expenditures, peacekeeping, land-mine clearance, free and fair elections, civil society, biodiversity protection, HIV/AIDS, drug trafficking, and refugee movements—and causally distant (or causally unrelated) outcomes like economic growth and infant mortality, the reality is that such research probably obscures more than it reveals.[10] Biodiversity aid is not designed to accelerate short-term economic growth. Nor is democracy assistance intended to reduce infant mortality. Therefore, future research should evaluate the impact that *specific* types of aid have on *specific* development outcomes. The PLAID database enables researchers to do just that.[11]

However, to truly understand the impact of individual projects and specific interventions, a great deal of project-level research will also be needed. Development research is increasingly drawing upon the kinds of methods that are employed in modern medicine—in particular, random selection of treatment and comparison groups, but also regression discontinuity analysis, propensity score matching, and difference-in-difference analysis.[12] These types of methods enable researchers to answer the key counterfactual question: How would the 'treatment group' have fared in the absence of a donor-financed project?[13] For example, Esther Duffo and several of her colleagues at MIT's Poverty Action Lab are currently analyzing the impact of a randomized 'clean stove' program in Orissa, India.[14] Chomitz and Wertz-Kanounnikoff (2005)

---

[9] Fungibility (using the freed-up cash from aided sectors to fund other parts of the budget) is also a key issue that will require serious examination in the future. The peculiarities of implementing agencies also shape final project outcomes. Although studying these parts of the chain may require an entirely different approach, we hope our global study will inspire strategically chosen cases and help put these cases into comparative context.

[10] Boone (1996); Burnside and Dollar (2000a); Hansen and Tarp (2001); Easterly et al. (2004a, 2004b); Collier and Dollar (2002); Easterly (2003); Roodman (2003).

[11] While we do not focus on aid effectiveness in this book, PLAID data collection and coding at the project level will enhance efforts to identify the causes of and conditions for aid effectiveness. For early efforts to do this type of sector-specific analysis of aid effectiveness see Bermeo (2006); Clemens et al. (2004).

[12] Duflo (2004).

[13] For example, one would not want to conduct a simple pre-program and post-program analysis of a reforestation project, as deforestation may have declined or improved, independently of the program, due to a change in climatic conditions or agricultural prices Chomitz and Wert-Kanounnikoff (2005).

[14] Dufflo et al. (2007).

have evaluated an innovative Brazilian licensing and enforcement system that was designed to reduce deforestation. Their difference-in-difference research design enabled them to determine that, while deforestation increased during their study period, there were 'post-program declines in deforestation in high-priority enforcement areas relative to other areas.'[15]

A third limitation of this study is our reliance on national-level variables, such as GDP per capita or water pollution. Most recipient countries possess significant variation across regions and districts, in terms of both environmental quality and number of environmental aid projects. A next step in environmental aid research would be to look at sub-national regions or states and their levels of wealth or biodiversity or water pollution in order to examine whether aid to particularly needy or threatened areas is allocated there, and if so, whether it is effective.

A fourth shortcoming of this study is its inability to account for the 'marbling,' or 'mainstreaming,' of environmental aid into larger projects, and the difficulty of assigning one project category in counting schemes like ours. Many projects now include infrastructure and environmental elements together in one project. This issue is extremely difficult to resolve, as different views are provided by different systems of categorization. We stand by the value of developing one coding list (as we showed in Chapter 2) and counting all projects in those categories the same way: this method maintains consistent categories which are applied over the entire time period and the whole spectrum of donors. Ideally, we would be able to count the percentage of the project budget given for each element of the project in each of our tally categories.[16] However, the problem with allowing one large project to be counted in multiple sectors is that the information for doing the categorization is not evenly supplied across donors and time. Some donors provide detailed descriptions, while others provide only a title; some provide more data in recent years than in earlier times; and some now provide online files with detailed project descriptions, implementation documents, budgets, and impact evaluations. The World Bank is one of the few donors that provide detailed financial data on the total amount of environmental aid mainstreamed into its projects, and Nielson and Tierney (2003: 68–9) find that this type of environmental funding represents a significant amount of total environmental assistance. Providing searchable databases with all of this information is a future step for the larger PLAID (Project-Level Aid) project of which this book is a part.

[15] Chomitz and Wertz-Kanounnikoff (2005: 1). For an additional example, see Bandyopadhyaya et al. (2004).

[16] Dan Nielson and his research team at BYU are pioneering this type of work with data on multilateral donors where they employ PLAID sub-sector codes so that an individual project can have up to five ordinally ranked codes corresponding to different development sectors (e.g. environment, agriculture, transportation, gender...).

Fifth, as we discussed in the case study of the UK agency DFID, their internal accounting system for environmental aid provides a useful comparison with our own project categorization. In that case, a bilateral agency counted projects whose main goals were not primarily environmental (but which included an environmental element) as 'environmental.' As a result, their estimate of environmental aid was twice ours. We believe the same might be true for the 'Rio Marker' of environmental projects inconsistently categorized in the OECD DAC database, as this field is reported by donors and is not subject to external validation or uniform coding standards. Pressure on agencies to show they are 'doing something about the environment' suggests that donors have an incentive to overstate their environmental lending and grants. If countries, NGOs, scholars, or citizens are interested in assessing the real impact of aid on the environment, independent and systematic reviews of these types of assessments are needed.

Sixth, we are aware that our analysis fails to consider a complex dimension of aid contracts made between donors and recipients. For example, aid of different types tends to travel together: our results in Chapter 4 indicate that aid flows overall tend to be influenced similarly by conditions in recipient countries, regardless of the sector. While there are some exceptions, this finding provides evidence that the aid contract extends beyond sectors and that recipients may be induced to accept environmental aid only if some other type of aid is also a part of the package. We have not systematically investigated this type of recipient leverage, and want to caution readers that this leverage is probably very important for any type of project having global benefits and significant local costs.

Seventh, we sought to use the most comprehensive set of aid projects in our analysis. Therefore, our definition of international development assistance extends beyond that of official development assistance and includes projects with lower grant elements. Consequently, we may not be capturing differences across donors with respect to the component of each project that is a grant versus what must be repaid. This concern, while not perfectly addressed, is diminished to a great degree since our analysis is done with *shares* of aid flows. However, our summary statistics and totals do make comparisons across donors in ways that may conflate projects with markedly different grant elements. We recognize this limitation, but intentionally chose to have as comprehensive an analysis as possible. Readers can use the 'grant element' variable in the PLAID database to re-analyze specific claims. Such procedures may be appropriate depending on the research question being asked.

Finally, our aid allocation models in Chapters 4, 6, and 8 are based on a relatively short time period: 1990–9. We selected this time period because environmental measures used as explanatory variables in our models largely did not exist in significant numbers across countries prior to 1990. We therefore restricted our attention to the 1990s for most of the econometric models and this has hampered our ability to attempt more sophisticated techniques. It also made the identification of effects difficult. Even with these limitations, our models offer several interesting findings.

Climate Change and the Future of Environmental Aid

The latest trends in foreign aid are to 'make poverty history' with the achievement of the Millennium Development Goals, focus on Africa, and provide recipient governments with more 'budget support' and less project funding. Environmental aid also remains a salient issue because of the sharp increase in attention around the world to global climate change. A growing number of official and non-governmental aid agencies are now discussing how to 'climate-proof' their projects. Andy Atkins of Tearfund put it this way: 'Before governments embark on major agricultural projects, they must understand how increasingly erratic rainfall will affect water supply and crop yields. And as governments invest in health systems, they must be confident they will cope with changing patterns of disease linked to climate change. By the end of the decade this "climate-proofing" of development must become the norm, not the exception. Without urgent action billions of dollars of aid money could be wasted and many lives needlessly jeopardized.'[17]

The basic paradox of global climate change is that the poor countries did not create the problem, but they will suffer most of the negative consequences: rising sea levels, devastating droughts and storms, lower agricultural yields, and increased disease burdens.[18] They are also being pressured to swallow large short-run economic costs to reduce carbon emissions. Environmental campaigners fear that the burning of the Amazon and South-East Asian forests could destabilize these regional ecosystems, and that booms in automobile use and the construction of coal-fired power plants in China and India may soon outweigh any reductions in emissions that wealthy countries manage to achieve under the first round of the Kyoto Protocol. In short, the global North is pushing the global South to not do what it did: develop at the expense of forests, waters, and the air.

Built into the 1992 UN Framework Convention on Climate Change negotiations is the keystone principle of 'common and differentiated responsibility,' whereby the industrialized countries that caused the bulk of the emissions problem would act first, and only after doing so would poorer countries begin to take action. In 1972, Brazil called this the 'happy coincidence' that those who created the problems have the means to address them.

In order to ensure developing country participation and strengthen adaptive capacity in the face of the climate change, aid still seems to be the only

---

[17] Tearfund (2006).   [18] Roberts and Parks (2007a).

way forward. In late 2001, under the auspices of the Marrakech Accords, donor countries agreed to provide three funds to make participation in the Kyoto Protocol feasible for poorer countries. The first of these was an adaptation fund, to help countries likely to be hit by climate disasters to prepare, respond, and rebuild. This fund could soon become very large, as it will be financed with a 2 per cent levy on the proceeds from poor countries helping wealthy countries meet their Kyoto commitments through the selling of certificates that verify their emissions were reduced elsewhere.[19] Wealthy countries also established a special climate change fund to support technology transfer, greenhouse gas emitting sectors, and economic diversification in countries that might be hurt by addressing carbon emissions. A least developed country fund was also created to help such countries prepare national plans of action to prioritize how to prepare for an altered climate. However, these financial commitments were not mandatory, and there is no burden-sharing formula. The funds remain under-financed, and recipient countries are frustrated that to receive these funds they must implement projects that are 'additional' to what they would have done without the funds—a counterfactual that is nearly impossible to prove.

The Clean Development Mechanism (CDM) plan and the adaptation levy have been very slow in starting up but hold substantial promise. They could generate hundreds of millions of dollars by 2012.[20] But initial flows suggest that the money is narrowly targeting emission reductions in big countries like China and Brazil. These projects also seem to provide relatively few social and economic benefits to recipient countries. The 2006 'Stern Report' described why the CDM by itself is not a sufficient response to climate change in developing countries by discussing the major policy and program changes that will be needed: 'Programmes on this scale can take place only in the context of structural reforms and development policies implemented by national or regional governments. Investment in CDM projects tends to be directed towards countries where there is a strong enabling environment for private sector investment (for example, economic and political stability, liberalized markets, strong legal structures), and countries that have built up national capacity for using this source of funding.'[21] Individuals and companies buying carbon offsets through traders and NGOs face many of the same problems. Therefore, there will likely still be a role for official assistance, since market mechanisms will send money only to some of the areas of need.

The booming market for CDM credits has led to another intriguing set of proposals in which countries that slow or stop deforestation are able to sell carbon permits for 'avoided deforestation.' This UN-regulated, but market-based, proposal was raised by Papua New Guinea and fifteen other

---

[19] This is called the CDM, the Clean Development Mechanism.
[20] Muller and Hepburn (2006).   [21] Stern (2006: 508).

tropical forest countries at the November 2005 Montreal meetings of the UNFCCC/Kyoto Protocol.[22] In November 2006, Brazil introduced a competing proposal based on a standard amount of compensation for each hectare of forest preserved. This proposal is based on an entirely different model, relying on environmental aid of substantial proportions, not on the sale and purchase of permits. In either case, compensation for the avoidance of deforestation may be a huge new stream of environmental aid.

This brief look at the future role of aid in addressing climate change raises the wider question of what the future of environmental aid will look like. Will there be a shift toward market mechanisms (with some marginal adjustments like the 2 per cent adaptation tax on CDM projects), or will official assistance remain dominant? If market mechanisms are preferred, we suspect that significant development funding will still have to be channeled to institutions that track and monitor carbon reduction credits. There is vigorous debate about this issue at the moment.[23] We will argue shortly that truly 'climate proofing' countries will require a much bigger project: there will be a need for substantial amounts of aid that effectively integrate environmental and development objectives.

Policy Implications and Recommendations

When we summed our entire dataset of development projects, the total from the early 1970s to early 2000s was over $2.3 trillion. Aid budgets have increased, but donor countries are nowhere near the promise made in the 1970s to give 0.7 per cent of their GDP to developing countries through their foreign aid programs. Countries furthest away from meeting that goal, like the United States, often claim that private funds through NGOs, churches, universities, and family remittances constitute a significant portion of their country's generosity.[24]

As we suggested above, the question of what drives and sustains Western environmental aid budgets has profound 'downstream' consequences for poor countries. We posited that if Western citizens are primarily motivated by post-materialist values, we would expect their governments to promote environmental values abroad in an altruistic and non-discriminatory manner, rather than using environmental aid as a coercive policy instrument. We found this

---

[22] Santilli et al. (2005); Moutinho and Santilli (2005).

[23] The 2% adaptation tax will be insufficient to address the $10–50 billion financing gap that is allegedly needed to help countries adapt to climate change every year. This number itself is exceedingly contested, and illustrates just how difficult it is to know whether one is actually addressing environmental needs.

[24] USAID webpage, www.usaid.gov (2006); the claim is based on the Hudson Institute's 2006 *Global Index of Philanthropy* report.

to be partly true at best. We predicted that if Western support for environmental aid was tied to specific trans-boundary environmental threats, then a more selective allocation of environmental assistance—both among implementing agencies and recipient countries—would be observed. Our findings do suggest that interest groups influence the allocation to green environmental projects at the expense of addressing local environmental problems of greater concern to recipient countries.

Critics of the 'aid industry' also suggest that the dirtiest projects are shifting to agencies that are more difficult for environmentalists to target—like private banks and export promotion agencies, which have lower levels of transparency and oversight.[25] When it comes to financing the projects to which outside environmentalists most object, like the Three Gorges Dam and road-building in the Amazon, some developing countries, like Brazil and China, have turned to self-funding or private sources. Official development assistance will never reach all environmentally damaged areas or even all large projects in developing countries. However, the increased attention to the environment in multilateral banks and bilateral agencies is forcing many developing countries to consider the impacts of sweeping development plans much earlier in the planning process. The 'partial greening of aid' documented here has had implications far beyond the trends we documented from studying hundreds of thousands of projects for these twenty years. Developing country governments have had to change their approach on many more issues to meet environmental criteria if they wanted aid of any sort.

That said, many countries are being left behind in the effort to fund environmental projects. Some lack large or conspicuous natural resources that gain international attention. Some lack large populations, economic power, or geo-political significance. Some lack proximity to donor countries, or have been off the well-beaten trail of tropical biologists to their favorite field research stations.[26] These other countries need environmental aid as much as, or perhaps more than, the 'usual suspects.' Barbara Connolly argues that environmental aid can be used to specifically target those countries with poor environmental policies in order to enhance national concern for environmental protection and strengthen weak environmental institutions: 'Environmental assistance . . . [creates] . . . windows of opportunity: chances to augment financial resources in order to enable recipients to devote more attention to environmental problems; to build strong political coalitions in a position to protect the environment; to package a deal to make environmental protection appeal to actors whom it otherwise would not.'[27] She continues in proposing the ambitious but very delicate role for this kind of aid: '[n]ot only can environmental assistance alter the incentives of key actors, it can also

[25] Rich (2003).   [26] E.g. Vandermeer and Perfecto (1995); Roberts and Thanos (2003).
[27] Connolly (1996: 328).

contribute to a redistribution of capabilities and hence political clout behind actors who exhibit environmental concern.... By increasing the political and financial resources of strategic coalitions within recipient countries that share donors' environmental goals, environmental aid may simultaneously boost concern and capacity.'

An open question is whether multilateral agencies, particularly specialized ones like the Global Environment Facility, are able to allocate environmental aid more efficiently than others. Our preliminary analysis in Chapter 4 showed that bilateral agencies were more effective in allocating environmental aid to recipients that have demonstrated a credible commitment to environmental protection.

However, multilateral agencies have been the site of recent debates over whether there should be (*ex ante* or *ex post*) conditions placed on poor countries receiving aid, including environmental aid. Many recipient countries have adamantly opposed this idea, and in pursuing this approach there is great risk that these multilateral agencies will be seen as the handmaidens of global superpowers. This can damage the credibility of these agencies and undermine their ability to elicit the cooperation of recipient countries in the future.[28]

China and India loom ever larger in the story of aid and its impact on the environment. Both are major recipients, geopolitical players, and key actors in global environmental politics. Some initial analysis suggests that aid for efficiency of power stations is followed by measurable improvements in energy efficiency a few years later, so aid appears to have a key role in the issue.[29] China seems at the time of this writing to be making major shifts in its environmental policy, adopting efficiency and pollution requirements exceeding some wealthy countries (like the US). However, enforcement remains weak and this is a potential gap for environmental aid to attempt to fill. Another twist is that with huge financial reserves and trade surpluses, China is emerging as a leading donor, increasing investments and aid abroad, building on four decades of experience.[30] There have always been other donors outside the OECD DAC group, but with shifts in the global economy, this group may expand.

Our results have also shown that increases in national wealth and post-materialist values in donor countries correspond with declines in dirty aid, which could potentially have a huge impact on poor countries. Recipients generally want more dirty aid, since these are the key facilities they associate with accelerating economic growth: roads, power lines, power plants, mines, factories, and so on. The prospects from this analysis are dim for their access

---

[28] This is the case with the Global Environmental Facility and the Kyoto funds such as the Adaptation Levy, as was debated in the Nairobi 2006 meetings.

[29] Martinot (2001).   [30] Brautigam (2007).

to such funding in a future with wealthier and more post-materialist donor country citizens. The findings from the green, brown, and environmental side of the analysis have similarly grave implications for poor countries wishing to address core socio-environmental issues like land degradation and water supply. The rise of 'green and greedy' coalitions may result in the reduction of the bilateral funding available to these issues. Protected parks and climate change will most likely be better funded.

We argue that environmental aid should be reconsidered in the context of national development planning. In particular, some of the most polluting, energy- and resource-intensive stages in the production process of modern manufactures are being increasingly relocated to developing countries. Asking developing countries to curb emissions from these industries is therefore a tough sell and may require compensation and assistance to shift to 'alternative development pathways' for their participation in global initiatives on environmental protection.

The analysis in this book suggests some principles that aid agencies and donor governments should embrace if they are interested in the twin goals of promoting environmental protection and reducing poverty in developing countries. We propose that ten of these are particularly important.

Ten Principles for Improving the Environmental Performance of Aid Agencies

1. Environmental aid planning and allocation cannot be done outside of national development planning in recipient countries. Development and environmental planning need to be integrated.

2. The transfer of environmental assistance should be conceived of as a cooperative contract that implies mutual policy adjustment by both donor and recipient. Asking recipient governments to unilaterally clean up the environment and enforce new regulations without some compensation is unrealistic. Similarly, asking donors to allocate resources to developing countries without credible guarantees that recipients will alter their behavior is equally unrealistic.

3. Recipients of environmental assistance that actively address global environmental issues through planning, regulation, public education, or remediation should be rewarded with other types of aid that are more highly valued by the recipient government.

4. If recipient countries are going to transition to less pollution-intensive development pathways, then donor countries must recognize the political consequences of such economic changes and design aid programs to compensate firms, individuals, and groups who suffer as a consequence of these environmental reforms.

5. Aid allocations should be based on scientific assessments of environmental need as much as possible.

6. Environmental aid should be directed to areas where it is likely to be most effective.

7. Tied aid should be reduced or eliminated because it reduces the environmental rate of return on donor investments by artificially restricting competition for goods and services purchased with aid dollars.

8. Donor coordination requires better information on allocation and effectiveness. Specifically, the development community needs a single database that covers all donors (OECD bilateral donors, multilateral donors, emerging donors, and, ideally, private donors). The current data system is not sufficient for coordination in the field because it lacks real time information and because of gaps in the data and non-uniform standards for classifying different types of assistance.

9. Recipient countries must have greater say in the allocation of environmental aid.

10. Recipient governments and local groups within developing countries need to participate more in the planning and execution of aid projects. If recipients lack a sense of ownership, then the likely effectiveness of the project will be reduced.

These principles do not provide policy options for bilateral or multilateral agencies, but provide a guiding list of values with which to evaluate reform proposals now being considered in the development community.

Compared with the certainty expressed in the 1972 Stockholm Declaration about why we need environmental funding to flow from the global North to the South, the history documented here has been anything but certain. During the 1980s and 1990s, environmental aid increased substantially and aid with negative environmental effects declined as a share of total assistance; however, as described in Chapter 7, there are preliminary indications that funding for infrastructure and extractive industries could be on the rise again. Our analysis in Chapter 3 showed that the prescriptions for environmental aid made at Rio in the huge Agenda 21 document have largely not been implemented. Looking ahead to the issues of climate change and biodiversity loss, the time may finally be arriving when environmental protection and economic development can be planned and managed together. Aid will play a crucial role in this effort: coordination and strategic planning among donors, and understanding the determinants of aid effectiveness, will require careful and complete analysis of aid and its environmental impacts.

The Project-Level Aid Database[1]

Introduction

The aim of the PLAID (Project-Level Aid) database is to collect and standardize data on every individual development assistance project committed since 1970. This appendix describes the procedures used in the data collection, standardization, and coding of projects within the version of the PLAID database used in this book. In addition, it provides a brief analysis to distinguish our contribution from previous work and to assist researchers in the use of our data. Section I details the donors that currently make up the database, as well as the sources from which we obtained the data. It also clarifies what we consider a project and what we do not, and what kinds of aid are included in the database. The primary variables in the PLAID database are described in Section II. Some have been compiled from a range of official sources, including the OECD CRS database, donor annual reports, and project documents from both bilateral and multilateral aid agencies, and so will be familiar to users of these sources. Additional variables have been created specifically for the PLAID database, including standardizations of traditionally problematic fields in previous diverse data collections (such as country names and dollar amounts). In the current version of the database, all projects have also been carefully coded for their expected environmental impact, the procedure of which is described in Section II. Subsequent iterations of the PLAID database will include coding schemes for other variables of interest, including health and education.

Section I: About PLAID Data

Data Sources

The majority of the PLAID data were obtained from the Organization for Economic Cooperation and Development's (OECD) Creditor Reporting System (CRS). The CRS data are the original source for 76.7 per cent of the project records in PLAID, covering the years 1973–2001.[2] The vast majority of the data taken from the CRS are bilateral aid projects, although a small portion of the multilateral aid data are also from OECD sources. The CRS data rely on the information that donor governments and multilateral organizations submit through the CRS system about their aid projects

---

[1] This Appendix closely follows sections of the document *Codebook and Users Guide to Project Level Aid Database (PLAID)*, McNamara et al. (2005).

[2] These data are available both online at www.OECD.org and from the OECD CD-ROM (2002).

each year. This reliance on donor reporting causes the OECD database alone to be incomplete, in particular for the early years of the CRS system.[3] The remaining 100,054 records included in the PLAID database were gathered directly from donor organizations.

A significant portion of foreign aid comes from many multilateral organizations that are not covered or covered incompletely in the CRS data. To fill these gaps, we collected project-level data from many multilateral organizations directly, including those already reporting using the CRS system for increased accuracy. The following is a complete list of independently collected multilateral donors as of January 2005:

African Development Bank (AFDB)
Asian Development Bank (ASDB)
Carbon Offset (World Bank Group)
Caribbean Development Bank (CDB)
Council of Europe Development Bank (COEB)
European Bank for Reconstruction and Development (EBRD)
European Investment Bank (EIB)
European Union (EU)
Global Environmental Facility (GEF)
Inter-American Development Bank (IADB)
Inter-American Investment Corporation—IADB Group (IIC)
International Bank for Reconstruction and Development—World Bank Group (IBRD)
International Development Association—World Bank Group (IDA)
International Finance Corporation—World Bank Group (IFC)
Islamic Development Bank (ISDB)
Montreal Protocol Fund (MPF)
Multilateral Investment Fund—IADB Group (MIF)
Multilateral Investment Guarantee Association—World Bank Group (MIGA)
Nordic Development Fund (NDF)
Nordic Investment Bank (NIB)
North American Development Bank (NADB)
OPEC Fund for International Development
Rainforest Trust (World Bank Group)
United Nations Children's Fund (UNICEF)
United Nations Development Programme (UNDP)
United Nations Population Fund (UNFPA)

As PLAID expands, more multilateral donors will be added to the database as well as increased coverage from directly contacted bilateral donors. For certain years particular donors did not send their surveys to the OECD, making reports collected directly from bilateral donors more complete than the CRS data alone. In addition, there are some PLAID variables that can only be coded by directly studying annual reports and project

---

[3] For a list of the specific gaps in coverage see Table A.1. These data were provided by OECD staff in July of 2003.

documents. To increase coverage on these variables, PLAID will continue to collect information that is not provided in the CRS survey.

Types of Aid Included in PLAID

The PLAID database covers approximately 90 per cent of commitments to development assistance projects from 1970 to 2000. We define development assistance as loans or grants from governments, official government aid agencies, and inter-governmental organizations (IGOs) with the promotion of the economic development and welfare of developing countries as their main objective. With the exception of certain debt reorganization commitments, at least 25 per cent of a loan must consist of a grant in order to be considered official development assistance (ODA). However, PLAID also include loans at market rates if these loans are designed for the broad purpose of fostering international development. Our data therefore include commitments that offer finance to developing countries in the form of:

- grants
- mixed loans and grants
- loans at discretionary rates from multilateral agencies
- loans/loan guarantees at market rates
- technical assistance
- sector program aid transfers in cash or in kind

Where the loan terms were available, PLAID includes data on interest rate, repayment period, and co-financiers of the loan. For many projects it is possible to restrict the data selection criteria within the database to differentiate among project financing types using either the *flowcode* or *grantelement* variables. For donors where it is unclear whether an amount is a loan or a grant, PLAID provides no information in these fields.

The PLAID database does not include data from non-governmental organizations (NGOs) or contributions from private investors, banks, or foundations. The development assistance information in PLAID also does not currently include military aid from either bilateral or multilateral donors. The following is a list of the types of financing which PLAID does not currently include:

- Military equipment and services
- Military stock of debt
- Aid flows from non-governmental organizations[4]
- Private long-term capital
- Grants by private voluntary agencies
- Members' contributions to multilateral agencies
- Loans made out of funds held in the recipient country
- Foreign direct investment (FDI), unguaranteed bank lending, portfolio investment

---

[4] PLAID excludes projects that originate from NGOs. However, projects from bilateral and multilateral donors that are implemented by NGOs are included. Implementing agents, NGO or otherwise, are captured in the *beneficiary* field or may also be identified in the project description.

Interpreting Project-Level Data

To use PLAID it is necessary to understand the unit of observation of the data. The data contain observations of money flows from donor entities to recipient countries for specific purposes. In the majority of cases, this means that a row of data corresponds to a single donor giving a particular recipient money in a particular year for a specific project, resulting in one row of data per project. Under two conditions it is possible that a single project may appear multiple times in our data: (1) when multiple donors give to the same project, or when a single donor commits new money to the same project in more than one year, or (2) if the original project was scheduled to be disbursed in yearly increments or periodic tranches over multiple years, this is captured on a single project line. However, on some occasions donors commit additional funds to existing projects. As these represent new funding commitments and separate funding decisions they are listed as distinct projects. For researchers, this means the following:

- Assuming that each row in PLAID is a unique project will lead to an overestimate (although probably small) of the number of development projects.

- In some instances, PLAID allows users to track projects having multiple donors. In these instances it is possible to construct data queries that collapse the data by project in order to obtain more accurate project counts.

- For the large majority of our data, there is no project identifier, so it is impossible to know whether each row is indeed a unique project. This drawback is characteristic of all large multi-donor databases currently in existence.

- Assuming redundant projects are coded into sectors consistently, summing commitment dollar amounts across donor, recipient, year will lead to a good measure of a donor's commitments to particular recipients for a given year.

Section II: Sector Coding

Each project in the PLAID database was coded for its effect on the environment according to strict criteria developed by the research team.[5] The *Env_Impact* variable was coded as one of five values on an ordinal scale designed to measure both the general effect and immediacy of each project's environmental impact. These values range from the most eco-friendly to the most harmful. The scale is as follows: environmental strictly defined (ESD), environmental broadly defined (EBD), environmentally neutral (N), dirty broadly defined (DBD), and dirty strictly defined (DSD). For those projects with either an ESD or EBD designation, we then coded our *Env_Aid_Type* variable to provide information on the intended scope of the environmental problem targeted by the project. This variable has two values, green or brown, where green designates environmental aid for international public goods projects and brown environmental projects that have more localized impacts. The reasons for our environmental scales are described in more detail in Chapter 2.

---

[5] Undergraduate research assistants at the College of William and Mary coded the majority of these projects with faculty supervision. See the Coding Methodology section below for more details.

Coding Methodology for Environmental Fields in the PLAID Database

The database consists of approximately 430,000 rows of foreign aid projects. Projects were coded line by line using project descriptions given above and an exhaustive list of categorized examples (see Table A.2). Previous studies have often relied on OECD sector codes to categorize different types of aid projects. However, many OECD sectors include some projects that are environmentally friendly and others that are environmentally damaging. Therefore, in PLAID 1.1 we disaggregated every sector and separately coded every single project before entering an environmental impact code into the PLAID database.

Every row in the PLAID database was coded individually for our environmental variables by at least two members of the research team. Researchers were trained on a set of practice projects and were only able to begin coding after they reached an 85 per cent accuracy threshold. Subsequent tests put coder accuracy at above 95 per cent for every single coder. Each project was then coded twice by separate researchers to establish inter-coder reliability. Projects which did not receive matching codes were referred to two senior researchers for a final decision before being added to the master database.

However, many projects in the database contain only very brief and generic descriptions, and a few contain no description at all. Projects with short descriptions or which included only project titles were coded based on this limited information, while projects with no descriptive information received no code for our environmental variables. This decision makes our estimate of environmental aid very conservative, since a project description must specifically indicate that a project is environmental for us to code it as such—information which is not often included in short or incomplete project descriptions. If one calculates the total number or the percentage of environmental projects (or project dollars) with the total number of development projects in the denominator, then one undercounts the number of projects and the dollars spent on environmental foreign aid. However, since projects with no descriptions tend to fall early in the time series when there were fewer environmental projects being committed, we expect that excluding blanks from the denominator will overestimate the number of environmental projects and project dollars.

Table A.1. Coverage gaps in OECD data

Donor country	CRS coverage gaps
Austria	—Reported only loans except in 1991 and from 1996–2001
	—Incomplete data for 1998
Belgium	—Reported only loans prior to 1994
France	—Technical cooperation not covered except partially from 1994
	—Up until 1998 reporting covered the Ministry of Foreign Affairs and the former Ministry of Cooperation; from 1999 onwards data also include the Ministry of Education
Germany	—Until 1998, technical cooperation not covered, except partially in 1997–8
	—Full coverage since 1999
Greece	—No CRS reporting
Ireland	—Only began reporting in 2000
Japan	—Technical cooperation not reported

(cont.)

Table A.1. (*Continued*)

Donor country	CRS coverage gaps
Luxembourg	— No CRS reporting
New Zealand	— No CRS reporting
Portugal	— Until 1998, only reported loans
	— Technical cooperation not covered
	— Full coverage since 1999
Spain	— Reported only loans prior to 1996
	— Technical cooperation not covered
	— Full coverage since 1997
United Kingdom	— Started reporting technical cooperation in 1996
	— Provided data retroactively (excluding scholarships) for 1989–95
United States	— Until 1998, only reported USAID projects
	— Full coverage since 1999
European Commission (EC)	— The data cover grant commitments by the European Development Fund, but are missing for grants financed from the European Commission budget
	— Loans by the European Investment Bank (EIB) are covered only since 2001

Note: Effective January 2002. These data were obtained through email correspondance with OECD staff.

Table A.2. Environmental coding criteria

Environmental Strictly Defined (ESD) Projects
Access to Clean Water (not wells)
Acid Rain Prevention
Air Pollution
Biodiversity
Carbon Dioxide Reduction
CFC Reduction
Debt for Env./Nature
Drainage (for sanitation)
Ecosystems
Eco-tourism
Energy Conservation
Forest Fire Control
Forestation
Forestation/Reforestation (non-industrial)
General Environmental
Multi-sector Environmental
National Park Protection
Ocean/Int'l. Waterways Protection
Rainwater Harvesting
Recycling
Reducing Desertification
Renewable Energy (geothermal, wind, solar, biomass, photovoltaic)
Site Preservation (unless specified archeological)
Soil Conservation
Solid Waste Treatment, including commercial
Wastewater/Sewage Treatment
Water Conservation/Supply/Infrastructure
Watershed Protection

Environmental Broadly Defined (EBD) Projects
Agenda 21
Desalination
Drought Control
Energy Efficiency
Env. Health Hazards
Env. Improvements to Existing Dirty
Erosion Control
Genetic Diversity (non-agricultural)
Industrial Reforestation
Multi-sector Env. and Neutral
Natural Resource Mgmt.
Nuclear Safety
Population/Family Planning
Safe Handling of Toxics
Soil Fertility
Sustainable Development
Tree Health

Neutral (N) Projects
AIDS/STDs
Archeological Site Preservation
Banking/Finance
Business Services
Cottage Industries/Handicrafts
Debt for Development

Disaster Relief/Prevention
Education
Export Promotion
Food Safety/Quality
Food Security/Food Aid
Governance/Civil Society
Govt. Reform
Health
Hotel Construction
Housing
Humanitarian Aid
Illegal Drug Policy
Infectious Disease Control
Media (radio/newspaper)
Multi-sector Unspecified
Multi-sector: Env. and Dirty
Privatization
Remote Sensing
Research (unspecified)
Rural Development (general)
SMEs (unspecified)
Social Welfare Programs
Storage (general)
Telecommunications (general)
Tourism
Trade Policy
Urban Development (general)

Dirty Broadly Defined (DBD) Projects
Agricultural Credits/Financing
Agricultural Inputs
Agricultural Research
Agriculture (general)
Agro-industries
Aqueducts
Automotive Parts
Biotechnology
Cold Storage/Refrigeration
Construction/Commercial Development (general)
Electricity Transmission
Engineering
Farmer Cooperatives
Fisheries
Flood Control/Prevention
Food Crops
Food Processing
Forest Development
Forestry (general)
Halieutics (fishing) and Halieutics Research
Hydroelectric Power
Industrial Credit/Exports
Industrial Crops/Ag. (sugar, coffee, tea, cocoa, oil seeds, nuts, kernels, fiber crops, tobacco, rubber)
Industry (general)
Irrigation
Livestock
Manufacturing Electronics

Mass Transport
Methanol
Multi-sector: Dirty and Neutral
Multi-sector: DSD and Env.
Nuclear Power
Pest Control
Pharmaceuticals
Rail Transport
Rural Electrification
Textiles/Weaving
Transport
Unspecified Energy
Water Transport

Dirty Strictly Defined (DSD) Projects
Air Transport
All Metals
Chemicals
Dams
Dredging
Industries (brickmaking, plaster, tanneries and leather, fertilizer, rubber)
Logging
Minerals (baryte, limestone, feldspar, kaolin, sand, gypsum, gravel, ornamental stones, salt)
Mining (general)
Multi-sector: DBD and DSD
Natural Gas
Oil and Coal
Power Generation (unspecified)
Raw Material Extraction
Road Transport
Specific Industries (cement, paper, lime)
Thermal Power
Wells and Groundwater Removal

Green Projects
Acid Rain
Afforestation/Reforestation
Agenda 21
Carbon Dioxide Emissions
CFC Reduction
Desertification
Ecosystem Aid/Preservation
Eco-tourism
Energy Conservation
Energy Efficiency
Environment and Energy Programs
Environment Films
Environment Unspecified
Environmental Education
Forest Fire/Wildfire Protection
Nuclear Safety
Population/Family Planning
Protected Areas
Recycling
Renewable Energy
Site Preservation (non-archeological)
Sustainable Development—Energy

Water Conservation
Watershed Protection

Brown Projects
Air Pollution (not GW or acid rain)
Clean Water (sanitation generally)
Coastal Management
Desalination
Drainage
Drought Control
Environmental Health Hazards (local)

Erosion Control
General Environment/Ag. Sector
General Local Environmental Aid
Land Reclamation
Localized Natural Resource Mgmt.
Safe Handling of Toxic Materials
Sewage/Wastewater Treatment
Soil Fertility
Soil Protection/Conservation
Solid Waste Treatment
Urban Environmental Issues

APPENDIX B

Aid Flows to Recipients

Table B.1. Allocation of environmental aid to all recipients, as categorized by the PLAID research project, 1980–1999; 1980–1989; 1990–1999

	1980–1999		1980–1989		1990–1999	
	Recipient	Env. aid	Recipient	Env. aid	Recipient	Env. aid
1	CHINA	$10,994,597,489	BRAZIL	$2,790,257,955	CHINA	$10,100,336,643
2	BRAZIL	$9,325,450,243	EGYPT	$2,219,912,022	INDIA	$6,586,701,797
3	INDIA	$8,767,285,419	INDIA	$2,180,583,622	BRAZIL	$6,535,192,288
4	INDONESIA	$7,016,344,275	INDONESIA	$2,158,424,088	MEXICO	$5,212,238,543
5	MEXICO	$6,140,244,290	PAKISTAN	$2,026,999,142	INDONESIA	$4,857,920,186
6	EGYPT	$5,420,420,251	PHILIPPINES	$1,480,211,532	PHILIPPINES	$3,931,269,817
7	PHILIPPINES	$5,411,481,349	SOUTH KOREA	$1,436,609,961	EGYPT	$3,200,508,229
8	PAKISTAN	$3,673,259,052	ALGERIA	$1,200,729,566	ARGENTINA	$2,917,609,204
9	TURKEY	$3,643,655,298	BANGLADESH	$1,174,240,175	TURKEY	$2,549,709,943
10	ARGENTINA	$3,335,977,768	TURKEY	$1,093,945,354	LEAST DEV.	$2,513,471,694
11	BANGLADESH	$3,128,224,658	KENYA	$990,700,686	BANGLADESH	$1,953,984,484
12	LEAST DEV.	$2,744,107,311	MEXICO	$928,005,747	VIETNAM	$1,717,587,142
13	THAILAND	$2,335,723,237	CHINA	$894,260,845	THAILAND	$1,683,753,259
14	SOUTH KOREA	$2,002,903,359	COLOMBIA	$823,575,815	PAKISTAN	$1,646,259,909
15	MOROCCO	$1,960,217,990	THAILAND	$651,969,978	MOROCCO	$1,412,159,347
16	COLOMBIA	$1,891,102,531	NIGERIA	$573,621,342	PERU	$1,186,105,733
17	VIETNAM	$1,773,648,436	EL SALVADOR	$556,011,119	TUNISIA	$1,128,497,380
18	ALGERIA	$1,735,074,158	MOROCCO	$548,058,642	RUSSIA	$1,124,888,610
19	KENYA	$1,729,547,480	TUNISIA	$445,773,894	COLOMBIA	$1,067,526,716
20	TUNISIA	$1,574,271,273	DOM. REPUBLIC	$431,185,277	SRI LANKA	$967,758,909
21	PERU	$1,435,339,266	SRI LANKA	$424,959,196	BOLIVIA	$851,733,926

(cont.)

Table B.1. (*Continued*)

	1980–1999		1980–1989		1990–1999	
	Recipient	Env. aid	Recipient	Env. aid	Recipient	Env. aid
22	NIGERIA	$1,403,154,982	ARGENTINA	$418,368,564	NIGERIA	$829,533,640
23	SRI LANKA	$1,392,718,105	ETHIOPIA	$408,671,880	GHANA	$797,699,790
24	RUSSIA	$1,124,888,610	CONGO, DEM. R.	$389,713,922	JORDAN	$792,397,100
25	JORDAN	$1,096,189,021	TANZANIA	$369,392,685	KENYA	$738,846,793
26	TANZANIA	$1,060,889,730	HONDURAS	$360,129,056	TANZANIA	$691,497,045
27	GHANA	$1,034,893,977	ECUADOR	$336,976,568	GLOBAL	$684,882,940
28	ECUADOR	$959,659,299	JORDAN	$303,791,921	POLAND	$672,928,908
29	BOLIVIA	$952,656,475	HAITI	$297,751,116	LEBANON	$667,191,005
30	HONDURAS	$914,781,969	YUGOSLAVIA	$293,548,539	MOZAMBIQUE	$666,994,562
31	AFRICA	$855,203,255	COSTA RICA	$285,643,257	AFRICA	$665,403,144
32	SENEGAL	$854,356,014	SENEGAL	$283,800,354	GERMANY	$664,012,330
33	EL SALVADOR	$837,953,143	CHILE	$281,502,614	ECUADOR	$622,682,731
34	NEPAL	$810,278,024	MALAYSIA	$279,756,000	UGANDA	$588,916,077
35	ZIMBABWE	$775,125,837	NIGER	$273,561,600	NEPAL	$576,874,927
36	MOZAMBIQUE	$748,579,689	VENEZUELA	$268,533,181	SENEGAL	$570,555,660
37	UGANDA	$721,407,611	SUDAN	$260,868,043	SOUTH KOREA	$566,293,398
38	ETHIOPIA	$718,460,119	PERU	$249,233,533	BURKINA FASO	$557,802,370
39	LEBANON	$716,578,436	ZAMBIA	$242,591,729	HONDURAS	$554,652,913
40	BURKINA FASO	$711,390,499	GHANA	$237,194,188	NICARAGUA	$542,016,153
41	MALAYSIA	$706,776,679	ZIMBABWE	$237,080,111	ZIMBABWE	$538,045,726
42	GLOBAL	$690,714,658	YEMEN	$233,739,599	ALGERIA	$534,344,592
43	POLAND	$672,928,908	NEPAL	$233,403,097	PALESTINE	$522,991,562
44	WEST GERMANY	$664,012,330	LEAST DEV.	$230,635,617	MALAWI	$502,882,918
45	VENEZUELA	$656,971,193	SYRIA	$229,676,257	CYPRUS	$480,025,182
46	YEMEN	$643,671,388	MALI	$207,944,263	ASIA AND THE PACIFIC	$433,704,069
47	NICARAGUA	$615,411,632	RWANDA	$204,240,778	MALAYSIA	$427,020,680
48	MALAWI	$591,134,090	CÔTE D'IVOIRE	$203,834,464	MADAGASCAR	$421,434,425
49	DOMINICAN REPUBLIC	$587,600,287	AFRICA	$189,800,110	YEMEN	$409,931,789
50	COSTA RICA	$585,510,395	CAMEROON	$188,656,441	C. AND E. EUROPE	$404,321,376
51	CHILE	$578,307,533	LESOTHO	$180,423,606	PARAGUAY	$395,209,937
52	ZAMBIA	$574,811,105	URUGUAY	$174,084,337	FRANCE	$394,517,786

#					
53	MALI	$574,556,654	GUATEMALA	$166,303,018	VENEZUELA	$388,438,012
54	HAITI	$564,634,669	PARAGUAY	$155,926,022	IRAN	$374,481,612
55	MADAGASCAR	$555,687,316	GUINEA	$155,656,722	MALI	$366,612,391
56	NIGER	$551,872,067	BURKINA FASO	$153,588,129	CZECH REPUBLIC	$362,337,824
57	PARAGUAY	$551,135,959	MADAGASCAR	$134,252,891	ZAMBIA	$332,219,376
58	CYPRUS	$546,909,294	JAMAICA	$133,802,565	CÔTE D'IVOIRE	$321,925,105
59	CÔTE D'IVOIRE	$525,759,568	UGANDA	$132,491,535	LESOTHO	$316,864,623
60	PALESTINE	$522,991,562	BENIN	$129,523,460	GUINEA	$313,746,897
61	LESOTHO	$497,288,229	BOTSWANA	$129,039,774	ETHIOPIA	$309,788,238
62	ASIA AND THE PACIFIC	$491,776,185	BURUNDI	$118,389,443	GUATEMALA	$306,103,448
63	GUATEMALA	$472,406,466	TOGO	$112,882,677	COSTA RICA	$299,867,138
64	GUINEA	$469,403,620	BOLIVIA	$100,922,549	CHILE	$296,804,919
65	CONGO, DEM. REP.	$453,256,379	SOMALIA	$97,831,048	BULGARIA	$287,211,020
66	C. AND E. EUROPE	$404,321,376	MYANMAR	$91,495,930	MAURITIUS	$283,147,553
67	URUGUAY	$401,963,179	MALAWI	$88,251,173	EL SALVADOR	$281,942,025
68	FRANCE	$394,517,786	DJIBOUTI	$83,104,742	NIGER	$278,310,467
69	BENIN	$394,225,635	MOZAMBIQUE	$81,585,127	LATIN AM. AND CARIB.	$272,898,924
70	IRAN	$374,481,612	NICARAGUA	$73,395,480	SOUTH AFRICA	$267,337,041
71	CZECH REPUBLIC	$362,337,824	PANAMA	$69,763,549	HAITI	$266,883,554
72	CAMEROON	$360,282,069	MAURITANIA	$67,116,253	BENIN	$264,702,175
73	BOTSWANA	$358,248,800	CYPRUS	$66,074,111	UKRAINE	$247,222,806
74	JAMAICA	$339,009,396	GAMBIA	$63,280,149	BOTSWANA	$229,209,026
75	MAURITIUS	$337,050,226	ISRAEL	$62,768,431	URUGUAY	$227,878,842
76	SUDAN	$335,596,801	ASIA/PACIFIC	$58,072,116	CAMBODIA	$222,755,219
77	SYRIA	$324,358,250	VIETNAM	$56,061,294	ROMANIA	$218,899,372
78	RWANDA	$322,609,003	MAURITIUS	$53,902,673	JAMAICA	$205,206,831
79	LATIN AM. AND CARIB.	$320,018,652	OMAN	$51,494,024	LAOS	$201,596,922
80	YUGOSLAVIA	$293,548,539	SIERRA LEONE	$50,407,457	CROATIA	$199,977,731
81	BULGARIA	$287,211,020	CAPE VERDE	$49,406,304	HUNGARY	$192,329,389
82	SOUTH AFRICA	$267,337,041	LEBANON	$49,387,430	MONGOLIA	$187,543,069
83	BURUNDI	$257,863,115	LATIN AM./CARIB.	$47,119,728	CHAD	$174,358,838
84	UKRAINE	$247,222,806	PORTUGAL	$41,430,000	ISRAEL	$173,752,382
85	MAURITANIA	$236,909,002	CHAD	$40,265,731	UZBEKISTAN	$172,614,765
86	ISRAEL	$236,520,813	GABON	$38,077,192	CAMEROON	$171,625,628
87	PANAMA	$228,332,479	BAHAMAS	$37,265,310	NAMIBIA	$169,933,959
88	HUNGARY	$226,210,645	CONGO	$36,804,983	MAURITANIA	$169,792,749
89	CAMBODIA	$226,109,456	LIBERIA	$35,217,291	PANAMA	$158,568,931
90	ROMANIA	$218,899,372	HUNGARY	$33,881,256	DOM. REPUBLIC	$156,415,010

(cont.)

Table B.1. (Continued)

	1980–1999		1980–1989		1990–1999	
	Recipient	Env. aid	Recipient	Env. aid	Recipient	Env. aid
91	LAOS	$215,774,414	BELIZE	$33,255,167	GREECE	$155,584,479
92	CHAD	$214,624,569	C. AFRICAN REP.	$32,120,287	TRINIDAD AND TOBAGO	$148,781,296
93	CROATIA	$199,977,731	MALDIVES	$29,373,631	SPAIN	$148,087,048
94	TOGO	$194,303,975	GUINEA-BISSAU	$26,777,298	BURUNDI	$139,473,672
95	MONGOLIA	$187,543,069	SEYCHELLES	$25,914,002	GUYANA	$139,467,935
96	UZBEKISTAN	$172,614,765	THE NETHERLANDS ANTILLES	$24,863,972	ANGOLA	$123,581,604
97	NAMIBIA	$170,582,362	ST LUCIA	$24,389,499	PAPUA NEW GUINEA	$122,586,517
98	SOMALIA	$158,445,819	CAYMAN IS.	$22,621,335	RWANDA	$118,368,225
99	GREECE	$155,584,479	BARBADOS	$20,351,769	AZERBAIJAN	$117,141,042
100	DJIBOUTI	$154,273,055	BHUTAN	$19,769,638	ALBANIA	$108,452,334
101	TRINIDAD AND TOBAGO	$149,214,231	PAPUA NEW GUINEA	$16,527,257	LITHUANIA	$104,335,158
102	SPAIN	$148,087,048	FIJI	$14,717,971	ARMENIA	$97,259,754
103	GUYANA	$141,886,962	ANTIGUA AND BARB.	$14,404,576	C. AFRICAN REP.	$96,882,881
104	PAPUA NEW GUINEA	$139,113,774	LAOS	$14,177,491	ITALY	$96,208,135
105	ANGOLA	$135,715,814	SWAZILAND	$12,650,977	KAZAKHSTAN	$95,625,963
106	C. AFRICAN REP.	$129,003,167	ANGOLA	$12,134,210	SYRIA	$94,681,992
107	CAPE VERDE	$128,128,145	ST KITTS-NEVIS	$11,949,200	LATVIA	$94,127,608
108	AZERBAIJAN	$117,141,042	SAMOA	$10,297,369	FINLAND	$92,609,809
109	GAMBIA	$116,986,591	AFGHANISTAN	$9,615,365	BARBADOS	$88,744,940
110	SIERRA LEONE	$112,631,117	KIRIBATI	$9,177,372	EUROPE UNSPEC.	$87,764,993
111	BARBADOS	$109,096,710	N. MARIANAS	$8,843,381	ERITREA	$81,983,252
112	ALBANIA	$108,452,334	SOLOMON IS.	$8,796,772	TOGO	$81,421,298
113	GABON	$104,661,003	TONGA	$8,585,069	CAPE VERDE	$78,721,841
114	LITHUANIA	$104,335,158	COMOROS	$8,128,221	SUDAN	$74,728,758
115	BAHAMAS	$101,444,109	MIDDLE EAST	$6,994,113	DJIBOUTI	$71,168,313
116	ARMENIA	$97,259,754	SOUTH YEMEN	$6,776,251	BHUTAN	$67,948,440
117	ITALY	$96,208,135	SÃO TOMÉ AND PR.	$6,684,792	ESTONIA	$67,641,855
118	KAZAKHSTAN	$95,625,963	DOMINICA	$6,058,497	MOLDOVA	$67,074,790
119	LATVIA	$94,127,608	GLOBAL	$5,831,718	GABON	$66,583,811
120	BELIZE	$93,561,019	GRENADA	$5,014,554	BAHAMAS	$64,178,800
121	FINLAND	$92,609,809	NEW CALEDONIA	$4,578,139	CONGO, DEM. REP.	$63,542,457

#	Country	Amount	Country	Amount	Country	Amount
122	MYANMAR	$92,541,614	MAYOTTE	$4,519,018	SIERRA LEONE	$62,223,661
123	EUROPE UNSPECIFIED	$87,764,993	ANGUILLA	$4,310,030	GUINEA-BISSAU	$60,946,884
124	GUINEA-BISSAU	$87,724,182	EQ. GUINEA	$4,200,761	SOMALIA	$60,614,770
125	BHUTAN	$87,718,078	CAMBODIA	$3,354,237	BELIZE	$60,305,852
126	ERITREA	$81,983,252	TUVALU	$3,253,131	SURINAME	$56,750,818
127	ESTONIA	$67,641,855	LIBYA	$3,211,628	GAMBIA	$53,706,442
128	MOLDOVA	$67,074,790	VANUATU	$2,942,482	SLOVENIA	$53,180,512
129	MALDIVES	$62,714,809	GUYANA	$2,419,028	GEORGIA	$48,406,275
130	CONGO	$61,358,948	MONTSERRAT	$2,144,282	TURKMENISTAN	$43,296,769
131	ST LUCIA	$59,014,942	IRAQ	$1,371,118	SWAZILAND	$41,915,158
132	SURINAME	$56,794,370	ARUBA	$1,327,691	SLOVAKIA	$37,884,348
133	SWAZILAND	$54,566,135	ST VINCENT AND GR.	$1,022,554	ST LUCIA	$34,625,443
134	SLOVENIA	$53,180,512	REUNION	$887,134	BOSNIA-HERZ.	$33,711,364
135	OMAN	$51,940,586	US VIRGIN IS.	$870,932	MALDIVES	$33,341,178
136	GEORGIA	$48,406,275	NAMIBIA	$648,403	SOLOMON ISLANDS	$32,333,694
137	TURKMENISTAN	$43,296,769	COOK ISLANDS	$638,740	KIRIBATI	$31,169,172
138	SEYCHELLES	$42,318,744	NIUE	$468,971	SAUDI ARABIA	$31,147,015
139	PORTUGAL	$41,430,000	TRINIDAD AND TOB.	$432,935	SAMOA	$31,048,073
140	SAMOA	$41,345,441	FR. POLYNESIA	$377,032	DOMINICA	$30,145,221
141	SOLOMON ISLANDS	$41,130,466	TURKS AND CAICOS	$169,211	MICRONESIA	$28,494,482
142	KIRIBATI	$40,346,544	SINGAPORE	$113,102	MARSHALL ISLANDS	$26,909,227
143	FIJI	$40,029,259	SURINAME	$43,552	FIJI	$25,311,288
144	SLOVAKIA	$37,884,348			CONGO	$24,553,965
145	LIBERIA	$36,637,681			BAHRAIN	$22,591,072
146	DOMINICA	$36,203,718			MIDDLE EAST	$20,113,127
147	BOSNIA-HERZEGOVINA	$33,711,364			COMOROS	$19,097,763
148	SAUDI ARABIA	$31,147,015			FRENCH POLYNESIA	$18,057,537
149	MICRONESIA	$28,494,482			CUBA	$17,385,740
150	NETH. ANTILLES	$28,001,157			EQUATORIAL GUINEA	$17,033,053
151	COMOROS	$27,225,983			SEYCHELLES	$16,404,742
152	MIDDLE EAST	$27,107,240			MACEDONIA	$16,134,916
153	MARSHALL ISLANDS	$26,909,227			SÃO TOMÉ AND PR.	$15,961,566
154	CAYMAN ISLANDS	$24,905,867			GRENADA	$15,399,336
155	SÃO TOMÉ AND PRÍNCIPE	$22,646,357			BELARUS	$13,540,807
156	BAHRAIN	$22,591,072			VANUATU	$11,923,714
157	EQUATORIAL GUINEA	$21,233,814			N. MARIANAS	$11,778,388
158	NORTHERN MARIANAS	$20,621,769			MAYOTTE	$11,593,561

(cont.)

Table B.1. (Continued)

1980–1999		1980–1989		1990–1999	
Recipient	Env. aid	Recipient	Env. aid	Recipient	Env. aid
159 GRENADA	$20,413,891			ST VINCENT AND GR.	$10,993,906
160 ANTIGUA/BARBUDA	$20,057,146			TONGA	$10,138,967
161 TONGA	$18,724,037			TURKS AND CAICOS	$9,025,255
162 FRENCH POLYNESIA	$18,434,569			PALAU	$8,265,221
163 CUBA	$17,385,740			KOSOVO	$7,429,395
164 MACEDONIA	$16,134,916			MONTSERRAT	$6,540,094
165 MAYOTTE	$16,112,579			NEW CALEDONIA	$6,062,977
166 ST KITTS-NEVIS	$15,917,176			SOUTH YEMEN	$5,789,623
167 VANUATU	$14,866,196			ANTIGUA AND BARBUDA	$5,652,570
168 BELARUS	$13,540,807			SERBIA AND MONT.	$4,575,308
169 AFGHANISTAN	$13,165,963			ANGUILLA	$4,493,435
170 SOUTH YEMEN	$12,565,874			TUVALU	$4,190,246
171 ST VINCENT AND GR.	$12,016,460			ST KITTS-NEVIS	$3,967,976
172 NEW CALEDONIA	$10,641,116			NORTH KOREA	$3,874,020
173 TURKS AND CAICOS IS.	$9,194,466			KYRGYZSTAN	$3,598,288
174 ANGUILLA	$8,803,465			AFGHANISTAN	$3,550,598
175 MONTSERRAT	$8,684,376			NETH. ANTILLES	$3,137,186
176 PALAU	$8,265,221			TAJIKISTAN	$2,754,029
177 TUVALU	$7,443,376			EAST TIMOR	$2,659,161
178 KOSOVO	$7,429,395			COOK ISLANDS	$2,407,798
179 SERBIA AND MONT.	$4,575,308			CAYMAN ISLANDS	$2,284,533
180 NORTH KOREA	$3,874,020			ST HELENA	$2,193,089
181 KYRGYZSTAN	$3,598,288			LIBERIA	$1,420,389
182 LIBYA	$3,291,418			US VIRGIN ISLANDS	$1,403,196
183 COOK ISLANDS	$3,046,538			SINGAPORE	$1,388,650
184 TAJIKISTAN	$2,754,029			NIUE	$1,350,122
185 EAST TIMOR	$2,659,161			GIBRALTAR	$1,067,058

186	US VIRGIN ISLANDS	$2,274,128	MYANMAR	$1,045,683
187	ST HELENA	$2,193,089	MALTA	$931,594
188	IRAQ	$1,888,821	BRUNEI	$853,459
189	NIUE	$1,819,093	IRAQ	$517,703
190	ARUBA	$1,786,384	ARUBA	$458,693
191	SINGAPORE	$1,501,752	KUWAIT	$448,649
192	GIBRALTAR	$1,067,058	OMAN	$446,562
193	MALTA	$931,594	MACAO	$395,108
194	REUNION	$887,134	CZECHOSLOVAKIA	$211,922
195	BRUNEI	$853,459	QATAR	$155,851
196	KUWAIT	$448,649	TOKELAU	$120,822
197	MACAO	$395,108	LIBYA	$79,790
198	CZECHOSLOVAKIA	$211,922	NAURU	$61,969
199	QATAR	$155,851	TAIWAN	$42,705
200	TOKELAU	$120,822		
201	NAURU	$61,969		
202	TAIWAN	$42,705		

Technical Details

This appendix provides supplementary information concerning (1) our use of development finance data for calculating total aid flows, (2) econometric modeling details, and (3) independent variable selection. First, there are several overarching methodological considerations which must be explained. It is important to note that our use of the PLAID data in this book pools different types of financial arrangements. For example, some projects are essentially grants, with no expectation for repayment, while others have only small parts that are grants and include detailed contractual arrangements on repayment dates and loan terms. Still others are entirely loans whose terms may be dictated solely by market rates. Unlike other studies that calculate the percentage of a project commitment that is effectively a grant (termed grant element), we pool commitment amounts from the broadest possible set of donors without converting to grant element. We do this because some data does not contain the financial terms necessary to calculate grant element, and we decided to go for the most comprehensive assessment of aid allocation.

Another important point to note is that in this book donors are treated equally in all econometric models, since we are modeling aid flows in terms of shares of budgets. A country with a large green aid budget giving 10 per cent of its green funds to Brazil in a year will receive the same weight as a country with a very small green aid budget also giving 10 per cent of its green funds in a year to Brazil. We do this because we are interested in the average donor preferences with respect to independent variables in models and aid allocation. If the emphasis is on money flows versus average donor preferences then donor-specific models are more appropriate, with the noted caveat that sector-level models at the donor level often stratify data very thinly.

Finally, in this study we treat aid allocation decisions as being separable across sectors and, due to data limitations, ignore the marbling of aid. For example, in Chapter 4, our models assume that the amount of aid received from a donor in one sector does not influence allocation decisions in some other sector. It is likely that to induce recipients to accept environmental projects (and in particular green projects), donors give aid packages that include support for multiple sectors. This allows recipients to accept the local costs of environmental packages by receiving aid in more 'productive' aid sectors. Alternatively, this type of interaction may result in more marbled projects. In this book we are forced to ignore such strategic interactions, although they undoubtedly exist.

Chapter 4: The Empirical Aid Allocation Model

The goal in this chapter is to empirically examine how donor countries allocate their environmental aid, and see if their allocation rule depends in part on environmental, economic, and political factors in the recipient country. A glance at patterns of environmental aid-giving over recent decades reveals that a significant proportion of countries receive no aid in given sectors for long periods while others receive large amounts of aid consistently in the same sectors. This lends itself to thinking about aid allocation as a two-step process.[1] In the gate-keeping stage, a donor country decides whether to give a recipient country some positive amount of aid. Once a recipient country has passed the gate-keeping stage, the donor country then allocates a portion of their overall aid budget to the recipient country in the allocation stage. Consequently, when one asks how donor preferences and recipient characteristics affect aid allocation, one needs to think about how both of these factors affect the gate-keeping and allocation stage of the donor process.

We construct the share of aid, given by bilateral or multilateral donors (i) to recipient countries (j) for a given year (t) and aid sector (s).[2] Denote this share as:

$$SH_{ijts} = \frac{P_{ijts}}{\sum\limits_{k \in R} P_{ikts}} \tag{1}$$

where P_{ijts} is the total value of projects committed by donor i to recipient j in year t for sector s.[3] The denominator sums all project monies given across all R recipients for a sector and year. Consequently, we are modeling donor, recipient, year triads and are investigating how shares of funds are allocated by donors in each sector.

Using equation (1), we construct a binary variable based upon the values of SH_{ijts}. This variable accounts for the issue of zeros inherent with dyadic donor–recipient models. Many donor–recipient pairs correspond to no aid given, since not all donors give money to all recipients every year. In the gate-keeping model, define $gate_{ijts} = 1$ if a positive share of aid was given by donor i to recipient j in year t, otherwise, $gate_{ijts} = 0$. We model the gate-keeping stage using a probit model as follows:

$$gate_{ijts} = X^R_{ijt-1s}{}'\alpha_b + X^D_{ijt-1s}{}'\beta_G + \varepsilon_{ijts}$$

where the independent variables in the model are partitioned according to whether they are recipient-specific (X^R_{ijt-1s}) or dyadic (X^D_{ijt-1s}) and are lagged by one year. When modeling multilateral allocations in this chapter, all of the dyadic variables, which by definition are donor- and recipient-specific, are excluded from the analysis. The complete list of independent variables in the two-stage model is found in Table 4.1, while variables considered are in Table B.1.

---

[1] Meernik and Poe (1996); McGillivray and Oczkowski (1991, 1992); Tarp et al. (1998); Dudley and Montmarquette (1976).

[2] Note that aid sector refers to the unique environmental typology developed in the PLAID database rather than substantive sectors, such as health, education, or infrastructure.

[3] In this book, all financial flows are expressed in 2000 dollars.

Conditional on receiving some positive share of a donor aid, the amount equation uses the same variables. The share of environmental aid that a donor country i gives to recipient j in year t for sector s is modeled as:

$$SH_{ijts} = X_{ijt-1s}^{R}{}'\alpha_A + X_{ijt-1s}^{D}{}'\beta_A + \varepsilon_{ijts}.$$

Notice that the parameters from the gate-keeping model (α_G and β_G) are not restricted to be equal to those from the share equation model (α_A and β_A).

While we considered using other models to deal with truncation including the well-known Heckman and Tobit models that have been used in other aid allocation contexts (Neumeyer 2003c), a variation of the Cragg model was ultimately used in all of the truncated analyses in the book. There are several reasons for this. Unlike the Tobit model that restricts the *same* variables to affect the gate-keeping and amounts equations in the *same* way, the Cragg model allows different variables to drive each stage and further the signs impact of variables can be different at each stage. The Heckman model also allows for these types of differences and has the further advantage that the gate-keeping and amount stages are modeled simultaneously, and admits to some correlation among the two stages. However, a well-known limitation of the Heckman model is the identification of each stage of the analysis; it often requires some variable to impact only the gate-keeping stage in a fundamental way without having large impacts on the amounts equation. We had a difficult time envisioning a variable like this and hence used the modified Cragg specification.[4] A further limitation of the Cragg model is that the amounts equation is modeled only over those donor, recipient, year combinations where a positive share of aid is given. Consequently, the sample sizes in the amount equations are smaller than if a Tobit or Heckman model is used. The Cragg model is easy to implement in the multiple imputation framework we use in Chapter 4 to account for missing data. A very comprehensive discussion of the tradeoffs associated with these models in an aid allocation context is given in Neumeyer (2003d).

Multiple Imputation for Missing Data

An important innovation in this chapter is the use of multiple imputation techniques for handling the missing data that are a part of most international panel data studies. Prior work has either performed listwise deletion, a procedure that removes observations with any missing values, or has imputed missing data in unsystematic ways.[5] While our work is less affected by selection bias associated with listwise deletion and ad hoc imputation, the use of multiple imputation also introduces noise in the estimation process, since imputed datasets are considered random and drawn from the underlying distribution of data. Therefore, estimates and standard errors are subject to the researcher's uncertainty regarding the independent variable data. However,

---

[4] Cragg (1971) spends most of the article discussing a truncated regression model as the model to use in the amounts stage of the regression. These models are notoriously difficult to estimate, so many employ a log-linear model instead, which is briefly discussed in the paper and described by equation (10).

[5] See for example, Burnside and Dollar (2000a); Easterly et al. (2004a); Neumeyer (2003c).

recent research on the use of multiple imputation indicates it is still likely the best research tool for the missing data problems abundant in most cross-national time-series analyses.

We employ the multiple imputation techniques described by Little and Rubin (1987), Rubin (1976, 1987, 1996), and Schafer (1997) using software written by Honaker et al. (2006). This technique uses available data to estimate the distribution of the independent variables in the model using Monte Carlo Markov Chain Bayesian simulation techniques. To summarize, this approach estimates numerous datasets by imputing missing values from the estimated distribution of data and the model, in turn, is estimated using each imputed dataset. Overall inference is accomplished by combining estimation results obtained from each imputed dataset.

The distribution of missing data should be estimated with the dependent variable included. For our application, this means that the panel nature of the dataset is destroyed since each donor, recipient, and year combination is assumed to be independent from other observations when generating imputed datasets. Consequently, measures of recipient-specific dependent variables for a given year and recipient may differ across donors. Instead, we imputed recipient–year-specific data separately from donor–recipient–year-specific data (e.g. trade importance or colonial status) and combined them to construct the final imputed dataset. This retained the panel nature of the dataset but increased the computational time and expense required to implement the estimator. All results in Chapter 4 are recovered using five imputed datasets.

It is common practice to consider a number of variables that may capture a particular effect before final model selection. In a multiple imputation context, when including similar (and often correlated) variables, the MCMC algorithm often fails to converge to a stable distribution. Consequently, robustness checks must proceed in parallel with unique imputed datasets for each set of independent variables considered by the analyst. This adds a considerable amount of effort to such exploratory analysis.

In an online technical companion document, we present a set of results for bilateral and multilateral models run only over non-missing data. By performing listwise deletion, these results do not rely on imputed data and hence are a useful benchmark upon which the imputed results can be compared to methods commonly employed in the literature. Substantial summary statistics and correlations are available there for the models.

Elasticities

The elasticities reported in Chapter 4 represent the recipient's estimated percentage change in aid share received from a donor due to a change in an independent variable in the model. It is important to note that our elasticities are *not* conditional, but rather combine both the gate-keeping and amounts equation estimates. Further, we provide confidence intervals for the elasticities that include both the uncertainty associated with the beta vector and associated with imputed data. To be more specific, for any given aid sector, s, let the estimated elasticity ($ELAS_{ik}^s$) for each row of each imputed dataset i associated and dependent variable x_k^i be defined by

$$ELAS_{ik}^s(\beta, \mathbf{X}^i) = \left[\frac{\partial P(SH^s > 0|\beta, \mathbf{X}^i)}{\partial x_k^i} E(SH^s|\beta, \mathbf{X}^i, SH^s > 0) + P(SH^s > 0|\beta, \mathbf{X}^i) \right.$$

$$\left. \times \frac{\partial E(SH^s|\beta, \mathbf{X}^i, SH^s > 0)}{\partial x_k^i} \right] \frac{P(SH^s > 0|\beta, \mathbf{X}^i)E(SH^s|\beta, \mathbf{X}^i, SH^s > 0)}{\bar{\mathbf{X}}^i},_6$$

where $P(\cdot)$ is the probability of observing a positive aid share and $E(\cdot)$ is the expectation operator, both of which are a function of the estimated parameter vector, β. We explicitly write the elasticity to be a function of an imputed data, $\mathbf{X}^i$, to motivate the next step in accounting for the researcher's uncertainty concerning the independent variables in the model due to missing data. The expected value of the elasticity given the estimated probability distribution function of $\mathbf{X}$ is

$$E\left(ELAS_{ik}^s\right) = \iint ELAS_{ik}^s(\beta, \mathbf{X}) f(\mathbf{X})g(\beta)d\mathbf{X}d\beta$$

where $f(\mathbf{X})$ and $g(\beta)$ are the probability density function of the missing data and the parameters, respectively. This expression does not have a closed form solution, so we use the multiple imputed datasets, combined with a simulation of estimated parameters using the Krinsky Robb method to numerically simulate the elasticity distribution that reflects variation as a result of sampling error associated with the model and missing data. Using the simulated distribution, we recover the means and confidence intervals in the chapter.[7]

Chapter 6: Environmental Aid Sector Budgets

As with the other models reported in this book, we measure environmental aid projects categorized as ESD and EBD dirty aid over projects in the DSD and DBD categories. Any project that received an ESD or EBD designation was also coded as either green or brown. While the descriptive statistics in Chapters 2 and 3 cover more than twenty years of aid projects, the quality of data on our independent variables limits us to the later half of that time series. Therefore, in the results in this chapter we are investigating the behavior of seventeen bilateral donor countries for the period 1988–99. Because we lag independent variables and since we have a few missing data points, this limits us to approximately 160 observations.

[6] This expression follows from the expected value of the dependent variable in the Cragg model, $P(SH^s > 0|\beta, \mathbf{X}^i)E(SH^s|\beta, \mathbf{X}^i, SH^s > 0)$.

[7] We use 200 draws from the estimated parameter distribution combined with the five imputed datasets, to evaluate the elasticity distribution at 1,000 points for each elasticity reported in Chapter 4.

To construct the dependent variables in the model, we define a share variable for each aid sector (k) as

$$SH_{itk} = \frac{\sum\limits_{j \in c} P_{itj}}{\sum\limits_{c \in C} \sum\limits_{j \in c} P_{itj}} \tag{1}$$

where P_{itc} is the value of a project (normalized to 2000 US$) committed by country i in year t for category c. In the numerator, we are calculating the total amount spent on aid category c, while in the denominator, we are summing over all aid categories (C) to capture the total amount of bilateral aid given by country i in year t.

When investigating why some countries allocate more aid dollars for environmental projects and others allocate more for dirty projects, there are undoubtedly many differences from one country to another that drive the observable pattern of aid allocation. Some of these factors are fixed within a country; yet the fixed factors play an important role in explaining patterns across countries. The fixed effects estimator we use controls for the multitude of fixed factors within a country that, taken collectively, are likely an important determinant of aid allocation. To differentiate between fixed factors and those that influence aid share through time requires independent variables that vary through time within a country. Variables that do not vary through time will capture the fixed effects associated with a country and it is therefore not possible to identify the variable of interest separately from the other fixed effects associated with the country. In practice, this means that if a variable is measured in only one time period, it cannot be included in the regression analysis. In addition, if variables do not change during the time period of analysis, they must also be dropped from the regression. For example, though a country's geography generally does not change through time, its effect on aid allocation will be fully captured by the fixed effects model. We also estimate ordinary least squares models that include these time-invariant data as a robustness check on our results.

To empirically estimate aid allocation patterns, we collect independent variables ($\mathbf{X}_{it}$) from a wide variety of sources. Table 6.3 summarizes the variables used in the analysis, the unit and direction of measurement, and the source. The model we estimate is given as follows

$$\ln(SH_{itj}) = \gamma_j + a_{ij} + \beta_j t + \mathbf{X}_{it-1j}\delta_j + \varepsilon_{it} \tag{2}$$

where γ is a constant, a_i is country i's fixed effect, with positive values indicating a larger share of aid in sector k given by country i. β is a time trend estimate, with values greater than zero indicating that shares of aid going to category k are increasing through time. Notice that β is estimated over all donor countries and therefore is the average trend observed across all donors. Positive estimates of δ_j indicate that as X_{it-1j} increases, the share of aid increases. Further, these coefficients can be interpreted as elasticities, allowing for a meaningful comparison of the magnitudes of parameter estimates across models. For example, a parameter estimate of 2 on a variable of interest implies that, should that variable increase by 1 per cent, the share of aid would increase by 2 per cent.

Chapter 8: Delegating Aid

As we describe in Chapter 8, this book examines two key delegation decisions made by donor governments. We model donor governments as deciding how much of its total aid portfolio in a sector should be delivered via its own versus multilateral channels. The donor government then decides which of the many multilateral agencies should disburse its 'multilateral' portion of aid, by shopping among the various MDBs and MGAs (and/or discuss with other donors the need to create new IOs) in search of a multilateral agent that will maximize the government's policy interest while minimizing its agency losses.[8] To test the hypotheses outlined in Chapter 8, we continue to maintain the simplifying assumption that aid allocation is separable across sectors, given the choices made by bilateral donors described in Chapter 4. It is also important to note that we are modeling the choices of donor governments which, in all cases, have imperfect control over the multilateral allocation process.

First, consider the issue of why certain bilateral donors might want to distribute more aid monies through their own bilateral agencies rather than multilateral channels. This decision may well depend on what type of aid is given. For example, a bilateral donor may prefer to implement environmental and social projects through bilateral channels while perhaps allocating more money for infrastructure projects through multilateral channels. Consider the amount of money spent by donor i in year t through bilateral channels (i) and multilateral channels (m). By differentiating financial flows based on implementation by the donor government's own agencies and multilateral institutions, we can construct the share of bilateral aid given for a given sector and year as

$$SH_{it}^s = \frac{\sum\limits_{j \in R} P_{itj}^s}{\sum\limits_{j \in R} P_{itj}^s + \sum\limits_{k \in M} a_{ikt} \sum\limits_{j \in R} P_{ktj}^s} \tag{3}$$

where P_{itj}^s is the value of all bilateral projects committed by country i in year t for category s. Notice we are summing over all j recipients (where the set of recipients is denoted by R). In the denominator, we construct the total amount of aid spent on sector s by first considering the bilateral monies, but also the aid monies channeled via all multilateral donors (denoted by M). An important consideration in this calculation is the amount of a multilateral institution's aid budget 'given' by member governments. Since aid flows out of multilateral institutions are significantly easier to measure than money flows into multilateral institutions we construct a_{ikt}, to denote the share of a given IO's budget funded by donor country i. We then use this term to transform all aid given by a multilateral institution into the amount effectively given by donor i (for any given donor country i and multilateral institution k, this is written as $a_{ikt} \sum_{j \in R} P_{ktj}^s$—we sum over all of the monies given to recipient countries by multilateral k devoted to sector s for all recipients and transform that total into the effective amount given by donor country i).

---

[8] On forum shopping, see Jupille and Snidal (2005) and Hawkins and Jacoby (2006). On minimizing agency slack, see Hawkins et al. (2006).

Constructing the weights, a_{ikt}, required data on one of two factors. For MDBs where countries typically subscribe to the bank by investing sums of money, the weight was constructed using capital subscriptions. The logic of this assumption is that for institutions like the World Bank, the amount of money flowing from this investment pool is roughly proportional to the amount of money invested in the bank. Consequently, we rely on the flow of resources out of this multilateral to calculate total aid flows from a given bilateral and year. This assumption admittedly is restrictive when one considers that aside from capital subscriptions, which typically do not vary from year to years; voluntary contributions might be made to these institutions from donor countries that are poorly approximated by examining capital subscriptions alone.[9] For MGAs and other agencies that do not rely on capital subscriptions, we use the actual sum of money given by a country to the multilateral agency for calculating the shares in equation (3). These data were collected directly from the multilateral institutions.

To investigate the reasons behind bilateral versus multilateral aid delivery, we estimate the following simple regression model:

$$\ln (SH_{it}) = \gamma + x'_{it-1}\delta + \varepsilon_{it} \tag{4}$$

The independent variables (x_{it-1}) considered in the equation are listed in Table 4.1. Equation (4) was estimated using OLS with robust standard errors over individual donors. Results of these regressions can be found in Table 8.2.

Notice that the bilateral allocation model includes donor performance scores recovered from Chapter 4's donor-specific models.[10] These scores (on government effectiveness, trade, UN affinity, and natural capital index) were estimated from separate bilateral donor-specific allocation models similar to those reported in Chapter 6. These elasticity measures do not vary through time—they represent the average responsiveness of each multilateral donor for the 1990s.[11] We hypothesize that as the responsiveness of a country's own aid institutions increases, donor governments are likely to allocate more of their funding via bilateral channels, all other factors held equal.

To investigate which multilateral agencies receive money from donor governments, we must use similar techniques to construct shares going to a given multilateral m in year t for sector s from donor country i. To construct the dependent variable for this

---

[9] We were able to construct the shares for the following multilateral institutions: Asian Development Bank, Asian Development Bank Special Fund, the European Bank for Reconstruction and Development, European Union, the European Investment Bank, the Council of Europe Bank, the Global Environmental Facility, the International Fund for Agriculture and Development, the Nordic Development Fund, the World Bank IBRD, the World Bank IDA, the World Bank MIGA, the Rainforest Trust Fund, the International Finance Corporation, the African Development Bank, the African Development Fund, the Caribbean Development Bank, the Inter-American Development Bank, the Inter-American Development Bank Special Operations Fund, the MIF, the IIC, the Montreal Protocol Fund, and the NIB.

[10] For the sake of brevity, these country-specific results are not reported either in this chapter or in Chapter 5, but are available from the authors in the Technical Appendix.

[11] Fixed effects regression was not possible because the elasticity variables, which are donor-specific, do not vary through time. Fixed effects regressions are available in the Technical Appendix.

analysis, consider the share of multilateral development assistance given by a donor country i to multilateral m in year t in sector s as

$$SH^s_{itm} = \frac{\alpha_{imt} \sum_{j \in R} P^s_{mtj}}{\sum_{k \in M} \alpha_{ikt} \sum_{j \in R} P^s_{ktj}} \tag{5}$$

where $\alpha_{imt} \sum_{j \in R} P^s_{mtj}$ is the total amount of aid allocated by donor country i through multilateral m in year t since the multilateral total uses the effective aid weight (α_{imt}) as above. The denominator simply calculates the effective aid given by a donor country to each multilateral institution by sector and year. The set M of multilateral institutions varies by donor country i and consists of only those countries that are 'eligible' to give money to a particular IO. For example, Japan is not eligible to give money to the Nordic Development Fund. Notice that we sum each multilateral donor's aid dollars in a sector and year given to all recipients, R.

Since there are many cases of multilateral institutions not receiving any money from specific donors, we estimate the Cragg model described earlier in this appendix. This model accounts for the problems that arise when a high proportion of observations of the dependent variable mass at zero and the associated problems with parameter bias. In practical terms, our approach models the probability of a country allocating money to a multilateral organization as a two-step process. First, the multilateral organization must pass the gate-keeping stage, and conditional on that, it receives some positive amount of money. This is necessary since a significant portion of multilateral organizations do not receive any monies from some bilateral donors.

Like the Bilateral Allocation model from Chapter 6, the Multilateral Allocation model includes donor performance scores recovered from donor specific models. However, unlike the bilateral/multilateral model where scores were taken from bilateral models, the scores included here are the performance scores for *each* multilateral organization. Elasticity scores are recovered on government effectiveness and natural capital score. These elasticity measures do not vary through time—they represent the average responsiveness of each multilateral organization for the 1990s. We hypothesize that as the responsiveness of any given multilateral institution increases, bilateral donors are more likely to allocate more of their multilateral funding to that multilateral organization, all other factors held equal. The caveats noted in the preceding section concerning the use of these elasticity estimates should be noted here as well.

Summary Statistics for Main Analyses

Table C.1a. Chapter 4 summary statistics: inter-recipient models. Gate-keeping stage

Variable name	Observations	Mean	Std. dev.	Min.	Max
Green aid	14903	0.0064	0.0419	0	1
Environmental aid	15765	0.0072	0.0384	0	1
Brown aid	15765	0.0076	0.0451	0	1
Dirty aid	16169	0.0075	0.0346	0	0.8855
Score on Environmental Policy Index	21324	56.628	146.61	1	1225
Water quality (org_water_~s)	12715	0.1965	0.0487	0.07	0.38
Environmental treaty ratifications (count_ratif)	11248	0.1986	0.1603	0.125	0.875
CITES reporting (cites-repo~g)	15498	69.445	23.578	11	100
Recipient gov't effectiveness (government)	9366	-0.3378	0.6312	-2.136	1.489
Democracy index for recipient (democ)	14914	6.1546	2.855	0.0342	10
Importance of recipient in donor trade (trade_impo~e)	19399	0.0001	0.0004	0	100
Recipient UN voting with donor (S2un)	27588	0.774	0.2199	-0.326	1
Distance from donor to recipient (distance)	29113	7.509	4.072	0.1447	19.586
Recipient was colony in 1945 (col45)	29113	0.0264	0.1605	0	1
GDP per capita (gdp_cap)	20732	3715.6	3083.862	403.89	17771

Table C.1b. Amount stage

Variable	Observations	Mean	Std. dev.	Min	Max
Green aid	6534	0.0098	0.0696	0	1
Environmental aid	7800	0.0114	0.0627	0	1
Brown aid	5809	0.0129	0.0758	0	1
Dirty aid	6702	0.0127	0.0449	0	1
Score on Environmental Policy Index	8453	58.96	151.38	1	1225
Water quality	5243	0.1978	0.0497	0.07	0.38
Recipient UN voting with donor (S2un)	27588	0.774	0.2199	−0.326	1
Distance from donor to recipient (distance)	29113	7.509	4.072	0.1447	19.586
Recipient was colony in 1945 (col45)	29113	0.0264	0.1605	0	1
GDP per capita (gdp_cap)	20732	3715.6	3083.862	403.89	17770.55
Water quality (org_water_)	5243	0.1978	0.0497	0.07	0.38
Environmental treaty ratifications (count_ratif)	4994	0.1983	0.1631	0.125	0.875
CITES reporting (cites-repo~g)	6198	70.357	22.17	11	100
Recipient gov't effectiveness (government)	4038	−0.3092	0.5905	−2.136	1.489
Democracy index for recipient (democ)	6562	6.139	2.872	0.0342	10
GDP per capita (gdp_cap)	8812	3705.84	3021.99	403.89	17770.55

Table C.2. Chapter 6 summary statistics

Variable	Observation	Mean	Standard deviation	Minimum	Maximum
Dirty aid	189	0.338922	0.1009958	0.1316618	0.6094122
Green aid	189	0.031872	0.017493	0.0024456	0.1112532
Brown aid	189	0.069698	0.0299394	0.0224802	0.2226019
Env. aid	189	0.101569	0.0356777	0.0301495	0.2902631
Donor environmental policy index [ln(EPI)]	170	0.8724	0.1811139	0.268	1
Veto players	160	2.661493	1.538074	1	6
Percentage of environmental treaties ratified ([ln(treat%)]	239	0.457927	0.3163656	0	0.7777778
Post-materialist values [ln(WorldValues)]	170	2.568195	0.1893515	2.237347	3.127193
National wealth [ln(GDP per capita)]	170	21425.95	7309.303	12444.38	106430.6
Strength of environmental lobby [ln(enviro lobby)]	170	1.76 e-08	1.32 e-08	7.85 e-10	5.42 e-08
Kenwcoor	160	3.2875	1.437973	1	5
Power of left in legislative branch [ln(LEFTS)]	170	37.47471	15.87316	0	64
Strength of industrial lobby [ln(IGC)]	170	0.426632	0.0683927	0.2962999	0.5635208

Table C.3. Chapter 8 summary statistics

Variable	Observation	Mean	Standard deviation	Minimum	Maximum
Green_share	3468	0.049	0.111	0.000	0.981
Env_share	3468	0.049	0.093	0.000	0.733
Brown_share	3468	0.049	0.103	0.000	0.758
Dirty_share	3468	0.049	0.088	0.000	0.787
Donor's vote share	3901	0.051	0.075	0.000	0.594
Multilat.'s technical experience	5049	0.074	0.262	0.000	1.000
Multilat.'s years in existence	5049	23.589	15.832	0.000	55.000
Government effectiveness score (elasticity) [green share model]	5049	0.084	0.187	−0.161	0.415
Donors target recipients high in natural capital index (elasticity) [green share model]	5049	0.199	0.357	−0.027	0.967
Government effectiveness score (elasticity) [enviro share model]	5049	0.142	0.353	−0.391	0.857
Donor's target recipients high in natural capital index (elasticity) [enviro share model]	5049	−0.063	0.244	−0.726	0.472
Government effectiveness score (elasticity) [brown share model]	5049	0.202	0.344	−0.145	1.012
Donors target recipients high in natural capital index (elasticity) [brown share model]	5049	−0.128	0.378	−1.250	0.209
Government effectiveness score (elasticity) [dirty share model]	5049	0.050	0.264	−0.235	0.581
Donors target recipients high in natural capital index (elasticity) [dirty share model]	5049	−0.067	0.153	−0.045	0.308
Double majority voting	5049	0.037	0.189	0.000	1.000

References

'About ADB.' Asian Development Bank. www.adb.org/About/default.asp (accessed July 2006).

'African Housewives Stranded in Debt.' *Copenhagen Post Online*, 10 February 2002. www.cphpost.dk/get/85814.html.

'A Great Wall of Waste.' *The Economist*, 24 August 2004.

'Aid and the Environment—Outlook: Cloudy.' *The Economist*, 12 February 1994, 42.

'Aid that Doesn't Help.' *Financial Times*, 23 June 2000.

'Beijing Ministerial Declaration on Environment and Development, 1991 (accessed 11 June 2007).

'Book Reviews—Environment: Costa Rica: The Ecotraveller's Wildlife Guide.' *Canadian Field-Naturalist* 114, no. 1 (2000): 171.

'Bush Administration Declines to Endorse Plan for World's Poor.' *Associated Press Worldstream*, 17 December 2001 (accessed 9 July 2006).

'Bush Plan Ties Foreign Aid to Free Market and Civic Rule.' *New York Times*, 25 November 2002 (accessed 9 July 2006).

'Clearing the Deck, and the Forest.' *The Economist*, 29 March 2001.

'Closing in for the Kill?' *The Economist*, 16 May 2002.

Congressional Presentation Fiscal Year 2000: Kenya. United States: United States Agency for International Development, 2000, www.usaid.gov/pubs/cp2000/afr/kenya.html (accessed 1 August 2006).

Fact Sheet on the U.S. Contribution to the Global Environment Facility. Washington, DC: US Bureau of Oceans and International Environmental and Scientific Affairs, 2002 (accessed 9 July 2006).

'Foreign Aid Bill to Fund Controversial UN Agencies.' *OneWorld US*, 24 January 2004.

Foreign Relations. *Economic Freedom and U.S. Development Aid Programs*. Second sess., 1996.

'Give UNESCO a Second Chance.' *New York Times*, 25 October 1987, sec. The Week in Review.

'Good Times Increase Foreign Aid.' *Copenhagen Post*, 16 June 2006.

'Help in the Right Places.' *The Economist*, 16 March 2002.

'India Country Fact Sheet.' The World Bank (accessed 20 July 2006).

'India: Thanks, but no Thanks, to Aid.' *Copenhagen Post Online*, 4 June 2004.

International Public Goods: Incentives, Measurement, and Financing, edited by Marco A. Ferroni and Ashoka Mody. Washington, DC: Kluwer Academic Publishers and World Bank, 2002.

References

'Learning from Narmada.' World Bank Independent Evaluation Group. wbln0018. worldbank.org/oed/oeddoclib.nsf/e90210f184a4481b85256885007b1724/12a795722 ea20f6e852567f5005d8933 (accessed 24 July 2006).

'Leave USAID Alone.' *Buffalo News*, 1997, sec. City Edition, Viewpoints.

'O liberal.' *Belém*, 14 November 1989.

'Personal Interview with Mohamed Al Ashry.' Washington, DC, 2004.

'Pilot Program to Conserve the Brazilian Rain Forests.' Global Mechanism (GM) of the United Nations Convention to Combat Desertification (UNCCD). www.gm-unccd.org/FIELD/Multi/WB/Pilot.pdf (accessed 9 July 2006).

'Polluter Says' Principle: Global Environment Facility.' In *Green Politics: Global Environmental Negotiation—1: Green Politics*, edited by A. Agarwal, Sunita Narain, and S. Sharma. New Delhi: Centre for Science and Environment, 1999.

Public Law no. 101–167: Foreign Operations, Export Financing, and Related Programs Appropriations Act, 1990. Translated by House of Representatives. Vol. Public Law 101-1671989.

'Russia to Create Development Bank under German Scenario.' *SKRIN Market & Corporate News*, 27 April 2006.

'Senators Fed up with Diplomats Abusing Privilege.' *States News Service* (1993).

'The Greening of Giving: Aid and the Environment.' *The Economist*, 25 December 1993, 53–6.

'The IMF and the World Bank: Bribing Allies.' *The Economist*, 29 September 2001.

'The Ivory Paradox.' *The Economist*, 2 March 1991.

'The Sardar Sarovar Case (Narmada River).' International Emvironmental Law Research Center. www.ielrc.org/india/narmada.php (accessed 20 July 2006).

'The United States and the Withdrawal from UNESCO.' *Time Magazine*, 9 January 1984, 17.

The USAID FY 1998 Congressional Presentation. United States Agency for International Development, 1998, www.usaid.gov/pubs/cp98/afr/countries/ke.htm (accessed 1 August 2006).

'Third World Aid as Refugee Policy Tool.' *Copenhagen Post Online*, 4 August 2004.

'Tired of the Same Old Body.' *Time Magazine*, 16 December 1985, 42.

'USAID Protest.' *USA Today*, 2 August 1996, International Edition, sec. News (accessed 14 July 2006).

'USAID's Strategy for Stabilizing World Population Growth and Protecting Human Health.' *Population and Development Review* 20, no. 2 (1994): 483–7.

'Will the Bush Administration make Life More Difficult for the IMF and the World Bank?' *The Economist*, 17 February 2001.

Abbott, Kenneth W. and Duncan Snidal. 'Why States Act through Formal International Organizations.' *Journal of Conflict Resolution* 42, no. 1 (1998): 3–32.

Acharya, Arnab, Ana Fuzzo de Lima, and Mick Moore. *Aid Proliferation: How Responsible are the Donors?* Institute of Development Studies, 2004.

Adam, C. S. and J. W. Gunning. 'Redesigning the Aid Contract: Donors' Use of Performance Indicators in Uganda.' *World Development* 30, no. 12 (2002): 2045–56.

Albin, Cecilia. 'Negotiating International Cooperation: Global Public Goods and Fairness.' *Review of International Studies* 29, no. 3 (2003): 365–85.

References

Alesina, Alberto N. and David N. Dollar. 'Who Gives Foreign Aid to Whom and Why?' *Journal of Economic Growth* 5, no. 1 (2000): 33–63.

al-Nasser, Nassir Abdulaziz. *Submission of the Group of 77.* New York: The Group of 77, 2004.

Altbach, Eric. 'Japan's Foreign Aid Program in Transition: Leaner, Greener—with more strings Attached?' *Japan Economic Institute Report* 5 (1998).

Alterman, Jon B. 'Review of U.S. Assistance Programs to Egypt:' Statement before the House International Relations Committee, Subcommittee on the Middle East and Central Asia. 21 June 2006.

Anand, P. B. 'Financing the Provision of Global Public Goods.' *World Economy* 27, no. 2 (February 2004): 215.

André, Catherine and Jean-Phillipe Platteu. 'Land Relations under Unbearable Stress: Rwanda Caught in the Malthusian Trap.' *Journal of Economic Behavior and Organization* 34, no. 1 (1998): 1–47.

Aparecida de Mello, Neli. 'Between Conservation and Development: Innovations and Paradox in Amazon Environmental Policy.' In *Global Impact, Local Action: New Environmental Policy in Latin America*, edited by Anthony Hall, 74–80. London: University of London, 2005.

Arase, David. *Buying Power: The Political Economy of Japan's Foreign Aid.* Boulder, Colo.: Lynne Rienner Publishers, 1995.

Arce, D. G. and Todd Sandler. *Regional Public Goods: Typologies, Provision, Financing, and Development Assistance.* Vol. 1. Stockholm: Almquist & Wiksell International, 2002.

Asher, Robert E. 'Multilateral Versus Bilateral Aid: An Old Controversy Revisited.' *International Organization* 16, no. 4 (1962): 697–719.

Asian Development Bank (ADB). 'Board of Directors.' http://adb.org/BOD/default.asp (accessed 13 June 2007).

——'Funding and Lending.' www.adb.org/About/FAQ/funding.asp#source (accessed 15 June 2007).

——'Organization.' http://adb.org/About/organization.asp (accessed 26 July 2006).

——'Environment Community Practice.' www.adb.org/about/environment.asp (accessed 26 July 2006).

——*Environmental Policy: Policies and Procedures.* Manila: Asian Development Bank, 2002. http://www.asiandevbank.org/documents/policies/environment/default.asp?p=policies.

Asia-Pacific Forum for Environment and Development. 'Overview Paper on Issues and Challenges in the Financing of Sustainable Development in Asia and the Pacific.' Bangkok, 2002.

Auer, Matthew. 'Agency Reform as Decision Process: The Reengineering of the Agency for International Development.' *Policy Sciences* 31, no. 2 (1998): 81–105.

Ayubi, Nazih H. 'Government and the State in Egypt Today.' In *Egypt under Mubarak*, edited by Charles Tripp and Roger Owen. London: Routledge, 1989.

Azfar, Omar. *The NIE Approach to Economic Development: An Analytical Primer.* Washington, DC: Working Paper, USAID, 2002.

Babb, Sarah. 'The IMF in Sociological Perspective: A Tale of Organizational Slippage.' *Studies in Comparative International Development (SCID)* 38, no. 2 (2003): 3–27.

Baldwin, David A. *Economic Statecraft.* Princeton: Princeton University Press, 1985.

References

Balls, Andrew. 'Congress Asked to Raise Contribution.' *Financial Times*, 23 June 2004a, USE Ed2, sec. News Digest.

Balogh, T. 'Multilateral Versus Bilateral Aid.' *Oxford Economic Papers* 19, no. 3 (1967): 332–44.

Bandyopadhyaya, Sushenjit, Michael N. Hwuavindu, Priya Shyamsundar, and Limin Wang. 'Do Households Gain from Community-Based natural Resource Management? An Evaluation of community Conservancies in Namibia.' World Bank Working Paper, 2004.

Barder, Owen. *Reforming Development Assistance: Lessons from the UK Experience.* Center for Global Development, 2005.

Barnett, Michael N. *Eyewitness to a Genocide: The United Nations and Rwanda.* Ithaca, NY: Cornell University Press, 2003.

——and Margaret Finnemore. *Rules for the World: International Organizations in Global Politics.* Ithaca, NY: Cornell University Press, 2004.

—— —— 'The Power, Politics, and Pathologies of International Organizations.' *International Organization* 53, no. 4 (1999): 699–732.

Barrett, Scott. 'Creating Incentives for International Cooperation: Strategic Choices.' In *Providing Global Public Goods: Managing Globalization*, edited by Inge Kaul, P. Conceição, Katell Le Goulven, and Ronald U. Mendoza, 308–28. New York: Oxford University Press, 2003a.

——*Environment and Statecraft: The Strategy of Environmental Treaty-Making.* Oxford: Oxford University Press, 2003b.

——'A Theory of Full International Cooperation.' *Journal of Theoretical Politics* 11, no. 4 (1999a): 519–41.

——'Montreal v. Kyoto: International Cooperation and the Global Environment.' In *Global Public Goods: International Cooperation in the 21st Century*, edited by I. Kaul, I. Grunberg, and M. A. Stern. New York: Oxford University Press, 1999b.

Barry, Tom. *Aiding the Environment: U.S. Policy and Practice.* Silver City, NM: IRC Bulletin 43, 1996.

Bates, Robert H. *Markets and States in Tropical Africa: The Political Basis of Agricultural Policies.* Berkeley and Los Angeles: University of California Press, 1981.

Baumert, Kevin A. *Building on the Kyoto Protocol: Options for Protecting the Climate.* Washington, DC: World Resources Institute, 2002.

BBC News. 'Third of China Hit by "Acid Rain".' n.d. http://bbcnews.co.uk/ (accessed 27 August 2006).

Beck, T., G. Clarke, A. Groff, Philip Keefer, and P. Walsh. 'New Tools in Comparative Political Economy: The Database of Political Institutions.' *World Bank Economic Review* 15, no. 1 (2001): 165–76.

Bell, Jennifer. 'Egyptian Environmental Activists' Uphill Battle.' *Middle East Report* (Fall 2000).

Bell, Michael Mayerfield. *An Invitation to Environmental Sociology.* 2nd edn. Thousand Oaks, Calif.: Pine Forge Press, 2004.

Bell, Ruth Greenspan, Jane Bloom Stewart, and Magda Toth Nagy. 'Fostering a Culture of Environmental Compliance through Greater Public Involvement.' *Environment* 44, no. 8 (October 2002): 34–44.

Bergman, Torbjörn, Wolfgang C. Müller, and Kaare Stroslash. 'Introduction: Parliamentary Democracy and the Chain of Delegation.' *European Journal of Political Research* 37, no. 3 (2000): 255–60.

Bering-Jensen, Henrik. 'Foreign Aid: From Waste to Investment.' *Insight on the News* 10, no. 5 (1994): 6–11.

Bermeo, Sarah. 'Foreign Aid, Foreign Policy, and Development: Sector Allocation in Bilateral Aid.' Paper presented at the Annual Meeting of the International Studies Association, Chicago, 2006.

Bernheim, B. D. and M. D. Whinston. 'Common Agency.' *Econometrica* 54, no. 4 (1986): 923–42.

Bernstein, Johannah and Melissa Bluesky. 'Highlighting Southern Priorities for Earth Summit 2002.' Workshop Final Report. Brussels: The Heinrich Böll Foundation and the Stockholm Environment Institute, 16–18 June 2000.

Binder, S. and Eric N. Neumayer. 'Environmental Pressure Group Strength and Air Pollution: An Empirical Analysis.' *Ecological Economics* 55, no. 4 (2005): 527–38.

Bird Graham and Dane Rowlands. 'IMF Lending: How is it Affected by Economic, Political and Institutional Factors.' *Journal of Policy Reform* 4, no. 3 (2001): 243–70.

———— 'The Catalyzing Role of Policy-Based Lending by the IMF and the World Bank: Fact or Fiction?' *Journal of International Development* 12, no. 7 (2000): 951–73.

———— 'The Catalytic Effect of Lending by the International Financial Institutions.' *World Economy* 20, no. 7 (1997): 967–91.

Bøas, Morten. 'Environmental Policy in the African Development Bank and the Asian Development Bank.' In *Handbook of Global Economic Policy*, edited by Stuart S. Nagel, 38. New York: Marcel Dekker Incorporated, 2000.

Bocchi, Stefano, Stefano P. Disperati, and Simone Rossi. 'Environmental Security: A Geographic Information System Analysis Approach—the Case of Kenya.' *Environmental Management* 37, no. 2 (2006): 186–99.

Boehmer-Christiansen, Sonja. 'Climate Change and the World Bank: Opportunity for Global Governance?' *Energy & Environment* 10, no. 1 (1999): 27–50.

Boli, John and George M. Thomas, eds. *Constructing World Culture: International Nongovernmental Organizations since 1875.* Stanford, Calif.: Stanford University Press, 1999.

Bolt, K., Kir Hamilton, Kiran Pandey, and David Wheeler. 'The Cost of Air Pollution in Developing Countries: New Estimates for Urban Areas.' World Bank Development Research Group Working Paper, Forthcoming.

Boockmann, B. and Axel V. Dreher. 'The Contribution of the IMF and the World Bank to Economic Freedom.' *European Journal of Political Economy* 19, no. 3 (2003): 633–649.

Boone, P. 'Politics and the Effectiveness of Foreign Aid.' *European Economic Review* 40, no. 2 (1996): 289–329.

Bornschier, Volker, Christopher Chase-Dunn, and Richard Rubinson. 'Cross-National Evidence of the Effects of Foreign Investment and Economic Growth on Inequality.' *American Journal of Sociology* 84 (1978): 651–83.

Boulding, Carew. 'The Foreign Aid Puzzle: Bilateral Versus Multilateral Development Assistance.' Chicago, APSA, 1–5 September 2004.

Bowles, Ian A. and C. F. Kormos. 'The American Campaign for Environmental Reforms at the World Bank.' *Fletcher Forum of World Affairs* 23, no. 1 (1999): 211–25.

References

Bowles, Ian A. and C. F. Kormos. 'Environmental Reform at the World Bank: The Role of the US Congress.' *Virginia Journal of International Law* 35, no. 4 (1995): 777–839.

Boyd, Emily, Nathan E. Hultman, J. Timmons Roberts, Esteve Corbera, and Johannes Ebeling. 'The Clean Development Mechanism: Current Status, Perspectives, and Future Policy.' Working Paper, Environmental Change Institute and Tyndall Centre for Climate Change, Oxford 2007.

Bradley, Curtis A. and Judith Kelley. 'The Concept of International Delegation.' *Law and Contemporary Problems* (forthcoming 2007).

Bradsher, Keith and David Barboza. 'Pollution from Chinese Coal Casts a Global Shadow.' *New York Times*, 11 June 2006.

Brady, Henry E. and David Collier. *Rethinking Social Inquiry: Diverse Tools, Shared Standards.* Lanham, Md.: Rowman & Littlefield, 2004.

Brandon, Katrina, Kent H. Redford, and Steven E. Sanderson, eds. *Parks in Peril: People, Politics, and Protected Areas.* Washington, DC: Island Press, 1998.

Brautigam, Deborah. 'China, the World Bank, and the Global Aid Regime.' Paper presented at the University of Oxford/Cornell University conference on 'New Directions in Development Assistance', Oxford, 2007.

Brazil, World Wildlife Fund, World Bank, and Global Environmental Facility (GEF). 'Brazil to Triple Amount of Protected Amazon Rainforest over Ten Years.' Press release, 2002.

Brechin, Steven R. 'Objective Problems, Subjective Values, and Global Environmentalism: Evaluating the Postmaterialist Argument and Challenging a New Explanation.' *Social Science Quarterly* 80, no. 4 (1999): 793–809.

——Peter R. Wilshusen, Crystal L. Fortwangler, and Patrick C. West, eds. *Contested Nature: Promoting International Biodiversity Conservation with Social Justice in the Twenty-First Century.* Albany, NY: SUNY Press, 2003.

Breitmeier, Helmut, Marc A. Levy, Oran R. Young, and Michael Zürn. *The International Regimes Database as a Tool for the Study of International Cooperation.* Laxenburg: International Institute for Applied Systems Analysis, 1996.

Bruner, A., R. E. Guilison, and A. Balmford. 'Financial Costs and Shortfalls of Managing and Expanding Protected Area Systems in Developing Countries.' *Bioscience* 54 (2004): 1119–26.

Bruno, Kenny, Joshua Karliner, and China Brotsky. 'Greenhouse Gangsters vs. Climate Justice.' San Francisco: Transnational Resource & Action Center, 1999.

Buchanan, J. M. 'The Samaritan's Dilemma.' In *Altruism, Morality, and Economic Theory*, edited by E. S. Phelps, 71–85. New York: Russell Sage Foundation, 1975.

Bueno de Mesquita, Bruce, Alastair Smith, Randolph M. Siverson, and James D. Morrow. *The Logic of Political Survival.* Cambridge, Mass.: MIT Press, 2003.

Bunker, Stephen G. *Underdeveloping the Amazon: Extraction, Unequal Exchange, and the Failure of the Modern State.* Urbana: University of Illinnois Press, 1985.

Burnside, Craig and David N. Dollar. 'Aid, Policies, and Growth: Revisiting the Evidence.' World Bank Policy Research Working Paper 3251, World Bank, Washington, DC.

——'A Reply to New Data, New Doubts: A Comment on Burnside and Dollar's "Aid, Policies, and Growth".' *American Economic Review* 94, no. 3 (2004): 781.

——'Aid, Policies and Growth.' *American Economic Review* 90, no. 4 (2000a): 847–68.

References

——— 'Aid, the Incentive Regime, and Poverty Reduction.' In *The World Bank: Structure and Policies*, edited by Christopher L. Gilbert and David Vines. Cambridge: Cambridge University Press, 2000b.

——— 'Aid, the Incentive Regime, and Poverty Reduction.' Policy Research Working Paper 1937, Washington, DC: World Bank, 1998.

——— 'Aid, Policies, and Growth.' Policy Research Working Paper 1777, Washington, DC: World Bank, 1997.

Bush, George W. *Speech at Inter-American Development Bank*. Washington, DC: 2002.

Buthe, Tim. 'Institutional Persistence and Change in International Delegation.' Paper presented for the Workshop on Delegating Sovereignty at the Duke Law School, Durham, NC, 2006.

Butterfield, Samuel Hale. *U.S Development Aid—an Historic First: Achievements and Failures in the Twentieth Century*. 1st edn. Westport, Conn.: Praeger Publishers, 2004.

Cahn, Jonathan. 'Challenging the New Imperial Authority: The World Bank and the Democratization of Development.' *Harvard Human Rights Journal* 6 (1993): 159–94.

Caimcross, Sandy. 'Handwashing with Soap: A New Way to Prevent ARIs?' *Tropical Medicine and International Health* 8, no. 8 (2003): 677–9.

Calvo, Guillermo. 'Comment on "Why is there Multilateral Lending" by Dani Rodrik.' Washington, DC: World Bank, 1995.

Caplen, Brian. 'The Scalp-Hunters of Capitol Hill.' *Euromoney* 365 (1999): 170–7.

Carey, John M. and Matthew S. Shugart. *Presidents and Assemblies: Constitutional Design and Electoral Dynamics*. New York: Cambridge University Press, 1992.

Cassen, R. *Does Aid Work?* Oxford: Clarendon Press, 1994.

Center for Global Development. 'Commitment to Development Index.' www.cgdev.org/section/initiatives/_active/cdi (accessed 28 June 2006).

Chan, Gerald. 'China's Compliance in Global Environmental Affairs.' *Asia Pacific Viewpoint* 45, no. 1 (2004): 69–86.

Chase-Dunn, Christopher and V. Rubinson. 'Cross-National Evidence of the Effects of Foreign Investment and Aid on the Economic Growth and Inequality: A Survey of Findings and a Reanalysis.' *American Journal of Sociology* 84, no. 3 (1978): 651–83.

Chatterjee, Pratap and Matthias Finger. *The Earth Brokers: Power, Politics and World Development*. London: Routledge, 1994.

Checkley, W., R. H. Gilman, R. E. Black, L. D. Epstein, L. Cabrera, C. R. Sterling, and L. H. Moulton. 'Effect of Water and Sanitation on Childhood Health in a Poor Peruvian Peri-Urban Community.' *The Lancet* 363, no. 9403 (2004): 112–18.

Chen, Sulan and Juhan I. Uitto. 'Governing Marine and Coastal Environment in China: Building Local Government Capacity through International Cooperation.' *China Environment Series* 6 (2002): 67–80.

Chomitz, Kenneth and Sheila Wertz-Kanounnikoff. 'Measuring the Initial Impacts on Deforestation of Mato Grosso's Program for Environmental Control.' World Bank Research Working Paper 3762, Washington, DC: World Bank, 2005.

Clapp, R. L. 'The Resource Cycle in Forestry and Fishing.' *Canadian Geographer* 42, no. 2 (1998): 129–44.

Clasen, Thomas F., Joseph Brown, Simon Collin, Oscar Suntura, and Sandy Caimcross. 'Reducing Diarrhea through the Use of Household-Based Ceramic Water Filters: A Randomized, Controlled Trial in Rural Bolivia.' *American Journal of Tropical Medicine and Hygiene* 70, no. 6 (2004): 651–7.

References

Clemens, M., Steven Radelet, and R. Bhavnani. 'Counting Chickens when they Hatch: The Short-Term Effect of Aid on Growth.' Center for Global Development Working Paper 44 (2004).

Cody, Edward. 'Chinese Police Kill Villagers during Two-Day Land Protest.' *Washington Post*, 9 December 2005a.

—— 'For Chinese, Peasant Revolt is Rare Victory: Farmers Beat Back Police in Battle over Pollution.' *Washington Post*, 13 June 2005b, sec. A1.

Cole, John C. and J. Timmons Roberts. 'Social Development Aspects of the Kyoto Protocol Clean Development Mechanism Projects: A Review of Six Hydroelectricity Projects in Brazil and Peru.' Draft manuscript, n.d.

Cole, Matthew A. and Eric N. Neumayer. 'The Impact of Poor Health on Factor Productivity: An Empirical Investigation.' *Journal of Development Studies* 42, no. 6 (2006): 918–38.

Collier, Paul, Shantayanan Devarajan, and David N. Dollar. 'Measuring IDA's Effectiveness.' Unpublished paper. Washington, DC: World Bank, 2001.

—— and David N. Dollar. 'Aid Allocation and Poverty Reduction.' *European Economic Review* 46, no. 9 (2002): 1475–1500.

Congleton, Roger D. 'Forthcoming. Agency Problems and the Allocation of International Environmental Grants: The Return to Rio.' *Economia delle scelte pubbliche* 20 (2003): 125–46.

Connolly, Barbara. 'Increments for the Earth: The Politics of Environmental Aid.' In *Institutions for Environmental Aid*, edited by Robert O. Keohane and Marc A. Levy, 340. Cambridge, Mass.: MIT Press, 1996.

—— Tamar L. Gutner, and Hildegard Bedarff. 'Organizational Inertia and Environmental Assistance in Eastern Europe.' In *Institutions for Environmental Aid*, edited by Robert O. Keohane and Marc A. Levy, 281–323. Cambridge, Mass.: MIT Press, 1996.

Cooley Alexander and James Ron. 'The NGO Scramble: Organizational Insecurity and the Political Economy of Transnational Action.' *International Security* 27, no. 1 (2002): 5–39.

Copelovitch, Mark. 'Master or Servant? Agency Slack and the Politics of IMF Lending.' Paper presented at Princeton University, 2006.

Cosgrove, W. J. and F. R. Rijsberman. 'Creating a Vision for Water Life and the Environment.' *Water Policy* 1 (1998): 115–22.

Cox, G. W. *The Efficient Secret*. Cambridge: Cambridge University Press, 1987.

Cragg, John G. 'Some Statistical Models for Limited Dependent Variables with an Application to the Demand for Durable Goods.' *Econometrica* 39, no. 5 (1971).

Crenson, Matthew A. *The Un-Politics of Air Pollution: A Study of Non-Decisionmaking in the Cities*. Baltimore: Johns Hopkins University Press, 1971.

Crepaz, M. M. L. 'Explaining National Variations of Air Pollution Levels: Political Institutions and their Impact on Environmental Policy-Making.' *Environmental Politics* 4, no. 3 (1995): 391–414.

Curmally, Atiyah. 'Environment and Rehabilitation.' In *India Infrastructure Report 2002: Governance Issues for Commercialization*. New Delhi: Oxford University Press, 2002.

Curtis, Val and Sandy Caimcross. 'Effect of Washing Hands with Soap on Diarrhoea Risk in the Community: A Systematic Review.' *Lancet Infectious Diseases* 3, no. 5 (2003): 275–81.

Cutler, David, Angus Deaton, and Adriana Lleras-Muney. 'The Determinants of Mortality.' NBER Working Paper 11963, National Bureau of Economic Research, Cambridge, Mass.

—— and Grant Miller. 'The Role of Public Health Improvements in Health Advances: The Twentieth-Century United States.' *Demography* 42, no. 1 (2005): 1–22.

Dalgaard, C. J. and Henrik Hansen. 'On Aid, Growth and Good Policies.' *Journal of Development Studies* 37, no. 6 (2001): 17–41.

Damania, Richard. 'When the Weak Win: The Role of Investment in Environmental Lobbying.' *Journal of Environmental Economics and Management* 42, no. 1 (July 2001): 1–22.

—— and Per G. Fredriksson. 'Trade Policy Reform, Endogenous Lobby Group Formation, and Environmental Policy.' *Journal of Economic Behavior and Organization* 52, no. 1 (2003): 47–69.

Danish International Development Agency (Danida). *New Danida Environment Guide 2006.* Copenhagen: Royal Danish Ministry of Foreign Affairs, 2006a.

—— *Danida's Annual Report 2004.* Copenhagen: Royal Danish Ministry of Foreign Affairs, 2005.

—— *Strategy for Denmark's Environmental Assistance to Developing Countries 2004–2008.* Copenhagen: Royal Danish Ministry of Foreign Affairs, 2003.

Darst, Robert G. 'Samaritan's Dilemma in International Environmental Politics: Lessons for the Climate Change Regime.' Paper prepared for presentation at the Annual Meeting of the International Studies Association, 25 February–1 March 2003.

—— *Smokestack Diplomacy: Cooperation and Conflict in East–West Environmental Politics.* Cambridge, Mass.: MIT Press, 2001.

Datong, Ning. 'An Assessment of the Economic Losses Resulting from Various Forms of Environmental Degradation in China.' University of Toronto, n.d., www.library.utoronto.ca/pcs/state/chinaeco/land.htm#top (accessed 14 June 2007).

Dauvergne, Peter. *Loggers and Degradation in the Asia-Pacific: Corporations and Environmental Management.* Cambridge: Cambridge University Press, 2001a.

—— 'The Rise of an Environmental Superpower? Evaluating Japanese Environmental Aid to Southeast Asia.' In *Japan and East Asian Regionalism*, edited by Javed Maswood, 51–67. London: Routledge, 2001b.

—— *Shadows in the Forest: Japan and the Politics of Timber in Southeast Asia.* Politics, Science, and the Environment Series. Cambridge, Mass.: MIT Press, 1997.

Davis, J. 'Corruption in Public Service Delivery: Experience from South Asia's Water and Sanitation Sector.' *World Development* 32, no. 1 (2003): 53–71.

Department for International Development (DFID). *DFID Departmental Report 2006.* London: DFID, 2006.

—— *Strategic Review of Resource Allocation Priorities.* London: DFID, 2003.

—— *Untying Aid, Background Briefing.* London: DFID Information Department, 2001.

—— *Eliminating World Poverty: Making Globalization Work for the Poor.* London: DFID, 2000.

—— *Eliminating World Poverty: A Challenge for the 21st Century.* London: DFID, 1997.

de Sherbinin, A. and C. Giri. 'Remote Sensing in Support of Multilateral Environmental Agreements: What have we Learned from Pilot Applications?' Paper prepared for presentation at the Open Meeting of the Human Dimensions of Global Environmental Change Research Community, Rio de Janeiro, 2001.

DeSombre, Elizabeth R. 'Environmental Sanctions in US Foreign Policy.' In *The Environment, International Relations, and US Foreign Policy*, edited by Paul G. Harris. Washington, DC: Georgetown University Press, 2001.

—— 'Developing Country Influence in Global Environmental Negotiations.' *Environmental Politics* 9 (2000a): 23–42.

—— 'The Experience of the Montreal Protocol: Particularly Remarkable and Remarkably Particular.' *UCLA Journal of Environmental Policy and Law* 1, no. 19 (2000b): 49–78.

——and Joanne Kauffman. 'The Montreal Protocol Multilateral Fund: Partial Success Story.' In *Institutions for Environmental Aid: Pitfalls and Promise*, edited by Robert O. Keohane and Marc A. Levy, 89–126. Global Environmental Accords: Strategies for Sustainability series. Cambridge, Mass.: MIT Press, 1996.

Dessler, David. 'Constructivism within a Positivist Social Science.' *Review of International Studies* 25 (1999): 123–37.

Development Assistance Committee (DAC). *Development Cooperation Review: Denmark*. Paris: Organization of Economic Cooperation and Development (OECD), 2003, www.oecd.org/dataoecd/23/63/2956543.pdf.

Djankov, S., C. McLeish, and Andrei Shleifer. 'Private Credit in 129 Countries.' NBER Working Paper, 2005.

Dollar, David N. and William G. Easterly. 'The Search for the Key: Aid, Investment and Policies in Africa.' *Journal of African Economies* 8, no. 4 (1999): 546–77.

——and Victoria Levin. *The Increasing Selectivity of Foreign Aid, 1984–2002*. Policy Research Working Paper 3299. Washington, DC: World Bank, Development Economics Senior Vice Presidency, Development Policy, 2004.

——and Lant Pritchett. 'Assessing Aid: What Works, What Doesn't and Why.' *World Bank Policy Research Report*. Oxford: Oxford University Press, 1998.

——and Jakob Svensson. ' "What Explains the Success or Failure of Structural Adjustment Programs?" ' *Economic Journal* 110 (2000): 894–917.

Dudley, L. and C. Montmarquette. 'A Model of the Supply of Bilateral Foreign Aid.' *American Economic Review* 66, no. 1 (1976): 132–42.

Duflo, Esther. 'Scaling Up and Evaluation.' In *Accelerating Development*, edited by François Bourguignon and Boris Pleskovic. Oxford: Oxford University Press, 2004.

—— Michael Greenstone, and Rema Hanna. 'Indoor Air Pollution: A Randomized Study in Orissa, India.' MIT Working Paper, 2007.

Dugger, Celia. 'Overfarming African Land is Worsening African Crisis.' *New York Times*, 31 March 2006, sec. A7.

Dunlap, Riley E., G. H. Gallup, and A. M. Gallup. 'Of Global Concern: Results of the Health of the Planet Survey.' *Environment* 35 (1993): 7–15–33–39.

——and Angela G. Mertig. 'Global Concern for the Environment: Is Affluence a Prerequisite?' *Journal of Social Issues* 51, no. 4 (1995): 121.

Easterly, William G. 'Are Aid Agencies Improving?' *Economic Policy* (forthcoming 2007).

—— 'How to Assess the Need for Aid: The Answer: Don't Ask.' Unpublished paper, 2005.

—— 'Can Foreign Aid Buy Growth?' *Journal of Economic Perspectives* 17, no. 3 (2003): 23–48.

—— 'The Cartel of Good Intentions: The Problem of Bureaucracy in Foreign Aid.' *Journal of Policy Reform* 5, no. 4 (2002): 223–50.

—— *The Elusive Quest for Growth: Economists' Adventures and Misadventures in the Tropics.* Cambridge, Mass.: MIT Press, 2001.

—— Ross Levine, and David Roodman. 'Aid Policies and Growth: A Comment.' *American Economic Review* 94, no. 3 (2004a): 774–80.

———— 'New Data, New Doubts: A Comment on Burnside and Dollar's "Aid, Policies, and Growth".' *American Economic Review* 94, no. 3 (2004b): 774.

—— and S. Rebelo. *Fiscal Policy and Economic Growth: An Empirical Investigation.* Cambridge, Mass.: National Bureau of Economic Research, 1993.

Eckstein, Harry. 'Case Study and Theory in Political Science.' In *Handbook of Political Science.* Vol. 7, 79–137. Boston: Addison-Wesley, 1975.

Economy, Elizabeth. *The River Runs Black: The Environmental Challenge to China's Future.* Ithaca, NY: Cornell University Press, 2004.

Eigen, P. and C. Eigen-Zucchi. 'Corruption and Global Public Goods.' In *Global Public Goods: International Cooperation in the 21st Century*, edited by Inge Kaul, Isabelle Grunberg, and Marc A. Stern, 576–97. New York: Oxford University Press, 2003.

Einhorn, J. 'The World Bank's Mission Creep.' *Foreign Affairs* 80, no. 5 (2001): 22–35.

Eldridge, Phillip J. *The Politics of Foreign Aid in India.* New York: Schocken Books, 1970.

Ellis, J., H. Winkler, J. Corfee-Morlot, and F. Gagnon-Lebrun. 'CDM: Taking Stock and Looking Forward.' *Energy Policy* 35, no. 1 (2007).

Esrey, S. A. 'Water, Waste, and Well-Being: A Multicountry Study.' *American Journal of Epidemiology* 143, no. 6 (1996): 608–23.

—— J. B. Potash, L. Roberts, and C. Shiff. 'Effects of Improved Water Supply and Sanitation on Ascariasis, Diarrhoea, Dracunculiasis, Hookworm Infection, Schistosomiasis, and Trachoma.' *Bulletin of the World Health Organization* 69, no. 5 (1991): 609–21.

Esty, Daniel C. and Michael Porter. 'National Environmental Performance: An Empirical Analysis of Policy Results and Determinants.' *Environment and Development Economics* 10 (2005): 391–434.

European Commission 2006. Environment Directorate-General of the European Commission Website. http://ec.europa.eu/environment/env-act5/chapt7.htm.

Evans, Peter. 'Japan's Green Aid Plan: The Limits of State-Led Technology Transfer.' *Asian Survey* 39, no. 6 (1999): 825–44.

—— 'Japan's Green Aid.' *China Business Review* (1994): 39–43.

Fairman, David. 'The Global Environment Facility: Haunted by the Shadow of the Future.' In *Institutions for Environmental Aid*, edited by Robert O. Keohane and Marc A. Levy, 55–88. Cambridge, Mass.: MIT Press, 1996.

—— and Michael Ross. 'Old Fads, New Lessons: Learning from Economic Development Assistance.' In *Institutions for Environmental Aid*, edited by Robert O. Keohane and Marc A. Levy, 29–51. Cambridge, Mass.: MIT Press, 1996.

Farnsworth, E. Allan. 'Uncitral—Why? What? How? When?' *American Journal of Comparative Law* 20, no. 2 (1972).

Fay, Marianne, Danny Leipziger, Quentin Wodon, and Tito Yepes. 'Achieving Child-Health-Related Millenium Development Goals: The Role of Infrastructure.' *World Development* 33, no. 8 (2005): 1267–84.

Fearnside, Philip M. 'Deforestation Control in Mato Grosso: A New Model for Slowing the Loss of Brazil's Amazon Forest.' *Ambio* 32, no. 5 (2003): 343–5.

—— 'Controle de desmatamento no Mato Grosso: um novo modelo para reduzir a velocidade da perda de floresta Amazonica.' Paper presented in the seminar

References

'Aplicacoes e Controle do Desmatamento na Amazonia Brasileira', Brasilia-DF, 2002.

Fearon, James D. 'Domestic Political Audiences and the Escalation of International Disputes.' *American Political Science Review* 88, no. 3 (1994): 577–92.

Federal Ministry on Cooperation and Development. 'Country Concentrations.' 2006. www.bmz.de/en/countries/laenderkonzentration/index.html (accessed 9 July 2006).

Ferejohn, J. N. *Pork Barrel Politics: Rivers and Harbors Legislation, 1947–1968*. Stanford, Calif.: Stanford University Press, 1974.

Ferroni, Marco A. *International Public Goods: Incentives Measurement and Financing*. Dordrecht: Kluwer Academic Publishers, 2002.

—— and A. Mody. *International Public Goods: Incentives, Measurement, and Financing*. Dordrecht: Kluwer Academic Publishers, 2002.

Feyzioglu, T., V. Swaroop, and M. Zhu. 'A Panel Data Analysis of the Fungibility of Foreign Aid.' *World Bank Economic Review* 12, no. 1 (1998): 29–58.

Fidler, Stephan. 'Who's Minding the Bank?' *Foreign Policy* 126 (2001): 40–50.

Fincher, Leta H. 'Worldwatch Institute: 16 of World's 20 Most-Polluted Cities in China.' n.d.www.voanews.com/english/archive/2006-06/2006-06-28-voa36.cfm (accessed 14 June 2007).

Finnemore, Martha. *National Interests in International Society*. Ithaca, NY: Cornell University Press, 1996.

Fiorina, M. P. *Retrospective Voting in American National Elections*. New Haven: Yale University Press, 1981.

Fistenet. 'Vietnamese Fisheries Sector Project List of Donor Funded Projects (Part I).' 2006. www.fistenet.gov.vn/details_e.asp?Object=2114112&news_ID=9264705 (accessed 14 July 2006).

Fitzgerald, Rachel and Jessica Sloan. 'Where the Donors Got it Right: The Effectiveness of Water and Sanitation Aid to Developing Countries.' Working Paper, Williamsburg, Va.: College of William and Mary, 2006.

Fleck, Robert, and Christopher Kilby. 'World Bank Independence: A Model and Statistical Analysis of US Influence.' *Review of Development Economics* 10, no. 2 (2006a): 224–40.

—— —— 'How Do Political Changes Influence US Bilateral Aid Allocations? Evidence from Panel Data.' *Review of Development Economics* 10, no. 2 (2006b): 210–23.

Flint, Michael, Paul Balogun, Ann Gordon, Richard Hoare, Doug Smith, Ben Voysey, and Anthony Ziegler. *Environmental Evaluation Synthesis Study, Environment: Mainstreamed or Sidelined?* London: DFID, 2000.

Florini, A. 'The Politics of Transparency.' Annual Meeting of the International Studies Association, Los Angeles (2000).

Food and Agriculture Organization (FAO). 'Convention to Combat Desertification and Drought.' 1993. www.fao.org/docrep/X5308E/X5308E00.htm (accessed 30 June 2007).

Forrest, R. A. 'Japanese Aid and the Environment.' *Ecologist* 21, no. 1 (1991): 24–32.

Foster, Andrew D. and Mark R. Rosenzweig. 'Economic Growth and the Rise of Forests.' *Quarterly Journal of Economics* 118, no. 2 (2003): 601–37.

Fox, Jonathan A. and L. David Brown, eds. *The Struggle for Accountability: The World Bank, NGOs, and Grassroots Movements*. Global Environmental Accord Series. Boston: MIT Press, 1998.

Fredriksson, Per G. 'The Political Economy of Pollution Taxes in a Small Open Economy.' *Journal of Environmental Economics and Management* 33, no. 1 (1997): 44.

French, Howard W. 'Anger in China Rises over Threat to Environment.' *New York Times*, 19 July 2005.

G-7 Finance Ministers. *Strengthening the International Financial Architecture*. Fukuoka: G7, 2000.

G-8 Gleneagles. 'Gleneagles Plan of Action.' Perthshire, Scotland, 6–8 July 2005.

Galiani, Sebastian, Paul Gertler, and Ernesto Schargrodsky. 'Water for Life: The Impact of the Privatization of Water Services on Child Mortality.' *Journal Political Economy* 13, no. 1 (2005): 83–120.

Gartzke, Erik and Dong-Joon Jo. *UN General Assembly Voting, Version 4.0. Dataset.* 2002.

———— and R. Tucker. *The Similarity of UN Policy Positions* (2002).

Gates, S. and A. Hoeffler. 'Global Aid Allocation: Are Nordic Donors Different?' CSAE Working Paper No. 2004–34, Oxford, 2004.

Gaubatz, Kurt Taylor. 'Democratic States and Commitment in International Relations' *International Organization* 50, no. 1 (1996): 109–39.

Georgieva, Kristalina. Lecture delivered at the London School of Economics, 2003.

Gerlak, Andrea K. 'The Global Environment Facility and Transboundary Water Resource Management: New Institutional Arrangements in the Danube River and Black Sea Region.' *Journal of Environment and Development* 13, no. 4 (2004a): 40–424.

—— 'One Basin at a Time: The Global Environment Facility and Governance of Transboundary Waters.' *Global Environmental Politics* 4, no. 4 (2004b): 108–41.

Gibson, Clark C. *Politicians and Poachers: The Political Economy of Wildlife Policy in Africa.* New York: Cambridge University Press, 1999.

—— K. Andersson, E. Ostrom, and S. Shivakumar. *The Samaritan's Dilemma: The Political Economy of Development Aid.* Oxford: Oxford University Press, 2005.

Gleditsch, Kristian S. 'Expanded Trade and GDP Data.' *Journal of Conflict Resolution* 46 (2002): 712–24.

Gleick, Peter H. 'Freshwater Systems—Water in Crisis: Paths to Sustainable Water Use.' *Ecological Applications: A Publication of the Ecological Society of America* 8, no. 3 (1998): 571.

Global Environment Facility (GEF). 'GEF Council.' www.gefweb.org/interior.aspx?id=66 (accessed 26 July 2006).

—— 'RAF at a Glance: GEF's New Framework for Allocating Resources.' www.gefweb. org/interior_right.aspx?id=82&menu_id=120 (accessed 26 July 2006).

—— *Project Database: Regional—Caribbean Planning for Adaptation to Global Climate Change (CARICOM).* Global Environmental Facility, 2006a, www.gefonline. org/projectDetails.cfm?projID=105 (accessed 1 August 2006).

—— 'GEF Council.' Washington, DC: Global Environmental Facility, 2006b. http://www.gefweb.org/interior.aspx?id=66 (accessed 26 July 2006).

—— OP53: *Progress Toward Environmental Results.* Washington, DC: GEF, 2005.

—— *Instrument for the Establishment of the Restructured Global Environment Facility.* Washington, DC: Global Environment Facility, 2004b, http://thegef.org/ GEF_Instrument3.pdf.

—— 'Submission of the Group of 77.' Paris, 27–8 September 2004b.

—— 'GEF Biodiversity Program Study 2004 (BPS2004).' Washington, DC: Global Environment Facility, September 2004c.

References

Global Environment Facility (GEF). *GEF Annual Report 2003: Making a Difference for the Environment and People.* Washington, DC: GEF, 2003.

——*Focusing on the Global Environment: The First Decade of the GEF: Second Overall Performance Study.* Washington, DC: GEF, 2002.

——'Incremental Costs.' Washington, DC: Global Environmental Facility, 1996. http://www.gefweb.org/interior.aspx?id=80 (accessed 26 July 2006).

——'Project Descriptions: Regional—Caribbean Planning for Adaptation to Global Climate Change (CARICOM).' www.gefonline.org/projectDetails.cfm?projID=105 (accessed 15 June 2007).

Gomaa, Salwa S. *Environmental Policy Making in Egypt.* Gainesville, Fla.: University Press of Florida, 1997.

Gómez-Lobo, Andres and Dante Contreras. 'Water Subsidy Policies: A Comparison of the Chilean and Columbian Schemes.' *World Bank Economic Review* 17, no. 3 (2003): 391–407.

Gould, Erica R. 'Money Talks: Supplementary Financiers and International Monetary Fund Conditionality.' *International Organization* 57, no. 03 (2003c): 551–86.

Gowan, P. 'Explaining the American Boom: The Roles of "Globalisation" and United States Global Power.' *New Political Economy* 6, no. 3 (2001): 359–74.

Greenpeace. 'Asian Development Bank Bankrolling Climate Change, Says Greenpeace.' Greenpeace SE Asia 2006. www.greenpeace.org/seasia/en/news/asian-development-bank-bankrol (accessed 26 July 2006).

Grieco, Joseph. 'Anarchy and the Limits of Cooperation: A Realist Critique of the Newest Liberal Institutionalism.' *International Organization* 42, no. 3 (1988): 485–508.

Grossman, Gene M. and E. Helpman. 'Electoral Competition and Special Interest Politics.' *Review of Economic Studies* 63, no. 2 (1996): 265–86.

——'Protection for Sale.' *American Economic Review* 84, no. 4 (1994): 833–50.

Grossman, Sanford J. and Oliver D. Hart. 'The Costs and Benefits of Ownership: A Theory of Vertical and Lateral Integration.' *Journal of Political Economy* 94, no. 4 (August 1986): 691–719.

Grübacher, Armin. *Reconstruciton and Cold War in Germany: The Kreditanstalt für Wiederaufbau (1948–1961).* 1st edn. Vol. 1. Burlington, Vt.: Ashgate Publishing Company, 2004.

Grubb, Michael. *Energy Policies and the Greenhouse Effect.* Energy and Environmental Programme. Aldershot: Dartmouth, 1990.

Guerrero, Dorothy, ed. *A Handbook on the Asian Development Bank: The ADB and its Operations in Asia and the Pacific Region.* Essen: Asienstiftung/Asienhaus, 2003.

Guha, Ramachandra and Juan Martinez-Alier. *Varieties of Environmentalism: Essays North and South.* London: Earthscan Publications, 1997.

Guillaumont, P. and L. Chauvet 'Aid and Performance: A Reassessment.' *Journal of Devlopment Studies* 37, no. 6 (2001): 66–92.

Guimarães, Robert. *Ecopolitics of Development in the Third World: Politics and Environment in Brazil.* Boulder, Color.: Lynne Rienner Publishers, 1991.

Gundry, Stephen, Jim Wright, and Ronan Conroy. 'A Systematic Review of Health Outcomes Related to Household Water Quality in Developing Countries.' *Journal of Water and Health* 2, no. 1 (2004): 1–13.

Gupta, J. 'The Global Environment Facility in its North–South Context.' *Environmental Politics* 4, no. 1 (1995): 19–43.

Gutner, Tamar L. *Banking on the Environment: Multilateral Development Banks and their Environmental Performance in Central and Eastern Europe*. Cambridge, Mass.: MIT Press, 2002.

—— 'World Bank Environmental Reform: Revisiting Lessons from Agency Theory.' *International Organization* 59, no. 03 (2005): 773–83.

Haas, Peter M., Marc A. Levy, and T. Parson. 'Appraising the Earth Summit: How should we judge UNCED's Success?' *Environment* 34, no. 8 (1992): 26–33.

Haggard, Stephan and Robert R. Kaufman. *The Political Economy of Democratic Transitions*. Princeton: Princeton University Press, 1995.

—— and Andrew Moravcsik. 'The Political Economy of Financial Assistance to Eastern Europe, 1989–1991.' *After the Cold War: International Institutions and State Strategies in Europe 1989–1991* (1993).

Hall, Anthony. 'Agrarian Crisis in Brazilian Amazonia: The Grande Crajas Programme.' *Journal of Development Studies* 23, no. 4 (1987): 522–52.

—— ed. *Global Impact Local Action: New Environmental Policy in Latin America*. London: Institute for the Study of the Americas, 2005.

Han, Aung M. and Thein Hlaing. 'Prevention of Diarrhoea and Dysentery by Hand Washing.' *Transactions of the Royal Society of Tropical Medicine and Hygiene* 83 (1989): 128–31.

Hansen, Henrik and Finn Tarp. *Aid and Growth Regressions, Paper Presented at the OECD DAC Seminar on Aid Effectiveness, Selectivity and Poor Performers* (2001).

Hao, Jiming and Litao Wang. 'Improving Air Quality in China: Beijing Case Study.' *Journal of the Air and Waste Management Association* 55 (2005): 1298–305.

Hardin, Russell. *Collective Action*. Washington, DC: RFF Press, 1982.

Harris, Paul G. *The Environment, International Relations and U.S. Foreign Policy*. Vol. 1. Washington, DC: Georgetown University Press, 2001.

Hassler, Björn. 'Foreign Assistance as a Policy Instrument: Swedish Environmental Support to the Baltic States, 1991–96.' *Cooperation and Conflict* 37, no. 1 (2002): 25–45.

Hatton, T. 'Reconceptualizing Foreign Aid.' Review of International Political Economy 8, no. 4 (2007): 633–60.

Hawkins, Darren and Wade Jacoby. 'How Agents Matter.' In *Delegation and Agency in International Organizations*, edited by Darren Hawkins, David A. Lake, Daniel L. Nielson, and Michael J. Tierney. Cambridge: Cambridge University Press, 2006.

—— David A. Lake, Daniel L. Nielson, and Michael J. Tierney, eds. *Delegation and Agency in International Organizations*. Cambridge: Cambridge University Press, 2006.

———— 'Delegation under Anarchy: States, International Organizations, and Principal–Agent Theory.' Unpublished Manuscript, BYU and UCSD, 2003.

Hayes, Peter and Kirk R. Smith. *The Global Greenhouse Regime: Who Pays?: Science, Economics and North–South Politics in the Climate Change Convention*. London: Earthscan Publications, 1993.

Hayes, Tanya. 'Parks, People, and Forest Protection: An Institutional Assessment of the Effectiveness of Protected Areas.' *World Development* 34, no. 12 (2006): 2064–75.

Hayter, T. *Exploited Earth: Britain's Aid and the Environment*. London: Earthscan Publications, 1989.

Hayward, Steven F. *Index of Leading Environmental Indicators 2006: The Nature and Sources of Ecological Progress in the U.S. and the World*. San Francisco: Pacific Research Institute, 2006.

References

Hecht, Susanna and Stephen Schwartzman. 'The Good, the Bad, and the Ugly: Amazonian Extraction, Colonist Agriculture, and Livestock in Comparative Perspective.' Unpublished, 1988.

Heckelman, J. and S. Knack. 'Foreign Aid and Market-Liberalizing Reform.' *Economica* forthcoming.

Heltberg, Rasmus and Uffe Nielsen. 'Foreign Aid, Development and the Environment.' In *Foreign Aid and Development: Lessons Learnt and Directions for the Future*, edited by Finn Tarp and Peter Hjertholm. London: Routledge, 2000.

Henisz, Witold J. and Bennet A. Zelner. 'Interest Groups, Veto Points and Electricity Infrastructure Deployment.' *International Organization* 60, no. 1 (2006): 283–6.

Hewitt, A. and M. Sutton. 'British Aid: A Change of Direction.' *ODI Review* 1 (1980): 1–10.

Honaker, James, Gary King, and Matthew Blackwell. 'Amelia II: A Program for Missing Data.' Unpublished manuscript, Harvard University, 2006.

Hook, Steven W. and Charles W. Kegley. 'US Foreign Aid and UN Voting: An Analysis of Important Issues.' *International Studies Quarterly* 35 (1991): 295–312.

——Peter J. Schraeder, and Bruce Taylor. 'Clarifying the Foreign Aid Puzzle: A Comparison of Japanese, French, and Swedish Aid Flows.' *World Politics* 50, no. 2 (1998): 294–323.

Hopkins, R. F. 'Political Economy of Foreign Aid.' In *Foreign Aid and Development: Lessons Learnt and Directions for the Future*. London: Routledge 2000: 423–49.

Hoque, B. A., D. Mahalanabis, M. J. Alam, and M. S. Islam. 'Post-Defecation Handwashing in Bangladesh: Practice and Efficiency Perspectives.' *Public Health* 109, no. 1 (1995): 15–24.

Houghton, R. A. 'The Annual Net Flux of Carbon to the Atmosphere from Changes in Land Use, 1850–1990.' *Tellus B* 51, no. 2 (1999): 298.

Huntington, Samuel P. 'Foreign Aid for what and for whom.' *Foreign Policy* 1 (1970): 161–89.

Huttly, S. R. A., S. S. Morris, and V. Pisani. 'Prevention of Diarrhoea in Young Children in Developing Countries.' *Bulletin of the World Health Organization* 75, no. 2 (1997): 163–74.

Independent Evaluation Group. 'Learning from Narmada.' World Bank, 2006.

Indufor, Oy. 'Final Report of the Evaluatory Phase.' STCP Engenharia de Projetos Ltda, 2000. www.worldbank.org/rfpp/docs/rfpp-mtr_eng.pdf (accessed 9 July 2006).

Inglehart, Ronald. 'Public Support for Environmental Protection: Objective Problems and Subjective Values in 43 Societies.' *PS: Political Science and Politics* 28, no. 1 (1995): 57–72.

——*Culture Shift in Advanced Industrial Society*. Princeton: Princeton University Press, 1990.

Intergovernmental Panel on Climate Change (IPCC). *Third Assessment Report*. Cambridge: Cambridge University Press, 2001.

——*Assessment Report 4: Working Group I: The Physical Basis of Climate Change*. Cambridge: Cambridge University Press, 2007.

International Environmental Law Research Center. 'The Sardar Sarovar Case, Narmada River.' 2006. www.ielrc.org/india/narmada.php (accessed 20 July 2006).

Isham, J. and S. Kähkönen. 'The Importance of "Exit and Voice" in the Provision of Clean Water: Evidence from India and Sri Lanka.' In *Democracy and Development*, edited by Sunder Ramaswamy and Jeffrey Cason. Hanover, NH: University Press of New England, 2003.

———— 'Institutional Determinants of the Impact of Community-Based Water Projects: Evidence from Sri Lanka and India.' *Economic Development and Cultural Change* 50, no. 3 (2002): 667–92.

—— and Daniel Kaufmann. 'The Forgotten Rationale for Policy Reform: The Productivity of Investment Projects.' *Quarterly Journal of Economics* 114, no. 1 (1999): 149–84.

—— D. Narayan, and Lant Pritchett. 'Does Participation Improve Performance? Establishing Causality with Subjective Data.' *World Bank Economic Review* 9, no. 2 (1995): 175–200.

Islam, Shafiqul. 'Moscow's Rough Road to Capitalism.' *Foreign Affairs* 72, no. 2 (Spring 1993): 57–66.

Ivory, Ming. 'The Politics of US Environmental Assistance, 1976–1986.' *World Development* 20, no. 7 (1992): 1061–76.

Jalan, Jyotsna and Martin Ravallion. 'Does Piped Water Reduce Diarrhea for Children in Rural India?' *Journal of Econometrics* 112, no. 1 (2003): 153–73.

Japan International Cooperation Agency. *Annual Report* 1996.

—— *Annual Report* 1993.

—— *Carajas*. Tokyo: Japan International Cooperation Agency, 1983.

Jensen, Nathan. 'Democratic Governance and Multinational Corporations: Political Regimes and Inflows of Foreign Direct Investment.' *International Organization* 43, no. 3 (2003).

Jokela, Minna. 'European Union as a Global Policy Actor: The Case of Desertification.' In *Proceedings of the 2001 Berlin Conference on the Human Dimensions of Global Environmental Change*, edited by Frank Biermann, Rainer Brohm, and Klaus Dingwerth, 308–16. Potsdam: Potsdam Institute for Climate Impact Research, 2002.

Jupille, Joseph and Duncan Snidal. 'Forum Shopping and International Institutions: Cooperation, Alternatives and Strategies.' Paper read at American Political Science Association, Washington, DC, 2005.

Kanbur, Ravi. 'Aid Conditionality and Debt in Africa.' In *Foreign Aid and Development*, edited by Finn Tarp, 409–22. London: Routledge, 2000.

—— Todd Sandler, and K. M. Morrison. *The Future of Development Assistance: Common Pools and International Public Goods*. Overseas Development Council, 1999a.

———— 'The Context of Development Assistance.' In *The Future of Foreign Assistance: Common Pool Approach and International Public Goods*. Overseas Development Council, 1999b.

Kappagoda, Nihal. *The Asian Development Bank*. Boulder, Colo.: Lynne Rienner Publishers, 1995.

Kapur, Devesh. 'Do As I Say Not As I Do: A Critique of G-7 Proposals on Reforming the Multilateral Development Banks.' G-24 Discussion Paper Series. United Nations Conference on Trade and Development, 2003.

—— 'The Changing Anatomy of Governance of the World Bank.' In *Reinventing the World Bank*, edited by Jonathan R. Pincus and Jeffrey A. Winters, 54–75. Ithaca, NY: Cornell University Press, 2002a.

Kardam, N. 'Development Approaches and the Role of Policy Advocacy: The Case of the World Bank.' *World Development* 21, no. 11 (1993): 1773–86.

References

Katzman, M. T. 'Paradoxes of Amazonian Development in "Resource Starved" World.' *Journal of Developing Areas* 10 (1975): 445–59.

Kaufmann, David, Aart Kraay, and Massimo Mastruzzi. *Governance Matters III: Governance Indicators for 1996–2002*. World Bank, World Bank Institute, Global Governance Dept., and Development Research Group, Macroeconomics and Growth, 2003.

——and Yan Wang. 'Macroeconomic Policies and Project Performance in the Social Sectors: A Model of Human Capital Production and Evidence from LDCs.' *World Development* 23, no. 5 (1995): 751–65.

Kaul, Inge, Pedro Conceicao, Katell Le Goulven, and Ronald U. Mendoza. *Providing Global Public Goods: Managing Globalization*. New York: Oxford University Press, 2003.

——Isabelle Grunberg, and Marc A. Stern, eds. *Global Public Goods: International Cooperation in the 21st Century*. New York: Oxford University Press, 1999.

Kazis, Richard and Richard L. Grossman. *Fear at Work: Job Blackmail, Labor and the Environment*. New Society Publishers, 1990.

Keck, Margaret E. and Kathryn Sikkink. *Activists beyond Borders: Advocacy Networks in International Politics*. Ithaca, NY: Cornell University Press, 1998.

Keefer, Philip and Stuti Khemani. 'Democracy, Public Expenditures, and the Poor: Understanding Incentives for Providing Public Services.' *World Bank Research Observer* 20, no. 1 (2005): 1–27.

——and Stephen Knack. 'Boondoggles, Rent-Seeking, and Political Checks and Balances: Public Investment under Unaccountable Governments,' The Review of Economics and Statistics 89, no. 3 (2007): 566–72.

——Ambar Narayan, and Tara Vishwanath. 'Decentralization in Pakistan: Are Local Politicians Likely to be More Accountable.' In *Decentralization to Local Governments in Developing Countries: A Comparative Perspective*, edited by P. Bardhan and D. Mookherjee. Cambridge, Mass.: MIT Press, 2006.

Kegley, Charles W. and Steven W. Hook. 'U.S. Foreign Aid and U.N. Voting: Did Reagan's Linkage Strategy Buy Deference or Defiance?' *International Studies Quarterly: A Publication of the International Studies Association* 35, no. 3 (September 1991): 295.

Kenny, T. B. A. E. 'Republic of Ireland.' *Irish Political Studies* 21, no. 1 (February 2006): 15–84.

Kenworthy, Lane. 'Quantitative Indicators of Corporatism.' *International Journal of Sociology* 33 (2003): 10–44.

Keohane, Robert O. 'Analyzing the Effectiveness of International Environmental Institutions.' In *Institutions for Environmental Aid*, edited by Robert O. Keohane and Marc A. Levy, 3–27. Cambridge, Mass.: MIT Press, 1996.

——*After Hegemony: Cooperation and Discord in the World Political Economy*. Princeton: Princeton University Press, 1984.

——'The Study of Political Influence in the General Assembly.' *International Organization* 21, no. 2 (1967): 221–37.

——and Marc A. Levy. *Institutions for Environmental Aid: Pitfalls and Promise*. Global Environmental Accords. Cambridge, Mass.: MIT Press, 1996.

——and Joseph S. Nye. 'Introduction: The End of the Cold War in Europe.' In *After the Cold War: International Institutions and State Strategies in Europe, 1989–1991*, edited by Stanley Hoffmann, Robert O. Keohane, and Joseph S. Nye. Cambridge, Mass.: Harvard University Press, 1993.

KfW Bankengruppe. *Annual Report 2005*. Frankfurt: KfW Bankengruppe: Group Communication, 2005a, www.kfw.de/DE_Home/Service/OnlineBibl48/DieBank30/GB_05_E.pdf (accessed 9 July 2006).

—— *Annual Report on Cooperation and Development*. Frankfurt: KfW Bankengruppe, 2005b.

——'KfW Environmental Guideline.' www.kfw.de/EN_Home/Die_Bank/Our_Tasks/Environmen35/KfWsPublic20/Guidelines49/Rahmenrichtlinie_engl_180602.pdf (accessed 9 July 2006).

Khemani, Stuti. 'Political Cycles in a Developing Economy: Effect of Elections in the Indian States.' *Journal of Development Economics* 73, no. 1 (2004): 125–54.

Kiewiet, D. R. and Mathew D. McCubbins. *The Logic of Delegation: Congressional Parties and the Appropriations Process*. Chicago: University of Chicago Press, 1991.

Kilby, Christopher. 'Donor Influence in MDBs: The Case of the Asian Development Bank.' *Review of International Organizations* 1, no. 2 (2006): 173–95.

——'Donor Influence in MDBs: The Case of the Asian Development Bank.' Working Paper, Vassar College and Haverford College, 2005.

Killeen, Timothy J. *A Perfect Storm in the Amazon Wilderness: Development and Conservation in the Context of the Initiative for the Integration of the Regional Infrastructure of South America (IIRSA)*. Arlington, Va.: Conservation International, 2007.

Kim, Soyeun. The 'Greening' of Aid: The Political Ecology of Japan's Bilateral International Cooperation with the Philippines. Ph.D. thesis, King's College London, 2006.

Kim, Soo Yeon and Bruce Russett. 'The New Politics of Voting Alignments and United Nations General Assembly.' *International Organization* 50, no. 4 (1996): 629–52.

King, Gary, Robert O. Keohane, and Sidney Verba. *Designing Social Inquiry: Scientific Inference in Qualitative Research*. Princeton: Princeton University Press, 1994.

Kishor, Nalin and Arati Belle. 'Does Improved Governance Contribute to Sustainable Forest Management?' *Journal of Sustainable Forestry* 19 (2004): 55–80.

Knack, Stephen. 'Does Foreign Aid Promote Democracy?' *International Studies Quarterly* 48, no. 1 (2004): 251–66.

——'Aid Dependence and the Quality of Governance: Cross-Country Empirical Tests.' *Southern Economic Journal* 68, no. 2 (2001): 310–29.

—— and Aminur Rahman. *Donor Fragmentation and Bureaucratic Quality in Aid Recipients*. The World Bank, Policy Research Working Paper Series 3186, 2004.

Kotov, V. and E. Nikitina. 'Implementation and Effectiveness of the Acid Rains Regime in Russia.' In *Implementation and Effectiveness of International Environmental Commitments*, edited by D. Victor, K. Raustiala, and E. Skolnikoff. Cambridge, Mass.: MIT Press, 1998.

Krasner, Stephen D., ed. *International Regimes*. Ithaca, NY: Cornell University Press, 1983.

——'Power Structures and Regional Development Banks.' *International Organization* 35 (1981): 303–28.

Krauthammer, Charles. 'The Failure of Multilateralism.' *Guardian Weekly*, 6 December 2001.

Krueger, Anne O. 'Whither the World Bank and the IMF?' *Journal of Economic Literature* 36, no. 4 (1998): 1983–2020.

Kydd, Andrew. 'Trust, Reassurance, and Cooperation.' *International Organization* 54, no. 2 (2000): 325–57.

References

Lahiri, Sajal and Pascalis Raimondos-Møller. 'Lobbying by Ethnic Groups and Aid Allocation.' *Economic Journal* 110, no. 462 (2000a): 62–79.

Lai, Brian. 'Examining the Goals of US Foreign Assistance in Post-Cold War Period, 1991–96.' *Journal of Peace Research* 40, no. 1 (2003): 103–28.

Lake, David A. 'International Political Economy: A Maturing Interdiscipline.' In *The Oxford Handbook of Political Economy*, edited by Barry R. Weingast and Donald A. Wittman, 757–77. New York: Oxford University Press, 2006.

—— *Entangling Relations: American Foreign Policy in its Century*. Princeton: Princeton University Press, 1999.

—— 'Anarchy, Hierarchy, and the Variety of International Relations.' *International Organization* 50, no. 1 (1996): 1.

—— 'Powerful Pacifics: Democratic States and War.' *American Political Science Review* 86, no. 1 (1992): 24–37.

—— and Mathew D. McCubbins. 'The Logic of Delegation to International Organizations.' In *Delegation and Agency in International Organizations*, edited by Darren G. Hawkins, David A. Lake, Daniel L. Nielson, and Michael J. Tierney. New York: Cambridge University Press, 2006.

Lancaster, Carol. *Transforming Foreign Aid: United States Assistance in the 21st Century*. Washington, DC: Institute for International Economics, 2000.

Leakey, Richard and Virginia Morell. *Wildlife Wars: My Fight to Save Africa's Natural Treasures*. New York: St. Martin's Press, 2001.

Léautier, Frannie, ed. *Cities in a Globalizing World: Governance, Performance, and Sustainability*. Washington, DC: World Bank, 2006.

Leeds, Brett Ashley. 'Domestic Political Institutions, Credible Commitments and International Cooperation.' *American Journal of Political Science* 43, no. 4 (1999): 979–1002.

Lensink, Robert and Howard White. 'Are there Negative Returns to Aid?' *Journal of Development Studies* 37, no. 6 (2001): 42–65.

Levy, David L. and Daniel Egan. 'Capital Contests: National and Transnational Channels of Corporate Influence on the Climate Change Negotiations.' *Politics and Society* 26, no. 3 (September 1998): 337–61.

—— and Aseem Prakash. 'Bargains Old and New: Multinational Corporations in Global Governance.' *Business and Politics* 5, no. 2 (2003): 131–50.

Levy, Marc. 'East–West Environmental Politics after 1989: The Case of Air Pollution.' In *After the Cold War: International Institutions and State Strategies in Europe 1989–1991*, edited by Robert O. Keohane, Joseph S. Nye, and Stanley Hoffman. Cambridge, Mass.: Harvard University Press, 1993.

—— Catherine Thorkelson, Charles Vorosmarty, Ellen Douglas, and Macartan Humphreys. 'Freshwater Availability Anomalies and Outbreak of Internal War: Results from a Global Spatial Times Series Analysis.' Conference Paper presented at the Human Security and Climate Change International Workshop, Oslo, 2005.

Lewis, Paul. 'Pact on Environment Near, but Hurdles on Aid Remain.' *New York Times*, 12 June 1992.

Lewis, Tammy L. 'Environmental Aid: Driven by Recipient Need or Donor Interests?' *Social Science Quarterly* 84, no. 1 (2003): 144–61.

Lieberthal, Kenneth. 'China's Governing System and its Impact on Environmental Policy Implementation.' *China Environment Series* 1 (1997).

Little, R. J. A. and D. B. Rubin. *Analysis with Missing Data*. New York: John Wiley & Sons, Inc., 1987.

Lofstedt, Ragnar E. 'What Factors Determine Sweden's Provision of Environmental Aid to Eastern Europe?' *Global Environmental Change* 5, no. 1 (1995): 41–9.

—— 'Environmental Aid to Eastern Europe: Swedish and Estonian Perspectives.' *Post-Soviet Geography* 35 (1994): 594–607.

—— and Gunnar Sjostedt. *Environmental Aid Programmes to Eastern Europe: Area Studies and Theoretical Applications*. Brookfield, Vt.: Ashgate Publishing, 1996.

—— 'Environmental Aid to Eastern Europe: Problems and Possible Solutions.' *Ambio* 24, no. 6 (1995): 366.

—— —— and Magnus Andersson. 'Environmental Aid Programmes to Eastern Europe.' *International Environmental Affairs* 9, no. 2 (1997): 173.

Long, Marybeth. 'Expertise and the Convention to Combat Desertfication.' In *Innovations in International Environmental Negotiation*, edited by Lawrence E. Susskind, William R. Moomaw, and Teresa L. Hill, 88–111. Cambridge, Mass.: Program on Negotiation at Harvard Law School, 1997.

Loud, J. and C. O'Keefe. 'Faith and Foreign Aid.' Paper presented at the annual meeting of the American Political Science Association, Philadelphia.

Lowenthal, Mark. *U.S. Foreign Aid in a Changing World: Options for New Priorities*. Washington, DC: US Government Printing Office, 1991.

Lu, S. and R. Ram. 'Foreign Aid, Government Policies and Economic Growth: Further Evidence from Cross-country Panel Data for 1970 to 1993.' *International Economics* 54 (2001): 15–29.

Lumsdaine, David. *Moral Vision in International Politics: The Foreign Aid Regime, 1949–1989*. Cambridge: Cambridge University Press, 1993.

Lupia, A. and Mathew D. McCubbins. *The Democratic Dilemma: Can Citizens Learn what they Need to Know?* New York: Cambridge University Press, 1998.

Luterbacher, Urs and Detlef F. Sprinz. *International Relations and Global Climate Change*. Global Environmental Accord. Cambridge, Mass.: MIT Press, 2001.

Lyne, Mona M. *The Voter's Dilemma: Explaining the Democracy–Development Paradox*. University Park, Pa.: Pennsylvania State University Press, 2008.

—— —— —— 'Who Delegates? Alternative Models of Principals in Development Aid.' In *Delegation under Anarchy: States, International Organizations, and Principal–Agent Theory*, edited by Darren Hawkins, Daniel Nielson, and Michael J. Tierney. Cambridge: Cambridge University Press, 2006.

McCain, John. *Statement Concerning the Foreign Appropriations Bill for Fiscal Year 2002*. 2001.

McCully, Patrick. 'The Case against Climate Aid.' *Ecologist* 21, no. 6 (1991): 244–51.

MacFarquhar, Roderick. 'China's Half Century.' *Harvard Asia Quarterly* 3, no. 3 (1999).

McGillivray, Mark and Edward Oczkowski. 'A Two-Part Selection Model of British Bilateral Aid, 1960–1970.' *British Journal of Political Science* 8, no. 3 (July 1992): 313–22.

—— 'Modeling the Allocation of Australian Bilateral Aid: A Two-Part Sample Selection Approach.' *Economic Record* 197 (1991): 147–52.

McMichael, Phillip. *Food and Agrarian Orders in the World-Economy*. New York: Praeger, 1995.

References

McNamara, Douglas, Klaus Schultz, Jessica Sloan, and Michael Tierney. 'Codebook and Users Guide to Project Level Aid Database (PLAID), Versions 1.0 and 1.1.' Working Paper. Williamsburg, Va.: College of William and Mary, 2005.

Maizels, A. and M. K. Nissanke. 'Motivations for Aid to Developing Countries.' *World Development* 12, no. 9 (1984): 879–900.

Maliniak, Daniel, Amy Oakes, Susan Peterson, and Michael J. Tierney. *The View from the Ivory Tower: TRIP Survey of International Relations Faculty in the United States and Canada.* Williamsburg, Va.: College of William and Mary, 2007. www.wm.edu/irtheoryandpractice/trip/surveyreport06–07.pdf.

Mancin, Rinaldo C. 'Involving Civil Society: The Demonstration Projects Subprogram of the Pilot Program to Conserve the Brazilian RainForest.' 1998. http://srdis.ciesin.columbia.edu/cases/Brazil-Paper.html (accessed 9 July 2006).

Mansfield, Edward D. and Jack Snyder. 'Democratic Transitions, Institutional Strength, and War.' *International Organization* 56, no. 2 (2002): 297–337.

Margolis, Mac. 'Amazon Ablaze.' *World Monitor* (February 1989): 26.

Markandya, Anil. 'Water Quality Issues in Developing Countries.' In *Essays in Environment and Development*, edited by Joseph E. Stiglitz. New York: Columbia University Press, 2005.

Martens, Bertin. 'Why do Aid Agencies Exist?' *Development Policy Review* 23, no. 6 (2005): 643–63.

—— 'The Performance of the EC Phare Programme as an Instrument for Institutional Reform in the EU Candidate Member-States.' *Journal for Institutional Innovation, Development and Transition* 5, no. 35 (2001): 47.

—— U. Mummert, Peter Murrell, and P. Seabright. *The Institutional Economics of Foreign Aid.* Cambridge: Cambridge University Press, 2002.

Martin, Lisa. 'Agency and Delegation in IMF Conditionality.' In *Delegation and Agency in International Organizations*, edited by Darren Hawkins, David A. Lake, Daniel L. Nielson, and Michael J. Tierney. Cambridge: Cambridge University Press, 2006.

—— *Democratic Commitments: Legislatures and International Cooperation.* Princeton: Princeton University Press, 2000.

—— 'Interests, Power, and Multilateralism.' *International Organization* 46, no. 4 (1992): 765–92.

Martinot, Eric. 'World Bank Energy Projects in China: Influences on Environmental Protection.' *Energy Policy* 29, no. 8 (2001): 581–94.

Meernik, James and Steven C. Poe. 'US Foreign Aid in the Domestic and International Environments.' *International Interactions* 22, no. 1 (1996): 21–40.

Meier, Patrick and Doug Bond. 'Environmental Influences on Pastoral Conflict in the Horn of Africa.' Paper presented to the 47th Annual Convention of the International Studies Association, San Diego, 2006.

Meltzer, A. H. *Report to the US Congress on the Reform of the Development Banks and the International Finance Regime.* Washington, DC: International Financial Institution Advisory Commission, US Congress, 2000.

Meyer, John W., David John Frank, Ann Hironaka, Evan Schofer, and Nancy Brandon Tuma. 'The Structuring of a World Environmental Regime, 1870–1990.' *International Organization* 51, no. 4 (1997): 623–9.

Millennium Challenge Corporation. Press Release: *The Millennium Challenge Corporation Announces Fiscal Year 2005 Country Selection Process.* Washington, DC: Millennium Challenge Corporation, 2004.

Miller-Adams, M. *The World Bank: New Agendas in a Changing World.* London: Routledge, 1999.

Milner, Helen V. 'Why Multilateralism? Foreign Aid and Domestic Principal–Agent Problems.' In *Delegation and Agency in International Organizations*, edited by Darren Hawkins, David A. Lake, Daniel Nielson, and Michael J. Tierney, 107–39. Cambridge: Cambridge University Press, 2006.

—— 'Why Delegate the Allocation of Foreign Aid to Multilateral Organizations? Principal–Agent Problems and Multilateralism.' La Jolla, Calif., 19–20 September 2003.

—— and Dustin Tingley. 'The Domestic Politics of Foreign Aid: American Legislators and the Politics of Donor Countries.' Paper presented at the International Studies Association, San Diego, 2006.

Mitchell, Ronald B. 'Sources of Transparency: Information Systems in International Regimes.' *International Studies Quarterly* 42 (1998): 109–30.

—— 'Compliance Theory: A Synthesis, Review of European Community and International Environmental Law.' *Review of European Community and International Environmental Law* 22, no. 4 (1993): 328.

—— and Thomas Bernauer. 'Empirical Research on International Environmental Policy: Designing Qualitative Case Studies.' *Journal of Environment and Development* 7, no. 1 (1998): 4–31.

Moravcsik, Andrew. 'Theory Synthesis in International Relations: Real Not Metaphysical.' *International Studies Review* 5, no. 1 (2003): 131–6.

—— *The Choice for Europe: Social Purpose and State Power from Messina to Maastricht.* Ithaca, NY: Cornell University Press, 1998.

Morgenthau, Hans. 'A Political Theory of Foreign Aid.' *American Political Science Review* 56 (1962): 301–9.

Morrissey, Oliver. 'ATP is Dead: Long Live Mixed Credits.' *Journal of International Development* 10, no. 2 (1998): 247–55.

Moser, Christine. 'Poverty Reduction, Patronage, or Vote Buying? The Allocation of Public Goods and the 2001 Election in Madagascar.' Western Michigan University Working Paper, 2005.

Moutinho, P. and M. R. Santilli. 'Reduction of GHG Emissions from Deforestation in Developing Countries.' Belém, Brazil, 2005.

Mufson, Steven. 'Exxon Mobil Warming up to Global Climate Issue.' *Washington Post*, 10 February 2007, sec. D.

Muller, Benito. *Nairobi 2006: Trust and the Future of Adaptation Funding.* Oxford: Oxford Institute for Energy Studies, 2007.

—— and Cameron Hepburn. 'IATAL: An Outline Proposal for an International Air Travel Adaptation Levy.' *Oxford Institute for Energy Studies* EV 36 (October 2006).

Murdoch, James C. and Todd Sandler. 'Voluntary Cutbacks and Pretreaty Behavior: The Helsinki Protocol and Sulfur Emissions.' *Public Finance Review* 25, no. 2 (1997a): 139–62.

Murdoch, James C. and Todd Sandler. 'The Voluntary Provision of a Pure Public Good: The Case of Reduced CFC Emissions and the Montreal Protocol.' *Journal of Public Economics* 63, no. 3 (1997b): 331–49.

Murshed, Syed Mansoob. *When does Natural Resource Abundance Lead to a Resource Curse?* Discussion Paper 04–01; DP 04–01. London: International Institute for Environment and Development, Environmental Economics Programme, 2004b.

—— 'Strategic Interaction, Aid Effectiveness and the Formation of Aid Policies in Donor Nations.' *Journal of Economic Development* 28, no. 1 (June 2003): 189–203.

Najam, Adil. 'Dynamics of the Southern Collective: Developing Countries in Desertification Negotiations.' *Global Environmental Politics* 4, no. 3 (2004a): 128–54.

—— 2004b. 'The View from the South: Developing Countries in Global Environmental Politics.' In *The Global Environment: Institutions, Law, and Policy*, 2nd edn., edited by Regina Axelrod, David Downie, and Norman Vig, 225–43. Washington, DC: CQ Press.

—— 'Financing Sustainable Development: Crises of Legitimacy.' *Progress in Development Studies* 2, no. 2 (2002a): 153–60.

—— 'The Unraveling of the Rio Bargain.' *Politics and the Life Sciences* 21, no. 2 (2002b): 46–50.

—— Ioli Christopoulou, and William R. Moomaw. 'The Emergent "System" of Global Environmental Governance.' *Global Environmental Politics* 4, no. 4 (2004): 23–35.

Nandakumar, N. K., Michael Reich, Mukesh Chawla, Peter Berman, and Winnie Yip. 'Health Reform for Children: The Egyptian Experience with School Health Insurance.' *Health Policy* 50, no. 3 (2000): 155–70.

National Development Council of India. *Tenth Five Year Plan (2002–2007)*. New Delhi: Government of India, 2001.

Nelson, P.J. *The World Bank and Non-Governmental Organizations: The Limits of Apolitical Development*. New York: St Martin's Press, 1995.

Neumann, Roderick P. *Imposing Wilderness: Struggles over Livelihood and Nature Preservation in Africa*. Berkeley and Los Angeles: University of California Press, 2002.

Neumayer, Eric N. 'Are Left-Wing Party Strength and Corporatism Good for the Environment? Evidence from Panel Analysis of Air Pollution in OECD Countries.' *Ecological Economics* 45, no. 2 (2003a): 203–20.

—— 'The Determinants of Aid Allocation by Regional Multilateral Development Banks and United Nations Agencies.' *International Studies Quarterly* 47, no. 1 (2003b): 101–22.

—— *The Pattern of Aid Giving: The Impact of Good Governance on Development Assistance*. London: Routledge, 2003c.

—— 'What Factors Determine the Allocation of Aid by Arab Countries and Multilateral Agencies?' *The Journal of Development Studies* 39, no. 4 (2003d): 134–47.

—— 'Do Human Rights Matter in Bilateral Aid Allocation? A Quantitative Analysis of 21 Donor Countries.' *Social Science Quarterly* 84 (2003e): 650–66.

—— *Explaining the Pattern of Aid Giving: The Impact of Good Governance on Development Assistance*. London: Routledge, 2003f.

—— 'Do Democracies Exhibit Stronger International Environmental Commitment? A Cross-Country Analysis.' *Journal of Peace Research* 39, no. 2 (2002g): 139–64.

Nielson, Daniel L. and Michael J. Tierney. 'Principals and Interests: Common Agency and Multilateral Development Bank Environmental Lending.' Paper presented at the International Political Economy Society, Princeton University, November 2006.

—— 'Theory, Data, and Hypothesis Testing: World Bank Environmental Reform Redux.' *International Organization* 59, no. 3 (2005): 785–800.

—— 'Delegation to International Organizations: Agency Theory and World Bank Environmental Reform.' *International Organization* 57, no. 2 (Spring 2003): 241–76.

—— 'Green and Brown Lending at the World Bank.' Paper presented at Duke University's Seminar on Globalization, Equity, and Democratic Governance, 2001.

Niemeijer, David and Valentina Mazzucato. 'Soil Degradation in the West African Sahel: How Serious is it?' *Environment* 44, no. 2 (2002): 20–31.

North, Douglass Cecil. *Structure and Change in Economic History*. 1st edn. New York: Norton, 1981.

O'Driscoll, G. *2003 Index of Economic Freedom*. The Heritage Foundation, 2003.

O'Keefe, Christopher, and Daniel Nielson. 'Islamic Development Bank Lending: The Effects of Domestic Politics, Norms, and the Hegemon's Absence.' Paper presented at the annual meeting of the International Studies Association, San Diego, Calif., 2006.

Olsen, Gorm Rye. 'Danish Aid Policy in the Post Cold War Period: Increasing Resources and Minor Adjustments.' Centre for Development Research Working Paper, Copenhagen, 2002.

Olson, Mancur. 'Dictatorship, Democracy, and Development.' *American Political Science Review* 87, no. 3 (September 1993): 567–76.

OPEC (Organization of Petroleum Exporting Countries). 'Agreement Establishing the OPEC Fund for International Development.' Vienna.

OPEC Fund for International Development. *Annual Report 2005*. Vienna: 2006, www.opecfund.org/publications/PDF/annual_report_2005/English.pdf.

—— *Annual Report 2000*. Vienna: 2001a.

—— *1981 Annual Report*. 1982.

—— *Annual Report 1980*. Vienna, Austria: 1981.

Organization of Economic Cooperation and Development (OECD). 'Dataset 1: Official and Private Flows.' OECD. http://stats.oecd.org/wbos/default.aspx?DatasetCode=TABLE1 (accessed 5 July 2006).

—— *Development Co-operation Review of the United States*. Paris: OECD, 2002a.

—— *The Global Environmental Goods and Services Industry*. Paris: OECD, 2001.

—— International Development Statistics CD-ROM. Paris: OECD, 2002b.

Ostrom, Elinor. *Governing the Commons: The Evolution of Institutions for Collective Action*. Cambridge: Cambridge University Press, 1990.

—— Clark C. Gibson, S. Shivakumar, and K. Andersson. 'Aid, Incentives, and Sustainability: An Institutional Analysis of Development Cooperation.' *Sida Studies in Evaluation* 2, no. 01 (2002): 1.

Ostrom, Vincent and Elinor Ostrom. 'Public Goods and Public Choices'. In *Polycentricity and Local Public Economies*, edited by Michael D. McGinnis, Ann Arbor: University of Michigan Press, 2001.

Oye, Kennete and James H. Maxwell. 'Self-Interest and Environmental Management.' In *Environment in the New Global Economy, ii: Applications*, edited by Peter M. Haas, 67–98. Elgar Reference Collection. International Library of Writings on the New Global Economy, vol. 1. Cheltenham: Elgar, 2003 [1994].

Pack, H. and J. R. Pack. 'Is Foreign Aid Fungible? The Case of Indonesia.' *Economic Journal* 100, no. 399 (1990): 188–94.

Parenti, M. *The Sword and the Dollar*. New York: St Martin's Press, 1989.

References

Pargal, Sheoli, Mani Muthukumara, and Mainul I. Huq. *Inspections and Emissions in India: Puzzling Survey Evidence on Industrial Water Pollution*. Washington, DC: World Bank, 1997.

Park, Susan. 'Accessing the Accountability of the World Bank Group.' Paper presented at the annual American Political Science Association meeting, 2006.

—— 'Norm Diffusion within International Organisations: A Case Study of the World Bank.' *Journal of International Relations and Development* 8, no. 2 (2005): 114–41.

—— 'World Bank Group: Championing Sustainable Development?' *Global Governance*, forthcoming.

Parks, Bradley C. and Michael J. Tierney. ' "Out-Sourcing" the Allocation and Delivery of Foreign Aid.' Paper presented at the annual meeting of the American Political Science Association. Chicago, 2004.

Pascha, Werner. 'The Asian Development Bank in the Context of Rapid Regional Development.' In *Economic Globalization, International Organizations and Crisis Management*, edited by Richard Tilly and Paul Welfens, 155–83. Berlin: Springer, 2000.

Paterson, M. *Global Warming and Global Politics*. London: Routledge, 1996.

Pauly, Mark V. 'Overinsurance and Public Provision of Insurance: The Roles of Moral Hazard and Adverse Selection.' *Quarterly Journal of Economics* 88, no. 1 (1974): 44–62.

—— 'The Economics of Moral Hazard: A Comment.' *American Economic Review* 58, no. 3 (1968): 531–7.

Payer, C. *The World Bank: A Critical Analysis*. New York: Monthly Review Press, 1982.

Pearson, Lester B. *Pearson Commission*. Washington, DC: World Bank, 1969.

Pei, Minxin. 'China's Governance Crisis.' *Foreign Affairs* 81, no. 5 (2002).

People's Daily. '10 Year Efforts in Soil Erosion Achieved Great Success.' 2001. http://english.people.com.cn/english/200108/10/eng20010810_76994.html (accessed 15 June 2007).

Peterson, E. and Wesley F. 'The Design of Supranational Organizations for the Provision of International Public Goods: Global Environmental Protection.' *Review of Agricultural Economics* 22, no. 2 (2000): 355–69.

Petterson, Jan. 'Foreign Aid Fungibility, Growth, and Poverty Reduction.' Stockholm University Working Paper, Stockholm, 2004.

Phillips, Michael M. 'IMF, World Bank Face Mounting Attacks: House Presents Bills to Alter Debt Plan to Poor Countries.' *Wall Street Journal*, 26 October 1999.

Pincus, Jonathan R., Mancur Olson, and R. Zeckhauser. *Economic Aid and International Cost Sharing*. Baltimore: Johns Hopkins University Press, 1965.

—— and Jeffrey A. Winters, eds. *Reinventing the World Bank*. Ithaca, NY: Cornell University Press, 2002.

Pinto, Lucio Flavio. *Carajas: o ataque ao coracao da Amazonia*. 2nd edition. Rio de Janeiro: Studio Alpha, 1982.

Pion-Berlin, David. 'The Political Economy of State Repression in Argentina.' In *The State as Terrorist: The Dynamics of Governmental Violence and Repression*, edited by Michael Stohl and George A. Lopez, 99–123. Westport, Conn.: Greenwood Press, 1984.

Poe, Steven C. and James Meernik. 'US Military Aid in the 1980s: A Global Analysis.' *Journal of Peace Research* 32, no. 4 (1995): 399–411.

Pollack, Mark A. 'Delegation, Agency, and Agenda Setting in the European Community.' *International Organization* 51, no. 1 (1997): 99–134.

—— *The Engines of European Integration: Delegation, Agency, and Agenda Setting in the EU.* Oxford: Oxford University Press, 2003.

Porter, Gareth, Pamela S. Chasek, and Janet W. Brown. *Global Environmental Politics.* Boulder, Colo.: Westview Press, 2000.

Powell, L. *Evaluating Strategies: Foreign Foundations and Russian Environmental NGOs.* New York: Columbia University, Working Paper.

Pritchett, Ian and Michael Woolcock. 'Solutions when the Solution is the Problem: Arraying the Disarray in Development,' *World Development* 32, no. 2 (2004): 191–212.

Radelet, Steven. 'Bush and Foreign Aid.' *Foreign Affairs* 82, no. 5 (September/October 2003): 104.

—— M. Clemens, and R. Bhavnani. 'Aid and Growth: The Current Debate and Some New Evidence.' Maputo, 14–15 March 2004.

Rajan, M. G. *Global Environmental Politics: India and the North–South Politics of Global Environmental Issues.* New Delhi: Oxford University Press, 1997.

Ram, Rahul N. 'Benefits of the Sardar Sarovar Project: Are the Claims Reliable?' In *Toward Sustainable Development? Struggling over India's Narmada River*, edited by William F. Fisher, 113–34. Armonk, NY: M. E. Sharpe, 1995.

Ram, Rati. 'Roles of Bilateral and Multilateral Aid in Economic Growth of Developing Countries.' *Kyklos* 56, no. 1 (2003): 95–110.

Ranis, G. and S. A. Mahmood. *The Political Economy of Development Policy Change.* Oxford: Basil Blackwell, 1992.

Raustiala, Kal. 'States, NGOs, and International Environmental Institutions.' *International Studies Quarterly* 41, no. 4 (1997b): 719–40.

Redwood, John. 'World Bank Approaches to the Brazilian Amazon: The Bumpy Road towards Sustainable Development.' In *Global Impact, Local Action: New Environmental Policy in Latin America*, edited by Anthony Hall, 81–125. London: Institute for the Study of the Americas, 2005.

Reiff, Fred M., Mirta Roses, Linda Venczel, Robert Quick, and Donald A. Wittman. 'Low-Cost Safe Water for the World: A Practical Interim Solution.' *Journal of Public Health Policy* 17, no. 4 (1996): 389–408.

Reis, Arthur Cezar Ferreira. *A Amazonia e a cobica internacional.* Rio de Janeiro: Grafica Record Editors, 1968.

Reuters. *Reuters News Service*, 31 March 1995.

Rich, Bruce. *Worse than the World Bank? Export Credit Agencies—The Secret Engine of Globalization.* Washington, DC: Institute for Food and Development Policy, 2003.

—— 'Still Waiting: The Failure of Reform at the World Bank.' *The Ecologist* 30, no. 6 (2000): 8–16.

—— *Mortgaging the Earth: The World Bank, Environmental Impoverishment, and the Crisis of Development.* Boston: Beacon Press, 1994.

Ringskog, Klas and Nola Chow. *India: Environmental Sustainability in the 1990s. A Country Assistance Evaluation.* Washington, DC: Operations Evaluation Department, World Bank, 2002.

Rix, Alan. 'Japan's Foreign Aid Policy: A Capacity for Leadership?' *Pacific Affairs* 62, no. 4 (1989): 461–75.

Roberts, J. Timmons. 'Predicting Participation in Environmental Treaties: A World-System Analysis.' *Sociological Inquiry* 66, no. 1 (1996): 38–57.

References

Roberts, J. Timmons. 'Squatters and Urban Growth in Amazonia.' *Geographical Review* 82, no. 2 (1992): 441–57.

—— and Amy Bellone Hite. *The Globalization and Development Reader: Perspectives on Development and Social Change*. Malden: Blackwell Publishing, 2007.

—— and Bradley C. Parks. *A Climate of Injustice: Global Inequality, North–South Politics, and Climate Policy*. Cambridge, Mass.: MIT Press, 2007a.

—— 'Fueling Injustice: Globalization, Ecologically Unequal Exchange, and Climate Change.' *Globalizations* 4, no. 3 (2007b): 193–210.

—— —— and Alexis Vasquez. 'Who Ratifies Environmental Treaties and Why? Institutionalism, Structuralism and Participation by 192 Nations in 22 Treaties.' *Global Environmental Politics* 4 (2004), 22–64.

—— and Nikki Demetria Thanos. *Trouble in Paradise: Globalization and Environmental Crises in Latin America*. New York: Routledge, 2003.

Robinson, James A. 'Politician-Proof Policy.' *Desarrollo y sociedad* 55 (2005): 1–56.

—— and Ragnar Torvik. 'White Elephants.' *Journal of Public Economics* 89, nos. 2–3 (2005): 197–210.

Robinson, N. A., ed. *Agenda 21 and UNCED Proceedings*. Vols. 1 and 2. New York: Oceana Publications, 1992.

Rochester, J. Martin. 'The Rise and Fall of International Organization as a Field of Study.' *International Organization* 40, no. 4 (1986): 777–813.

Rodrik, Dani. 'Understanding Economic Policy Reform.' *Journal of Economic Literature* 34, no. 1 (1996): 9–41.

Roeder, Phil. *Red Sunset: The Failure of Soviet Politics*. Princeton: Princeton University Press, 1993.

Roginko, Alexei. 'Domestic Implementation of Baltic Sea Pollution Commitments in Russia and the Baltic States.' In *The Implementation and Effectiveness of International Environmental Commitments*, edited by David G. Victor, Kal Raustiala, and Eugene B. Skolnikoff. Cambridge, Mass.: MIT Press, 1998.

Rohrschneider, Robert. 'Citizens' Attitudes toward Environmental Issues: Selfish or Selfless?' *Comparative Political Studies* 21 (1988): 347–67.

Romer, Thomas and Howard Rosenthal. 'Bureaucrats Versus Voters: On the Political Economy of Resource Allocation by Direct Democracy.' *Quarterly Journal of Economics* 93, no. 4 (November 1979): 563–87.

Roodman, David. 'Aid Project Proliferation and Absorptive Capacity.' Research Paper No. 2006/04 UNU WIDER, 2006.

Roodman, R. 'The Anarchy of Numbers: Aid, Development, and Cross-Country Empirics.' Center for Global Development Working Paper #32, 2003.

Ross, Michael. 'Conditionality and Logging Reform in the Tropics.' In *Institutions for Environmental Aid: Pitfalls and Promise*, edited by Robert O. Keohane and Marc A. Levy, 167–98. Cambridge, Mass.: MIT Press, 1996.

Ross, S. and G. Wall. 'Ecotourism: Towards Congruence between Theory and Practice.' *Tourism Management* 20, no. 1 (1999): 123–32.

Rothenberg, Sandra and James H. Maxwell. 'Industry Response to the Banning of CFCs: Mapping the Paths of Technological Change.' *Technology Studies* 4, no. 2 (1997).

Rowe, Edward T. 'National Attributes Associated with Multilateral and US Bilateral Aid to Latin America: 1960–1971.' *International Organization* 32, no. 2 (1978): 463–75.

Rowlands, Ian. 'Transnational Corporations and Global Environmental Politics.' In *Non-State Actors in World Politics*, edited by Daphne Josselin and William Wallace. New York: Palgrave, 2001.

Rubin, D. B. 'Multiple Imputation After 18+ Years.' *Journal of the American Statistical Association* 91 (1996): 473–89.

—— *Multiple Imputation for Nonresponse in Surveys*. New York: John Wiley & Sons, Inc., 1987.

—— 'Inference and Missing Data.' *Biometrika* 63 (1976): 581–92.

Ruggie, John G. 'Multilateralism: The Anatomy of an Institution.' *International Organization* 46, no. 3 (1992).

Salim, Emil. 'The World Bank must Reform on Extractive Industries.' *Financial Times*, 17 June 2004, London Ed1.

Sanchez, Pedro, M. S. Swaminathan, Philip Dobie, and Nalan Yuksel. *Halving Hunger: It can be done*. United Nations Millenium Project Hunger Task Force Report. London: Earthscan, 2005.

Sandbrook, Richard and Jay Oelbaum. 'Reforming Dysfunctional Institutions through Democratisation? Reflections on Ghana.' *Journal of Modern African Studies* 35, no. 4 (1997): 603–46.

Sandler, Todd. 'Financing International Public Goods.' *International Public Goods: Incentives, Measurement, and Financing* 81 (2002): 117.

Santilli, M. R., P. Moutinho, Stephen Schwartzman, D. Nepstad, L. Curran, and C. Nobre. 'Tropical Deforestation and the Kyoto Protocol.' *Climatic Change* 71 (2005): 267–76.

Schafer, J. L. *Analysis of Incomplete Multivariate Data*. New York: Chapman and Hall, 1997.

Schellenhuber, John. 'Tipping Points in the World Climate System.' lecture, 2006.

Schelling, Thomas C. 'What Makes Greenhouse Sense? Time to Rethink the Kyoto Protocol.' *Foreign Affairs* 81, no. 3 (May–June 2002): 2–9.

—— 'American Foreign Assistance.' *World Politics* 7, no. 4 (1955): 606–26.

Schnaiberg, Alan and Kenneth A. Gould. *Environment and Society: The Enduring Conflict*. New York: Worth Publishers, 1994.

Schraeder, Peter J., Bruce Taylor, and Steven W. Hook. 'Clarifying the Foreign Aid Puzzle: A Comparison of American, Japanese, French, and Swedish Aid Flows.' *World Politics* 50, no. 2 (1998): 294–323.

Schultz, Kenneth A. and Barry R. Weingast. 'The Democratic Advantage: Institutional Foundations of Financial Power in International Competition, *International Organization* 57, no. 1 (2003): 3–42.

Schultz, Klaus, Douglas McNamara, Robert Hicks, Bradley C. Parks, J. Timmons Roberts, and Michael J. Tierney. 'The PLAID Codebook. Working Paper.' 2003.

Schwartz, Jonathan. 'The Impact of State Capacity on Enforcement of Environmental Policies: The Case of China.' *Journal of Environment and Development* 12, no. 1 (2003): 50–81.

Schwartzman, Stephen. *Bankrolling Disasters: International Development Banks and the Global Environment: A Citizen's Guide to the Multilateral Development Banks*. Washington, DC: Sierra Club, 1985.

References

Scruggs, Lyle. *Sustaining Abundance: Environmental Performance in Industrial Democracies.* Cambridge Studies in Comparative Politics. Cambridge: Cambridge University Press, 2003.

Seabright, Paul. 'Conflicts of Objectives and Task Allocation in Aid Agencies.' In *The Institutional Economics of Foreign Aid,* edited by Bertin Martens, Uwe Mummert, Peter Murrell, and Paul Seabright. Cambridge: Cambridge University Press, 2002.

Seers, D. 'What Types of Government should be Refused what Types of Aid?' *IDS Bulletin* 4, no. 2 (1972): 6–15.

Sell, Susan. 'North–South Environmental Bargaining: Ozone, Climate Change, and Biodiversity.' *Global Governance* 2, no. 1 (1996): 97–118.

Shahid, N. S., W. B. Greenough III, A. R. Samadi, Mainul I. Huq, and N. Rahman. 'Hand Washing with Soap Reduces Diarrhoea and Spread of Bacterial Pathogens in a Bangladesh Village.' *Journal of Diarrhoeal Disease Research* 14, no. 2 (1996): 85–9.

Shavell, S. 'On Moral Hazard and Insurance.' *Quarterly Journal of Economics* 93, no. 4 (1979): 541–62.

Shirk, Susan L. *How China Opened its Door: The Political Success of the PRC's Foreign Trade and Investment Reforms.* Integrating National Economies. Washington, DC: Brookings Institution, 1994.

Simmons, Beth A. 'Rules over Real Estate: Trade, Territorial Conflict, and International Borders as Institution.' *Journal of Conflict Resolution* 49, no. 6 (2005): 823–48.

Sjoberg, Helen. 'Restructuring the Global Environment Facility.' Working paper, 1999, http://thegef.org/Outreach/outreach-PUblications/WP13-Restructuring_the_GEF.pdf (accessed 11 June 2007).

Smil, Vaclav. *China's Environmental Crisis: An Inquiry into the Limits of National Development.* London: M. E. Sharpe, 1997.

Smillie, Ian, Henny Helmich, Tony German, and Judith Randels, eds. *Public Attitudes and International Development Coordination.* Development Center Studies. Paris: OECD, 1998.

Sonnenfeld, D. A. 'Vikings and Tigers: Finland, Sweden and Adoption of Environmental Technologies in Southeast Asia's Pulp and Paper Industries'. *Journal of World-Systems Research* 5, no. 1 (1999): 26–47.

Sprinz, Detlef F. and Yael Wolinsky-Nahmias, eds. *Models, Numbers, and Cases: Methods for Studying International Relations.* Ann Arbor: University of Michigan Press, 2004.

Steinke, Marita. 'Comments by Germany on the Performance Based Allocation Framework.' Letter to Dr Leonhard Good GEF Chief Executive Officer, Bonn, 2004, www.gefweb.org/Whats_New/PBA_Comments_-_Germany.pdf.

Stern, Nicholas. *Stern Report.* 2006.

Stiglitz, Joseph E. 'Globalization and the Logic of Institutional Collective Action: Reexamining the Bretton Woods Institutions.' In *Governing Globalization,* edited by Deepak Nayyar. New York: Oxford University Press, 2002.

—— 'The World Bank at the Millennium.' *Economic Journal* 109, no. 459 (1999): 577–97.

Stone, Randall W. *Lending Credibility: The International Monetary Fund and the Post-Communist Transition.* Princeton: Princeton University Press, 2002.

Strand, Jonathan R. 'State Power in a Multilateral Context: Voting Strength in the Asian Development Bank.' *International Interactions* 25, no. 3 (1999): 265–86.

Streck, Charlotte. 'The Global Environment Facility: A Role Model for International Governance?' *Global Environmental Politics* 1, no. 2 (2001): 71–94.

Strøm, Kaare., L. D. Longley, and R. H. Davidson. *The New Roles of Parliamentary Committees*. London: Frank Cass, 1998.

Struhsaker, T. T., P. S. Struhsaker, and K. S. Siex. 'Conserving Africa's Rain Forests: Problems in Protected Areas and Possible Solutions.' *Biological Conservation* 123 (2005): 45–54.

Suarez, Miguel. 'Asian Development Bank to Accept China, Keep Taiwan.' *Associated Press*, 28 November 1985.

Svensson, Jakob. 'Why Conditional Aid does Not Work and what can be done about it?' *Journal of Development Economics* 70, no. 2 (2003): 381–402.

—— 'Aid, Growth and Democracy.' *Sage Public Administration Abstracts* 27, no. 2 (2000a).

—— 'Foreign Aid and Rent-Seeking.' *Journal of International Economics* 51, no. 2 (2000b): 437–61.

—— 'When is Foreign Aid Policy Credible? Aid Dependence and Conditionality.' *Journal of Development Economics* 61, no. 1 (2000c): 61.

Swank, D. 'Political Strength of Political Parties by Ideological Group in Capitalist Democracies.' 21-Nation Pooled Time-Series Dataset, 2002. http://www.marquette.edu/polisci/ Swank.htm.

Taher, Nadia. 'In the Shadow of Politics: USAID–Government of Egypt Relations and Urban Housing Intervention.' *Environment & Urbanization* 13, no. 1 (2001): 61–76.

Tarp, Finn, Christian F. Bach, Henrik Hansen, and Søren Baunsgaard. *Danish Aid Policy: Theory and Empirical Evidence*. Copenhagen: Institute of Economics, University of Copenhagen, 1998.

Taylor, John. House Appropriations Subcommittee on Foreign Operations, Export Financing, and Related Programs. *Under Secretary of the Treasury for International Affairs Testimony. FY2005 Budget Request for Treasury International Programs*. 20 May 2004.

Taylor, Jonathan. 'Japan's Global Environmentalism: Rhetoric and Reality.' *Political Geography* 18, no. 5 (1999): 535–62.

Tearfund. 'New Report: Lives Will be Lost without Urgent Climate Action.' 2006. www.tearfund.org/News/Latest+news/New+Report+lives+will+be+lost+without+climate+action.htm (accessed 11 August 2006).

Thacker, S. C. 'The High Politics of IMF Lending.' *World Politics* 52, no. 1 (1999): 38–75.

Thibodeau, J. G. 'The World Bank's Procurement Myth.' *Cato Foreign Policy Briefing* 43 (1996).

Thompson, Louise Hodgden. 'Review of Lumsdaine, *Moral Vision in International Politics: The Foreign Aid Regime, 1949–1989.' Social Science Quarterly* 76, no. 1 (March 1995): 242.

Tierney, Michael J. 'Commitments, Credibility and International Cooperation: The Integration of Soviet Successor States into Western Multilateral Regimes.' Ph.D. dissertation, University of California, San Diego, 2003.

—— and Catherine Weaver. 'Clash of the Paradigms: Theoretical Stagnation and Scientific Progress in the Study of International Organizations.' Manuscript.

Tsebelis, George. *Veto Players: How Political Institutions Work*. Princeton: Princeton University Press, 2002.

US Department of the Treasury, Office of Public Affairs. 'U.S. Pledges $500 Million for Fund to Combat Global Environmental Threats,' Washington, DC: US Department of State, 7 August 2002.

Udall, Lori. 'The World Bank and Public Accountability: Has Anything Changed?' In *The Struggle for Accountability: The World Bank, NGOs, and Grassroots Movements*, edited by Jonathan Fox and David Brown, 391–436. Cambridge, Mass.: MIT Press, 1998.

United Nations. 'United Nations Convention to Combat Desertification.' www.gefonline.org/projectDetails.cfm?projID=105 (accessed 15 June 2007).

——'Agenda 21—Brazil.' United Nations Commission on Sustainable Development. www.un.org/esa/agenda21/natlinfo/countr/brazil/natur.htm (accessed 14 June 2007).

United Nations Conference on Environment and Development. *Rio Declaration on Environment and Development—Agenda 21*. Rio de Janeiro: United Nations General Assembly, 1992.

United Nations Development Programme. 2007. http://www.undp.org/gef/05/portfolio/biodiversity.html.

——*Human Development Report 2006*. Basingstoke: Palgrave Macmillan, 2006.

United Nations Environment Programme (UNEP). 'Global Environmental Outlook 3: Fact Sheet, Africa.' 2003. www.unep.org/geo/pdfs/GEO-3FactSheet-AFRICA.pdf (accessed 15 June 2007).

——'Global Ministerial Environment Forum: International Environmental Governance.' Cartagena, UNEP, 13–15 February 2002.

United Nations Millennium Project, Task Force on Water and Sanitation. *Health, Dignity, and Development: What Will it Take?* London: Earthscan, 2005.

United States Agency for International Development, USAID-Kenya website, 2007. http://www.usaid.gov/locations/sub-saharan_africa/ countries/kenya/.

——*Environmental Compliance Procedures*. 2005, www.usaid.gov/our_work/environment/compliance/reg216.pdf.

Urdal, Henrik. 'Population, Resources, and Political Violence: A Sub-National Study of India 1956–2002.' Review paper submitted to Development and Change, Center for the Study of Civil War and the International Peace Research Institute, Oslo, 2006, www.prio.no/files/file45244_india_urdal_dc.doc.

Vandermeer, John and Ivette Perfecto. *Breakfast of Biodiversity: The Truth about Rain Forest Destruction*. Oakland, Calif.: Food First Books, 1995.

VanDeveer, S. D. and Geoffrey D. Dabelko. 'It's Capacity, Stupid: International Assistance and National Implementation.' *Global Environmental Politics* 1, no. 2 (2001): 18–29.

Van de Walle, Nicholas. *Economic Reform in Africa, 1980–2000: Patterns and Constraints*. 2000, www.msu.edu/user/chapotoa/False%20Premise.pdf (accessed 11 June 2007).

Van Voorst tot Voorst, Sweden. 'GEF Council Member for the Netherland, to Leonard Good, Chief Executive Office of the GEF.' The Hague, 2004.

Varley, Robert C. G. *The World Bank and China's Environment 1993–2003*. Washington, DC: World Bank Operations Evaluation Department, 2005.

——J. Tarvid, and D. N. Chao. 'A Reassessment of the Cost-Effectiveness of Water and Sanitation Interventions in Programmes for Controlling Childhood Diarrhoea.' *Bulletin of the World Health Organizations* 76, no. 6 (1998): 617–31.

Vedeld, Paul, Arild Angelsen, Espen Sjaastad, and Gertrude Kobugabe Berg. 'Counting on the Environment: Forest Incomes and the Rural Poor.' Environmental Economics Paper 98. Washington, DC: World Bank, 2004.

Victor, David G. 'Enforcing International Law: Implications for an Effective Global Warming Regime.' *Duke Environmental Law and Policy Forum* 10, no. 1 (1999): 147–84.

—— Kal Ranstiala, and Eugene B. Skolnikoff, eds. *The Implementation and Effectiveness of International Environmental Commitments.* Cambridge, Mass.: MIT Press, 1998.

Vogel, David. *Trading Up: Consumer and Environmental Regulation in a Global Economy.* Cambridge, Mass.: Harvard University Press, 1995.

Wade, Robert H. 'International Organizations and the Art of Hypocrisy: The World Bank and its Critics.' Unpublished manuscript, 2004a.

—— 'Lecture on Global Economic Governance.' Lecture delivered at the London School of Economics, 2004b.

—— 'US Hegemony and the World Bank: The Fight over People and Ideas.' *Review of International Political Economy* 9, no. 2 (2002): 215–43.

—— 'Making the World Development Report 2000: Attacking Poverty.' *World Development* 29, no. 8 (2001a): 1435–41.

—— 'Showdown at the World Bank.' *New Left Review* 7 (2001b): 124–37.

—— 'US Treasury must Share Blame for World Bank's Predicament.' *Financial Times,* 4 September 2001d.

—— 'The World Bank is for Borrowers.' *Financial Times,* 14 February 2001e.

—— 'The World Bank as a Necessarily Un-forthright Organization.' Washington, DC, 17–18 April 2001f.

—— Money-Go-Round. *The Economist,* 4 May 1991.

Waltz, Kenneth. *Theory of International Politics.* New York: McGraw-Hill, 1979.

Wang, T. Y. 'U.S. Foreign Aid and UN Voting: An Analysis of Important Issues.' *International Studies Quarterly* 43, no. 1 (1999).

Watkins, Joanna A. 'When does Environmental Aid Work? Assessing the Effectiveness of Environmental Assistance to Brazil and China.' Honours thesis, College of William and Mary, 2004.

Weaver, Catherine. *Hypocrisy Trap: The Rhetoric, Reality, and Reform of the World Bank.* Princeton: Princeton University Press, 2008.

—— and R. Leiteritz. 'Organizational Culture and Change at the World Bank.' Unpublished manuscript, University of Kansas, 2002.

Weinbaum, Marvin G. *Egypt and the Politics of U.S. Economic Aid.* Westview Special Studies on the Middle East. Boulder, Colo.: Westview Press, 1986.

Weingast, Barry. 'A Rational Choice Perspective on the Role of Ideas: Shared Belief Systems and State Sovereignty in International Cooperation.' *Politics & Society* 23, no. 4 (1995): 449.

Weinthal, Erika. *State Making and Environmental Cooperation: Linking Domestic and International Policies in Central Asia.* Cambridge, Mass.: MIT Press, 2002.

Weiss, Edith Brown and Harold K. Jacobson, eds. *Engaging Countries: Strengthening Compliance with International Environmental Accords.* Cambridge, Mass.: MIT Press, 1998.

Weisskopf, Michael and Eugene Robinson. 'Rio Summit Highlights North–South Schism.' *Washington Post* 3 June 1992: A21, 23.

White, Howard. 'British Aid and the White Paper on International Development: Dressing a Wolf in Sheep's Clothing in the Emperor's New Clothes?' *Journal of International Development* 10, no. 2 (1998): 151–66.

Whittington, Dale. 'Muncipal Water Pricing and Tariff Design: A Reform Agenda for South Asia.' *Water Policy* 5 (2003): 61–76.

Williamson, Oliver E. *The Economic Institutions of Capitalism*. New York: Free Press, 1985.

—— 'Transaction Cost Economics: The Governance of Contractual Relations.' *Journal of Law and Economics* 22 (1979): 233–61.

Wilson, J. M., G. N. Chandler, Muslihatun, and Jamiluddin. 'Hand-Washing Reduces Diarrhoea Episodes: A Study in Lombok, Indonesia.' *Transactions of the Royal Society of Tropical Medicine and Hygiene* 85, no. 6 (1991): 819–21.

Withanage, Hemantha. *Annual Report 2005*. Diliman, Philippines: NGO Forum on ADB, 2006, www.forum-adb.org/pub/Annual%20Reports/Annual%20Report%202005.pdf.

Wittkopf, Eugene. 'Foreign Aid and United Nations Votes: A Comparative Study.' *American Political Science Review* 67, no. 3 (1973): 868–88.

Wonacott, Peter. 'Polluters in China Feel no Pain—but Watchdog Seeks Changes by Holding Officials Accountable.' *Wall Street Journal*, 24 March 2004.

Woods, Ngaire. 'Good Governance in International Organisations.' *Global Governance* 5, no. 1 (1999): 39–61.

World Bank. *Water Supply and Sanitation: Bridging the Gap between Infrastructure and Service*. Washington, DC: World Bank, 2006.

—— *Improving the World Bank's Development Effectiveness: What does Evaluation Show?* Washington, DC: World Bank Operations Evaluation Department, 2005c.

—— *World Development Report 2004: Making Services Work for Poor People*. Washington, DC: World Bank and Oxford University Press, 2004b.

—— *Efficient, Sustainable Service for All? An OED Review of World Bank Assistance for Water Supply and Sanitation*. Washington, DC: World Bank, 2003.

—— *Poverty in Pakistan: Vulnerabilities, Social Gaps, and Rural Dynamics. Poverty Reduction and Economic Management, South Asia Region*. Washington, DC: World Bank, 2002b.

—— *China: Air, Land, and Water*. Washington, DC: World Bank, 2001a.

—— *Mexico Country Evaluation*. Washington, DC: World Bank, 2001b.

—— *Operations Evaluation Department Report*. Washington, DC: World Bank, 1999.

—— *Assessing Aid*. Washington, DC: World Bank, 1998.

Yardley, Jim. 'Thousands of Chinese Villagers Protest Factory Pollution.' *New York Times*, 13 April 2005.

Yeoman, Barry. 'Statesmanship Vs. Helmsmanship: A Single Senator Holds the World Hostage.' *The Nation* 262, no. 5 (1996): 11.

Young, Oran R. *The Institutional Dimensions of Environmental Change: Fit, Interplay and Scale*. Cambridge, Mass.: MIT Press, 2002.

—— 'The Politics of International Regime Formation: Managing Natural Resources and the Environment.' *International Organization* 43, no. 3 (1989).

—— Michael Brecher, and Frank Harvey. 'Are Institutions Intervening Variables or Basic Causal Forces? Causal Clusters Vs. Causal Chains in International Society.' In *Reflections on International Studies at the Dawn of the New Millennium*. Ann Arbor: University of Michigan Press, 2002.

Young, Zoe. *New Green Order? The World Bank and the Politics of the Global Environment Facility*. London: Pluto Press (UK), 2003.

——George Makoni, and Sonja Boehmer-Christiansen. 'Green Aid in India and Zimbabwe: Conserving Whose Community?' *Geoforum* 32, no. 3 (2001): 299–318.

Zanini, Gianni. *India: The Challenges of Development. A Country Assistance Evaluation*. Washington, DC: Operations Evaluation Department, World Bank, 2001.

Zhao, Jimin. 'The Multilateral Fund and China's Compliance with the Montreal Protocol.' *Journal of Environment & Development* 11, no. 4 (2002): 331–54.

Index

Appendices, figures, notes and tables are indexed in bold.